"As the impact of climate change progresses, relatively likely and foreseeable events, such as production shocks in the food systems as a result of disease, weather-related yield loss, infrastructure failures due to physical or digital issues, need to be better modelled and understood. This new understanding of risk, as a dynamic topography where sub-acute and acute trends and events may come together rapidly and at large scales requires new analytical foundations. The model, ERRE, presented in this book offers the foundation to simulate and query how these shocks may occur, and may cascade through the global social and financial systems. These insights are key to building the physical, community, and financial resilience that must be at the heart of humanity's efforts in the 21st century."

Molly Jahn, *Professor at University of Wisconsin-Madison, USA*

"Nearly 50 years have passed since the publication of the first world model, the famous report to the Club of Rome titled 'The Limits to Growth.' Today, we see a remarkable return of interest in this subject and one result is this book by Pasqualino and Jones that extensively reviews the earlier work and includes the description of an improved world model called ERRE. We badly need formal models to understand a world that's becoming way too complex for our intuition to grasp. This book is a considerable step forward in the right direction."

Ugo Bardi, *Professor at University of Florence, Italy*

"Roberto Pasqualino and Aled Jones have produced a hugely ambitious and timely piece of work. In its time, the original 'Limits to Growth' was hugely influential, and as we lurch towards a climate emergency, this thoughtful and thorough approach to modelling the world deserves to have as much impact, not least in its challenge to the dominant reductive economic thought."

Nick Silver, *Chairman, Climate Bonds Initiative, UK*

"The Anthropocene demands a fresh approach to analysing the real risks to humanity of a destabilising Earth System. This book is a big step towards meeting that challenge, exploring the shocks, feedbacks, tipping points and other disruptive surprises that might lie ahead."

Will Steffen, *Emeritus Professor at the Australian National University, Australia*

"The importance of modelling is not being right, it's about helping us think more correctly. The Club of Rome's 1970s modelling, revisited in this book, was meant to explore highly uncertain long term futures to help us think more correctly about ecological limits. This book continues that tradition, along the way exploring the limits of modelling as well as the benefits of non-linear dynamics in understanding the dramatic environmental choices facing us."

Michael Mainelli, *Executive Chairman, Z/Yen Group*

Resources, Financial Risk and the Dynamics of Growth

This book presents a new system dynamics model (the ERRE model), a novel stock and flow consistent global impact assessment model designed by the authors to address the financial risks emerging from the interaction between economic growth and environmental limits under the presence of shocks.

Building on the World3–03 Limits to Growth model, the ERRE links the financial system with the energy, agriculture, and climate systems through the real economy, by means of feedback loops, time lags and non-linear rationally bounded decision making. Prices and their interaction with growth, inflation, and interest rates are assumed to be the main driver of economic failure while reaching planetary limits. The model allows for the stress-testing of fat-tail extreme risk scenarios, such as climate shocks, energy transition, monetary policies, and carbon taxes. Risks are addressed via scenario analyses, compared to real available data, and assessed in terms of the economic theory that lies behind. The book outlines the case for a government-led system change within this decade, where the market alone cannot lead to sustainable prosperity.

This book will be of great interest to scholars of climate change; behavioural, ecological, and evolutionary economics; green finance; and sustainable development.

Roberto Pasqualino is Visiting Researcher of the Global Sustainability Institute at Anglia Ruskin University, UK. Roberto's research interest is in feedback modelling of industrial policies for the analysis of financial risk and sustainability. This involves the nexus between food security, energy transition, and those environmental and economic shocks that have the potential to disrupt systems in a complex world.

Aled Wynne Jones is the inaugural Director of the Global Sustainability Institute (GSI) at Anglia Ruskin University, UK.

Resources, Financial Risk and the Dynamics of Growth

Systems and Global Society

Roberto Pasqualino and
Aled Wynne Jones

LONDON AND NEW YORK

First published 2020
by Routledge
2 Park Square, Milton Park, Abingdon, Oxon OX14 4RN

and by Routledge
52 Vanderbilt Avenue, New York, NY 10017

Routledge is an imprint of the Taylor & Francis Group, an informa business

British Library Cataloguing-in-Publication Data
A catalogue record for this book is available from the British Library

Library of Congress Cataloging-in-Publication Data
A catalog record for this book has been requested

ISBN: 978-1-138-18735-1 (hbk)
ISBN: 978-0-367-49763-7 (pbk)
ISBN: 978-1-315-64318-2 (ebk)

DOI: 10.4324/9781315643182

To Elisabetta
Among those who change the world for the better
To Vaughan and Lewis
Parts of society's next generation

Contents

List of figures   x
List of tables   xiv
List of equations   xvi
Acknowledgements   xvii
Foreword   xxii
Preface   xxiv

PART I
World models and limits   1

1   The first formal world models   3

2   A calibration analysis of World3-03   47

3   Welcome to the real world!   64

PART II
Economic Risk, Resources and Environment
(ERRE) model   129

4   Economic thinking and system modelling   131

5   System structure and theory   177

6   Data, statistics, and scenario analysis   218

7   Conclusion   268

Index   284

Figures

1.1   Standard run of World3–03 model   6

1.2   Normalised values of World3 (Meadows et al. 1972) and trend
on historical time series   7

1.3   Definition of databases in system modelling   10

1.4   Focus of system dynamics modelling   12

1.5   Feedback loop to explain desired system behaviours   13

1.6   Stock and flows within the feedback structure   16

1.7   An example of stock and flow structure of agriculture and
climate interaction   17

1.8   Top-down view on the World3–03 model   20

1.9   Major feedback loops and accumulation processes in
the World3–03   22

1.10   Production and investment function in the World3–03   26

1.11   Allocation of industrial investments in agriculture and impact
on food production   28

1.12   Non-linear impact of food and services change on the
life expectancy   29

1.13   Negative effect of industrial output growth on food output and
sensitivity   31

1.14   Non-linear impact of industrial output per capita on life
expectancy via crowding   32

1.15   Balancing feedback loop of resource availability on industrial
capital growth, and adaptive technology effect   34

1.16   Limits to Growth non-linear relationships controlling feedback
loops in the agricultural sector   35

1.17   Non-linear impact of persistent pollution on land fertility   37

1.18   Negative impact of persistent pollution on life expectancy   38

1.19   Non-linear effects of technology scenarios on the reduction of
the industrial output   40

1.20   Standard run scenario of the World3–03 showing collapse of
human society due to conservative assumption on resource limits   42

1.21   Scenario 2 of World3–03 showing the world collapsing due to
exponential accumulation of persistent pollutants in
the atmosphere   42

1.22 Scenario 6 of the World3–03; adaptive technology scenario as the closest representation of an expected future of the world as depicted in the Limits to Growth   43

2.1 Sensitivity parameterisation of allocation of investments to services for the World3–03-Edited calibration   52

2.2 Sensitivity parameterisation of effects of land productivity on the land erosion for the World3–03-Edited calibration   53

2.3 Estimate of the food production loss for processing   54

2.4 Calibration of the World3–03-Edited model   58

3.1 McKelvey diagram used for geological exploration to assess economic availability of mineral resources   83

3.2 Hubbert peak model theory   84

3.3 Historical peak in production of coal production in the UK   87

3.4 Coal production by global regions from 1980 to 2015   90

3.5 Real global prices of crude oil, coal, and natural gas from 1970 to 2016   91

3.6 Global price of crops (maize, rice, wheat), fertilizers, and crude oil from 1990 to 2016   93

3.7 Correlation between CO_2 concentration and global average temperature   95

3.8 Population projections by region over time   100

3.9 Number of nuclear reactors in operation and electricity capacity of those reactors   102

3.10 Reinforcing feedback loops from market forces generating technological path dependency   108

3.11 Power load of electric energy during winter and summer in a developed country   111

3.12 Costs comparison between sources of energy   112

5.1 Interactions among the five basic economic sectors of World3   181

5.2 Physical flows in the energy transition and the economy model   183

5.3 ERRE model sector overview   185

5.4 ERRE model architecture   187

5.5 Hierarchical network view of the ERRE model   188

5.6 Reinforcing feedback loops in the financial dimension of savings deposits   191

5.7 Distribution of government debt between households and financial sector   192

5.8 Production function in the business sector of ERRE   201

5.9 Production function in the agriculture sector   203

5.10 Utility function in the household sector   204

5.11 Reinforcing feedback loop from cash availability to interest rate in the private sector   212

5.12 Balancing feedback loops counterbalancing interest rate within firm   213

5.13 From resource constraints to financial risk feedback loop structure   214

6.1	Population growth as input to the model	226
6.2	Exogenous money creation from central bank	226
6.3	Exogenous government deficit and government debt as input for money creation	226
6.4	Technology change for every sector in the model	227
6.5	Energy intensity of new capital and goods for the household sector	228
6.6	Forest land comparison between historical and simulated behaviour	233
6.7	Selected variables in the base run of the ERRE model	235
6.8	ST Scenario 1 – Input: Fossil fuel production shock	237
6.9	ST Scenario 1 – Output: Impact of fossil fuel production shock on selected variables	239
6.10	ST Scenario 2 – Input: Agricultural capacity shock	240
6.11	ST Scenario 2 – Output: Impact of agricultural capacity shock on selected variables	241
6.12	Decision tree for uncertain extreme risk analysis of long-term scenarios	243
6.13	LT Scenario 1 – Input: Impact of climate on food production and hot house effect	244
6.14	LT Scenario 1 – Output: Impact of climate on food system and Real GDP	246
6.15	LT Scenario 2 – Input: High risk scenarios of climate impact on food	247
6.16	LT Scenario 2 – Output: High risk scenario of climate impact on food	248
6.17	LT Scenario 3 – Input: Resource availability initial condition	249
6.18	LT Scenario 3 – Output (1/3): Impact of resource depletion on economic activity and energy transition	250
6.19	LT Scenario 3 – Output (2/3): Impact of resource depletion on energy prices and market shares	251
6.20	LT Scenario 3 – Output (3/3): Impact of resource depletion on carbon emissions and temperature anomaly	251
6.21	LT Scenario 4 – Input: Green technology productivity exponential growth	253
6.22	LT Scenario 4 – Output (1/3): Impact of green technology growth on selected variables	255
6.23	LT Scenario 4 – Output (2/3): Impact of green technology growth on employment, market shares, and prices	256
6.24	LT Scenario 4 – Output (3/3): Impact of green technology growth on temperature anomaly	256
6.25	LT Scenario 5 – Input: Carbon tax on fossil fuels	258
6.26	LT Scenario 5 – Output (1/4): Impact of 2030 carbon tax on selected variables	259
6.27	LT Scenario 5 – Output (2/4): Impact of 2030 carbon tax on selected variables	260

6.28 LT Scenario 5 – Output (3/4): Impact of 2020 carbon tax on
      selected variables   261
6.29 LT Scenario 5 – Output (4/4): Impact of 2020 carbon tax on
      selected variables   262
6.30 LT Scenario 6 – Input: Combined effects of green growth and
      carbon tax   263
6.31 LT Scenario 6 – Output (1/2): impact of combined effects of
      green growth and carbon tax on selected variables   264
6.32 LT Scenario 6 – Output (2/2): impact of combined effects of
      green growth and carbon tax on selected variables   265

Tables

1.1 Exponential growth at 3.6% per year over 20 years; the calculation is 1.036^{Years} 22

1.2 Exponential growth of a doubling economy every 20 years becomes 1024 bigger in two centuries; the calculation is $2^{Year/20}$ 22

1.3 World3 parameters that quantify the impact of natural constraints on economic growth   40

2.1 Metadata comparison between historical data and World3 variables   49

2.2 Parameters and variable additions between World3–03 and World3–03-Edited   50

2.3 List of the 16 parameters used in the calibration and sub-group division according to their role in the model   56

2.4 Values of parameters to differentiate between 'without limits' and 'with limits' scenarios   57

2.5 Result of the calibration process in relation and parameter variation between calibrated runs and Scenario 2 of World3   58

3.1 Share of energy consumption by sector and technology   109

5.1 Balance sheet matrix of the closed system economy   194

5.2 Summary of financial flows in the model   196

5.3 Type of output that each productive sector supplies to every other sector   205

5.4 Supply chain equilibrium system of equation   206

6.1 Time series used to calibrate the ERRE model   221

6.2 Accounting for time in Vensim software   223

6.3 Exponents on production functions   224

6.4 Sensitivities of key parameters for model calibration   229

6.5 Statistical comparison of model output to real data   231

6.6 ST Scenario 1 – Input parameter: Fossil fuel production shock   238

6.7 ST Scenario 2 Input parameters: Agricultural capacity shock   240

6.8 LT Scenario 1 – Input switches: Impact of climate on food production and hot house effect   245

6.9 LT Scenario 2 – Input switch: High risk scenarios of climate impact on food   247

6.10 LT Scenario 3 – Input parameter: Resource availability initial
 condition 250
6.11 LT Scenario 4 – Input parameter: Green technology
 productivity exponential growth 253
6.12 LT Scenario 5 – Input parameters: Carbon tax on fossil fuels 258
6.13 LT Scenario 6 – Input parameter: Combined effects of green
 growth and carbon tax 263
7.1 Skill set to develop and update the ERRE model 274

Equations

3.1   Net present value   107
4.1   Damage function and production in DICE   147
5.1   Cobb-Douglas production function   198
5.2   Marginal productivity in Cobb-Douglas production function   199
5.3   Constant elasticity of substitution production function   199
5.4   Leontief production function   200
5.5   Effective capital in ERRE   202
5.6   Effective labour in ERRE   202
5.7   Second level CES production function in ERRE   202
5.8   Effective agricultural land   203
5.9   Second level CES production function in agriculture   203
5.10   Utility function in households   204
5.11   Relation between costs and price   205
5.12   Cobb-Douglas condition of exponents   207
5.13   Value share of energy in capital   207
5.14   Value share of capital   207
5.15   Value share of energy   207
5.16   Value share of labour   207
5.17   Unit cost of energy   207
5.18   Unit cost of labour   207
5.19   Unit cost of capital   208
5.20   Amount of capital production to balance agriculture stock   208
5.21   Capital charge rate formulation   210
5.22   Discount rate in the capital charge rate formulation   210
5.23   Nominal interest rate   211
5.24   Interest rate with risk premium   211

Acknowledgements

We would like to thank the Peter Dawe Foundation and the Economic and Social Research Council (ESRC), as part of the Centre for the Understanding of Sustainable Prosperity (CUSP) grant (ESRC grant no: ES/M010163/1), for the funding that has supported this work.

From the time this book was conceived until the time it was completed, lots of events and people impacted its evolution who should be acknowledged.

First we would like to acknowledge all those who influenced the outcome of this work, both in quality and content.

We would like to thank the CUSP community and team of scientists in all their MAPSS themes (meanings and moral framings, arts and culture, political and organisational dimensions, social and psychological understandings, and systems analysis). It is much more what we gained from your work than what we gave back to you, and we hope this book will support your work going forward beyond CUSP. Particular thanks goes to the systems analysis team, involving Sarah Hafner, Andrew Jackson, Simon Mair, Ben Gallant, Craig Rye, Angela Druckman, Martin Sers, and Peter Victor, whose many conversations helped to shape the role of system dynamics in the economic community. Particular thanks go to Linda Gessner, who ensured that the CUSP message was widely shared, and to Ian Christie, who every Friday for the four years managed to provide the updates on the whole world of sustainability. Lastly, of course, Professor Tim Jackson who led the CUSP team and provided the inspiration to explore a future of sustainable prosperity as well as keeping a tight hold on that 'thin red line' that provided a link across all who have engaged with CUSP.

We would like to thank all those who worked in the Global Resource Observatory project that initiated the work proposed in this book. In particular, Irene Monasterolo for her energy and her ability to create networks and the passion she brought to the role. Davide Natalini and Efundem Agboraw for sharing their experience as well as the journey through a PhD. Julie-Anne Hogbin for her passion in managing the project. Tracey Zalk and Alexander Phillips in providing help with data. The advisory group composed of Catherine Cameron, Nick Silver, and Victor Anderson, who helped in shaping the important questions to be tackled, and the wider steering committee of the project. We would like to thank Peter Dawe, who kept supporting and believing in the success of this project (and continues to do so!).

We would like to acknowledge the wider Global Sustainability Institute team, a place where the project could be shaped. Initially started by Aled, in addition to sharing an amazing culture for collaboration and passion for sustainability, the team demonstrates an openness for interdisciplinary work and a passion for the activism. In particular, Roberto would like to thank Rosie Robison, who helped in structuring a PhD thesis out of this work, Chris Foulds, who supported him with the greatest mentorships over his early career position stage. Felicity Clarke for her passion for sustainability and role in keeping the team together. Listing the all GSI members is a difficult task, and we would love to list all people involved in here but there have been many over the years!

We would like to thank the team of professionals at Exoshock who helped to gather knowledge and understanding from the real world, and supported with additional feedback and model reviews, with the final aim to influence decision making in the real world. These include Barry McGovern, Ketan Bhimani who helped simplify the model communication to meet the needs of the real world, James Butterfill who helped reviewing some energy structures to improve the scenarios included in this book, Keith Eubanks who worked alongside Roberto and showed the secrets of system modelling for professional environments. Keith's review of the work performed was detailed and invaluable for directing amendments and improvements in the model. Some of these, and many more dependent on his advice, and lessons learnt from his experience, helped out to improve greatly the model we see here today. We would like to thank Faraz Helmi, who helped to complete a database from public available sources. We would like to thank Andrei Korolev, and the interesting insights on the functioning of the financial system. In addition, Michael Mainelli, who linked in to the real world in many ways.

Secondly, we would like to acknowledge all those people whose work was not directly linked to the content of this book, but without whom this work could have never been achieved. Three of them are among the true initiators of this work even if we never had the fortune to meet them in person. These are Professor Jay Forrester (1918–2016) and Professor Donella Meadows (1941–2001), whose rigorous approach, wisdom, and impressive achievements in life shaped the results of this work. We are also grateful to Aurelio Peccei (1908–1984), tremendous source of inspiration for the sustainability movement, and initiator of the Club of Rome.

We would like to particularly acknowledge Professor Jorgen Randers and Ulrich Golüke, who partially shaped the way for us, and provided important insights and feedback on earlier versions of the ERRE model. We are grateful to Professor Dennis Meadows for providing feedback on our 2015 paper, sharing invaluable wisdom, direction for further development, and an unpublished work written by Donella Meadows. This last has been integrated in the core text in Chapter 3 of this book to provide insights on the financial system and pathways towards sustainability.

We would like to acknowledge David and Laura Peterson, Tom Fiddaman, and Larry Yeager from Ventana Systems Inc., who provided wisdom, training, a library of models, and technical support on the software side that allowed this work to be possible. In particular, Roberto would never be grateful enough to both David and Laura for the one week of stories and anecdotes in relation to the early years of the system dynamics community. Conversations about the style of modelling, and the provision of a technology that could allow that have been extremely useful. We are profoundly grateful to Tom Fiddaman for his availability in providing advice during the system dynamics conferences and during a training at Ventana. In particular, without his online library (metasd.org), inclusive of a version of the models World3–03 and the Energy Transition and the Economy models, this work could have never even been started. To all the team, we believe your wisdom and passion over the years has affected this work greatly, and we hope we will be able to carry some of it through our careers in the future.

We would like to thank the Italian chapter of system dynamics, in particular, Stefano Armenia, Ugo Bardi, Edoardo Mollona, Alberto Stanislao Atzori, for sharing their experience with us, and the members of the UK chapter of system dynamics, including John Morecroft and Kim Warren, for providing informal advice at the beginning of this project. We are grateful to Matteo Pedercini and Pål Davidsen, who provided training on the modelling of social planning and nations using system dynamics at the University of Bergen. We also would like to thank the system dynamics society in general for their constant support and maintenance of the community over the years. In particular, we are particularly grateful to John Sterman for his passion for excellence, and terrific contribution to the community over the last 40 years.

We would like to thank the international community of those linked to the Institute for Manufacturing at Cambridge University, and their passion to link manufacturing and sustainability. In particular, Steve Evans for his advice who indirectly affected some assumptions placed in this model, Catherine Tilley for the enthusiasm and passion for applying sustainability in business practices, Maria Holgado and Dai Morgan for their energy in managing the Peak District Program.

People who have to be acknowledged for their help include some who are not among us anymore. This includes Professor Anthony Janetos (1954–2019), director of the Pardee Centre for the Study of Longer Range Futures at Boston University, who provided feedback on some initial versions of the agriculture sector of the ERRE model.

This work is the culmination of six years' of Roberto's research, which includes his PhD and subsequent research fellowship with CUSP. Roberto's detailed passion for systems modelling and dedication to delivering such a complex and all encompassing (and massive!) ERRE model should not be underestimated and I (Aled) would like to thank him for this attention to detail over those years.

As this is the culmination of Roberto's PhD and fellowship he would like to add some more personal acknowledgements here.

I (Roberto) would like to express my gratitude to:

- Aled, for the trust, wisdom, resources allocated, and patience to respond to my questions and doubts over these years. I have been learning a lot from him, both by writing this book and absorbing his careful amendments to all my work, as well as by immersing myself in the sustainability life through the Global Sustainability Institute, which he created and sustained. I would never be grateful enough for his inspiration for delivering sustainability at the global scale, as well as creating and letting it to grow at his feet.

- Professor Paolo Taticchi, who introduced me to MBA schools to teach sustainability and global dynamics to his students, and supported me over the years both as academic reference point and a link to the business world.
- Flavio Tonelli, Professor of Engineering for Sustainability at the University of Genoa who first introduced me to the problem of sustainability from an engineering perspective, and opened my way towards the Limits to Growth, as well as providing advice over the years.
- Marco Raberto, Professor of Finance at the University of Genoa, for sharing his experience in agent based modelling of the financial system, so that I could take the best decisions I could in the modelling of the ERRE.
- Giovanni Gambardella, who first introduced me to the world of entrepreneurship, and taught me how not to give up in the face of any challenge.

I would also love to thank all the people who supported me in my day to day life over the writing and development of this project, and which simple conversations helped me to find the energy for dealing with the challenge of global scale sustainability. In particular, I would like to express my gratitude to:

- Maribel Calvó Martinez and Zachariah Mark Iskander, who shared their life with mine, supporting with active energy, passion for environmental and social change, and fun. I would also like to thank Mariusz Baniak as a source of motivation to achieve impressive results, and Thea Marcellia Sletten for sharing insights from her work at the Ministry of Environment.
- Christian Steinruecken and Aleksandra Kulesza for their passion for changing the world for the better, the positive energy I could gain from you, and the nice touch in sustaining the society around you.
- Heidi Serra for the practical insights and ideas on food security from a biotechnology research perspective, and the politics of the food industry.
- Natalia Ferreira De Castro for leading by example in choosing a better world of a simple life, and providing insights through her work in human rights in international organisations.
- Stefania Ferrucci for the positive attitude towards improving the state of the world in every place she goes, and focus on those who are in need.
- Martina Kunz for sharing a PhD journey alongside mine, always ready to discuss ideas and futures on how we can make a difference in this world.
- Angel Garcia, who showed me feedback thinking to improve the connection with other people and society as a whole.
- Giacomo Caroli for sharing experience from the mechanical engineering world in support of my research, and doing that alongside cultivating his vegetable garden every day.

- Luca Occhi for sharing thoughts on the state of global pollution from the perspective of a material scientist.
- Matteo Milite for his energy in dealing with migration challenges from African countries to Europe, which is a problem we should all be taking care of.

Finally, I would like to thank my family for never being upset with me for the time I have been taking from them over these past years, thus reducing my carbon footprint in international travels. Thanks Maria Carmela, Giuseppe, Marco, Sara, Salvatore, Raffaella, and Ruggero.

Last but not the least, I would like to thank Elisabetta Sciacca, my beloved partner. She kept supporting me in the last months of writing, and provided some of her expertise by writing the R code necessary to produce all the images that are presented in Chapter 6 of this book (in just a few hours of effort!). She also opened my way to a dimension of spirituality and set the path towards new horizons to be reached together.

Thank you all. Let's go save the world.

Foreword

Fifty years ago I fortunately chose to attend a physics colloquium at MIT and met a small team of researchers under the leadership of Jay W. Forrester. Two years later, as part of this team, we published *The Limits to Growth*. This study for the Club of Rome changed the world, by raising awareness about the physical limitations of planet Earth.

Economics, most other academic disciplines, and most governments up until that point did not consider nature, and – more specifically – the world's natural resources, as an integral part of the human enterprise. The world was still seen as very big, with little impact on the dynamics of society. *The Limits to Growth* sought to explore, and showed, that conventional economic growth would tend to expand the human ecological footprint so rapidly that it would overshoot the ability of the planet to supply the resources needed or overload land and oceans with pollution that would reduce their ability to keep up with human demands. In overshoot, society either collapses or organises managed decline. Today – some 50 years after *Limits* – the world finds itself in overshoot and tending to ignore this fact.

With my many colleagues around the world, I have spent the years since the publication of *Limits* advocating for humanity to live in sustainable harmony with the rest of nature.

That is not to say that the future is totally broken. It is to say that human society needs to actively think about these challenges and ensure governance systems that manage them rather than just hoping a solution will land from somewhere at some point. While there have been huge improvements in how industry works – we no longer have black soot billowing out of industrial chimneys in the middle of New York – there is still a long way to go.

And there are signs of progress in other areas. In this book – for example – we see a new global model that can explore a different set of scenarios to those presented in *Limits*. In my book *2052* I presented a forecast for global developments towards the middle of this century. It is a slightly more optimistic educated guess than the darkest scenarios of *Limits*. The risks are all still there, but some of the trends are bending in the right direction. In this book some of those risks are explored through a new model and a new set of scenarios – and with a time horizon all the way to the end of this century. Importantly, it explores the approach to those limits and risks and helps us understand how society might respond, either proactively or reactively.

I am optimistic a better world can be created. However, we need to actually plan that better world. If we don't actively manage the risks we will see shocks in our economic and financial system. Some of these shocks might be large enough to create a paradigm shift in human history.

Finally, it is important to stress that these models do not forecast the future. They test different possible outcomes based on a set of assumptions and the likely impact of a set of policies or processes that govern society. The idea is that these scenarios can then inform society on how to change those policies and processes to avoid some of the worst outcomes.

How did *The Limits to Growth* change the world? It opened up space for discussing these challenges. It created an argument for setting up international governmental processes to manage environmental challenges. It inspired, and continues to inspire, generations of sustainability champions. But more importantly it annoyed a lot of people.

So, as I did in *2052* I offer a final word of encouragement – in particular to the younger of the authors as he sets out on his journey into this world of modelling and advocacy. Hope for the unlikely! Work for the unlikely! And be bold.

Jorgen Randers
Professor Emeritus
Climate strategy
Department of Law and Governance
BI Norwegian Business School
Oslo

Preface

Models and decisions

You can think of the world as an imaginary box. The simple action of associating a non-existent box with the world within the mind might be considered of little use to the scientific community or policy makers. However, such an action represents the beginning of a journey to understanding global systems through the creation of a mental model of the entire world.

By definition, a model is a simplified, reductionist representation of reality. Our mind cannot give attention to everything surrounding us. A model can capture some particular details of the observed environment allowing people to interact with it. These representations are models of the reality in the mind, or better, mental models.

For example, let us say that one child would like to move a box full of toys from a position A to B. The box is heavy enough that the child cannot lift it up, but light enough they can drag it on the ground. They would not need to know every single detail of the toy box to achieve their desire of moving the box. Details such as the exact number of toys in the box, their colours, who manufactured them, would not help in dealing with the issue they are facing. Intuitively, the child would make a calculation of the relative mass and volume of themselves and the ones of the box. By simply touching and approaching the box physically, they would make some tests to adjust the initial calculations to the ones necessary to perform the action correctly. Then, they would push (or pull) the box from A to B. The child created a mental representation of themselves interacting with the box and the ground in relation to the purpose of the action. They gave some attributes to every participant (nothing detailed), applied some testing thus improving the initial mental model, used such a model to decide what to do and how to do it, and performed the action. The mental model was in the mind of the child for the full duration the action was taken. Once the action was completed, the mental model vanished, dragging the child's attention to something different (for example the toys in the box).

Mental models are a part of being human. They can be created, evolve, and get discarded at the speed of thought without even realising we are using them. The main purpose of a mental model is supporting us in taking decisions which drive our actions that interfere with the dynamics of our environment. Whereas decisions can be taken without any support from mental models – i.e. the reason why the child wants to move the box can be completely irrational – we often face situations where the cost of failure can be prohibitive in comparison to what we believe is acceptable. Our feelings alone do not help much in turning such a situation towards the desired path.

Our world is a dynamic system and we are part of it. As individuals we keep evolving and interacting with the elements of the environment that surround us. The food we eat, the air we breathe, the people we socialise with are all elements of our environment and we are part of theirs. As groups we also keep evolving and interact with elements of world ecosystems as well as with other groups of people. As a society we organise ourselves in many different ways with the final aim of satisfying each other's needs both locally and internationally. We extract resources to produce goods and warm houses up, use land and its nutrients to produce the food we eat, use science to innovate our society towards a more desirable future, and so on.

Both as individuals and as a society we are part of wider systems. A 'system' can be defined as a set of interconnected elements (both living and non) that interact one to another over time towards a purpose. A mutual relationship (both direct and indirect) among two elements of a system is referred to as a 'feedback.' At the individual level, examples of feedback may include tasting food (direct feedback from food to our brain through our sense), or a teacher providing corrections to a student based on their homework. At the societal level, we can consider the population of a nation that votes for its preferred political representatives, or a government that goes into war (the feedback would be less direct here, for example involving first a lack of resources, then a persistent financial and economic crisis, and then a decision to engage into war with someone else). Feedbacks are our means for adaptation to our environment and the foundation for learning. Thus they form the basis for the experience we cumulate in our lifetime that drives the actions we take in particular situations.

Modelling is an activity we all do when facing a new situation that requires our attention and input. If we focus on a particular real system, there exist an infinite number of mental models that can help us understanding it. When we feel comfortable with a particular mental model of reality we take an action and interact with it. The reality, in most cases, feeds back to us in one way or another, showing if the mental model was mostly wrong (the feedback of the reality is something we were not expecting with potential negative consequences) or mostly right (somehow the consequences of our actions were expected and have a positive outcome). In the first case we would reject the model, and in the second we would accept it, aggregating it to previous ones to develop a deeper understanding of what we believe is surrounding us and how we can live with it. Because we mostly learn through feedback from the environment we can perceive, we are naturally forced to learn mostly from our past experiences, and have trouble in solving situations we have never faced before.

One of the most successful outcomes of our global society is the way we were able to accumulate and spread knowledge and information over space and time.

Nowadays our mental models are mostly formed through education, personal relationships, and as an outcome of the exposure to daily events and information from media, while filtered from the lens of the mental model that we currently own. When we face a new challenging situation we would normally look for advice among the people who know more than us about that specific problem. When people cannot be reached directly, information tends to be gathered through literature, consulting reports available within the extremely large amount of knowledge we have created and deposited, or, at last resort, interacting with the environment by mean of tests and experiments with tools. This is also the way we manage risk of failure, increasing our likelihood of success to reach the desired results within the available time. Still feedback from reality remains the key for learning, helping us to deal with similar situations in the future. It is worth noting that despite the individual modelling activity being carried out at a minimum level in relation to the problems we face, we are still all modellers who accept and reject information within our set of beliefs and mental architectures.

All models are questionable. As such they must be continuously tested in comparison to the reality they aim at representing, and should be effectively shared among communities to both influence their mental models (learning), and being influenced by those. Most important, because our environment is dynamic (it changes over time), it is fundamental to innovate models of the past because they might not be suitable for the problems of the present and the future. The most common ways to share and influence each other's mental models is through simple conversation and communication. Words, diagrams, pictures are all tools that can be used to rationalise concepts that can be shared and influence mental models of others as well as your own. They are useful ways to drag mental models out of the mind of people and welcome criticisms from others. In so doing it is possible to create a shared and agreed understanding of real-world systems among different communities, forming the basis for human institutions and a tiny certainty within our uncertain world.

Computer models are one of the ways to formalise the mental models in a format that is sharable among many. Computer models can also use calculation power to capture some characteristics of the reality that the mind finds difficult to catch. Characteristics of the reality that people can measure, interpret, or formulate hypothesis on, in relation to their possible evolution over time. Computer models can be seen as extensions of mental models, and can play an important role in structuring a better society. By using computer models to drag mental models out of people's mind, it is possible to create models built by the aggregation of the mental models of many, test and improve those over time, and use the models for pursuing some objective for the community.

The world and the society

Coming back to the box as a mental representation of the entire world, we might use it to start developing a computer model. As an empty box, the model is static (does not change over time) and does not capture any information about the state and evolution of any system in the world. The practical use we can make of it is none. Higher success can be achieved by exploring what there is inside the box, some relations among such elements, and possibly their behaviour over time in particular conditions.

When opening the box, it is easy to list everything that comes into our mind that would be part of it. We can range from the atoms of hydrogen to entire oceans, from the consciousness of one person to the information captured in their DNA, from a tiny village in the countryside in Africa to the network of 214 nations defining the geopolitics of our planet. Some of these aspects can be approached with certainty, others would be less clear since they are not yet understood by humanity or not scientifically attainable. Some elements can be listed, but it would be not feasible to define how they interact with other elements of the whole.

Two simple ways to differentiate systems of the world can be on the basis of the time they take to evolve and their scale of impact. While some ecosystems on Earth take thousands to millions of years to exhibit significant changes (for example, the time to form crude oil and coal in the ground, the time for Earth to absorb carbon dioxide (CO_2), or the time for new forms of life to emerge), the time frame taken into account for people dealing with daily activities, businesses, and politics ranges from hours to a few decades. It takes less than two decades for a new born to be considered an adult; it takes a few years to receive an education and set up a career to have a role in society; it takes about two decades to spread technologies and products in society after they have been discovered for the first time; it takes about five years for a government to be responsible for managing nations in democratic societies; it takes months to a few years to substitute goods and appliances in your house; it takes generations to change culture in a society; it takes years to deal with conflicts and wars among nations; it takes days, or even hours to take decisions in the financial market to invest the next dollar profitably. But the leftovers of human passage on Earth can take hundreds to millions of years to be reabsorbed into the environment. Together as a dominant species on the planet we were able to become a planetary force strong enough to change the climate from the era of the Holocene (a period of relatively stable climate that started about 11,700 years ago) to the Anthropocene due to emissions generated from a massive economy founded on the paradigm of growth (this is considered to have started with the Industrial revolution in the 18th century).

Society itself can be thought of in many different ways as well. Culture, wealth, and religion are common ways to differentiate groups of people, one to another. From a global perspective, we can see the world divided in 214 countries covering different geographies and interacting one to another through the exchange of commodities and services (and people). It is also possible to see the world in terms of a financial district controlled by central banks, each with a different currency, sometimes involving multiple countries (see Europe). Seen both as countries and a financial district the main philosophy unifying all of those is the interconnection and the ability of some to solve the problems of others in a gigantic supply-demand network of global communities driven by production, trade within global markets, and the overall tendency to expand towards the next challenge. Based on the assumption of increased well-being for all, reduction in inequality among rich and poor, eradication of food insecurity and poverty in the long term, and the assurance of maximum employment levels for all, more and more power has been given to the financial system which was designed to address the disequilibrium of the world society and move towards growth. In so doing, the paradigm of economic growth became the strongest force dominating human development since James Watt invented the steam engine.

Despite this approach, which allowed for the widespread deployment of new technologies and modified the socio-economic environment to the point of being unrecognisable from just a few decades ago, all production still relies on the extraction and depletion of some natural ecosystem. In particular every material good we use uses minerals, every house needs energy for lighting and heating, every business needs energy for operating machines, every farm needs water, land and fertilizers to produce food, and so on. Each of these processes has the peculiarity of generating waste and pollutants as well as depleting the natural resources at a pace that leaves less time before reaching the limits of the planet. Such an approach is unsustainable and actions should be taken collectively and urgently if we are to avoid the worst impacts.

Governments have an extremely important role in the sustainability challenge. Despite technological change, the process of decision making and policy development remains firmly based on a traditional humanistic approach. Although information is more easily available to decision makers in shorter time frames, and despite an increasing use of computerised algorithmic decision making, the final decision is based on the mental models of the decision makers informed through dialogue and feedback from the various elements of the society they aim at supporting. Based on the understanding and knowledge relative to the systems composed of businesses, citizens, and finance, it is clear that, in its current state, decision makers cannot effectively deal with important global trends which have the potential to negatively feedback on our society such as systemic crises, recessions, and conflicts. Such a global system needs to be reformed. A new mental model is needed.

Sustainability, resilience, and global models

Given a variety of systems in the world evolving with different time scales and affects, how can we define correctly the right granularity and content of a computer model? It is the purpose of the model that determines its content. For example, if we want to study the world from the angle of climate interaction with the oceans, the physical characteristics of a single person might not be relevant. The knowledge available to inform the model and the methodology adopted are also important constraints defining the format of the model and its capability to study some particular world dynamics. In turn its format and accessibility will determine whether it influences the mental models of decisions makers.

The models that are presented in this book look at the problems of sustainability, systemic risk, and resilience based on current behaviour of human society dealing with the resources of the finite planet in the context of major shocks. One of the earlier definitions of sustainable development was provided by the Bruntland report in 1987 as: "development that meets the needs of the present without compromising the ability of future generations to meet their own needs." Such a definition remains hard to interpret by policy makers and businesses when they make decisions, and unfortunately, the long term in the year 1987 has become the short term in the year 2020. In fact, the concept of resilience, the ability of an ecological system to absorb and react to perturbations and return to its normal state, became fundamental for a transition towards a more sustainable world.

Sustainability and resilience must be seen as multidisciplinary challenges involving different systems interconnected through mutual feedbacks. A system characterised by the presence of closed loop feedbacks takes the name of 'complex system,' indicating that the evolution of every component should not be considered in isolation but as outcome of its interactions with the other components. In the case of global scale models, we can consider those as 'complex macro-systems' involving knowledge coming from social, biological, political, environmental, and economic perspectives among others.

In Part I of this book, we explore a revisit of the Limits to Growth model, presented in its last version (Meadows et al. 2003). As the analysis focuses on sustainability, the model is relatively small, with a focus on the dynamics of real output and population growth in a finite planet between the years 1900 and 2100 (Chapter 1). A comparison of world limits with current global trends (Chapter 2) and current literature (Chapter 3) has also been performed. Part II of the book focuses on the development of a novel model named Economic Risk, Resources and Environment (ERRE). ERRE is a larger and more detailed model than the World3, that includes finance, energy, food, and climate systems. The aim is to tackle both political problems related to resource availability in the short time scale (one to five years), as well as stress-test long-term scenarios and risks emerging from the interaction between the dynamics of growth and global resources limits until the end of this century.

The ERRE model has been formulated based on the work of Professor Jay Forrester in the 1970s and early 1980s. In particular, it is a formal update on the PhD Thesis of Professor John Sterman from the MIT School of Management, while integrating a food system based on the World3–03 land structure. During the modelling process, many updates based on current state of the art, in particular around the structure of financial flows and closed loop economic system, have been performed.

Part II of the book starts from a detailed review of the economic modelling literature, while comparing the system dynamics approach to other economic modelling methods (Chapter 4), and is followed with a general description of the ERRE model (Chapter 5). Chapter 6 provides a review of the dataset used to calibrate the model, and a statistical validation of the model output with the dataset. In addition, short-term shock scenarios are assessed, and long-term stress testing, to explore the dynamics of the world economy within the limits of the planet by the end of the century, is performed. The analysis is performed under deep uncertain conditions, while engaging in the debate of uncertainty and fat-tail extreme scenario risk assessment. The ERRE model simulates from the year 2000 to 2030 to capture short-term shock dynamics, and extend the simulation until the year 2100 to capture long-term risk fat-tail scenarios. Both Chapters 5 and 6 are extended with supporting online material describing the structure and equations of the ERRE model in detail, and some key leverage behavioural tests performed on the ERRE model, to address how its dynamics compare to economic literature. All these are accompanied with the entire model, at the https://doi.org/10.25411/aru.10110710. The book concludes with our thoughts and proposals to engage in global system change both from a top-down approach to decision making, and from a bottom-up businesses and citizens' perspectives (Chapter 7).

The models are presented in order to welcome criticism from the reader. We are interested in making our models transparent and accessible. We believe that through questioning the limited structures of the models presented here, a system's view on the current state of the world can be reached. Most important we encourage debate and feedback, which ultimately, improve the models as well as change our mental models. Please take your time to read this book and be open for changing your view on world systems.

Part I
World models and limits

1 The first formal world models

"What we meant in 1972 in 'the Limits to Growth' and what is still true, is that there is simply no endless growth in a finite planet" (Meadows 2012). The need for developing a world model was recognised and actively encouraged by the Club of Rome (CoR) in 1970 (Club of Rome 1970). The CoR is an informal, multinational, non-political group of scientists, intellectuals, educators, and business leaders sharing a common vision and concern for the future of humanity. It was formed in 1968 at the instigation of Aurelio Peccei, an Italian anti-fascist industrialist (Pauli 1987; Meadows et al. 1972). With the aim of engaging in the social problems generated by humankind and finding a way to create an economic paradigm that could generate sufficiency for all in the indefinite long term, they gained global visibility after their first report entitled 'The Limits to Growth' was published in 1972 (Meadows et al. 1972).

After decades of prosperous global industrial and business activities and an unprecedented accumulation and spread of capital and technology worldwide, it became clear that such an orthodox approach was also causing problems that would require a different way of thinking from that used to generate such 'prosperity.' They named such a concept the 'problematique of mankind' and referred to it as the "fragmentation of reality into closed and well-bounded problems which creates a new problems whose solution is clearly beyond the scope and the concepts we customarily employ" (Club of Rome 1970, p. 13). Today, the CoR has its headquarter in Winterthur, Switzerland, and involves more than 100 members ranging from heads of state, UN bureaucrats, high-level politicians and government officials, diplomats, scientists, economist and business leaders around the globe. They all share a common mission: "to act as a global catalyst for change through the identification and analysis of the crucial problems facing humanity and the communication of such problems to the most important public and private decision makers as well as the general public" (Weizsäcker 2014).

The first world computer model was driven by the need for a unifying integrated vision that could be shared among collaborating countries and economies that were getting bigger, more complex, more intelligent, at faster increasing rates, but were still based on resources extraction, unable to cope with (probably being the cause of) social and environmental problems, including overpopulation,

DOI: 10.4324/9781315643182-2

widespread poverty and malnutrition, loss of traditional values in the society, and the rise of pollution. The need generated a research demand which, accompanied by the rise in cybernetic technologies previously applied to the study of social and industrial complexity, allowed for the feasibility of such an ambitious and unprecedented project (Club of Rome 1970).

Following the development of a research proposal in March 1970, the group asked Professor Jay Forrester at the Sloan School of Management at the Massachusetts Institute of Technology (MIT) to assess the potential of industrial dynamics (thereafter named system dynamics) (Forrester 1961, 1968, 1971a) as a possible methodology to approach the problematique. On 29th June 1970, Forrester was invited to the conference of the Club of Rome in Bern. After an introduction to the problematique, Forrester generated a sketch of a world model (sometimes called World1) while on his flight back to the US. On 20th July, the Club of Rome was invited to a two-week conference at MIT, to review the World2 model, the first functioning formal computer world model ever developed (Forrester 1971b; Meadows et al. 1982).

Phase One of the Predicament of Mankind could formally start. Dennis Meadows, who had recently attained his PhD at MIT under Forrester's supervision, was appointed as team lead for the development of the World3 model. Based on the initial work of Professor Forrester, a team of 16 scientists, with active support from the Club of Rome members, was engaged for 18 months to answer the complex interconnected set of needs of the Club of Rome and its stakeholders using SD. In March 1972 the research was presented to the Club of Rome committee, and the first report of the Club of Rome entitled "The Limits to Growth" (1972) was published to the wider public.

Limits to growth achievements

The main findings of the Limits to Growth were sobering. By means of scenario analysis through simulation, the team at MIT opened a discussion proposing social and economic shifts away from the most basic paradigm that governed global society dynamics till then, i.e. the paradigm of growth.

The belief that economic growth based on resource extraction and use could have been the engine for spreading well-being across societies and cultures for an indefinite time horizon was demonstrated as being naïve in nature and was even the driver of widespread problems generated by the interaction between growth and the ecological physical constraints of the planet (limits). Population and industrial growth could overshoot the planet's limits within the first half of the 21st century with a possible drastic collapse of human society in terms of well-being including the early deaths of a significant portion of the population on the planet.

Large uncertainty in estimating structural relations and limits were considered in the publication. In particular, scenarios relaxing the effects of growth on the use and depletion of natural resources were proposed. Unless the effects could be reduced to zero the dynamics of growth could still reach the limits of the planet within the time frame of the simulation. Most important, Limits to Growth (LtG) recognised the importance of delays in the adaptation of humankind to develop and spread new technologies globally. The emphasis on time delays showed that the earlier actions are taken to address the limits, the better the outcome could have been for all.

On the basis of such findings, the team of scientists tried to reach multiple aims. First, to answer the needs of the Club of Rome and the Problematique. Second, to provide the scientific community with a model of the world that could be criticised, improved, and updated as well as to form the basis for further research. Third, to communicate the results of the work to everyone potentially interested in its findings, that is, the whole world population from then onwards.

According to Meadows et al. (1982), the work was very successful in all three aspects. By the year 1980, the LtG was translated in 23 languages and sold over three million copies worldwide; it accounts for more than 12 million copies sold to date (Jackson 2016). Seven months after the LtG publication, the representatives of 12 national scientific organisations met in London to affix their signatures to the charter of a new and unique international scientific organisation: the International Institute for Applied System Analysis (IIASA). Concerned with the findings of the LtG, IIASA opened a call for global models to different scientific communities as a series of symposiums. The aim was to run a careful comparison between models that were developed based on paradigms different from the one of system dynamics (SD). Having multiple perspectives on the state of the future of humankind may potentially generate a unifying vision to drive actions. Such a symposium is recognised as one of the most intense efforts up to that point in global modelling (Sterman 1991).

In addition to the World3 Forrester-Meadows model, another six models were included in the comparative analysis. Although World3 was considered as having answered the needs of the Club of Rome, new directions were highlighted and new initiatives were taken. Among those models we find the Mesarovic-Pestel model that is a follow up on the LtG from the Club of Rome, and also formed the basis for the second report to the Club of Rome (Mesarovic and Pestel 1974).

With the publication of the Dynamics of Growth in a Finite World (Meadows et al. 1974), World3 became one of the most fully documented among the global models (Meadows et al. 1982) at that time. World3 is also probably one of the most criticised models of all time. In the words of Donella Meadows, "those who believed that continued growth was essential to the preservation of Western industrial society and to the improvement of the state mankind attacked the principal conclusions. Scientists and political leaders from the Third World argued that the model was essentially an ideological statement from the developed world. Economists attacked the world view of

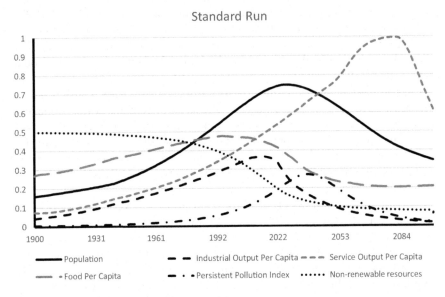

Figure 1.1 Standard run of World3–03 model

systems dynamics, which differed fundamentally from their own" (Meadows et al. 1982, p. 24).

It is worth noting that despite the effort of IIASA and the engagement of different scientific communities in developing new global models, only World3 received such global visibility. The simplicity of the LtG message can be viewed through its 'base run' scenario (or 'standard run' or 'scenario 1') proposed as a starting point for the analysis (see Figure 1.1). The 'base run' depicts the behaviour of seven key variables (population, birth and death rates, industrial output per capita, food per capita, non-renewable resource fraction remaining, persistent pollution index), and was proposed as the most likely among the scenarios presented in the LtG if the dynamics of growth seen at the time did not change. Under this scenario, the portion of greatest interest lies between the years 2000 and 2050. During this period, both population and industrial output per capita grow 'beyond sustainable levels' and start to decline. Depletion of non-renewable resources, leading to a generally depressed economy, is the principal cause of this decline.

More recent work by Graham Turner (2008, 2012) presented a comparison of the outcomes of the base run of LtG scenarios with the trends over the 40 years since the models were originally run. Figure 1.2 shows the results of his analysis. By mean of comparison of normalised trends of key measurable global variables with the outputs of the base run scenario of World3 in 1972, he observed that the world was following the same path as the 'base run.' The

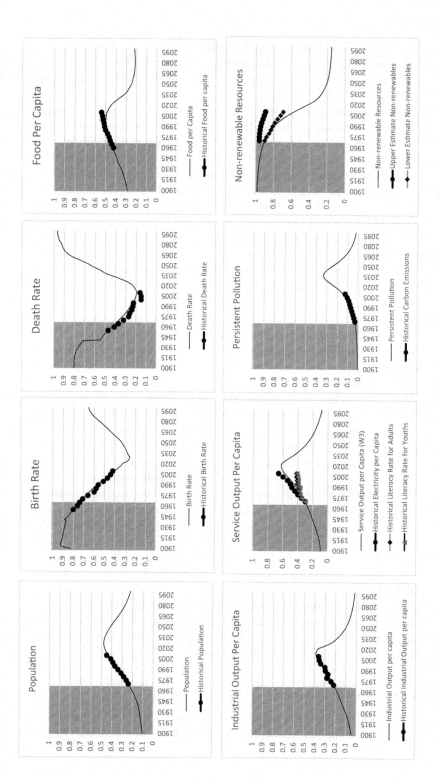

Figure 1.2 Normalised values of World3 (Meadows et al. 1972) and trend on historical time series

Source: Adapted from Turner (2012)

'base run,' of course, runs towards a global collapse towards the middle of this century. Castro (2012) criticised the superficial use of the World3 model to give premature results in informing policy although this was countered by Turner (2013).

As one of its originators argues, the 'standard run' represents only the beginning of the process of using the model (Meadows et al. 1982). The purpose was to better understand possible outcomes of mankind's attempt to deal with growth on a limited planet, and to identify strategies that could lead to more favourable futures using multiple scenario analysis. The base run shows a general decrease in terms of economic output and population on the planet because the estimate of non-renewable resources that could be extracted to support human activity was conservative (Meadows et al. 1982, 1992, 2003).

In fact, LtG policy recommendations were set on the basis of Scenario 2 that, differently from the 'standard run' scenario, assumed enough resource availability to sustain economic growth for a longer time. In this case the overshoot and collapse of economic and population dynamics was due to the unsustainable accumulation of persistent pollution in the environment linked to resource use. Other runs showed how the solution to one limit could lead to overshoot and collapse because of reaching another limit (generated by the complex interaction between available land, food production, and persistent pollution). Randers – another of the World3 originators argued that "It now appears that the tightest constraint on physical growth is not resource scarcity, or vulgar shortage of raw materials. Rather the most pressing limit seems to be on the emission side. To be concrete, the world appears to have much more fossil fuels than was assumed, indeed more than man can burn without causing serious climate change" (Randers 2000, p. 215).

LtG showed that the current trend of growth could easily reach the physical limits of the planet in terms of available resources, quality and availability land, and the Earth's capacity to absorb emissions from industrial activity and agriculture within the time frame of a few generations. In every realistic scenario, these limits force an end to economic growth in the World3 sometime during the 21st century. The study did not specify exactly which resource scarcity or what emission type might end growth simply because such detailed predictions cannot be made on a scientific basis in the huge and complex population-economy-environment system that constitutes our world (Meadows et al. 2003).

Before getting into the details of the model and the most important knowledge aspects that can be reused and readapted to current society, it is important to look at the use of the systems dynamics paradigm as a foundation to understand the assumption taken for developing the World3 model.

The basics of system dynamics

System dynamics (SD) is an approach to real complex systems by means of system thinking, computer modelling with emphasis on feedback loops, accumulation processes and non-linearities, and computer simulation and testing (Forrester 1980; Richardson 1991; Sterman 2000). First developed by Forrester at MIT for the study of high level industrial management problems (Forrester 1958, 1961), system dynamics demonstrated particular applicability to multidisciplinary problems and the study and design of social structures (Richardson 1991). Over the years SD has grown as a profession linking engineers, policy scientists, ecologists, sociologists, economists, and others. SD found application in studies of sustainability (Meadows et al. 1972), the dynamics of urban stagnation and decay (Forrester 1968), research and development (Warren 2008), commodity cycles (Meadows 1969; Morecroft 2007), economic development and fluctuations (Sterman 1985; Forrester 1980; Jackson 2016), energy life cycles and transitions (Morecroft 2007; Sterman 1981), dynamics and management of ecosystems (Costanza and Daly 1992; Fiddaman 1997), among others.

When systems are complex (this is the case for most social interactions) the sort of thinking that is required takes the name of 'system thinking.' In contraposition to the mechanistic, reductionist, or atomistic view where emphasis is given to elements that compose one part of the system, system thinking (or holistic, or organismic, or ecological) gives emphasis to the whole. According to such a view, the essential properties of an ecosystem emerge from the interaction and relationships between parts. Although we can discern individual parts in every system, these are not isolated, and the nature of the whole is always different from the mere sum of its parts (Capra and Luisi 2016).

The information used for taking decisions within social systems that can be incorporated in SD models are formalised in Figure 1.3. The larger depository of information and knowledge is what is contained within people's head (mental database). It is the depository of information formed through recording experience, observation, and participation in life. Such information can be formalised for the purpose of communication through written documentation. Such documentation can be further described with the use of numerical data. Emphasising such a concept, Forrester (1980a) states that the scale of reduction of information moving from mental data to written data, and from written data to numerical data is of the order one million.

The information available to decision makers can be organised in different ways. The perspective taken in SD aims to explain systems behaviour through endogenous feedback loop structures within the boundaries of the system under analysis. The feedback loops identify the system structure and the shifts in feedback loop dominance explain the change in system behaviour over time. Non-linearities remain key components in the formalisation of SD models, but at the same time SD models generate structures that are deterministic in nature. SD models are often used for tackling major improvements and large systems changes rather than to deal with problems related to volatility and randomness within smaller parts of systems. From a feedback loop perspective, the socio-political system is a "high order multi-loop, non-linear feedback system" where

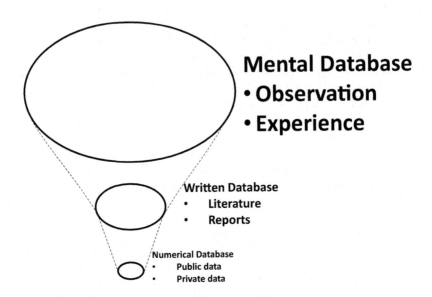

Mental Database
• Observation
• Experience

Written Database
•   Literature
•   Reports

Numerical Database
•   Public data
•   Private data

Figure 1.3 Definition of databases in system modelling

Source: Adapted from Forrester (1980)

behaviour and reaction to policy making is often misleading and counterintuitive (Forrester 1971a, 1980). The feedback from reality becomes hard to measure and the formation of resilient mental models becomes mostly a matter of action and reaction based on intuition, experience and the culture of the decision makers.

Nowadays, there exists several computer modelling techniques (for example econometrics, discrete-events, agent-based or complex networks) which influence and filter the way complex systems can be thought of. The approach of SD favours a particular view on systems that reflects its feedback loop structure. According to Richardson (1991), the way SD looks at decision processes is not detailed enough to deal with human thought and discrete actions, but neither far enough to signal ignorance of the pressures the system is subjected to. Such a view justifies the use of continuous time modelling, assuming that discrete decisions at the process level can be seen as flows of decisions, and discrete events can be approximated with aggregated continuous processes over time.

When feedback structures and relationships are formulated and incorporated in an SD model, computer simulation becomes the only practical way to test its meaningfulness. The comparison between model outcomes and the expectations formed through the mental models is the best way to allow for adjustment between one and the other. Simulation becomes essential when experimentation in the real system is not possible, and when it is important to speed up the learning feedback, which can too often be too slow. All models have to pass through a variety of tests (Forrester 1980; Sterman 2000) before the modelling process can be considered concluded and useful for the reason the model was originally built. Emphasis is given to rigorous and disciplined testing of models to avoid ideology and unconscious bias to generate useful information (Forrester and Senge 1980).

Some important characteristics and elements of system dynamics models are described next. These aspects are included here as they are critical for framing the systems dynamics approach to help understand the usefulness of this approach for our defined problem. For a deeper review of such components, work such as Forrester (1961, 1968), Ford (1999), and Sterman (2000) is suggested. A historical comparison of SD with other modelling methods, and wider evolution of the field in comparison to economic methods, is provided in Chapter 4 of this book.

Views and elements of system dynamics models

Purpose, boundaries, and time horizon

In the words of Donella Meadows (1982, p. 7): "the very best model would be the one containing only the information required for the purpose of the model itself." SD models are normally built around one or more research question that the model is supposed to help answer. The research questions emerge from one or more dynamic problems assumed to be generated by a complex set of interconnections within a particular unit of analysis (e.g. a business, an economy, an ecosystem). The behavioural problem might be revealed by past historical data, an intuition on possible future trends that have not been experienced yet, or the need for the development of a strategy to deal with a particular challenge.

A clear model purpose is the key to framing a model between (i) a set of interconnected elements that are assumed to participate in the dynamic evolution of the issue under study (endogenous), and (ii) a set of elements that are assumed to influence the dynamic under study but are not affected by its evolution (exogenous). By considering these different elements, the model gets bounded both in terms of space and time. The modeller places themselves in the special position of observer that allows them to see the dynamic of interest evolving as continuous time events. Such a top-down view allows the study of a dynamic system from an endogenous perspective based on its feedback loop structure. Exogenous elements are considered as those that are not affected by the endogenous structure of the system (i.e. they would not change over time). A simulation time is set such that it allows for a comparison with available historical data, and carries on long enough after present time to allow for a particular desired (or undesired) dynamic behaviour to show up. Such a view is depicted in Figure 1.4.

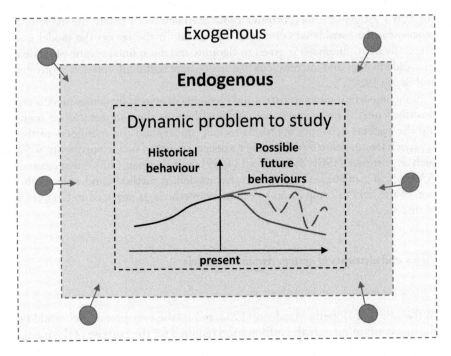

Figure 1.4 Focus of system dynamics modelling

Causal loop diagram and feedback loop structure

Within the endogenous frame of the model boundaries, feedback thinking can help sketch the structure of the model. In particular the interacting elements can be identified and their causal relationships drawn as arrows indicating the dependence of one element to another. Causal dependencies can be differentiated according to a polarity: a 'plus sign' (+) indicates that a positive/negative variation of one element would increase/decrease the element it is feeding into, whereas a 'minus sign' (-) would indicate that a positive/negative variation would decrease/increase the subsequent element. SD models focus on the identification of powerful feedback loops (circular causal relationships that bring one element back to itself passing through other system elements). These feedback loops generate the dynamic behaviour and compose the complexity of the system model.

Feedback loops can be distinguished between positive (or reinforcing) and negative (or balancing). The positive feedback loops are the most powerful instruments that must be identified within a system's study, since those are the ones that can generate disequilibrium in the system and can potentially amplify dynamics that bring the system farther away from any initial condition. The negative feedback loops can be seen as dynamic controls over the positive feedback loop that can generate balancing effects bringing the systems towards equilibrium. It is a

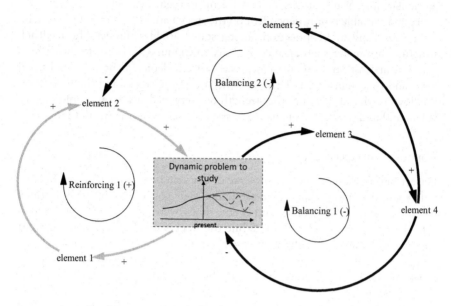

Figure 1.5 Feedback loop to explain desired system behaviours

battle among reinforcing and balancing forces that the system dynamics modeller attempts to capture within the system structure. As seen in Figure 1.5, the sign of every feedback loop can be found by multiplying the signs of the causal relationships that compose the circular causality.

Accumulation within the feedback loop structure

On the basis of the feedback loop structure it becomes possible to identify major accumulation processes within the system. Everything that we can identify as a tangible element of our reality is the result of some sort of accumulation. For example, the size of a city changes as the outcome of new construction, and is reduced by demolished buildings, whereas the size of a forest is reduced by cutting trees, and increased with new planted ones over time. The difficulty in perceiving this accumulation within a system increases the larger the system and the longer the time it takes to evolve.

The group of accumulations within a system represent the system's state, i.e. the system's condition at a particular time. It is because of the understanding of the system's state and its evolution over time that it is possible to take actions, and apply policies to control it towards desired states into the future. In SD, the accumulation is represented with the notion of stock (or state, or level) and flow (or rate) variables. In particular the stocks represent the state of the system at every time step, and the flows the degree of change of such states at every particular time. While stocks are dependent on their own inflows and outflows, every flow variable is only dependent on the stock variables (state) of the system.

The resulting interconnection among state variables through the feedback structures are major sources of complexity in SD models. Every feedback loop contains at least an accumulation process that is depicted through stocks and flows and their mutual relationships. The size of the stocks and their effect on the flows is what determines the strength of every feedback loop (reinforcing or balancing) and the degree of change of system's state at any point in time.

Flows as natural and decision processes

Perfect information on the current state of a system is not sufficient for effective policy and decision making. Understanding their possible evolution over time, based on the natural processes and events that govern the dynamics of a system into the future, are fundamental. While the stock variables capture the current condition of the system, the flow variables capture its dynamic change at any point in time. Flows either indicate natural dynamic changes (flows as natural processes), or human desired changes in the system (flows as decision processes and policy rules).

All natural systems, both physical and biological, evolve over time as a result of the interaction with other elements in their environment. Such dynamic change can be depicted with the support of the 'flows' as input or output from stock variables – we refer to this kind of flow as a 'flow as natural process.' Some examples might include the formation of crude oil in the ground – it can be thought as an inflow to the stock 'crude oil already present on Earth,' a natural process that took millions of years.

People also participate in the dynamic change of the systems that surround them. We call the flows dependent on human action 'flows as decision processes.' Some examples of flows between humans and ecosystems include an outflow from the stock 'crude oil' dependent on how it is extracted from the ground; an inflow to the stock 'amount of carbon dioxide in the atmosphere' because of anthropogenic emissions. Flows between human systems can include flow of money from a government to a business as subsidy – in this case the stocks involved would be 'available cash to government' and 'available cash to business'; flows of products and money for payments within a supply chain – in this case the stocks would be material ('inventory for delivery' and 'inventory for purchases' of two partners with the supply chain) and financial (stocks of cash available to the customer and supplier). Both in case of 'natural processes' and 'decision processes,' stocks are connected to flows by mean of feedback mechanisms. Whereas in the case of natural processes, the feedback structure describes the physical characteristics of the system under study, the feedback structure involving flows as decision processes mostly comes from the information gathered from the system that is to be controlled.

Within the context of system dynamics modelling, it is important to remember that decisions processes are seen as discrete processes that can be approximated as continuous flows of sums of decisions and actions from a top-down perspective.

Such decisions are differentiated from the concept of policy, which is seen as the 'guiding rule' that yields the stream of decisions (Forrester 1961). For example, the policy of following 'free market' as a rule to run an economy determines a series of human behaviours that prioritise certain flows of decisions over others within global supply chains.

Non-linear relationships, delays, goal-seeking structures, and tests

The connections among stocks and flows in the system provide a visual representation of its structure but may hide the relationships among system elements which drive the model behaviour. In particular, system dynamics allows for the modelling of both linear and non-linear relationships. SD uses delays within relationships to indicate the non-immediate availability of information and material adaptation that drive both decision and natural processes within the system model.

Linear relationships are the simplest way to describe a causal effect between one variable and another. If one quantity is dependent on another quantity with a linear relationship, it indicates that every change in the second implies a change in the first that is proportional to it. The constant of proportionality is made explicit as a 'parameter.' The assumption of a linear relationship is often used as a means to simplify reality. Constant coefficients on linear relationships corresponds to factors that remain exogenous to the dynamic of the system under study and can be approximated as invariant parameters over the time of the simulation. When the assumption of linear behaviour does not hold system dynamics allows for the inclusion of non-linear relationships for the study of systems.

Non-linear relationships are fundamental tools in SD because they help set the conditions that generate compensating feedbacks which shift loop dominance over the simulation time. Feedback systems driven by reinforcing feedback loops have the capacity to increase the strength of compensating feedback over time. This is the case in the LtG models (Forrester 1971b; Meadows 1972 – as illustrated in the next section), in which natural adjustments initially ineffective become major factors of world collapse over longer time frames in the simulation.

Non-linear relationships can be incorporated in different ways within the model structure. Mathematical equations quantified by external parameters can be used, and multiplications among different stock variables could generate non-linear behaviours. The most common use of non-linearities within system dynamics modelling is through the use of 'table functions' (or lookup functions), i.e. a non-linear function of an input variable giving an effect on the output variable. The use of non-linear relationships is the fundamental tool which differentiates a standard neoclassical economic model from an SD model of the economy. Whereas the first is often based on the use of linear relationships, and rationality of agents, an SD applies non-linearities in the attempt to describe human cognitive capabilities and non-linear feedback to system states (Morecroft 1985), and ecological boundaries to the economy (Costanza 1991).

Another tool for increased realism in SD is the presence of time delays. Relationships including delays generate lagged responses from the system to the input variables. Delays exist both in the physical (time for producing output for a company, time for the construction of a plant) and informational areas (time for the measurement of the state of the system, or time to take an investment decision). Every delay contains an accumulation (stock) by definition: since their outcome is to generate a lagged response of whatever input (both material and informational). Time delays can generate complex behaviours, including oscillations or even collapse if responses are too slow.

Delays and non-linearities are very useful tools in providing realism for decision processes over time. Decision processes are normally goal oriented and desired outcomes of decision processes should also be well specified within system dynamics models. A policy can be recognised as a local goal toward a decision point, which, by comparing the goal with the apparent system condition to detect any discrepancy, uses the discrepancy to guide an action. As such, goal-seeking structures recognise bounded rationality of agents working in the system and can be depicted with the use of time delays and non-linear relationships. Goal-seeking structures are balancing feedback loops which aim at helping systems to adapt to their environments.

Linear and non-linear relationships, and delays can be better estimated with econometric techniques, or running sensitivity tests to give ranges of variability on such relationships. Examples of estimation techniques can be found in Sterman (2000) and Senge (1978).

Figure 1.6 shows a stock and flow diagram as a result of the causal loop diagram of Figure 1.5, and Figure 1.7 proposes a real case dynamic problem on the basis of the proposed causal loop diagram.

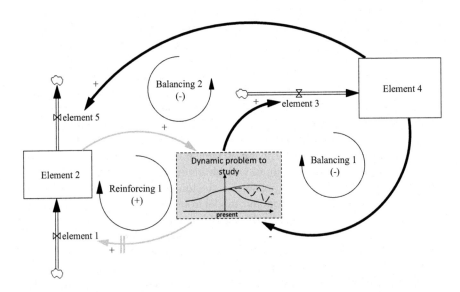

Figure 1.6 Stock and flows within the feedback structure

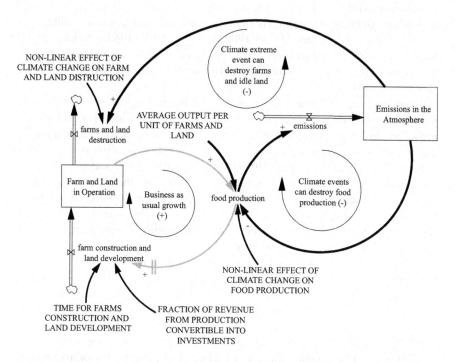

NON-LINEAR EFFECT OF
CLIMATE CHANGE ON FARM
AND LAND DISTRUCTION

Climate extreme
event can
destroy farms
and idle land
(-)

AVERAGE OUTPUT PER
UNIT OF FARMS AND
LAND

Emissions in the
Atmosphere

farms and land
destruction

+ emissions

Farm and Land
in Operation

Business as
usual growth
(+)

food production

Climate events
can destroy food
production (-)

farm construction and
land development

NON-LINEAR EFFECT OF
CLIMATE CHANGE ON
FOOD PRODUCTION

TIME FOR FARMS
CONSTRUCTION AND
LAND DEVELOPMENT

FRACTION OF REVENUE
FROM PRODUCTION
CONVERTIBLE INTO
INVESTMENTS

Figure 1.7 An example of stock and flow structure of agriculture and climate interaction

Model simulation, policy testing, and recommendations

From a mathematical standpoint, system dynamics modelling consists of capturing a complex system via dynamic differential equations (i.e. a system of equations where derivatives – flow or rate variables – are written as dependent on the integral functions – stocks or state variables). Historically, differential equation models have been constrained by the complexity of finding a mathematical solution unless the problem is formulated as linear and relatively small (Richardson 1991). System dynamics, being explicitly non-linear, require simulation as the only means of solving the model. On the other hand, it allows for the representation of much larger models than those approached by the scientists of the time (Richardson 1991).

The first use of model simulation is in the model design. Models are supposed to pass a variety of tests before being considered able to fulfil the purpose they were built for (Forrester and Senge 1980; Sterman 2000). Some tests that involve simulation include (i) the reproduction of historical data or past behaviour, (ii) extreme condition tests, and (iii) behaviour anomaly tests. The aim of all tests is to reveal that models can generate the right behaviour for the right reason, and fulfil their purpose to influence decision making (Barlas 1989, 1996; Barlas and Carpenter 1990).

Model structures and behaviours are tightly intertwined, but such a connection is hard to be depicted using human mental capabilities, as empirically demonstrated in several studies (Dörner 1980; Sterman 1989a, 1989b; Brehmer 1992; Kleinmuntz 1993; Diehl and Sterman 1995). Even when starting from the correct model structures, it is easy to draw the wrong conclusions on system behaviours (Forrester 1968).

Therefore, the simulation of dynamic models can help infer system behaviour from assumptions with greater confidence than that which is possible with mental simulations (Sterman 2000). At the most basic level, a simulation model can be used as a learning tool (see the use of C-Roads to sensitise policy makers about climate change – Sterman 2014). At a higher level it would be possible to test policies before actual implementation. In this case, the simulation can be seen as a tool for speeding up the learning process. Most important, when experimentation in real systems is not feasible or not acceptable, simulation becomes the main, and probably the only, way to test the validity of possible policies and assumptions before actual implementation.

'What if' scenario analysis remains the most widely used form of analysis within SD models. In particular, exogenous parameters and inputs can be modified in line with future unknown trends and events, such as population growth or climatic shocks. On the one hand, it would be important to identify significant leverage policies useful in mitigating negative effects on important system variables. On the other hand, it can be used just as a mean for exploring future possibilities and forecasting. The use of calibrations and optimisation techniques can also be beneficial. Other kinds of analysis focus on the identification of high leverage parameters and policies that can have major effects on the dynamics of the system. Sensitivity analysis on the main uncertainties in the models or more recent exploratory modelling techniques for the study of deep uncertainty are often used for these purposes (Pruyt 2015; Kwakkel and Pruyt 2015).

In the history of SD, models have always been used to try to approach the complexity of real systems and many different ways have been used to allow people to engage with these models. These include participatory modelling (Videira et al. 2003, 2010), flight simulators that allow people to explore leverage points within virtual realities (Sterman 2014; Meadows et al. 1993; Morecroft 1988), and development of narratives for engagement with global change (Jackson 2016).

The World3 model in practice

The World3 model is a system dynamics model developed to study the dynamics of human population and material economy growth within the limits of the finite planet. The model was constructed to be as compact and focused as possible for the purpose of communication to the wider public and non-expert audiences. In order to stress the importance of the dependency of human systems on natural resources, several aspects of the economy were not explicitly represented. Aspects of human behaviour and adaptation within the economy, such as financial activity, processes governing technological change, labour productivity, or resource prices can be considered as implicit and hidden within the structural relationship of the model.

The World3 model has been updated twice over the last 48 years. The model we refer to as World3 in this book corresponds to the last version published by the MIT group and called World3–03 (Meadows et al. 2003). The World3–03 presents minor updates to coefficients and relations in comparison to the previous version World3–91 (Meadows et al. 1992), which in turn presents minor updates from the original version used to publish *The Limits to Growth* (Meadows et al. 1972). The updates of each version were outlined in the appendices of each new publication, whereas the original World3 has been fully documented in *Dynamics of Growth in a Finite World* (Meadows et al. 1974). The latter presents all the hypotheses on which the LtG was grounded. It includes model testing, sensitivity analysis, the possibility to extend some model structures with more refined ones, and provides the structures to test technology development scenarios with various degrees of adaptation. Such structures that were initially neglected from the LtG (Meadows et al. 1972) have been further included in the updated version of the model because of initial criticisms.

Macro systems view and major assumptions in the World3

A simple way to start thinking about the World3 is to pretend to look at the world from a distance, distinguishing some major global aggregated processes evolving and interacting. Before defining the details of the accumulation processes and their interactions it is useful to first group and frame those as major macro-systems, and link those with mutual relationships. Some relationships among macro systems can be identified and qualitatively interpreted as carrying positive or negative effects between one system to the other. Finally it is possible to identify the major forces (feedback loops) within each system that can influence positively or negatively their internal dynamics.

In the World3, the major components, their relationships, and the major internal forces within each of them, can be represented as in Figure 1.8. The macro-systems can be seen as:

- Biological – human population;
- Economic – industries, services, agriculture and food production, and technology development;
- Natural resource based – land availability and fertility, resources in the ground;
- Waste generated by human activity which can be toxic to people and natural ecosystems – persistent pollution.

Focusing on material quantities that can be exchanged among different systems in the world, one can define every economic activity as dependent on extraction and transformation of resources from the ground into products and services useful for people. Industries are employed to extract resources and use those to build up

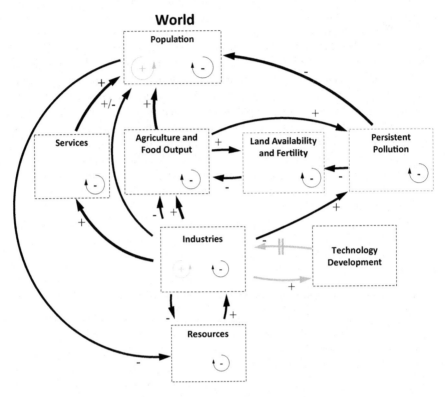

Figure 1.8 Top-down view on the World3–03 model

factories, service facilities, farms and agricultural equipment and consumption goods to support and satisfy the needs of the population. The aim of the economy is to increase the wealth of people, and wealth generation is linked to resource consumption. Therefore, World3 assumes that the entire economy is sustained via the forces that generate industrial output growth (see positive feedback loop in Industries). While the average population becomes wealthier, their material consumption needs rise. At the same time, facilities do not last forever. They need to be discarded and replaced with new ones (see negative feedback loops within Industries, Services, and Agriculture).

Agricultural systems rely on land. Based on modern farming techniques, they receive equipment and inputs supplied by industry. Such input is then used for developing agricultural lands out of forest land and increasing land productivity with the use of industrial fertilizers and pesticides. Land availability remains globally limited, and can be subjected to natural erosion processes (see negative feedback loop within Land Availability and Fertility). In addition, the overexploitation from inappropriate farming techniques can amplify erosion.

Despite all efforts to maintain high efficiency in production processes, there is always a certain amount of waste generated by industries and agriculture which is dispersed in the environment, damages ecosystems, and can be harmful for living organisms. Such waste can take the form of particulates which can be quickly absorbed by the environment (non-persistent pollutant), or waste that need considerable time (decades or centuries) to be reabsorbed by the environment in a form that is not harmful to biological systems (e.g. nuclear radioactive waste). In the World3, non-persistent particulates that do not involve any form of accumulation are generated from industrial production. This non-persistent pollution directly affects food output and the well-being of people (see negative causal relationships between industries and food production and population). The accumulation of persistent pollution (harmful waste) is assumed to slow down the normal ability of ecosystems to absorb harmful substances. At the same time persistent pollutants also constrain the production of healthy food, and affect people's well-being.

In World3, Population is seen as a biological system. In this sense, population increases in value because of births and decreases in value because of deaths, which are dependent on the amount of living people and represent two counteracting forces (see positive and negative feedback loops within Population in Figure 1.9). The effects on population from the other macro-systems can be seen as variants on the death and birth rates. Whereas improvements in food availability and health services per capita are drivers for increased life expectancy, the accumulations of persistent pollution above certain thresholds, which negatively impact food and health, can lower life expectancy, and pollute lands.

The world view in World3 puts the economy and every person as continuous users of material resources, constantly demanding more land, increasing soil erosion, and polluting the environment. When population and the economy are small in comparison to the planetary ecosystem, the effects of human systems can be absorbed or are almost not perceivable. However, there exist thresholds in ecosystems exploitation and resource depletion that can dramatically change the relationship between human activity and ecosystems over time. Such effects can become relevant when the population and the economy become large enough that their rate of exploitation of natural systems become greater than the bio-capacity of the planet. Still, assumptions of possible adaptive behaviour of humanity have been considered within the World3. Technology development and deployment can alter the strength of interaction between human activity and ecosystems. Seen from the perspective of governments, such technologies require investment into research and development (see delay between 'Technology development' and 'Industries') and, while the output of research and development can increase output over time, this investment itself constraints the output from other sectors of the economy in the short run.

Exponential growth and major forces generating behaviour

The observation that population and industrial growth was following a long-term exponential pattern lies at the heart of the Limits to Growth message. Coupled with the exploitation of ecosystems in a non-sustainable way, exponential growth represents a dangerous threat to humanity. The best way to feel the power of exponential growth is to do the calculation. For example, assuming economic growth maintains a constant real growth rate at 3.6% per annum (this is the case of the average growth rate of the global economy from the 1960), it takes about 20 years to double the size of the economy, as shown in Table 1.1.

In turn, a continuous doubling up of the size of the economy every 20 years for two centuries would correspond to an economy that is 1024 times bigger than its initial value as shown in Table 1.2.

While population and the economy become bigger, the rate of resources depletion and pollution rise proportionally. Even relatively small initial values of

Table 1.1 Exponential growth at 3.6% per year over 20 years; the calculation is 1.036^{Years}

Year	Present 1	2	3	... 16	17	18	19	20
Value	1	1.036 1.073296 1.111935		... 1.760987	1.824382	1.89006	1.958102	2.028594

Table 1.2 Exponential growth of a doubling economy every 20 years becomes 1024 bigger in two centuries; the calculation is $2^{Year/20}$

Year	Present	20	40	60	80	100	120	140	160	180	200
Value	1	2	4	8	16	32	64	128	256	512	1024

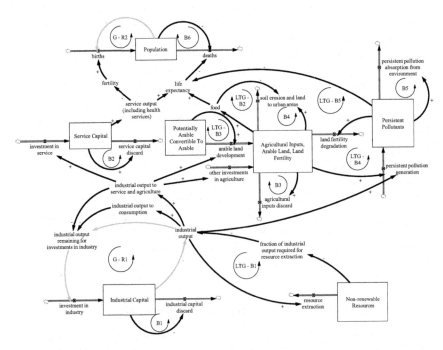

Figure 1.9 Major feedback loops and accumulation processes in the World3–03

an economy and population living non-sustainably on the finite planet would become impossible to contain without a fast transition towards a non-material extractive and non-polluting economy.

Some of the most important feedback loops and accumulation processes in the World3 are represented in Figure 1.9. In comparison to Figure 1.8, Figure 1.9 includes some major accumulation processes, aggregates together Land and Agricultural equipment as a unique accumulation, partially considers the effects of technology development, and brings in some auxiliary variables and major feedback loops as forces that generate the dynamic behaviour of World3 over time.

The reinforcing feedback loops generating growth in World3 are G – R1, assuming that industrial capital generates output that can be diverted to investments which then increase industrial capital, and G – R2, assuming that a larger population leads to more births that in turn increases the population. These loops capture the power of exponential growth.

The World3 model, as depicted in Figure 1.9, can be described as follows. Industrial Capital represents the amount of factories and equipment necessary for industrial production and is responsible for every material output that can be exploited within the economy. Through use, factories get discarded (they depreciate and need to be replaced or renewed) in proportion to the amount of industrial capital itself (balancing loop B1). Industrial output is then diverted into several sectors according to the needs of the economy. The first fraction is diverted for the extraction of energy and material resources. The non-renewable resources of World3 increase in cost the more they get extracted. Such a cost is assumed to increase the fraction of industrial output diverted to energy and material extraction (see balancing feedback loop LTG – B1). One fraction of the remaining industrial output is used for improving services and agriculture. A fraction of the remaining is then provided to people for consumption. The remaining fraction can be reintroduced, or reinvested, to industry, closing the reinforcing feedback loop generating economic growth (see reinforcing feedback loop G – R1).

The investments in service and agriculture are then allocated to the two sectors. In the case of services, new investments increase the stock of service capital which is subject to discard because of use and depreciation in a similar manner to industrial capital (see balancing feedback loop B2). The service output generated by service capital is used as an indicator for, amongst others, health services in the economy. Health services are linked to increasing life expectancy of people and provide services for maintaining family size close to desired levels. With regards to agriculture, machineries, chemicals and farms provided by industry are used for developing additional arable land, maintaining high fertility, and increasing productivity for satisfying the food needs of a growing population. Available food per capita is in turn assumed to increase the life expectancy of people. All factors involved in agricultural production, such as equipment, are subjected to discard and degradation (see balancing feedback loop B3). These inputs can have very different discard or degradation rates with some equipment having a long life while fertilizers or pesticides have a relatively short life. At the same time arable land is subject to a natural process of soil erosion (see feedback loop B4), which can be worsened by the exploitation of lands with food production (see feedback loop LTG – B2). This latter force, together with the increase in cost of land when the potentially arable land is fully converted to arable land (see balancing feedback loop LTG – B3), represents two major feedback loops in the agriculture sector that are involved in the Limits to Growth scenarios presented in Meadows et al. (2003).

Output from industry and agricultural activity also generate pollutants that accumulate in the environment and can be harmful to biological systems. Industries generate output for a growing and wealthier population, and agriculture disperses chemicals on land for the purpose of production. World3 assumes a natural capability of the environment to absorb such pollutants in a way that is not harmful to living systems, but such capability slows down the higher the accumulation of pollutants is (see balancing feedback loop B5). Above certain thresholds pollutants can degrade the available land and reduce people's life expectancy, generating two important balancing feedback loops that constraint growth (see balancing feedback loops LTG – B4 and LTG – B5).

Population is governed by two major forces that together generate the population dynamics. On the one side there is the reinforcing feedback loop involving births (G – R2) and on the other side the balancing feedback loops involving deaths (B6). When the first is stronger than the latter the population grows, whereas if the second is stronger, the population goes down. Historically births have remained higher than deaths on average, assuring a maintained growth in population over the centuries. The past increase in services and food per capita for a growing population, have assured increased life expectancy of people and widened the gap between births and death rates. The net increase in population per year has thus widened and the population dynamics followed exponential growth with increasing growing rates (Meadows et al. 1974).

The resulting picture depicts two forces of growth that are constantly challenged with a multitude of balancing forces that tend to bring the growth down and the system to decline and collapse. In particular, the overall system is governed by continuous discard processes (B1, B2, B3, B4, B6) that are always active and work to bring every accumulation down to zero. At the beginning of every simulation, the reinforcing processes are stronger than the sum of all such balancing forces and the system grows, generating better services and food to allow for a prosperous population growth. At the same time, ecosystems get depleted and the Limits to Growth feedback loops that are initially very weak and almost imperceptible become stronger (see LTG – B1, LTG – B2, LTG – B3, LTG – B4, LTG – B5). The rate of change in ecosystems, determined by a bigger economy and population, amplifies the strength of the Limits to Growth feedback loops as well. When such forces constrain growth, there is a shift in paradigm in the simulation that make the reinforcing feedback loops G – R1 and G – R2 weaker than the various discard processes B1, B2, B3, B4, B6, which then have enough power to bring the system down towards zero.

For example, when LTG – B1 becomes strong enough to require most of the industrial output, there remains nothing left for other sectors, meaning that no resources can be diverted into new investments, and the system follows the dynamic of collapse determined by B1, B2, B3. This implies a reduction in life expectancy that strengthens the balancing feedback loop B6 assuring population collapse. When persistent pollution gets very high (LTG – B4, LTG – B5), it reduces the production of food by degrading lands, resulting in an increased death rate, amplifying the effects of the balancing feedback loop B6 that leads to population collapse. When potential arable land reaches the limits (the costs associated with bringing new land into production increase dramatically), and existing arable land gets eroded because of natural processes and exploitation (see LTG – B2, LTG – B3), it affects both food production and industrial investments, increasing the strengths of B6 and weakening G – R1 at the same time, and driving the system to decline. The use of non-linearities in the model allows a shift in loop dominance between each simulation, from the reinforcing loops to the balancing ones, generating the dynamic of overshoot and collapse as a key assumption in every World3 scenario. The use of technology improvements is then applied to deal with the dynamics of exponential growth and exponential depletion of natural ecosystems.

The eight macro-systems (as depicted in Figure 1.8), and some major accumulation processes and feedback loops (as depicted in Figure 1.9), have been captured in World3 using more than 300 elements inclusive of stocks, flows, nonlinear relationships, parameters and several policy levers to run scenarios and test major uncertainties within the model. The following section aims at expanding on this generic view by highlighting the 14 non-linear relationships that play a key role in determining the dynamic behaviour of World3 scenarios. The diagrams used in this section recall the stock and flow structures of the World3 model, but remain largely simplified and generic in nature without requiring any mathematical understanding of the equations.

A process view on the World3

In order to facilitate the understanding of the structures of the model, three different categories that can be considered to affect the model behaviour in different ways are used. These are:

- Growth – structures that generate the exponential growth in the system based on industrial investments and population births;
- Negative effects of growth – structures that do not make the system collapse but can generate undesired effects on growth in relation to wealth per capita, and non-persistent pollution in particular. These are depicted in Figure 1.8 as negative effects of industrial growth on food production and well-being;
- Limits to growth – structures that represent ultimate natural limits on growth that can bring all human systems down to very low levels.

The use of technology structures is fully captured in the section, providing insights on how technological advancements have been included in the model and how the key non-linearities and effects in adaptive and discrete technology scenario analysis have been used.

Growth

The growth structures presented in this section are based on the non-linear relationships that govern the way investments are generated and allocated to improve life expectancy and support population growth. In particular, we highlight how the dynamics generating growth act in synergy to the Limits to Growth structure to trigger the dynamics of collapse in the World3.

INDUSTRIAL OUTPUT AND INVESTMENTS

Figure 1.10 shows the major non-linear relationships governing growth and eventual collapse of the economy when limits are reached in World3. The sustainability of growth in the industrial system is assured whenever the investments in industrial capital are higher than the industrial capital discard. Such flows are

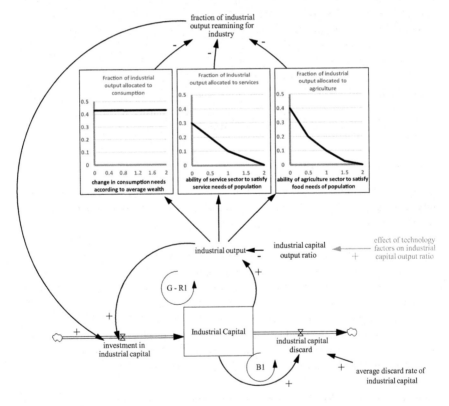

Figure 1.10 Production and investment function in the World3–03

governed by the feedback loop forces G – R1 and B1 as depicted in Figure 1.9 and Figure 1.10. The Industrial Capital Output Ratio indicates the units of industrial capital required to provide one unit of output to the economy. Such an output is then allocated to agriculture, services and consumption on a fractional base in comparison to the total, and the remaining industrial output is used as investments in industry to counteract the outflow of industrial capital discard.

The two non-linear relationships indicating the fraction of industrial output that should be allocated to the relative sectors are dependent on the performance of each sector. When the food output per person is close to the level required to feed the population, and the services provided are close to the one indicated in relation to the current level of wealth per capita (measured with industrial output per capita in World3), then the input to the non-linear relationship is close to 1, and the fractional industrial output allocated to that sector is close to 10% of the total. In the case where the two sectors provide about double the output required then the investments from industry would go down to zero, indicating the low interest of an economy to expand sectors that provide larger output than demanded. However, in the case where the two sectors would not be able to fulfil the demand of the population, more and more entrepreneurs and businesses would be attracted by high prices of commodities in those markets as a result of a mismatch in supply to demand. As a result, they would demand additional output from industry to build up facilities and infrastructures. In case of collapse, investments would be allocated more to food production than services to satisfy the need of a starving population. This is reflected in the non-linear increase towards the 30% and 40% of industrial investments to services and agriculture respectively when their satisfaction capabilities go towards zero. Beside the two non-linear relationships, it is assumed that a constant 43% of material output would end up as consumer goods every year (such an assumption can be challenged assuming adaptive consumer behaviour on the basis of average wealth in World3).

The productivity of capital is determined by the Industrial Capital Output Ratio representing the amount of capital units necessary to produce one unit of output. In the base run, the capital output ratio is assumed constant over the two centuries of the simulation. The assumption of decreasing marginal productivity of capital has been neglected by assuming that continuous technology improvements in the economy would innovate capital to maintain its productivity at constant levels. However, such an assumption is challenged when technology scenarios are proposed and affect the parameter. When agriculture and services run at satisfactory levels of performance according to current demand, only 63% (43% for consumption, 10% for agriculture, 10% for services) of the output is allocated to the rest of the economy and the remaining to industry. Based on such non-linearities, it becomes evident how temporary decreases in satisfactory levels of services and agriculture can trigger the dynamic of collapse in the model. For example, a strong effect of pollution on food output would start requiring larger and larger fractions of industrial capital until the point that the remaining fraction allocated to industry would be less than the discarded bringing the system

down to zero. Most important, when technology costs and industrial output allocated to resource extraction is accounted for, the constraint on output becomes
even more severe, leading to the collapse of the World3 model scenarios.

INVESTMENTS WITHIN AGRICULTURE

Figure 1.11 shows how investments from industry are allocated among the three
productive factors in agriculture to produce food in World3. In particular, agricultural inputs, that in World3 are an aggregate of fertilizers, pesticides, machines,
and farms, are assumed to increase the natural productivity of one hectare of
land, and remain subjected to discard. The high fraction of chemicals within
agricultural inputs that is subject to leaching and plant intake, leads to the agricultural inputs being completely discarded in a time scale that is much lower in
comparison to industrial and service capital.

Land fertility represents the natural capability of land to produce food, including land nutrients, acidity and quality of topsoil. It can be degraded by pollution,
but farmers can allocate investments to land maintenance to support the natural
potential for fertility regeneration. Agricultural inputs and land fertility determine the land yield in the model, which is the measure of productivity of every
hectare of land. In the adaptive technology scenarios, land productivity can be
increased through the implementation of new technologies.

In the model, fertile land can be converted to arable land through investments
diverted to land development. However, the use of land is subject to land erosion,

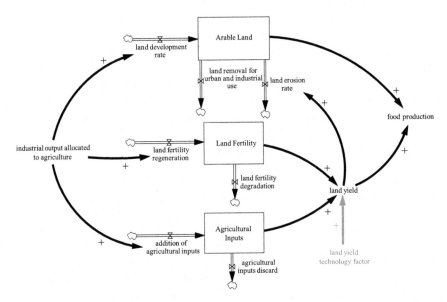

Figure 1.11 Allocation of industrial investments in agriculture and impact on food
production

and land removal to urban and industrial use. The resulting arable land and land yield are the main factors driving food output in World3. Figure 1.11 presents a few of the positive relationships that link growth in investments to growth in output in agriculture. For example, land yield is also affected by other effects that will be explained later in this section, and food production accounts for production constraints linked to arable land shift and food loss.

FOOD, HEALTH SERVICES, AND LIFE EXPECTANCY

Figure 1.12 shows two major non-linear relationships that describe the way population growth is influenced by the growth of service and agricultural outputs. Such non-linear effects govern the dynamics of life expectancy, which in turn decrease the deaths, and the strength of the feedback loop B6. This latter leads to population collapse in several Limits to Growth scenarios.

The two non-linear relationships are multiplicative effects whose product determines the fractional change in life expectancy over time. Their inputs are the normalised food per capita in comparison to subsistence food per capita (representing the abundance or scarcity of food per person in relation to that needed for a normal life), and the effective health services per capita. In the model it is assumed that a large abundance of food per person would, globally, be a driver for

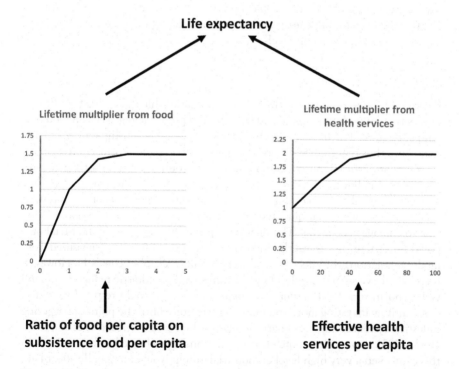

Figure 1.12 Non-linear impact of food and services change on the life expectancy

increased life expectancy until it reaches 50% more than subsidence level. Food scarcity (below subsistence level) would decrease life expectancy until zero, so assuming no food in the world corresponds to no humans surviving no matter what health services are in place. On the side of health services per capita, it is assumed that every increase in services above zero would correspond to a fractional increase that would bring average life expectancy from the current level (multiplier equals 1) to double (multiplier equals 2) the current level.

The underlying determinants of life expectancy in the model are explained in the rest of this section. It is worth noting that, while the economy grows in the simulation, the service output per capita and the food output per capita tend to grow as well, resulting in increased life expectancy. However, any decrease in those quantities would also start to decreasing life expectancy leading to a slowdown in population growth and eventually the beginning of population collapse. Only at low levels of services and food per capita would the population be drastically reduced.

Negative effects of growth

The negative effects of growth are described by two non-linearities within two feedback loops. These bring the same forces that generate growth to counteract themselves, decreasing the production of food, and negatively affecting life expectancy. Such relationships come from the effects of non-persistent pollutants (particulate dispersed in the air and in the soil) caused by industrial production when it raises above certain levels.

NON PERSISTENT POLLUTION AND LAND YIELD

Figure 1.13 shows the shape of the non-linear relationship indicating the effect of non-persistent pollutants generated by industrial production growth on food output per hectare. The impact of technology on such a relationship remains highly uncertain, thus requiring a scenario comparison to explore possible outcomes.

The relationship implicitly assumes that every output from industry generates some sort of pollutant that gets dispersed in the air and in the soil. Such pollutants are assumed to be harmful to soil only at very high levels of emissions, as small amounts would be quickly reabsorbed by the environment before being able to damage ecosystems. The relationship indicates that while industrial output is lower than ten times the industrial output level in 1970 (measured from model simulation) the effect on land yield is null (multiplier equals 1). However, increases above such a threshold would correspond to a drastic reduction of land yield, and in turn food output. The industrial system would respond to such a constraint by investing more and more in agriculture until the point of triggering industrial system collapse. Scenario analysis is then used in Meadows et al. (1972, 1992, 2003) to provide a more positive relationship indicated in Figure 1.13. In this case, even a very high level of industrial output would marginally affect land yield negatively.

Land yield

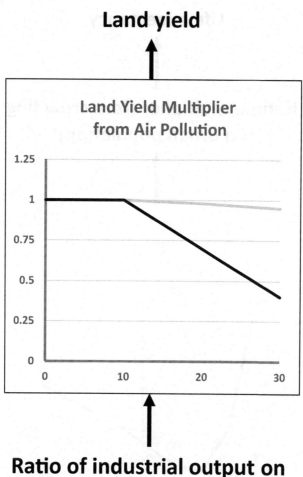

Ratio of industrial output on industrial output in 1970

Figure 1.13 Negative effect of industrial output growth on food output and sensitivity

NON PERSISTENT POLLUTION AND HYGIENE ON LIFE EXPECTANCY

Figure 1.14 depicts the non-linear effects of material wealth (measured with industrial output per capita) on the life expectancy of urban populations.

Such a crowding multiplier effect can be divided in three parts. When industrial output per capital is very low (less than 200 units per person), it is assumed that people are so poor that hygiene and diseases can have negative consequences for their life expectancy in cities. The higher the material output the lower the negative effects until reaching null value (no effect) near 200 units per person. Further

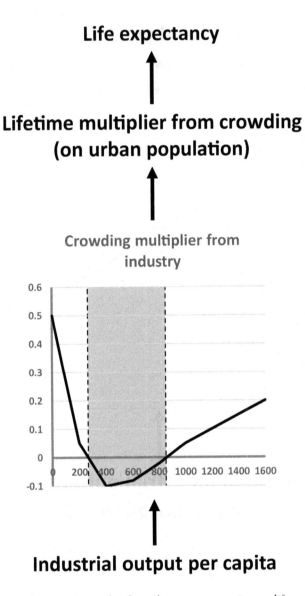

Figure 1.14 Non-linear impact of industrial output per capita on life expectancy via crowding

increases generate positive effects to life expectancy, reaching a maximum positive effect near 400 World3 capital units per person. Any additional increase in output per person is assumed to decrease the positive effect of material output due to increased air pollution in industrial cities. The effect reaches a null value at approximately 800 capital units per person, and keeps decreasing life expectancy for every output value beyond that.

For most of the simulations of the World3 model, the industrial output per person ranges in between the 200 to 800 units per person, affecting the average life expectancy mostly positively. However, when the economy collapses, the reduction in industrial output per capita below 200 units per person increases population death rates, supporting the global collapse even further.

Limits to Growth

In this section, we present the Limits to Growth structures and the key non-linear relationships governing their effects in the World3. These are non-renewable resources, persistent pollution, and available land. In addition, we provide a summary of the adaptive technology advancement scenarios whose effect is to remove limits at the cost of reduced economic growth.

RESOURCES AND DEPLETION

Figure 1.15 shows the balancing feedback loop involving resource scarcity, and the non-linear relationship used to model the scarcity effect on economic output. Resource extraction and use is dependent on the population of the planet and the average amount of resources every person uses. In World3, it is assumed that the higher the industrial output per capita, the higher is the per capita demand in terms of material products. Such an assumption indicates that the burden of every person on resource extraction increases while society gets richer. While population and resources use per person increase, extraction rises, increasing the speed of resource depletion. The lower the amount of resources the more difficult it is to extract those. This results in more capital and labour being allocated to extract resources.

The non-linearity indicates that while resources are abundant (fraction of resource remaining range from 60% and 100% of original total), only 5% of total industrial output would need to be used for extracting more resources. However, when resources available decrease below 60% of what was initially available, the output that has to be allocated to resource extraction must rise, indicating that more capital and labour are used for such a task. While the resources remaining approach zero, the industrial output allocated to resource extraction approaches 100% of the total, leaving nothing for the other sectors of the economy. In other words, all material output and energy is prioritised towards resource extraction. Of course without resource extraction the other sectors of the economy could not work anyway. When resources are impossible to extract with available technology the economy would have to run without those, collapsing the entire economic system based on industrial production.

Assumptions aimed at relaxing such constraints are considered within the World3 simulations. On the one hand, the non-linear relationship is substituted with another (see Figure 1.15) which requires a lower fraction of industrial output being used for resource extraction despite the decrease of resources remaining.

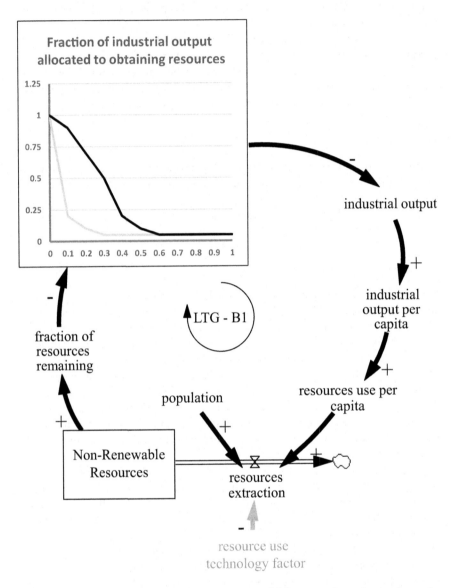

Figure 1.15 Balancing feedback loop of resource availability on industrial capital growth, and adaptive technology effect

The non-linearity assumes 5% of industrial output allocated to resource extraction until only 30% of resources are left, and then a rise to 100% more steeply because of resource unavailability. On the other hand, the resource use technology factor is applied, simulating the possibility of creating technologies that would not require any other resource to be extracted from the ground while still being able to run the economy as usual. For example, the use of closed loop supply chains, the assumption of recycling and reusing resources, or the possibility to run the economy using infinite energy resources. Such scenarios are explored among the business as usual adaptive technology scenarios, and can reduce the effect of resource depletion as marginal in terms of economic output reduction.

LAND AVAILABILITY AND EROSION

Figure 1.16 shows the three forms of land and two major non-linearities in the land system in World3. As it can be seen, there exists a global limit to the potentially arable land that can be converted for agriculture purposes. The land

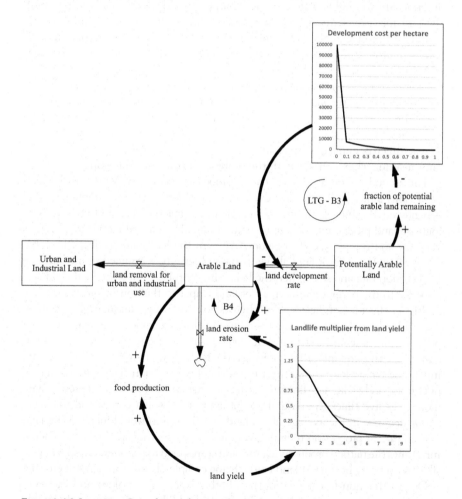

Figure 1.16 Limits to Growth non-linear relationships controlling feedback loops in the agricultural sector

development rate indicates the rate of conversion to arable land (land used for food production) and it is dependent on the industrial investments in agriculture (see Figure 1.11). In World3, it is assumed that the urban and industrial areas are built on agricultural areas, and that arable land in use is subjected to a natural erosion rate (see flows out of arable land in Figure 1.16).

Arable land is a key determinant of food production, and the dynamics governing its availability are essential components to understand the Limits to Growth within agriculture. The more the 'potentially arable land' is converted for agricultural uses, the higher is the cost of converting additional land. This dynamic behaviour is controlled with the 'development cost per hectare' non-linearity. When the 'potentially arable land' decreases below 100% in comparison to its initial value, the cost of converting every hectare in new arable land rises slowly and non-linearly. When the convertible land approaches 10% of the initial total, the cost for converting starts rising steeply. This indicates that human society would start producing food on lands that are difficult to be converted to agriculture with proportional rising costs (for example, bringing water to very arid areas or cultivating land within steep and rocky mountains). The more the cost rises, the lower is the arable land development rate (see balancing loop LtG – B3). If food needs exceed the maximum potential from global arable land, the constraint would limit production and in turn the positive effects of food availability on the well-being of the population (i.e. life expectancy in World3). The issues related to reaching the limits of convertible arable land on the planet assume an important meaning when coupled with the problem of rising land erosion.

The second important determinant of food production in World3 is the land yield. This indicates the level of exploitation of every hectare of arable land and depends on the use of innovative technologies, machineries, and chemicals to increase land productivity above its natural rate. The natural land erosion rate is very low and is represented in Figure 1.16 with the balancing feedback loop B4. The overexploitation of land above its natural fertility is assumed to increase the land erosion rate and strengthen the balancing loop B4. When the land yield corresponds to the natural productivity of land (input to the non-linearity is 1), the multiplier effect is 1, indicating that there is no effect of agriculture exploitation on natural land erosion. If land yield is reduced below such a level (agricultural output is below natural productivity), it would result in a betterment of land erosion and reduce the strength of B4. However, the higher the application of agricultural inputs and technology, the stronger the effect of land erosion. The 'land life multiplier from land yield' non-linearity, indicates that an increase of land productivity more than five times the natural productivity level would correspond to a very strong decrease in the average life of land, which in turn would increase the land erosion rate in proportion to arable land in use. When the land yield approaches nine times the natural productivity, it would correspond to just a few decades of possible use of every hectare of land before being completely lost through soil erosion.

Due to this non-linear relationship, both adaptive technology and increases in agricultural inputs relative to arable land, would drastically reduce the arable land, constraining food production. In turn, this would initiate the dynamics of population and economic collapse, as explained under the 'Growth' section of this chapter. Still adaptive technology is assumed to improve land management practices, in a smooth transition for the 'land life multiplier from land yield' non-linear relationship. Such a technological improvement would correspond to a decrease in the average life of land to about 20% of its normal value when land yield is improved to nine times the natural productivity of land, and removing one of the major Limits to Growth in agriculture.

PERSISTENT POLLUTION

Figure 1.17 and Figure 1.18 show the two major non-linear relationships describing the effects of persistent pollution on land fertility (thus constraining land yield and food production) and life expectancy (thus increasing death rate and reducing population). While it is well known that persistent pollution has an effect on a number of variables, quantifying this effect is difficult. Therefore, within World3 the parameters in the non-linear relationships have been estimated in relation to persistent pollution in the year 1970 (the reference year in the original World3 model).

The non-linear effect of persistent pollution on land fertility is described in Figure 1.17. In World3, every quantity of persistent pollution in the environment is assumed to decrease land fertility. On the other hand, farmers are assumed they can allocate investment to restore land fertility to natural levels, thus counter-balancing the fertility loss. The more the persistent pollution accumulates, the larger is the negative burden on fertility, reaching 10% of fertility loss when the

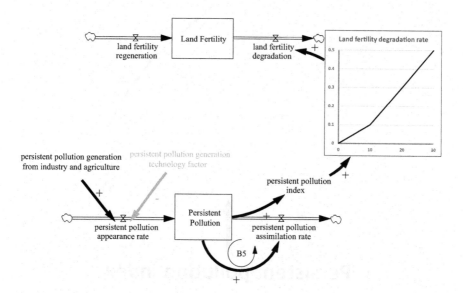

Figure 1.17 Non-linear impact of persistent pollution on land fertility

persistent pollution reaches ten times the amount in the reference year (1970). Continuous increases in the persistent pollution beyond this level would increase the fertility loss until a maximum of 50% per year if pollution reaches 30 times the amount in 1970. It is worth noting that a fertility loss of this scale would halve the food production, which in turn would demand a larger fraction of industrial investment into agriculture. If such a condition would be maintained for a few years (which would be the case due to the long delay in absorbing persistent pollution) the functioning of the full economy would be undermined and potentially result in collapse.

Figure 1.18 shows the effect of persistent pollution on life expectancy. The non-linearity implies that low increases above 1970 persistent pollution value

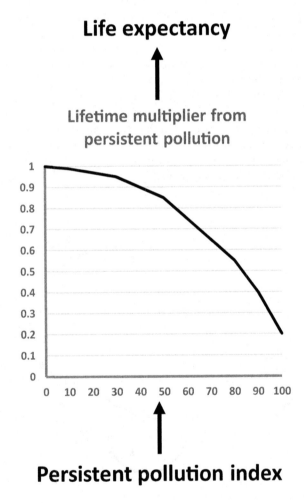

Figure 1.18 Negative impact of persistent pollution on life expectancy

would have a very low effect on life expectancy. Above 30 times the persistent pollution of 1970 (by this time it has reduced food production by half) the effect on life expectancy becomes larger, reaching 80% reduction when persistent pollution increases to 100 times in comparison to 1970. The adaptive technology scenario decreases the amount of persistent pollution generated by industry and therefore lowers the impact of industrial output on life expectancy.

Technology development scenarios

The technology development scenarios presented in Limits to Growth are simulated on the basis of both adaptive and discrete behaviours by performing changes in key parameters. Their effect is to simulate adaptive technology development to solve environmental problems at the cost of reduced economic growth.

The parameters affected are indicated in Figure 1.11, Figure 1.15, Figure 1.17 as multiplicative factors to the elements determining land yield (and in turn controlling the outflow of land erosion rate out of arable land), resource extraction (called 'resource usage rate' in the World3 model), and persistent pollution generation from industry and agriculture. All factors are assumed to have value 1 in the base run, which corresponds to a null multiplicative effect on the elements they aim at controlling. This implies that the effect of each of these limits to growth remain as outlined in the base run.

However, with the adoption of new technology, each factor is then changed to reduce the impact of the limits on the future runs. The land yield technology factor is assumed to have a maximum effect of doubling (increasing up to the value of 2) the land yield on the basis of available agricultural inputs per hectare and land fertility. The resource technology factor can decrease to 0, nullifying resource extraction in the model simulation and corresponding to infinite resources. The persistent pollution generation technology factor can decrease to 0, nullifying every effect of persistent pollution in the model.

The technology factors and their effects are summarised in Table 1.3. Coupling the adaptive change of these factors with the substitution of the non-linear relationships to those that have lower negative impact on growth (see Figure 1.13, Figure 1.15, Figure 1.16) has the potential to eliminate all effects of the Limits to Growth in the model, as well as allowing indefinite growth in the World3 simulation time horizon.

In World3, every adaptive technology improvement is assumed to have a cost in terms of economic output. Such a cost is modelled as an increase in the parameter Industrial Capital Output Ratio, imposing a limited availability of industrial output to the rest of the economy (see Figure 1.10 and Figure 1.19). This acts as a proxy for technology investment, and represents a simulated prioritisation for responding to environmental challenges before targeting economic growth.

Figure 1.19 shows how the accumulation of knowledge affects each technology factor, and how each of those implies non-linear change in the industrial output

Table 1.3 World3 parameters that quantify the impact of natural constraints on economic growth

Technology factor	Value in standard run	Range	Meaning and use of the parameter
Resource use technology factor	1	1 to 0	It controls the burden of resource extraction. Setting it to zero correspond to null resource depletion and infinite resources.
Land yield technology factor	1	1 to 2	It controls the productivity of one hectare of land based on agricultural inputs per hectare and land fertility. Setting it to two corresponds to assume a greater land yield of double to its normal value.
Persistent pollution generation technology factor	1	1 to 0	It controls the amount of persistent pollution generated from the combined effects of agricultural and industrial activities. Setting it to zero assumes null persistent pollution generation.

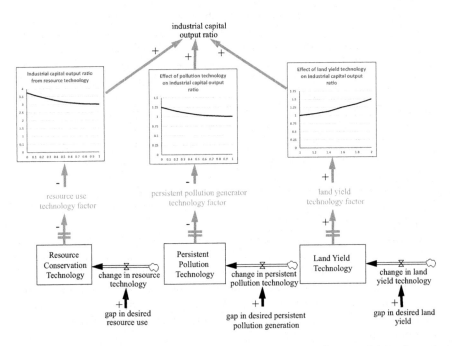

Figure 1.19 Non-linear effects of technology scenarios on the reduction of the industrial output

ratio. World3 assumes an adaptive approach based on research and development, and business application to solving limits to growth problems. A gap in performance between a desired and current levels of technology is measured and used to improve the environmental problem for every limit. A 20-year time delay is assumed between knowledge creation and technology deployment. The final result is to gradually remove the global limits by changes in each of the three parameters indicated in Table 1.3, Figure 1.11, Figure 1.15, and Figure 1.16. This implies an increase to the Industrial Capital Output Ratio that, together with resources depletion and investments to agriculture and services, reduces the ability of the economy to grow.

Scenarios of the World3

In Meadows et al. (2003) the World3 model analysis is presented using ten scenarios. First, the 'standard run' presents a world constrained by the availability of resources, and does not account for any attempt by society to develop better systems to deal with environmental problems. Assuming economic growth as the social development paradigm for the full duration of the simulation, the world systems grow, overshoot, and collapse because of hitting the planetary resource limit. Scenario 2 shows a world with more abundant non-renewable resources (the initial availability of resources is double that in the standard run) which allows for the extraction of those resources at lower cost for a longer time (see non-linearity in Figure 1.15). Still, assuming economic growth and no attempt to adaptively develop any technology to solve the burden of the issues caused by growth, the world collapses because of a pollution crisis. By gradually including all technological non-linear relationships (see Figure 1.13, Figure 1.15, and Figure 1.16) and assuming the approach of adaptive technology development (see Figure 1.10, Figure 1.11, Figure 1.15, Figure 1.17, and Figure 1.19) starting in the year 2002, all limits are challenged and presented in Scenarios 3, 4, and 5 of the Limits to Growth. The aggregation of all technological policies is presented in Scenario 6. Figure 1.20, Figure 1.21, and Figure 1.22 show the Scenarios 1, 2, and 6 of the World3–03 respectively.

Scenario 6 represents the most likely scenario of the Limits to Growth study in relation to possible human developments until the year 2100. Scenario 6 includes a reliance on economic growth as paradigm for developing technologies to solve environmental problems caused by growth. It represents a world in which technological advancements are successful in avoiding an abrupt decline in world population by 2100, but are not sufficient to avoid several food failures because of the delay in dealing with persistent pollution globally (see Figure 1.22 between 2030 and 2050). In addition, resources allocated to technology deployment generate a decline of services and industrial output per capita indicating a decrease in the average well-being of the living population by the end of the century. Other scenarios involve social policies aimed at stabilising population and investments. Figure 1.20, Figure 1.21, and Figure 1.22 show the 'standard run,' the Scenario 2 and the Scenario 6 as presented in Meadows et al. (2003).

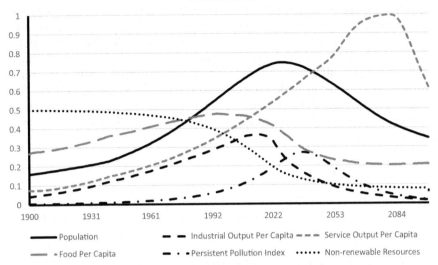

Figure 1.20 Standard run scenario of the World3–03 showing collapse of human society due to conservative assumption on resource limits

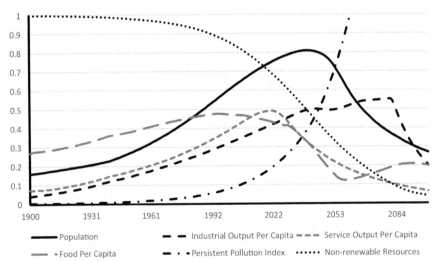

Figure 1.21 Scenario 2 of World3–03 showing the world collapsing due to exponential accumulation of persistent pollutants in the atmosphere

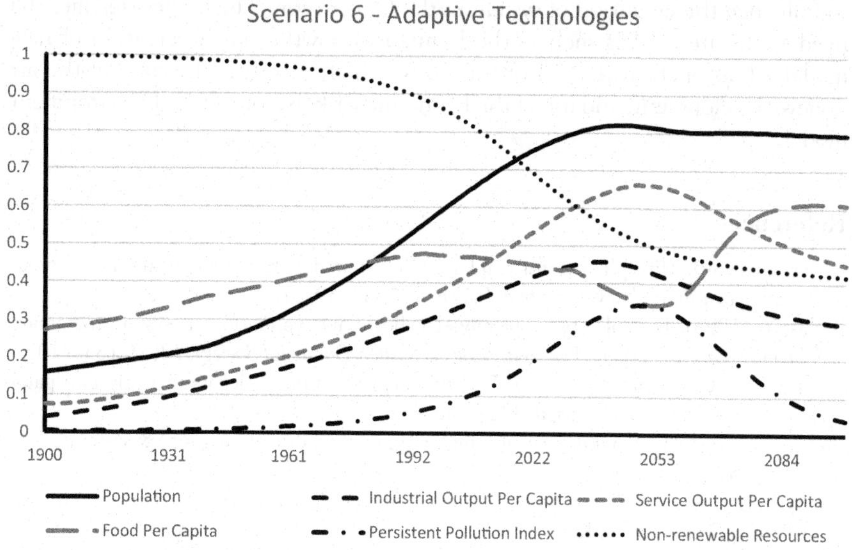

Figure 1.22 Scenario 6 of the World3–03; adaptive technology scenario as the closest representation of an expected future of the world as depicted in the Limits to Growth (Meadows et al. 2003)

Summary

In this section, the Limits to Growth (Meadows et al. 1972, 1974, 1992, 2003) has been reviewed in detail. Starting from the reasons that motivated this work (CoR 1970), the impact of this line of research was reported from the experience of the model originators (Meadows et al. 1982; Randers 2000). Thus the system dynamics approach is defined and its most basic concepts revealed so as to introduce the technical description of the World3–03 (Meadows et al. 2003).

Starting from a top-down perspective, the World3–03 is described. After highlighting the purpose of the model, the sub-sectors of the model and major feedback loops are shown. Thus we describe the elements of the World3 that generate behaviour in the model, capturing only those elements that can explain why the model behaves in a certain way in each scenario of the Limits to Growth. After presenting the major feedback loops, and the 14 non-linear relationships that impact the model behaviour, the Scenarios 1, 2, and 6 are proposed, aiming at linking model output with system structure.

This attempt is important in order to realise both strengths and weaknesses of the approach of modelling in World3. The next chapter provides first a calibration of the World3–03 to compare the output of the model to the historical data from 1995 to 2012, and follows with a description of the current state of the world systems as it is today. This approach is aimed to help the reader in grasping the difference between models and reality, and the effectiveness of forecasting to influence the evolution of system in the longer term. The process justifies the need to update models such as the Limits to Growth and the creation of new models. This opens to Part II of this book, which describes the state-of-the-art review, development, and use of the Economic Risk, Resources and Environment model.

References

Barlas, Y. (1989). Multiple tests for validation of system dynamics type of simulation models. *European Journal of Operational Research, 42*(1), 59–87.

Barlas, Y. (1996). Formal aspects of model validity and validation in system dynamics. *System Dynamics Review: The Journal of the System Dynamics Society, 12*(3), 183–210.

Barlas, Y., & Carpenter, S. (1990). Philosophical roots of model validation: Two paradigms. *System Dynamics Review, 6*(2), 148–166.

Brehmer, B. (1992). Dynamic decision making: Human control of complex systems. *Acta Psychologica, 81*(3), 211–241.

Capra, F., & Luisi, P. (2016). *The systems way of life: An unifying vision.* Cambridge University Press, Cambridge, UK.

Castro, R. (2012). Arguments on the imminence of global collapse are premature when based on simulation models. *GAIA-Ecological Perspectives for Science and Society, 21*(4), 271–273.

Club of Rome. (1970). *The predicament of mankind: A quest for structured responses to growing world-wide complexities and uncertainties.* Proposal to the Club of Rome, Geneva, Switzerland.

Costanza, R. (1991). The ecological economics of sustainability. In *Environmentally sustainable economic development: Building on Brundtland* (pp. 83–90). UNESCO, Paris.

Costanza, R., & Daly, H. E. (1992). Natural capital and sustainable development. *Conservation Biology, 6*(1), 37–46.

Diehl, E., & Sterman, J. D. (1995). Effects of feedback complexity on dynamic decision making. *Organizational Behavior and Human Decision Processes, 62*(2), 198–215.

Dörner, D. (1980). On the difficulties people have in dealing with complexity. *Simulation & Games, 11*(1), 87–106.

Fiddaman, T. S. (1997). *Feedback complexity in integrated climate-economy models.* Massachusetts Institute of Technology, Cambridge, MA, US.

Ford, A. (1999). *Modeling the environment: An introduction to system dynamics models of environmental systems.* Island Press, Washington DC, US.

Forrester, J. W. (1958). Industrial dynamics: A major breakthrough for decision makers. *Harvard Business Review, 36*(4), 37–65.

Forrester, J. W. (1961). *Industrial dynamics.* Pegasus Communications, Waltham, MA, US.

Forrester, J. W. (1968). *Principles of systems* (Vol. 1, p. 51). Wright-Allen Press, Inc., Cambridge, MA, US.

Forrester, J. W. (1971a). Counterintuitive behavior of social systems. *Technological Forecasting and Social Change, 3*, 1–22.

Forrester, J. W. (1971b). *World dynamics.* Wright-Allen Press, Cambridge, MA, US.

Forrester, J. W. (1980). Information sources for modeling the national economy. *Journal of the American Statistical Association, 75*(371), 555–566.

Forrester, J. W., & Senge, P. M. (1980). Tests for building confidence in system dynamics models. *System Dynamics, TIMS Studies in Management Sciences, 14*, 209–228.

Jackson, T. (2016). *Prosperity without growth: Foundations for the economy of tomorrow.* Routledge, London, UK.

Kleinmuntz, D. N. (1993). Information processing and misperceptions of the implications of feedback in dynamic decision making. *System Dynamics Review,* 9(3), 223–237.

Kwakkel, J. H., & Pruyt, E. (2015). Using system dynamics for grand challenges: The ESDMA approach. *Systems Research and Behavioral Science,* 32(3), 358–375.

Meadows, D. H. (2012, June 3). *Dennis meadows: "There is nothing we can do."* Format, Germany. Available online: http://churchandstate.org.uk/2013/04/dennis-meadows-there-is-nothing-that-we-can-do/

Meadows, D. H., Meadows, D. L., & Randers, J. (1992). *Beyond the limits: Global collapse or a sustainable future.* Earthscan Publications Ltd, London, UK.

Meadows, D. H., Meadows, D. L., & Randers, J. (2003). *The limits to growth: The 30-year update.* Routledge, London, UK.

Meadows, D. H., Meadows, D. L., Randers, J., & Behrens, W. W. (1972). *The limits to growth.* Universe Books, New York, NY, USA.

Meadows, D. L. (1969). *The dynamics of commodity production cycles: A Dynamic Cobweb Theorem.* Massachusetts Institute of Technology, Cambridge, MA, US.

Meadows, D. L., Behrens, W. W., Meadows, D. H., Naill, R. F., Randers, J., & Zahn, E. (1974). *Dynamics of growth in a finite world.* Wright-Allen Press, Cambridge, MA.

Meadows, D. L., Fiddaman, T., & Shannon, D. (1993). *Fish banks, Ltd: A microcomputer assisted group simulation that teaches principles of sustainable management of renewable natural resources* (pp. 698–706). Laboratory for Interactive Learning, Hood House, University of New Hampshire, Durham, NH.

Meadows, D. L., Richardson, J., & Bruckmann, G. (1982). *Groping in the dark: The first decade of global modelling.* John Wiley & Sons, Hoboken, New Jersey, US.

Mesarovic, M., & Pestel, E. (1974). *Mankind at the turning point.* The second report to the Club of Rome. Dutton, New York, US.

Morecroft, J. D. (1985). Rationality in the analysis of behavioral simulation models. *Management Science,* 31(7), 900–916.

Morecroft, J. D. (1988). System dynamics and microworlds for policymakers. *European Journal of Operational Research,* 35(3), 301–320.

Morecroft, J. S. M. (2007). *Business dynamics a feedback systems approach.* John Wiley &Sons Ltd, Hoboken, New Jersey, US.

Pauli, G. A. (1987). *Crusader for the future: A portrait of Aurelio Peccei, founder of the club of Rome.* Pergamon, Oxford, UK.

Pruyt, E. (2015). *From modelling uncertain surprises to simulating black swans.* Paper presented at the Proceedings of the 33-rd International Conference of the System Dynamics Society, Cambridge, MA.

Randers, J. (2000). From limits to growth to sustainable development or SD (sustainable development) in a SD (system dynamics) perspective. *System Dynamics Review: The Journal of the System Dynamics Society,* 16(3), 213–224.

Richardson, G. P. (1991). *Feedback thought in social science and systems theory.* Pegasus Communications, Waltham, MA.

Senge, P. M. (1978). *The system dynamics national model investment function: A comparison to the neoclassical investment function.* Massachusetts Institute of Technology, Cambridge, MA, US.

Sterman, J. D. (1981). *The energy transition and the economy: A system dynamics approach* (2 Vols.). MIT Alfred P. Sloan School of Management, Cambridge, MA.

Sterman, J. D. (1985). A behavioral model of the economic long wave. *Journal of Economic Behavior & Organization,* 6(1), 17–53.

Sterman, J. D. (1989a). Misperceptions of feedback in dynamic decision making. *Organizational Behavior and Human Decision Processes, 43*(3), 301–335.

Sterman, J. D. (1989b). Modeling managerial behavior: Misperceptions of feedback in a dynamic decision making experiment. *Management Science, 35*(3), 321–339.

Sterman, J. D. (1991). A skeptic's guide to computer models. *Managing a Nation: The Microcomputer Software Catalog, 2,* 209–229.

Sterman, J. D. (2000). *Business dynamics: Systems thinking and modeling for a complex world.* McGraw-Hill, New York, USA.

Sterman, J. D. (2014). Interactive web-based simulations for strategy and sustainability: The MIT sloan learning edge management flight simulators, part I. *System Dynamics Review, 30*(1–2), 89–121.

Turner, G. M. (2008). A comparison of the limits to growth with 30 years of reality. *Global Environmental Change, 18*(3), 397–411.

Turner, G. M. (2012). On the cusp of global collapse? Updated comparison of the limits to growth with historical data. *GAIA-Ecological Perspectives for Science and Society, 21*(2), 116–124.

Turner, G. M. (2013). The limits to growth model is more than a mathematical exercise. *Gaia, 22*(1), 18.

Videira, N., Antunes, P., Santos, R., & Gamito, S. (2003). Participatory modelling in environmental decision-making: The ria Formosa natural park case study. *Journal of Environmental Assessment Policy and Management, 5*(3), 421–447.

Videira, N., Antunes, P., Santos, R., & Lopes, R. (2010). A participatory modelling approach to support integrated sustainability assessment processes. *Systems Research and Behavioral Science, 27*(4), 446–460.

Warren, K. (2008). *Strategic management dynamics.* John Wiley & Sons, Cambridge, MA, US.

Weizsäcker, E. U. (Ed.). (2014). *Ernst Ulrich Von Weizsäcker: A pioneer on environmental, climate and energy policies.* Springer, Berlin.

2 A calibration analysis of World3-03

In this chapter we present the work published in Pasqualino et al. (2015), to recalibrate the World3–03 model using historical data from 1995 to 2012. In the context of this book, the World3–03 calibration highlights the differences between the evolution of the real world and what was modelled in Limits to Growth by means of numerical analysis of the model output. This links well to the following chapter, where a full description of today's world ecosystems and constraints for an economy to grow are explained. The model used for the analysis presented in this chapter is available online at https://doi.org/10.25411/aru.11341697.v1.

Since the first publication in 1972, new time series related to the World3 variables have been recorded allowing for new analysis and updates of World3. The World3–03 and World3–91 versions of the model were proposed as minor numerical changes in parameters and non-linear relationships to assure historical data and model simulation match (Meadows et al. 1992, 2003). Their use remained equivalent to the original, proposing a series of scenarios aimed at showing the possible dynamic behaviours of material output growth in a finite world.

More recently, Turner (2008, 2012) compared normalised trends of major global variables to three scenarios of World3 (Meadows et al. 1972), concluding that we are on the path of Scenario 1. While this analysis provides evidence that the understandings developed in World3 are valid and remain true up to present day, it does not test the Limits to Growth hypothesis given that many assumptions of actual limits have not yet been observed. Indeed the original scenarios as presented were not meant to be a forecast (Meadows et al. 1974, 1982, 1992; Randers 2000; Meadows et al. 2003). Additionally Turner (2008, 2012) compared the output of World3 with current trends within global variables and therefore, while validating some of the assumptions within World3, the study did not provide any new insights for refinements to the World3 model itself.

An alternative use of newly available data has been proposed (Pasqualino et al. 2015). Rather than comparing data with the outputs of the scenario analysis, the study proposes a way to allow the World3–03 model to generate the parameters that are required to replicate the historical data from 1995 to 2012. This calibration of World3–03 using recent data changes the scenario outputs from the model so that they generate more closely current pathways and therefore follow

DOI: 10.4324/9781315643182-3

any changes to key variables or parameters that determine particular behaviours. A comparison between the parameters that generate the run replicating historical patterns and those that generate the original base line scenario can be used to indicate positive or negative states of the world system as compared to that originally envisaged and depicted in Limits to Growth.

The analysis presented here is based on the three following observations:

1   Scenario 2 should be taken as a baseline scenario in a similar way to the adaptive technology analysis proposed in Meadows et al. (2003).
2   Available time series do not include any overshoot dynamics depicted in the longer term of World3 runs.
3   The use of relatively short (in comparison to the simulation run) time series would allow the approximation of non-linearities relative to technological change as single parameters, i.e. substituting non-linear relationships with linear relationships in the time frame of the simulation would have limited effect.

Therefore, this analysis does not look into the future and is intended to be a static representation of the dynamic reality as depicted within World3 for 1995 to 2012. The process of estimating the model parameters to obtain a match between observed and simulated structures and behaviours is generally referred to as model calibration (Oliva 2003). Available software platforms for system dynamics models allow for automated calibrations of parameters given a model structure and historical datasets. However, important considerations have been made to define a methodology which assured the model output could converge to a meaningful set of parameters.

In particular, based on the understanding of the complex structure of World3, historical data trends have been selected to give a thoughtful set of constraints to model behaviours and assure the parameters of different sub-systems (e.g. demographic, economic, and land related) could be calibrated separately. The variables match has been performed through metadata comparison between public available datasets and Meadows et al. (1974). Such an approach allowed for the inclusion of additional scaling parameters necessary to correctly match model output to historical data (the final version of the model has been called World3–03-Edited), including currency or conversion between units of measurement. The identification of the 16 most important parameters generating behaviours, and controlling convergence of model behaviours to time series by mean of several calibration of subsets of World3 parameters was then possible.

The World3 variables used for the analysis are (i) industrial output, (ii) service output, (iii) population, (iv) birth rate, (v) life expectancy, and (vi) arable land. The choice has been determined after a metadata comparison on the basis of World3 variables definition as reported in Meadows et al. (1974) and available historical data as reported in United Nations' public available datasets (see Table 2.1). The time series include data from 1995 to 2012 for each variable, which constrained the simulation to run over the same time frame.

Table 2.1 Metadata comparison between historical data and World3 variables

World3 variable	Dataset variable	Reference dataset	Stock variables covered
Population	Population, total	United Nations Population division	Population 0 to 14 Population 15 to 44 Population 45 to 64 Population 65 plus
Birth Rate	Birth rate, crude (per 1000 persons)	United Nations Population division	Population 0 o 14 Population 15 to 44 Industrial Capital Service Capital
Life Expectancy	Life expectancy at birth, total (years)	United Nations Population division	Population stocks Arable Land Service Capital
Industrial Output	Industry value added 2005 constant	World Bank National account Data	Industrial Capital Population 0 to 14 Arable Land
Service Output	Service value added 2005 constant	World Bank National account Data	Service Capital Population stocks
Arable Land	Arable Land (hectares)	Food and Agriculture Organization (FAO) data	Arable Land Potentially Arable Land Urban and Industrial Land

The lack of data in relation to World3 non-renewable resources and persistent pollution quantities required the analysis to be performed twice. First, the effects of those structures have been neglected and a set of calibrated parameters identified. Based on such set of newly calibrated parameters, the limits have been included again and their effects initialised as simulated in the Scenario 2 of Limits to Growth. The two calibrations have been called 'without' and 'with limits' and generated two sets of parameters which strengthened the value of the analysis performed.

From World3–03 to World3–03-Edited

The metadata comparison assured the correspondence between World3 and real variables counterparts. In order to create the match between historical and World3 variables for the calibration, scaling parameters and additional variables had to be created. Such minor updates resulted in a new version of the model World3–03-Edited used for this analysis. In order to reduce the amount of parameters to be calibrated at minimum, a manual update of those that could be found in literature or within available datasets in the year 1995 has been applied. Table 2.2 summarises the variables and parameters additions on the World3–03 model structure resulting in the World3–03-Edited version, used in this study.

Table 2.2 Parameters and variable additions between World3–03 and World3–03-Edited

Additional elements in the model structure	Role of parameter
Parameter 'Lifetime Multiplier From Services Correction Factor'	Controls the effect of Service Output on Health Services
Parameter 'Investment in Services Correction Factor'	Controls the fraction of Industrial Output allocated to Service capital
Parameter 'W3-Reality Exchange Rate'	Exchange rate which allows a comparison with World3 capital measures with 2005 dollar values
Auxiliary variable 'Industrial Output 2005 Value'	Allows a comparison between current World Bank data and World3 Industrial Output
Auxiliary variable 'Service Output 2005 Value'	Allows a comparison between current World Bank data and World3 Service Output
Auxiliary variable 'Arable Land Harvested'	Used to compare FAO's data with World3 Arable Land
Parameter 'Arable Land Erosion Correction Factor'	Used as indicator for current use of lands in relation to Arable Land Erosion Rate

Demographic sub-system

The variables 'population,' 'birth rate,' and 'life expectancy' perfectly match between the metadata provided in the public dataset of the United Nations Population Division and the World3 variables definitions (Meadows et al. 1974). Total population is the aggregated value of all the populations of every country estimated at midyear. Birth rate indicates the number of live births per year every 1000 persons. Life expectancy at birth indicates the number of years children would live if the prevailing patterns of mortality at the time of its birth were to stay the same throughout its life.

In World3, population is governed by the dynamics of 'deaths' and 'births.' The variable 'deaths' is dependent on the variable 'life expectancy' only, which in turn is affected by four different factors as previously described: (i) health services, (ii) crowding effect, (iii) food per capita, and (iv) persistent pollution. Neglecting the effect of persistent pollution in the initial part of analysis, the first three variables are in turn dependent on (i) 'service output per capita,' (ii) 'industrial output per capita,' and (iii) 'food production.' On the other side, 'births' is dependent on a more complex structure which derives from the dynamics of 'industrial output per capita' and 'service output per capita.' The use of 'birth rate' and 'life expectancy' from the United Nations dataset (UNPD 2015) help in constraining the model in relation to all three (industrial, services, and agriculture) economic sectors of World3.

In order to facilitate the analysis, the parameters indicating the initial values of the population age cohorts of the World3 have been manually updated with 1995 values of the United Nations datasets (UNPD 2015).

Economic sub-system

The match between real data and World3 variable definitions was possible using the World Banks public dataset (WB 2015). In particular, the following two variables have been taken and aggregated from national available data:

- Service, etc., value added (constant 2005 US dollars): "this includes ISIC divisions 50–99 which are value added in wholesale and trade (including hotels and restaurants), transport, and government, financial, professional, and personal services such as education, health care, and real estate services. Also included are imputed bank service charges, import duties, and any statistical discrepancies noted by national compilers as well as discrepancies arising from rescaling" (WB 2015).
- Industry, value added (constant 2005 US dollars): "this includes ISIC divisions 10–45, which comprises value added in mining, manufacturing, construction, electricity, water, and gas" (WB 2015).

In Meadows et al. (1974) it is possible to find the definition of the capital stock variables of industry and services which are responsible for respective outputs:

- "Service capital in the model is associated with the activities listed under ISIC (International Standard Industrial Classification) divisions 6 through 9: Wholesale and retail trade, restaurants and hotels; transport, storage, and communication; financing, insurance, real estate, and business services; and community, social, and personal services" (Meadows et al. 1974).
- "Industrial capital stock provides the output in ISIC divisions 2 through 5: Mining and quarrying, manufacturing; electricity, gas, and water; and construction" (Meadows et al. 1974).

Despite a change in the ISIC divisions in the last four decades, the metadata represents the same quantities. However, it is 'service output' and 'industrial output' World3 variables that have to be matched with historical data. In the model, those are respectively obtained as a division between the two capital stock variables and the parameters 'service capital output ratio' and 'industrial capital output ratio,' which represent the unit of capital required to produce one unit of output in both sectors.

In addition, economic variables in World3 are represented in 1972 real dollars. To allow a comparison with the available data, the model structure was extended with one additional parameter and two variables. The parameter is 'W3-reality exchange rate' whose role is to convert the value of the variables 'industrial output' and 'service output' into 2005 dollars as a multiplicative factor. The resulting values are recorded in the new variables 'industrial output 2005 value' and 'service output 2005 value,' which in turn are used for the comparison with the historical data.

Based on the historical data constraints and performing some initial sensitivity analysis with available parameters, it was clear that sufficient degrees of freedom

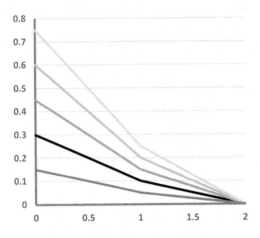

Fraction of industrial output allocated to services

Ability of service sector to satisfy service needs of population

Figure 2.1 Sensitivity parameterisation of allocation of investments to services for the World3–03-Edited calibration

(i.e. available parameters to vary) were not available to allow the model behaviour to converge to the historical data. Thus, two additional correction factors influencing two important non-linear relationships have been added to allow for the correct match. The parameter 'investments in services correction factor' has been included as a multiplier of the non-linear relationship 'fraction of industrial output allocated to services' (see Figure 1.10). The value of 1 corresponds to the curve indicated in Figure 1.10, whereas its variation correspond to moving to a different curve as shown in Figure 2.1. Similarly, the parameter 'lifetime multiplier from services correction factor' has been included to enhance the degrees of freedom of the non-linear relationship between the variables 'service output per capita' and 'health services per capita.'

Land sub-system

The FAO's metadata definition of the variable 'arable land' (FAO 2015) considers "land under temporary meadows for mowing or for pasture, land under market or kitchen gardens, and land temporary fallow. However, land abandoned as a result of shifting cultivation is excluded." In Meadows et al. (1974, p. 265), the variable 'arable land' is defined as "all areas which are used from time to time or full-time to grow crops and includes area under annual crops, area under permanent crops (tree crops, banana, sugar cane), area under temporary grass and fodder crops, and fallow." The differences in the two metadata requires the addition of the new variable 'arable land harvested,' which is derived from the multiplication of the variable 'arable land' in the World3 and the already existing parameter 'land fraction harvested.' The new variable depicts the fraction of arable land actually used for production out of the total as proposed by FAO (2015), and this is used for the match in the calibration.

The parameter 'arable land erosion correction factor' is also included to manage the uncertainty in the technology development related to good practices in agricultural land management. As shown in Figure 1.16 the Limits to Growth team managed such uncertainty by simulating a smooth switch between the two non-linear relationships indicating the burden of increased land yield on land erosion. The addition of the new parameter has been included to select the right curve among the two in a discrete manner for the calibration. The parameter has been set between 0 and 1 where 0 corresponds to the base run curve, 1 to the technological advancement curve, and all intermediate values to intermediate curves among the two as depicted in Figure 2.2.

The World3 parameter 'processing loss' is meant to take into account the percentage of produced food that is wasted in the food supply chain, plus a small percentage which considers area that is cultivated for purpose different from food production (for example, cotton). For the purpose of this study, this parameter has been manually set based on more recent work from FAO (2015) and excluded from the calibration analysis. The report proposed an estimation of the global fraction of food waste for major food commodities; i.e. cereals, roots and tubers, oil crops and pulses, fruits and vegetables, and meat. In order to

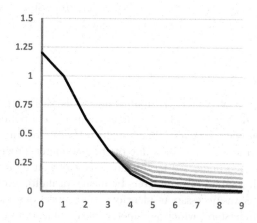

Figure 2.2 Sensitivity parameterisation of effects of land productivity on the land erosion for the World3–03-Edited calibration

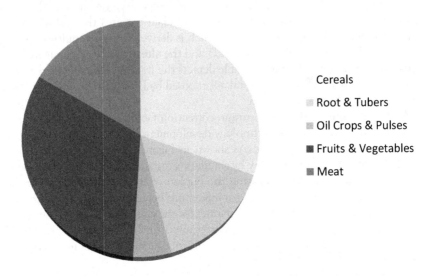

Figure 2.3 Estimate of the food production loss for processing
Source: FAO (2015)

convert those data into a single global loss figure as required in World3, the meat production value had to be multiplied by seven to account for its larger land footprint per unit of weight and then summed up to the other four categories (this is the same assumption used in Meadows et al. (1974) for aggregating meat and vegetables as a unique quantity). Figure 2.3 shows the relative waste from each type of food category. The resulting aggregate processing loss is 32%. An increase of 3% has been considered to take into account land cultivated for other purposes, resulting in setting the parameter 'processing loss' to 35%. This is widely different from the value of 10% of food waste as accounted for in the World3 scenarios.

Parameters selection

The total number of World3–03-Edited parameters is 59. By first neglecting the structures related to non-renewable resources and persistent pollution, this number was reduced to 44 parameters. By manually updating the initial values of the population cohort stocks and the value of the parameter 'processing loss,' the number of parameters subjected to this analysis was reduced to 39. A generic screening of such a group of parameters by means of multiple calibrations and sensitivity analysis was necessary to identify convergences of some parameters to certain values, understand which parameter most influences model behaviour, and identify a subset of parameters where the variation in their value could be used as output of the analysis.

In particular, the parameters 'W3-reality exchange rate' and 'land fraction harvested' converged to fixed values. 'W3-reality exchange rate' assumed a value of $7.19 in 2005 dollars for every World3–03 dollar. This compares favourably with the actual inflation figure for the United States over this period ($5.61), but it is not possible to externally validate the global figure as global inflation data does not exist for this whole period. Given inflation is likely to have been higher in emerging and developing countries, we feel this figure can be justified. 'Land fraction harvested' converged to the value 0.68 (in the standard scenario mode it was 0.7).

Where parameters did not show a particular change in relation to the ones used in Scenario 2 those have been left unvaried for the next phase of analysis. The final subset of parameters used for the actual calibration was reduced to 16 as listed in Table 2.3.

According to the role that every parameter had in the model behaviour, the final group was split into three sub-groups. For the purpose of this study these sub-groups were named:

1   'Economic' related parameters, concerned with the behaviours constrained between industrial output, service output, and life expectancy variables;
2   'Agricultural-food' related parameters that mainly affect the linkages constrained within arable land, industrial output, and life expectancy variables; and
3   'Demographic-social' related parameters which concern the model behaviours constrained by services output, industrial output, life expectancy, and birth rate variables.

Calibration with and without environmental limits

The model structures surrounding persistent pollution and non-renewable resources sub-systems can be easily included and omitted from the simulation by simply modifying the values of four parameters (see Table 2.4). By performing the calibration analysis on the basis of the 16 selected parameters, first neglecting and then including these structures, it is possible to test the robustness of the analysis.

The change in parameters was made in the model as follows:

- Resources Usage Factor 1 – controls the flow of material extraction in the model, and it is controlled by adaptive technology structures in the World3. Its value can range from 0 to 1, where 1 means no technology solutions are in place (With limits scenario) and 0 that resources are infinite (Without limits scenario).
- Persistent Pollution Generation Factor 1 – controls the persistent pollution generated by industry and agriculture, and it is controlled by adaptive technology structures in World3. Its value can range from 0 to 1, where 0 means that no pollution is generated at any time in the simulation (Without limits scenario) and 1 that no technology is in place to mitigate pollution generation (With limits scenario).

Table 2.3 List of the 16 parameters used in the calibration and sub-group division according to their role in the model

Parameter	Parameter role in World3–03-Edited model	Sub-system
Initial Industrial Capital	Initial value of Industrial Capital stock variable	Economic
Initial Service Capital	Initial value of Service Capital stock variable	Economic
Industrial Capital Output Ratio 1	Represents the ratio which defines the amount of output produced by every unit of Industrial Capital	Economic
Service Capital Output Ratio 1	Represents the ratio which defines the amount of output produced by every unit of Service Capital	Economic
Average Life of Service Capital 1	Represents the average amount of years the Service Capital can be used before depreciating	Economic
Investment in Services (*)	Acts as corrective factor in the allocation of investments form Industrial Output to Service Capital	Economic
Initial Arable Land	Initial value of Arable Land stock variable	Agriculture-Food
Initial Potentially Arable Land	Initial value of Potentially Arable Land stock variable	Agriculture-Food
Land Yield Factor 1	Determines the contribution of technology improvements in the food production in addition to conventional agricultural systems	Agriculture-Food
Arable Land Erosion Factor (*)	Determines how land are carefully used in relation to the level of exploitation in the food production	Agriculture-Food
Desired completed family size normal	Describes the desired family size by the average family	Demographic-Social
Lifetime Multiplier from Services (*)	A correction factor which defines the effect of Service Output on Health services	Demographic-Social
Income expectation averaging time	Average time spent from people to change their desires in family planning according to economic wages	Demographic-Social
Health services impact delay	Determines the delay between the changes in service output per capita and the time in which health facilities (hospital, doctors) are operative	Demographic-Social
Social adjustment delay	Determines the time population need to change their family planning to adapt to demographic changes	Demographic-Social
Lifetime perception delay	Determines the time spent by people to adapt to changes in relation to their expectation of life	Demographic-Social

Table 2.4 Values of parameters to differentiate between 'without limits' and 'with limits' scenarios

Parameter (unit)	1995 value in 'without limits' scenario	1995 value in 'with limits' scenario
Resource Use Factor (dimensionless)	0	1
Persistent Pollution Generation Factor (dimensionless)	0	1
Initial Persistent Pollution (pollution units)	0	349M (taken simulating the Scenario 2 till year 1995)
Initial Land Fertility (vegetable equivalent kilograms per year per hectare)	600 (correspondent to value of Scenario 2 at year 1900)	563 (taken simulating the Scenario 2 till year 1995)

- Initial Value of Persistent Pollution – determines the amount of persistent pollution at the beginning of the simulation. Every amount above zero generates negative effects on land fertility (see Figure 1.17). In the 'without limits scenario' the value is set to zero, that together with the removal of persistent pollution generation, allows its effect in the model to be neglected. In the 'with limits scenario' it is set to the same value of the simulated persistent pollution in 1995 of Scenario 2.
- Initial Value of Land Fertility – determines the natural productivity of land at the beginning of the simulation. Its value in the year 1900 is considered to be the natural level of land productivity. Persistent pollution can only decrease such a value. In the 'without limits scenario' this is set to the 1900 value of Scenario 2, which together with the elimination of pollution effects, results in no variation over time. In the 'with limits,' the parameter is set to the same value of the simulated land fertility in 1995 within Scenario 2.

Output of the calibration analysis

The results of the calibration process are shown in Figure 2.4, and Table 2.5. Figure 2.4 shows the six output variables used as a constraint for the calibration: Industrial Output, Service Output, Arable Land, Population, Life Expectancy, and Birth Rate. In particular, the historical data and the respective Scenario 2 values of the variables are pictured on the same unit scale, showing clear difference between simulated and historical data. The calibrations 'without limits' and 'with limits' are shown on the same graph and are mostly overlapping with themselves and with historical data as expected.

The difference between those and Scenario 2 is shown in Table 2.5. The generic nature of World3 does not allow the specification of exact values for the

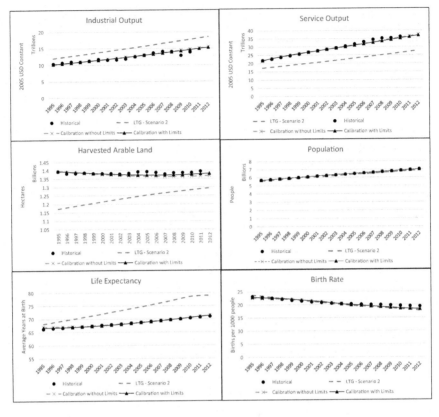

Figure 2.4 Calibration of the World3–03-Edited model

Source: Pasqualino et al. (2015)

Table 2.5 Result of the calibration process in relation and parameter variation between calibrated runs and Scenario 2 of World3

Parameter	Value scenario 2	Value calibration without limits	Value calibration with limits	Variation meaning
Industrial Capital-Output Ratio 1	3	3.64	3.64	There are lower rates of Industrial Output from every unit of Industrial Capital compared to the Scenario 2 of World3. This is due to more investment in technology to decouple industrial growth from planetary impacts.

Parameter	Value scenario 2	Value calibration without limits	Value calibration with limits	Variation meaning
Service Capital-Output Ratio 1	1	0.579	0.577	The productivity of Service Output per unit of Service Capital is higher than in the Scenario 2.
Investment in Services (*)	1 (not relevant)	2.07	2.02	There are higher investments in Service Capital than in the Scenario 2.
Average Life of Service Capital 1	20	24.07	24.02	Service Capital have longer life than in the Scenario 2
Land Yield Factor 1	1	1.634	1.672	There is a higher contribution from technology improvement resulting in higher food production from the same amount of available Arable Land
Arable Land Erosion Factor (*)	0	0.92	0.94	The Arable Land erosion factor more closely follows the good practice outlined within LTG
Initial Land Fertility	600 (1900 value)	600 (1900 value)	563 (1995 value)	Land Fertility is assumed to be lower when Persistent pollution is activated
Desired completed family size normal	3.8	3.42	3.48	Families desire are smaller than in Scenario 2
Lifetime Multiplier from Services (*)	1 (not relevant)	0.557	0.568	The Service Output has a smaller impact on life expectancy than in Scenario 2 due to the service sector having a disproportionate output from non-health sectors (the finance sector).
Income expectation averaging time	3	3.57	3.57	Assumes that people take a longer time to adapt to changes in wealth
Health services impact delay	20	24.97	20.86	Assumes higher delays between investments and having facilities in place to provide health services
Social adjustment delay	20	26	28	Assumes that global population is slower in adapting to demographic changes
Lifetime perception delay	20	23.54	28	Assumes that people perceive changes in life expectancy a bit less quickly

parameters to describe the state of our economic and ecological systems, but the variation in comparison to Scenario 2 can demonstrate the pattern the economy is taking in comparison to what was depicted in Scenario 2 of Meadows et al. (2003). Interestingly, the variation between 'with' and 'without' limits scenarios and Scenario 2 show agreement in the results for every parameter with variations of the same sign (positive or negative).

The most noticeable result of this analysis is that the economy has taken a shape that is different from the one assumed in the Limits to Growth study and further updates. A strong shift from an industrial to service economy has taken place. Driven by the rise of telecommunication, information technology and financial sectors, services have become a larger force of economic growth than expected. On the other side, the industrial sector has been producing less output than proposed in Scenario 2 of the Limits to Growth.

The shift in scenarios is demonstrated with the change in parameters. In particular, 'service capital' is approximately 70% more productive (whereas Scenario 2 assumed 1 unit of service capital to produce 1 unit of output, the calibrated scenario report that only 0.579 and 0.577 units of capital are used to produce 1 unit of output) than estimated in Meadows et al. (2003) alongside a more than doubling of the industrial investments in services ('investment in services correction factor' increase of more than 100%) and larger life of service capital (increased 'average life of service capital' parameter of more than 25%). Industries register a 17% lower productivity than in the calibrated scenarios (Industrial Capital Output Ratio moved from 3 to 3.64 capital units necessary to produce 1 unit of output). Based on Limits to Growth assumptions on pollution and technological change, this could be interpreted as a lower propensity of the industrial sectors to generate pollution allowing space for the assumption that humanity is currently dealing with ecological constraints by means of developing and deploying new technologies to a greater extent than envisaged in Scenario 2.

Significant changes are also registered in the agricultural sector of the model. The variable 'arable land' shows a barely constant trend in comparison to the growth behaviour of the Scenario 2. In World3, the dynamic of 'arable land' is subject to continuous land development that substitutes for what is eroded or diverted to urban and industrial uses (see Figure 1.16). Due to continuous population growth and increased food production, World3 would show a continuous erosion rate that, together with reaching the limit of land available for agriculture, would result in lower output levels in the food chain. Such dynamic behaviour is in agreement with Randers (2012) before the year 2052.

The parameter analysis suggests a significant improvement in food production technology to increase land yield ('land yield technology' factor increases to more than 60% in comparison to Scenario 2) and better land management techniques to maintain land erosion at low levels ('arable land erosion correction factor' is above 0.9 indicating that the curve measuring the effect of land yield to land erosion is almost the one of the technology improvement scenario of Meadows et al. (2003)).

It is worth noting that by setting the parameter 'processing loss' to be 35% before the calibration analysis rather than 10% as in the Scenario 2, the resulting effect of the model calibration is to increase the values of other parameters related to food production. This observation weakens the indication that the current level of technology is higher than in Scenario 2, but the conclusion of better land management practices because of a high value of the parameter 'arable land erosion correction factor' still holds true.

With regards to demographic variables, 'population' is demonstrated as being well represented in every scenario in comparison to historical data; 'life expectancy' results are overestimated in Scenario 2 in comparison to historical data; 'birth rate' remained difficult to be perfectly matched with historical data using World3 structures.

The analysis on the parameter shows 'lifetime multiplier from services correction factor' is largely lower than in Scenario 2, thus indicating an imbalance due to the large increase in the 'service output' in the model. In Scenario 2 it is assumed that if the world had the current level of 'service output,' we would expect to have a much larger health service than we do, with a bigger impact on life expectancy. This may be due to the oversized telecommunications and finance contribution to the current service sector than anticipated in Limits to Growth resulting in a smaller than anticipated share of services being dedicated to health.

With regard to the remaining parameters, their role is to link economic growth to the birth rate. The calibration indicates the average global family size represents a lower number of children per family ('desired completed family size' decrease to 3.42 and 3.48), and that people take more time to adapt to global economic trends (all delay parameters show significant increases in comparison to Scenario 2). However, given the complexity of the structure of this sub-system, the methodology used here is not able to be conclusive as to the interaction between, and absolute values of, these parameters. This is reinforced by the inability of the model in providing an exact match between historical data and calibrated runs.

From World3 to the real world

The Limits to Growth work was proposed as an analysis tool for an increasingly complex and problematic society as identified by the Club of Rome (1970). The system dynamics approach has been presented with emphasis on the use of systemic (top-down from a particular distance) view, feedback loops, accumulation processes and non-linearities as major instruments to depict system structures, and simulation. Then the World3 model assumptions have been described in a way to allow readers to find the sources of dynamic behaviours within the complex interconnection of elements captured in the model. This approach should:

- Allow other scientists to critique and analyse the model systematically challenging its most important assumptions and proposing updates to create a new personalised version of their global models;
- Propose an initial framework to understand how the world can be thought of as a system, starting from an empty box, and using available system thinking tools such as system dynamics.

Based on the interpretation of World3 assumptions, the most likely behaviours for the future have been represented as depicted in Meadows et al. (2003) and analysed using available historical data and calibration analysis as proposed in Pasqualino et al. (2015).

The outcome of this analysis can be summarised as follows:

- The most likely scenario proposed from the Limits to Growth team in relation to the future of society is the adaptive technology scenario (Scenario 6) of Meadows et al. (2003) and not Scenario 1 as often referred to (e.g. Turner 2008, 2012).
- Our world population and economy are growing in a finite planet, and the World3 model can be used to assess such a dynamic of growth.
- The pattern the economy is following demonstrates a radical economic shift to a system governed by services and improved technology rather the industries in comparison to what was expected in every scenario presented in the various publications of World3.
- Still growth remains the main paradigm the world society relies on, and such a growth remains based on the finite available resources of the planet. Resource scarcity as well as negative effects of the system, such as pollution, cannot be excluded in shaping the future possibilities of our world.

These findings are based on the underlying assumptions of the behavioural dynamics of World3 still holding true today. While a calibration of the model is shown to be able to fit current data, providing some assurance that these assumptions remain valid, further research is required to examine these in detail in light of new data and trends.

Summary

In this chapter, the World3–03 model has been compared to global historical data from the year 1995 to 2012 by means of model calibration and analysis of model output. This approach is different from the one proposed in Turner (2008, 2012), who made a comparison without considering the absolute values inherent in the World3 simulations. In fact, these are fundamental to determine model behaviour towards the future, as demonstrated in this study.

The world systems proposed within the World3 structures provides a picture that is aggregated in nature, generic, but still founded on science and case studies in order to estimate its relationships (Meadows et al. 1974). The whole economy is expressed in a single real currency, people are modelled as one single group, no countries are specified, the interaction among individuals and organisations in the design of new technologies or financial system are neglected, and so on. However, as pointed out in the various Limits to Growth reports, and supported with available data and the calibration analysis proposed in Pasqualino et al. (2015), the most fundamental statement emerging from these studies is that global society, and its economic footprint, still grows, and remains based on the finite available resources of this planet.

The next chapter puts aside the use of computer models and aims at developing some broad system understanding of the real world as it is shaped today. Its aim is to answer questions such as 'Why do we grow?' or 'How can we assess the impact of human growth on ecosystems?' Such a literature and real-world events review aims at providing material to help critique the World3 structures even more precisely, and can potentially allow one to develop a world system understanding by mean of narratives, pictures, and diagrams as tools to inform system thinking. This forms the foundation of the demand for novel global models, such as the one proposed in Part II of this book.

References

Club of Rome (1970). *The predicament of mankind: A quest for structured responses to growing world-wide complexities and uncertainties*. Proposal to the Club of Rome, Geneva, Switzerland.

Food Agriculture Organization (FAO). *Global food losses and food waste*. Available online: www.fao.org/docrep/014/mb060e/mb060e00.htm (accessed 9 May 2015).

Meadows, D. H., Meadows, D. L., & Randers, J. (1992). *Beyond the limits: Global collapse or a sustainable future*. Earthscan Publications Ltd, London, UK.

Meadows, D. H., Meadows, D. L., & Randers, J. (2003). *The limits to growth: The 30-year update*. Routledge, LONDON, UK.

Meadows, D. H., Meadows, D. L., Randers, J., & Behrens, J. (1972). *The limits to growth*. Universe Books, New York, NY, USA.

Meadows, D. L., Behrens, W. W., Meadows, D. H., Naill, R. F., Randers, J., & Zahn, E. (1974). *Dynamics of growth in a finite world*. Wright-Allen Press, Cambridge, MA.

Meadows, D. L., Richardson, J., & Bruckmann, G. (1982). *Groping in the dark: The first decade of global modelling*. John Wiley & Sons, Hoboken, New Jersey, Stati Unit.

Oliva, R. (2003). Model calibration as a testing strategy for system dynamics models. *European Journal of Operational Research*, 151(3), 552–568.

Pasqualino, R., Jones, A., Monasterolo, I., & Phillips, A. (2015). Understanding global systems today – a calibration of the world3–03 model between 1995 and 2012. *Sustainability*, 7(8), 9864–9889.

Randers, J. (2000). From limits to growth to sustainable development or SD (sustainable development) in a SD (system dynamics) perspective. *System Dynamics Review: The Journal of the System Dynamics Society*, 16(3), 213–224.

Randers, J. (2012). *2052: A global forecast for the next forty years*. Chelsea Green Publishing.

Turner, G. M. (2008). A comparison of the limits to growth with 30 years of reality. *Global Environmental Change*, 18(3), 397–411.

Turner, G. M. (2012). On the cusp of global collapse? Updated comparison of the limits to growth with historical data. *GAIA-Ecological Perspectives for Science and Society*, 21(2), 116–124.

United Nations Population Division Report, United Nations, Department of Economic and Social Affairs. Available online: http://esa.un.org/unpd/wpp/unpp/panel_population.htm (accessed 1 February 2015).

World Bank Databank (WB). Available online: https://data.worldbank.org/ (accessed September 2015).

3 Welcome to the real world!

"Give a fish to a man and you will feed him for one day. Teach him how to fish and he will deplete the oceans" (Bardi 2015). Today's paradigm of economic growth is founded on disequilibrium at both individual and societal levels. Capitalism, free trade, and consumerism are supported by most governments and businesses worldwide based on the assumption that they are key to alleviate unemployment, facilitate wealth distribution, reduce poverty, generate safer pensions, increase overall well-being for all, and create a more stable economy, amongst others (Maxton and Randers 2016; Capra and Luisi 2016). Unfortunately, uncontrolled economic growth is unsustainable, pushing society towards overshooting environmental limits. It depletes available resources and land quality, it generates pollution that accumulates in the ecosystems, and interferes with climate stability. It also generates social issues that it is supposed to tackle, such as increasing inequality (Piketty 2014; Stiglitz 2012; Jackson 2016), as well as being the main cause for political conflicts and the exploitation of underdeveloped countries by developed ones (Capra and Luisi 2016; Brown 2008; Randers 2012).

This chapter aims to picture today's world system considering social, economic, political, and technological aspects that underpin growth and provides evidence on the state of ecosystems' depletion. The paradigm of economic growth, which is driven by a capitalistic system governed by trade and technology development, characterised by instability, and sanctioned with the international structure of financial and debt money systems, is portrayed at the core of the sustainability dilemma. It shows how the issues related to resource scarcity have evolved, how land systems are performing, and how climatic change affects the complex interconnection among the two. It presents the state of pollution worldwide, sociopolitical implications of climate change, and how they reshape the world society. The need for an energy transition towards a green economy is introduced, and the fallacies in the current financial system as not able to help turn the world towards a sustainable path are identified.

Dynamics of growth – principles of the global economy

As creatures of nature, humans are needy entities from the day on which they are born. At the most basic level, needs can relate to nutrition, housing, and security,

DOI: 10.4324/9781315643182-4

and, on top of that, people's 'wants' can be satisfied with what are generally called commodities and services. Probably above all, and most often not even considered by many, the need to conduct a meaningful life remains fundamental to everyone (Druckman and Jackson 2010; Baumeister et al. 2013). Such a meaning is very relative in today's world: some examples might include the interest and passion for knowledge, art, and cultures; having and raising children; building up positive relationships with other people or affording time to enjoying a beer with friends. During their lifetimes people's needs change together with their want for commodities and services, as well as their interpretation of a meaningful life.

The possibility to work is the key in this context because it allows the expression of one's social value in the wider society and at the same time accommodates people's skills and personality, which keep evolving in a dynamic world (Jackson 2016). While people's needs generate demand, the work provided by the same people generate the supply to those needs. Efficient markets can then form the foundation for the allocation of resources and the satisfaction of the needs of every person on this planet in the long term. However, in today's global economic system a large number of countries are not able to deliver the basic needs for their population, most developed countries are overwhelmed with commodities and services they don't need, and the idea of reaching a meaningful life with a job seems a utopia for the vast majority of the global population.

The emergency of a capitalistic society founded on international trade and fossil fuels

The most familiar form of capital for most people is financial capital (i.e. money). Aristotle (384–322 BC) pointed out: "Money exists not by nature but by law," and as legal tender for every business transaction in the real world, financial capital is the main instrument of control on our economic system through centralised authorities who are responsible for supplying it – i.e. central banks as banknotes and electronic money. Money allows for a detachment of financial from real transactions on the basis of the social interest that communities place on certain items. Price is referred to as the valuation of commodities and services, whereas wage or salary as the compensation for the work of people involved in the production of those items.

In today's economic system, the term 'capital' refers to every input in the production process that contributes to economic output. A well-established framework (the Five Capitals Framework) aligns financial capital to four other fundamental forms of capital: (i) man-made capital (e.g. machines, buildings, software, and algorithms); (ii) human capital (i.e. labour and their skills); (iii) social capital (which emerges from the interaction among people); and (iv) natural capital (the world's ecosystems and resources). In a capitalistic view all those items for production can be valued in monetary terms. The legal power of those who own financial capital as a means of control is an important aspect of a capitalistic society. Set within an economic system, the financial sector intends to deliver public goods. However, as highlighted by John Maynard Keynes, the system of "Capitalism is the extraordinary belief that the nastiest of people, for the nastiest of motives, will somehow work for the benefit of all!" (as quoted in Maxton and Randers 2016, p. 32).

In such a system, people's needs of commodities and services (i.e. consumption) govern the consumer's flow of money to whom produces and distributes those over time. In turn, those involved in the production of commodities would employ workers and equipment (e.g. a machine, a building) and additional materials necessary for the manufacturing of the commodity. In so doing, the producer generates an additional demand that can be satisfied by further producers able to supply those equipment and materials, employ other labour and consume other material items for their production. The extended picture is a network of supply chains of industries and service providers that, at one end are the consumers and at the other end the suppliers of raw materials by mean of resource extraction from natural ecosystems. At each node, labour is required and the people who can provide it are given wages. The output is priced based on the demand it aims to fulfil, which tries to be higher than the cost of production. It is worth noting that while wages can be used for the consumption of commodities and services from labour, the price has to embed the cost of production and so the value of labour at every stage of the supply chain.

Among the various forms of capital employed in production, it is worth distinguishing between man-made or tangible capital (i.e. material such as a machine or a building) and human or knowledge capital (i.e. knowledge and skills of the people who create and operate the tangible capital). Commodities and services can be produced combining available labour and capital on the basis of existing knowledge. Man-made capital is subject to wearing, and has a limited amount of time that it can be used before becoming obsolete. However, knowledge capital accumulates the effort of everyone who contributes in its development. It can be archived and shared with other communities, who can use it to generate additional knowledge by means of extension and improvement, and apply it to new areas of interest. The accumulation of knowledge can create needs unknown before, thus creating demand for new capital, new commodities and services, and new knowledge. The continuous discard of old capital, allows for the displacement of new capital produced with renewed knowledge.

This dynamic interplay is fundamental for the increase of the well-being of society. The innovation of capital allows for the increase in productivity (amount of output produced by one worker in one unit of time) thus lowering the cost of production and distribution of output (accounted mostly by labour itself). In fact, the lower the amount of resources used in the production of a single commodity, the higher is its potential to be adopted by a vast amount of consumers.

In today's economic system, knowledge is created in both public and private sectors by employing people at the exchange of wages. The cost of knowledge generation is mostly represented by infrastructure and the labour necessary to create it, which must be repaid as taxes to governments or as mark-up on costs to the private sector. Due to its important role in shaping a society, legislation has been placed to protect and favour the creation of new knowledge by means of intellectual property rights and patents. This assures novel knowledge cannot be replicated by others within a certain amount of time after the invention was presented in the first place, promoting business development and implementation of novel ideas. In so doing, the creation of novel knowledge allows for the production of innovative capital and commodities, which in turn can be legally transferred using financial capital and trade.

Among the first to recognise the importance of international trade in the improvement of well-being across societies we find the Scottish and British economists Adam Smith (1723–1790) and David Ricardo (1772–1823), also known as the fathers of classical economics and neo-liberalism. Two of Smith's most important observations, as proposed in *The Wealth of Nations* (1776), are that the large poverty spread in the majority of economies of the time was due to the low productivity of labour that could not make goods and services affordable and widespread among the society, and that international trade could have significantly contributed to the rise of labour productivity.

Labour productivity increased significantly after the invention of James Watt's steam engine in 1781. The steam engine allowed for the employment of fossil fuel energy (coal) for performing the work that was initially delegated to people and animals (this is also the period in which abolition of slavery took place). By 1870 one steam engine could operate the work of 40 million British workers (Maxton and Randers 2016). The energy employed to operate such a machine could be used to extract more and more coal in areas that could not be reached before. The extraction of those allowed for the creation of new machines and led to the rise of the First Industrial Revolution.

While overall trade could evolve at a faster pace than ever before, David Ricardo formulated his theory of 'comparative advantage' within the *Principles of Political Economy and Taxation* (1891). In his view, a commodity free market composed of multiple nations could reach the maximum long-term benefit for all if every nation was specialising in the production of the commodities they could export at higher cost advantage in comparison to others.

In a world characterised by widespread poverty, high levels of unemployment, and large inequality among the rich and the poor, free markets, led by a capitalistic paradigm, were meant to alleviate all of those problems and effectively rise the well-being for various populations worldwide. The rise of a middle class of industrialists and businessmen could take place in both the poor and the nobility of the time. Indeed since the start of the first industrial revolution global poverty levels have declined and life expectancy has increased dramatically. Still the working conditions of labour were far from considered good, with long hours set by machines, and payments far below the minimum necessary for living a decent life (Maxton and Randers 2016).

By the 1850s, the economy was mostly fuelled with coal, which still presented some difficulty with transportation as well as being the cause of health issues because of its high particulate release that was polluting industrial cities. New ways of thinking around economic systems emerged as an answer to the fallacies of the theories proposed by Smith, Ricardo, and others in providing a satisfactory life for all. Among those we find the Prussian Karl Marx (1818–1883) who lived in Germany and England for a large part of his life. His theoretical thinking can be found in *Capital*, proposed in four volumes and written between 1861 and his death (Marx 1867). Volumes II and III were published after his death by his German friend and collaborator Friedrich Engels (1820–1895) (Marx 1885, 1894), whereas Volume IV (*Theories of Surplus Value*, 1905), which more than others contains the critique of liberalism and capitalism as depicted by previous thinkers, was published by the Czech-Austrian Karl Kautsky (Marx 1905).

In the meantime, the discovery of crude oil, the most disruptive fossil fuel of all time and the most responsible for sustaining the development of the society that we know today, enabled the beginning for a new energy transition in industrialised countries. The first oil well was drilled in 1859 in Pennsylvania by Edwin Drake. Oil was cheaper to transport, more versatile and more powerful than coal, but the installed capacity with existing technology was a barrier for the widespread substitution of oil for coal. The first application was found in the lighting of cities, allowing petroleum to substitute oil obtained from the fat of whales for that purpose (at the time whales were legally hunted and the oceans were almost depleted of whales). After the first few decades, new plants and new uses of oil were found. According to Smil (2010) it took approximately 50 years from the exploration stage in 1860s to reach 10% of energy supply in the United States, and another 30 years for crude oil to reach 25% of the national energy mix. The discovery of cheap crude oil is also considered as the base for the Second Industrial Revolution which lasted from 1870s to the beginning of World War I in 1914.

The engines of modern capitalism – debt money system and financial markets

As attributed to US President Woodrow Wilson after having signed the Federal Reserve into existence in 1913:

> I am the most unhappy man. I have unwittingly ruined my country. A great industrial nation is controlled by its system of credit. Our system of credit is concentrated. The growth of the nation, therefore, and all our activities are in the hands of a few men. We have come to be one of the worst ruled, one of the most completely controlled and dominated Governments in the civilized world; no longer a Government by free opinion, no longer a Government by conviction and the vote of the majority, but a Government by the option and duress of a small group of dominant men.
>
> (from Wijkman and Rockström 2013)

One of the engines of our economy lies in the process of borrowing and lending and in the creation of debt. The availability of cash for the purchase of material and non-material assets is a fundamental requirement in our society. The two most common forms of spending can be seen as consumption (referred to as the purchase of service and commodities that are subjected to wearing and have the role of providing short lasting utility to consumers) and investment (the purchase of long lasting assets that are assumed to provide higher future returns than the investment itself). Positive differences between income and spending are normally stored within banks as savings, and can be used as a means of cash accumulation towards higher future spending. Borrowing comes into play to raise the cash to the level necessary for the purchase of assets that are unaffordable with available cash. Financing practices based on borrowing are in use in our society since antiquity (Graeber 2014).

According to Jackson (2016), money itself evolved from debt-based exchange. The process consists of lenders who own liquidity (savings) and provide finance to borrowers in the form of loans at the cost of capital (i.e. interest rate), that is, what the borrower is supposed to pay back to the lender for the service received. The loan takes the name of *credit* (from Latin *belief*) from the point of view of the lender and *debt* from the point of view of the borrower. The interest rate is a measure of risk based on the assessment of the likely future capabilities of the debtors to repay its debt to the creditors in the time frame agreed by both parties, and is accounted as a fraction of the capital to be paid to the lender calculated on the monthly or yearly basis. The financial institution working as intermediary between lenders and borrowers is the bank, mainly responsible for assessing risk, based on which the borrower is supposed to pay debt service back to the lender. The higher the probability of failing to repay the debt, the higher the interest rate and the cost of financing.

The purchase of a house is the highest lump sum acquisition made by most people in the developed world and finance usually comes from borrowing in the form of a mortgage. In areas with expanding populations (in particular for urban areas) the demand for existing houses increases their price over time. When the future value of the house overcomes the cost of capital employed, the purchase of the house can easily be considered as an investment. Due to such a dynamic behaviour, the real estate market has become a priority in the banking sector.

On the business side, borrowing tends to be used as financial leverage to expand productive assets assumed to drive revenue streams in the business. Debt tends to increase the resiliency of firms allowing them to invest while mitigating risks dependent on future uncertainties within the markets they operate. In today's business world it is normal management practice to keep a fraction of financial assets available as financed with debt in order to approach new markets and without risking default of the entire business. However, markets are volatile, and the value that can be charged for produced commodities can decrease to levels that do not match the cost of production forcing firms to default. The fraction of assets belonging to the firm is called 'equity.' From the point of view of the lenders, the risk of default of the borrower has to be assessed a priori to minimise losses on the loans. The default of some producers can often result in a higher interest rate for the businesses operating in the same sector, which presents a barrier for new entrants in the market. Stronger firms result in lower default rates, and interest rates can be reduced back to lower levels. This is an important balancing feedback loop used by banks to stabilise the economic system today.

In a closed system economy, in which members of a supply chain produce output and provide income to households to consume such an output, borrowing has the effect of relaxing the constraint of keeping the cost of production to be always fully embedded in the price of output as well as relaxing the need to generate revenue before spending. Despite the cost of capital having to be incorporated in the price output for every producer at each node of the network, it is possible to see how the increase in liquidity determined by borrowing can increase the demand, consumption and investment patterns at every level of the supply chain. In turn, this generates inflation in the economy and supports stability and growth. In addition to this, it is fundamental to see that the requirement to service debt for businesses implies a minimum amount of growth that is necessary so as to not default on debt.

If all business operates, or desires to operate, in this way then the long-term dynamic at the system level is the one of exponential growth of the economy. The fraction of interest rate imposed from the average lender to the borrower represents a factor determining the desired exponential growth rate of the economy. In other words, a stable economy based on debt is forced to grow exponentially. If businesses fail in attaining exponential growth rates high enough to repay debt, lenders can renegotiate their conditions for debt return over a longer time frame, or take over the financial assets of the borrower. Every loss is also translated as an increase in the interest rate (measure of risk) for similar loans to other producers involved in the same sector. In so doing, they provide a negative feedback to growth in the attempt to rebalance the economy when things do not go well. Of course, the risk assessment of a bank is focused on avoiding such a situation from happening.

The pressure imposed by debt repayment can generate the need for market participants to create new technologies to decrease their costs of production, increase labour productivity, and thereby have enough revenue to repay debts. However, this pressure is environmentally unsustainable if producer activities are based on the exploitation of the limited non-renewable resources and create waste.

The continuous growth of the economic system coupled with the rise of inflation corresponds to a demand for new credit to be injected in the system over time. Historically, credit creation was based on a fixed amount of gold stored in the vaults of banks and central banks all over the world (e.g. the Federal Reserve Bank as central bank of the United States). However, the gold standard presented difficulties in assuring stability through growth in the economy, with particular focus on employment. In the early 1970s the gold standard started being abandoned in Europe (Italy, England, and Switzerland) and the US, initiating the transition towards the currently widely adopted debt money system. Nowadays, every central bank has the capability to create credit by printing money (quantitative easing), lend those at an interest rate, and records such a creation as debt money. Money creation in neoliberal economies has instead moved to private banks who create liabilities and assets on their balance sheets through loan activities (Silver 2017).

The inequality among the rich and the poor is a dynamic phenomenon, and the debt money system, as just presented, raises inequalities in different ways. In the first instance, access to liquidity favour the rich of society and presents a barrier to those who own less. The higher the amount of assets owned by the borrower, the lower their risk to return their debt, and in turn the interest rate imposed to them. This practice has the immediate effect of constraining access to liquidity by those who own less by increasing their interest rate and cost of capital (at the extreme level no ownership of money means no borrowing at all). Secondly, all payments for debt are given to the people who own the liquidity, that is, people who can earn enough to have savings deposited in their banks. In other words, the poor borrow from the rich and pay them back the cost of servicing capital, speeding up the wealth accumulation of the rich over time (Maxton and Randers 2016). Paradoxically, as inequality increases, poorer households become even less able to service loans. Today's global economic system has resulted in 1% of the population owning 48% of total assets (Credit Suisse 2015). Such inequality spread is even accentuated in periods characterised by fiscal policies focused on quantitative easing, often applied to maintain positive inflation rates and stabilise the economy. In those cases, the wealthy end up increasing their financial assets at much greater speed than the poorest of the society (Piketty 2014).

The inequality issue is equally stark when looking at the debt and credit distribution among countries. The debt of a country can be distinguished between private (debt of private firms to the households) and public debt (debt owned from the government to the private sector), and both can be distinguished as domestic (debt belonging to people resident in the same country borrower) or foreign debt (debt belonging to people living abroad). The private debt is what has been described so far in this section. It is about firms and people who are interested in achieving some goal (investment or purchase) through borrowing money. Public debt can be seen in a similar way, as the debt owned by the government to households who benefit from a surplus of cash deposited in banks. However, governments are in a different position from the private sector, as they are usually judged with much lower risk and therefore benefit from lower interest rates as well as being able to create debt at their will based on international regulation (Jackson 2016).

Governments have legislative power over the private sector and their aim is to regulate and provide infrastructure and services to the private sector to best perform their activities. In so doing, they collect taxes from the private sector, aiming at redistributing those by means of expenditure and subsidies. Public debt increases when the national income level is lower than expenditures plus other outflows from government treasury, and decreases in the opposite case. Austerity measures (lowering government expenditure, tax increases or both) are an instrument to deal with such a dynamic, although below a certain level they can constrain the economy towards recession. On the other hand, the issuing of bonds, or an increase in taxes can support higher expenditure. In a healthy economy in which the private and public sector find a good synergy to collaborate together, the growth of the private sector allows for higher resources to the government for expenditure and creates better infrastructure to allow stability and growth of the private sector. This is a positive feedback loop. However, this can also generate large inequalities between countries over time, favouring those able to grow based on their own strength and the natural resources they can rely on (Maxton and Randers 2016). A rising debt in a shrinking economy would be recipe for disaster (Jackson 2016).

If debt can be considered as an unbalancing force within the economy moving it towards growth, financial markets can be seen as the attraction point of such a disequilibrium, representing what we call here the second engine of capitalism. In fact, in order to run effectively, financial markets rely on the reinforcing feedback loop more money leads to more investments, that lead to more profit, that is more money and more investments. Financial markets play the role of a funding channel from the investor to corporations and the public sector, allowing those to finance their activities and grow. Financial markets operate through trading government and household debt (bond or credit market), corporate equity (stock market), primary commodities such as coffee, wheat or oil (commodity market), and, since the abandonment of gold standard in 1970s, currency (foreign exchange market). The foreign exchange market is the largest among those, followed by the credit market. The sophisticated use of information technologies allowed for the creation of more and more abstract financial products including future options, hedge funds and derivatives on the one hand, and for the automation of trading programs on the other hand. The speed of trade governed by electronic transactions is significantly faster than the one experienced at the level of real commodities and production systems. In so doing, financial markets operate as detached from the economy. Volatility and turbulence are key characteristics of financial markets, supporting short termism, speculation, and in the usual attempt of making profit out of market volatility, without any concern about the possible effects on the real economy (Capra and Luisi 2016).

Castells (1996) coined the term 'casino finance' to describe this phenomena. Today's markets are fundamentally shaped by machines with the only target of making money, whereas ethical considerations related to fairness and integrity have been gradually excluded. According to Capra and Luisi (2016) technology is not the problem, but rather politics and human values, which could be included as parameters of those machines as natural laws, rather than creating a system that supports inequality spread in favour of the rich (Maxton and Randers 2016).

Productivity growth and technological revolutions

The recognition that productivity growth is the most important determinant of long-term economic growth and rising living standards is well established in economics (Schwab 2017; Maxton and Randers 2016; Jackson 2016). Productivity growth represents incremental changes in the ability of one person to produce a certain unit of economic output. Human history has been characterised by several limited periods of time in which overall productivity increased more intensively than in others. For the purpose of this book, we use the term 'revolution' to describe short lasting innovation waves involving the widespread diffusion of technologies around the world, triggering profound change in economic systems and shifts in the way of living.

The first agricultural revolution, approximately 12,000 years ago, can be considered the first of those. The stable climate conditions after a glacial era, allowed the human transition from foraging to farming. The main innovation of the time was in the domestication of animals allowing people to exploit their muscle power, and supporting the development of the first cities and urban areas. This period is called the Holocene. Technological improvements in the Holocene include metallurgy practices improvements (from the stone-age to iron-age), employment of renewable energy in agriculture production (water and windmills) and for transportation, colonisation and trade (sailing and naval ships), architecture and construction (including sewerage), and political and social innovations (including democracy) among others.

Approximately 250 years ago, the embedding of fossil fuel energy into human activities, and the transition from muscle power to machine power, signalled the beginning of world development as we see it today. The first industrial revolution is marked with the use of coal in the powering of the steam engine in the late 18th century. Innovation in metallurgy, machines, lighting, and cements allowed for the widespread development of roads and industries, and started taking workers away from agriculture. The second industrial revolution in late 19th century was marked by the discovery of crude oil and the electrification of factories. Telecommunications were simplifying global communication through telegraph and telephone. Progress in metallurgy continued to allow the expansion of rail, whereas the newly invented combustion engine led to the creation of the first airplane and automobile. Henry Ford pioneered an industrial movement called 'Fordism,' consisting in reaching economies of scale and mass production by developing gigantic factories that could reduce the unit cost of production and increase the total output of the capital employed.

Probably the most disruptive innovation in agriculture of all time is represented by the Haber-Bosch process. Patented in 1909 to produce industrial fertilizers it consists in burning natural gas to separate ammonia and nitrogen. Still at the core of modern farming techniques, fertilizers increase the natural soil fertility and productivity of land, and supported population growth farther beyond the Malthusian hypotheses formulated in 1798. In Malthus' view, agriculture production should not have been able to keep up with the exponential growth of population and resulted in a future characterised by famine and food scarcity. From 1930s to 1960s the second agriculture revolution (or green revolution) took place. It consisted in the implementation of modern farming techniques including fertilizers and chemical application to increase land production, irrigation technologies, and improved land management techniques thereby keeping food prices low.

The major forces driving productivity growth during the first and second industrial revolutions were resource based innovations that allowed for the creation of new machines and infrastructures, and the design of better organised systems to apply those innovations efficiently. Continuous improvement of those technologies gradually increased productivity in the 20th century to the point where John Maynard Keynes (another of the most influential economists of the time) envisioned such a productive economy would allow the generation of his grandchildren to work only few hours a week to satisfy the consumption needs of the wider society (Keynes 1930). Research and development continued on this pace for decades, with a particularly large commitment and leadership demonstrated in the military sector (in particular in the US and Europe). Some examples include the aerospace industry and their engines developed by Rolls Royce and General Electric corporations, the Manhattan project including Enrico Fermi (1901–1954), Albert Einstein (1879–1955), and John Von Neumann (1903–1957) to conceptualise decades of research in atomic energy to create the first atomic bomb leading to the first nuclear reactor to power an electricity grid in 1954, and the invention of the first theoretical computer machine as ideated by Alan Turing (1912–1954) while developing a computing machine to break the German encryption machine called *Enigma*.

The next frontier of widespread technology change leading to increased productivity growth at the economic level came through the manufacturing of the first transistor in 1947 as a foundation for all electronic devices. The 1950s and 60s were characterised by the Cold War, with the United States and the Soviet Union as the two superpowers. The Advanced Research Projects Agency (ARPA – today called Defence Advanced Research Project Agency DARPA), funded by US Department of Defence, created the ARPAnet as the first technology able to use the protocol TCP/IP in order to connect the various supercomputers dispersed in the US to speed up research and development and communication among geographically dispersed teams. ARPAnet expanded quickly and in the 1980s, after TCP/IP was legitimated as its standard protocol of communication, it expanded towards a global network of super computers under control of militaries and academics. In the meantime computer calculation power was quickly increasing as a result of transistor technology manufactured at smaller and smaller scales. It is estimated that one square millimetre held approximately 200 transistors in 1970 and about 1 million in 2011, bringing with it the increased computation power.

The first personal computers were commercialised in late 1970s and took off in the 1980s with the invention of the first operating systems. Personal computers became a fundamental tool for every work environment, and spread all over the developed world. The concept of network externality that allowed a particular business to gather advantage through the users who were part of their network became common. Research at CERN, based on the ARPAnet technology in the 1980s, developed the HTML and HTTP languages that allowed for the creation, in 1989, of the World Wide Web. In 1990, ARPAnet was decommissioned, and the internet was opened to the public. In 1991 the Cold War ended and the Soviet Union dissolved.

The nature of the third industrial revolution is one of empowerment through interconnectivity and the fast exchange of information within a global network of individuals as well as exploiting the computation power of new algorithms and software for performing more and more sophisticated tasks. The study of mechanical engineering became gradually substituted with the study of mechatronics, highlighting the important role of automation and robotics in industry. Labour was gradually removed from the factory increasing the demand for higher educated personnel. Financial transactions on the global market could be automated with sophisticated trade algorithms. On this last note it is worth remembering the financial crash of the 19th October 1987 (Black Monday 1987) which saw a 22% decline in the values of stocks traded on US exchange in one day with the instantaneous spread to European and Asian Markets. Analysis revealed that automated trading programs, each analysing market singularly, acted in synergy towards a global financial crash (Krahmer and Meadows, unpublished).

The great contribution of the digitalisation era to industrial development has been in the empowerment of the knowledge base as driver of real capital innovation and displacement globally. The term 'knowledge economy', an economy driven by the innovation and knowledge of people, has been used (Drucker 1968). According to Capra and Luisi (2016) a new form of capital, very different from the one formed during the industrial revolution and Keynesian time, emerged. This knowledge economy is characterised by three fundamental features: (i) its core economic activities are global, (ii) the main sources of productivity and competitiveness are knowledge generation and information processing, and (iii) it is structured largely around networks of financial flows. In such an economy, capital moves in real time through global financial networks. Profit margins tend to be much higher in financial markets than in direct investments, hence supporting the convergence of all money flows back in the financial network in search for higher gains (Silver 2017). Such an out of equilibrium knowledge based system is what led us to the edge of the fourth industrial revolution, which is a new wave of technologies built upon the digital age.

Some of the key disruptive technologies characterising the fourth industrial revolution include the internet of things, artificial intelligence and machine learning, cryptocurrencies, humanoids as robots, and 3D printing (or additive manufacturing) technology. It is estimated that by 2030 more than 100 trillion sensors will be connected to the internet of things (Rifkin 2014). Radio-frequency identification (RFID) technology is spreading all over supply chains in global distribution channels to keep track, not only of commodities and materials, but also of vehicles and machines. The use of satellites can support the recognition and monitoring of such items all over the world. The internet of things would allow information on all those items to be virtually stored in the cloud, allowing centralised control of those from different parts of the world. It is worth noting that the current state of the art in robotics, allows a robots to gather the information they need to perform tasks just by 'watching' videos on the internet. Additive manufacturing (or 3D printing) has the potential to revolutionise the concept of factory. Today, 3D printing can be used to construct buildings, manufacture weapons, blade turbines, plastic components, using the technology of additive material rather than material removal, eliminating material waste from production processes. This series of innovations all contributed to the increase of average productivity globally. Rifkin (2014) proposes a vision in line with Keynes' thoughts for his grandchildren, indicating a Zero Marginal Cost Society in which productivity growth would allow people to work less and less over time.

The technology adopted in the last 30 years has allowed the creation of new products and services virtually at zero cost (Rifkin 2014; Schwab 2017). However, many challenges have been created in society. There is concern around the spread of inequality between those who own the capital and those who supply the labour. Every industrial revolution brought along concern for employment loss and there is no doubt the economic shift put at risk a large part of the current workforce (Jackson 2016). Castells (1996) distinguishes between two kinds of labour. Unskilled 'generic' labour, who are not required to access information and knowledge beyond the ability to execute orders that can be replaced at any moment by machines or by generic labour in other parts of the world, and 'self-educated' labour, who have the capability to access high levels of education, execute complex tasks, and can create and control knowledge.

According to Capra and Luisi (2016), since economic power resides in the global financial networks, which determine the fate of most jobs, unskilled labour that remains locally constrained in the real world has become disempowered and fragmented. The fear of having jobs moved abroad constrain those who fight for higher salaries and better working conditions whether they are unionised or not. On the other hand, within an economy in which information processing, innovation, and knowledge creation are the main sources of productivity, the skilled personnel is highly valued. Companies need to maintain long-term, secure relationships with those core workers to retain their loyalty and make sure their tacit knowledge is passed on within the organisation. As incentive to stay, such workers are increasingly offered stock options in addition to their basic salaries, which gives them a stake in the value created by the company, further undermining the traditional class solidarity of labour (Capra and Luisi 2016).

Despite the speed of change and the continuous embedding of new technology in the economic system, labour productivity growth has been falling over the last 70 years globally (Jackson 2016). The term 'secular stagnation' re-emerged in the developed economies indicating the possibility of slow economic growth due to low labour productivity growth. On the side of the less developed world it seems that the productivity rise has still not benefitting a large portion of the global population. In particular, 49% of the global population does not have energy access whereas only one-third benefits from the knowledge effects of the internet (UN 2019). Currently 2.4 billion people lack access to basic sanitation services (toilets and latrines) despite those being widely in use in the developed world since the Greek and Roman empires more than 2000 years ago (UN

2019), and over 800 million people remain in poverty and are undernourished (FAO 2015).

Geo-politics, trade unions, and boom and bursts in the past 100 years

The dynamics of the debt money system in imposing disequilibrium towards growth to every economic agent by means of interest rates, the continuous search for higher gains through investments in the financial markets, and the resulting knowledge development and productivity growth throughout global society, are all characteristics that form the trend of development and wealth creation in our global economy. The current system tends to mostly involve and benefit the rich part of the world, marginalises those who do not have control on capital and knowledge, and relies on the assumption that the trickle-down effect of such an activity would, in the long term, benefit the low income part of the world. In addition to the fallacies and limits of this system, its dynamics have been all but smooth as history of the last century, with multiple boom and bust and longer term cycles.

After World War I in 1918, Germany was supposed to pay war reparations to the victors. The solution of the Weimar Republic was to monetise debt by printing money and temporally abandoning the gold standard. Since its creation by Italian merchants and banks in the 12th century, the gold standard imposed on governments the need to maintain parity between gold and currency in the economy, thus reducing flexibility in tackling issues such as price instability and unemployment. Abandoning the gold standard, set off hyperinflation with prices rising on average 322% per month from August 1922 to November 1923, generated unemployment that brought the German economy to the brink of collapse, and created the conditions that enabled the rise of Hitler together with the end of the democratic republic. In the meantime, the USA of the 1920s saw a sharp rise in the value of their stock market. The high returns of the stock exchange market brought investors and brokers to use low amounts of liquidity to purchase large amount of stocks by borrowing 80% to 90% of their value. The expected return was able to pay for the cost of loans supporting continuous investments using the margin gained, creating more and more growth, as well as attracting more and more investors in emulating the same behaviour. This dynamics quickly overvalued the stock market despite low coverage of real money. When the bubble burst in 1929, the leveraged investors could not make the margin creating a global financial crash (Krahmer and Meadows, unpublished).

The financial crash created the conditions that brought the Second World War. Bank holdings of stocks, bonds, and real estate lost tremendous value overnight. Without a deposit insurance system, almost 40% of all US commercial banks defaulted. The money supply contracted by 25% and unemployment rose to 25% of total labour force in four years. Economic growth became stagnant worldwide for the following decade. US voters' sentiment for protectionism exploded after the crash, and the government started raising tariffs on imports to promote exports. European countries, which owed the US considerable debt for financing World War I, found themselves in the difficult position of not being able to generate a balance of payments surplus through exporting to their main global partner. Their response was to adopt the same policy, raising trade barriers to neighbour countries even further. Germany was forced to default on its reparations, the Weimar republic collapsed and Hitler took power in 1933. The continuous issuance of government bonds and debt was the only option for Germany recovery. Between 1933 and 1939, German debt increased to extreme levels in order to support economic growth and employment, while investing resources in the military sector. The financial fragility of the country and the inability to grow at the level to repay its debt was one of the drivers of racial laws, planned Jews expropriation of their financial assets and then subsequently the Holocaust during the World War II. In other words, Jews' persecution was seen as necessary to pay Germany debt created to finance their military power, and keep the well-being standard of other Germans high during hard times (Aly 2007).

With this backdrop the British John Maynard Keynes (1883–1946) was very concerned with the problem associated with the financial crisis, including economic stagnation, unemployment, and price stability. He found most of his solutions in studying the role of the state with austerity policies and targeted expenditures to reactivate the dynamic stability in the economy (Keynes 1936). Keynes' thinking led US president Roosevelt to demand for the first national accounting system, which was designed by Simon Kuznet in 1934. Aggregated measures were fundamental for monitoring the state of the economy and run targeted policies. In addition, the Gross Domestic Product (GDP) indicator was proposed as a measure to demonstrate that the US economy would be able to provide enough war supply whilst still maintaining enough output of goods and services to its citizens in the view of possible future conflicts. Despite Kuznet cautioning against using it as an indicator for general progress, GDP became widely used as an indicator for overall prosperity of an economy, and GDP growth as the driver (Maxton and Randers 2016).

Towards the end of the World War II, the design of a global system that could prevent war among super powers became the primary concern for the developed world. In July 1944, at the United Nations Monetary and Financial Conference held in Bretton Woods, New Hampshire, 44 nations gathered together to develop such international institutions thereafter named 'the Bretton Woods' agreement. John Maynard Keynes, who was present at the conference, is also considered one of its founding fathers. These institutions were the International Bank for Reconstruction and Development (IBRD), whose purpose was to make loans to war-devastated countries to allow reconstruction, now part of the World Bank (WB) Group, and the International Monetary Fund (IMF) facilitating international trade by stabilising and regulating currency flows and financially assisting countries with temporary trade imbalances. In October 1945, the League of Nations, which was created after World War I to prevent future global conflicts and promote global peace, was replaced with the United Nations (UN), which carried the same mission but relied on the financial structure of the Bretton

Woods agreement. In 1947 the General Agreement on Tariffs and Trade (GATT) was set up with the purpose of reducing trade barriers such as tariffs and quotas to avoid global crisis such as the one seen in 1929. Their overall role was to support economic expansion of balanced growth by setting caps of maximum debt issued by every country and regulating international markets under the hypothesis that this could increase employment and rise income globally.

The following decades were characterised by the greatest labour productivity growth in human history, and the creation of several cartels and institutions that reshaped the global international panorama. The North Atlantic Treaty Organization (NATO) was formed as an intergovernmental military alliance in 1949, and became the core of the United Nations Security Council. European Union construction begun with the Treaty of Paris and the creation of the European Coal and Steel Community (ECSC) in 1951. The creation of a common fundamental resource market was key to maintaining peace among member countries (West Germany, France, Luxemburg, Italy, the Netherlands, and Belgium). In 1957 the same countries institutionalised the European Economic Community (EEC) and the European Atomic Energy Community (EAEC). In 1960 the International Development Association (IDA) was formed as a counterpart of the IBRD to focus on developing country construction and forming the second body part of the World Bank. In the same year, the Organization of the Petroleum Exporting Countries (OPEC) was formed as the first cartel responsible for controlled oil production to the rest of the world. Its first members were Iraq, Iran, Kuwait, Venezuela, and Saudi Arabia. In 1967 the EEC was renamed European Community (EC) ready for the inclusion of neighbour countries.

One of the major economic shocks generating economic instability during this period was the 'peak oil' of the US economy in the year 1970. Global economic growth with the US at the centre of its development kept an exponential growth path for decades and, in turn, its production of oil for supporting production and growth. In 1970, the limit of production with available reserves reached its maximum, forcing the US to rely on other forms of energy to fuel its economy and at the same time making it more dependent on OPEC. This led to a concern about energy price rises, and any subsequent increase in the cost of production of all US-produced commodities, with possible increases in unemployment and inflation. At the time, the Bretton Woods were regulating international monetary system based on the gold standard. Unfortunately gold availability proved to be too constraining in relation to the flexibility required to deal with such extreme economic problems and in 1972–73 Italy, UK, Switzerland, and, finally, the US abandoned the gold standard signing the collapse of the first era of the Bretton Woods and the rise of the volatile era of floating currencies.

In 1972, the Limits to Growth findings strongly advocated for the possible limitations of growth in dealing with social development under the assumption of global environmental limits. If growth paradigms were supposed to carry economic development forward in the long-term future, not only could resources reach the peak of production globally, as experienced in the US with the case of oil, but also other limits could be reached such as land quality and availability and pollution could accumulate exponentially in the atmosphere causing irreversible damage to people and environment. Concern for the environmental sphere led to the creation of the United Nations Environmental Programme (UNEP) founded to support developing countries to create legislation to sustain environmentally policy and practices. The following year, the first scientific evidence of ozone layer damage caused by chemicals used in industrial production was discovered. This led to the first international convention held in Vienna to bring every country to sign the Montreal Protocol in 1987, the main outcome of which was to ban all of those substances causing the depletion of the ozone layer.

Between 1970 and 1980 Europe was enhancing its single market allowing for low barriers in the trade of commodities, capital and people and expanding to more and more countries. Energy markets, initially state regulated, saw a transition towards deregulation and privatisation under the assumption of greater efficiency and higher pace of innovation through free market competition. The US deregulated its market in 1982, whereas European countries followed in the 1990s.

Increasing evidence of environmental depletion and greenhouse gas emissions were supporting the creation of new scientific bodies and programmes. In 1988 the Intergovernmental Panel on Climate Change was set up by the UN to providing clear cut scientific evidence on the status of climate change. In 1992, the United Nations Conference on Environment and Development (the Rio Earth Summit) was held and the United Nations Framework Convention on Climate Change (UNFCCC) was signed by UN country members to regulate greenhouse gas emissions. The Conference of the Parties (COP) was introduced in 1995, and since then all country members meet annually to support the development of legislation on climate change. In 1997, the Kyoto Protocol bounded countries to control their anthropogenic emissions.

In the meantime projects for removing trade barriers were successful all over the world. The European Union (EU) was formed with the Maastrict Treaty in 1993, completing a unifying project of European peace based on trade after the end of the Cold War and the fall of the Berlin Wall. The North American Free trade Agreement (NAFTA) was signed to create a free market between Mexico, US, and Canada. With the collapse of the Soviet Union, NATO expanded to 19 countries by the year 1999. In 1995 the GATT agreement was substituted with the World Trade Organization (WTO) responsible for trade among countries. However, increasing evidence was shown about the impact of future climate change (IPCC 1990) and concern for eradicating poverty and increasing the well-being for the marginalised part of the world grew. The year 2000 saw the Millennium Development Goals set of indicators launched to highlight the need for more inclusive global development.

The major systemic unpredicted event of the early 2000s came endogenously from within the system in the form of the financial bubble and crash in the year 2007–2008. The policy response from governments was to nationalise some banks and in the refinancing of a growing economy through quantitative easing. The term 'secular stagnation' emerged again indicating difficulty in creating the condition for growth and issues around economic stability shaped the world. The year 2015 saw an important shift towards sustainability, while updating the Millennium Development Goals to the 17 Sustainable Development Goals (UN 2019) for the year 2030, and agreeing for the first time a climate target at +2 degrees Celsius at COP21, to be managed at the national level by 196 signatory countries. This implies cooperative countries, taking actions now, to invert the carbon footprint from today's overshoot back within the planetary boundaries by the year 2050.

Resources – evidence and perspectives on the status of world's ecosystems

Globally, economic activity is mainly targeted towards those who own financial assets. Attention to the ecosystems that surround the economy (including the state of mineral reserves, land degradation, pollution and climate stability) is given to the extent to which it is functional to the 'health' and 'purpose' of a stable economy.

The true picture is one of an economic system bounded within the ecosystem characterised by interconnections and a dynamic evolution of its components. Today, it is possible to give higher granularity to such a picture based on a continuous effort to gather new data on the health of ecosystems, including the condition of climate change.

This section presents the state of ecosystems and the interconnection among those. In particular it highlights the mineral resource system as a basis of all other activities within the economy. In this context, fossil fuels are a particular kind of mineral resource required for almost every economic activity including the extraction of other minerals. Even the possibility of recycling other mineral resources requires energy currently obtained from fossil fuels. Agriculture, which is the primary sector of the economy responsible for supplying nutrition to people, and for the production of energy from biomass and biofuels, is also tremendously dependent on mineral resources. The production of all fertilizers, that have been key driver for increasing agriculture output, requires the extraction of phosphorus from ores and employs natural gas for the separation of nitrogen for the production of industrial fertilizers. Mineral use within industries and fertilizer use both generate waste and pollutants and create emissions that can interfere with climate stability. Both resource depletion, climate system and pollution influence the stability of the economic system.

Mineral resources, production peaks, and prices

Mineral resources can be extracted, traded, and processed for the production of commodities. Despite most mineral resources being recyclable, they are by definition finite and non-renewable given that mineral formation is the result of geological processes that take millions of years (Prior et al. 2012; Campbell 2015; Bardi 2014). For example, fossil fuels – oil, natural gas, and coal – formed mostly from decaying organisms buried in the ground. It is estimated that coal forms in approximately 60 million years starting 360 million years ago, whereas oil and natural gas formed in two specific periods approximately 150 and 90 million years ago.

The inefficiency of current recycling processes implies that all mineral resources become scarcer over time. Most minerals are affected by down-cycling each time they are processed for recycle. Theoretically, some minerals, such aluminium, can be recycled almost infinite times, while others, such as fossil fuels, have no possibility of recovery (Swain and Mukherjee 2007; DOE 2011). Furthermore, waste and pollution, as well as energy consumption for extraction and recycling processes, are primary concerns that have to be addressed within the extracting industry. Resource pricing remains the key variable that is taken into account by various stakeholders as the metric to assess the health of the sector in relation to a particular mineral.

Minerals can be found all over the Earth at different levels of concentration. There exist 88 elements in the Earth's crust which can be classified according to their physical properties and concentration (Bardi 2014). Common elements have average concentrations over 0.1% in weight (1000 parts per million). Among those are various metals useful for modern industrial applications such as iron, aluminium, magnesium, silicon, and titanium. Elements present in the crust with average concentration lower than 100 ppm (parts per million), such as copper, zinc, lead, and phosphorus, are defined as rare. Very rare elements such as gold, platinum, uranium, and lithium are present in the crust with average concentrations below 0.01 parts per million. Deposits are defined as areas where chemical elements that exist in the Earth's crust can be found in greater-than average concentrations. Those deposits that are concentrated enough to be profitably mined are called 'ores' from the geologist point of view (different terms are used for specific kind of minerals, such as 'wells' for crude oil and 'seams' for coal), and 'reserves' in economic terms. The cost of production and price in the commodity market are the two key variables determining the viability of extraction of reserves in profitable terms.

The United States Geological Survey (USGS) is one of the most respected authorities in the monitoring and studying of mineral reserves globally, releasing public data every year (USGS 2000–2017). Figure 3.1 shows the framework used to classify resources based on their concentration on Earth as proposed by McKelvey (who also worked as a director of the USGS in 1970s). In relation to a particular mineral, the total amount of resources is often available at different levels of concentration, and in conditions that cannot be economically reached at current level of technology. The work of the geologist is to measure and infer the amount of possible reserves that are economically (i.e. dependent on the cost and the price of the resource) viable for production from the resources, and identify larger deposits that can be converted to reserves.

Modern mining follows a multistage process: (i) extraction, in which materials are extracted from the ground, (ii) beneficiation, in which valuable minerals are separated from worthless rocks, (iii) refinement for industrial purposes

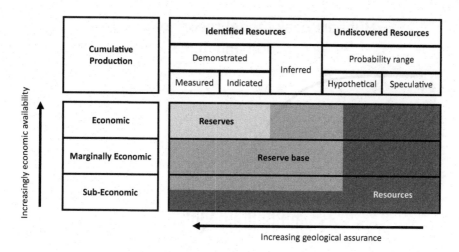

Figure 3.1 McKelvey diagram used for geological exploration to assess economic availability of mineral resources

(Bardi 2014). The mining industry first extracts and depletes ores that are easier to exploit at lower cost, which, most often, are those minerals present in larger concentrations. The mining activity would then divert its efforts to deposits at lower concentrations or deposits in geographic regions which are less accessible for physical or political reasons, implying higher cost of extraction. It is estimated that a factor of ten in the reduction of average concentration correspond to a tenfold increase in the energy use for extraction (Bardi 2014) – and consequent lower marginal economic productivity. Resources that were considered not economically viable can be exploited through technology improvements in extraction techniques. Even if we are not running out of mineral resources today, many mineral productions are found to be at the cusp of decline because of depletion leading to a rising cost of extraction (Bardi 2014).

The dynamics of resource extraction based on finite resources are well explained by the Hubbert peak theoretical model (Hubbert 1956, 1962) as shown in Figure 3.2. First applied to the study of 1970 peak oil in the US, the theory has become the key framework to study mineral depletion for every mineral resource on the planet. Assuming that all resources of a particular mineral are extractable with available technology, the theory explains that while the economy and the demand for a particular resource grows, the more easily available ores are extracted first. The more the resources are depleted the higher the cost (in terms of capital, technology, energy, and personnel) of extraction, forcing the production to slow down until a peak, and creating incentives for recycling. After the first phase of cheap abundant resources, production costs keep increasing along with a decline of the industry. The use of indicators such as reserves-to-production ratio (R/P), which measures total economically viable reserves divided by production at

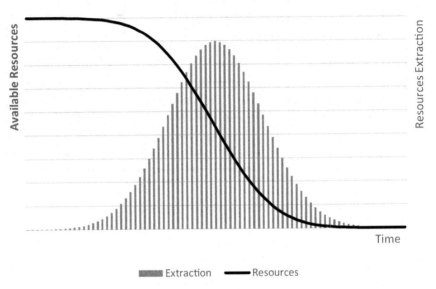

Figure 3.2 Hubbert peak model theory

present time, often hides the peak. In fact, both the reserves can rise as new technology is brought online while total resources deplete, and production quantities change depending on difficulty of extraction. In an optimistic view, in which all resources would be somehow available because of gradual improvements in technology, Calvo et al. (2017) applies the Hubbert model to estimate global production peak of 47 mineral commodities based on USGS resources (not reserves) data. Their analysis shows how two minerals (gold and antimony) have already reached their maximum theoretical peak, 30 are assumed to reach the production peak within 50 years (including lithium in 2037), and the rest within the century.

The price dynamics of minerals are influenced by multiple factors which make price forecasting a very hard task characterised by uncertainty and intuitive work. However, over the past few decades, widespread technology diffusion and the exploitation of high quality reserves have allowed for the price of most mineral commodities to decrease or at least stay stable. This led many to assume that this overall trend will always continue. At the same time, geopolitical factors (e.g. a war), trade policy (e.g. export and import bans), climatic catastrophic events (e.g. hurricanes, floods or tsunamis), as well as uncertainty around mineral reserves, resources, and discovery rates, have generated shocks and spikes in the price of mineral commodities as well as large differences in terms of estimated production peaks according to different scientists (Jones et al. 2013).

According to Campbell (2013) the global production peak of a particular commodity is often signalled by large price spikes due to the imbalance between a growing demand and a struggling supply. Every commodity is often produced by a few countries which have reserves (USGS 2017). Production can therefore be controlled to govern the price dynamics irrespective of the physical availability of a particular mineral. According to the British Geological Survey (BGS 2012), China is the leading producer of over 40 mineral commodities globally, many of which are rare minerals and fundamental for production in the semiconductor industry. China's mineral trade regulation (Mancheri 2015) should be compliant with the World Trade Organisation (WTO) rules which attempts to avoid the dominance of single players, while keeping global price stable (WTO 2017).

Although rising costs the substitution of one mineral commodity for another in particular applications could reduce the demand, and therefore price. Substitution is often used as an argument that new technologies will always bring down the cost of production, assuring the availability of products in the longer time range (Bardi 2014). Most often, substitution requires the sacrifice of properties of particular materials that are not available in others and reduces their applicability for solving particular issues. In addition, substitution often requires different industrial processes for obtaining similar results, which can be more energy intensive. Examples include the case of substitution of copper with aluminium, which presents both of the aforementioned characteristics (Bardi 2014).

Despite the geopolitical dynamics affecting the mining industry, today's reserves are sufficient to supply the global economy for the next few decades. In the shorter time frame, the availability of minerals is not a problem of the amount of resources dispersed in the ground, rather the amount of energy necessary for the extraction of those that increases while depletion rises. Oil, natural gas, and coal, minerals themselves, supply energy to over 80% of the full global energy mix today (IEA 2017a) and are becoming more costly to extract.

Fossil fuels as the foundation for today's economy

Oil, natural gas, and coal – generally referred to as fossil fuels or hydrocarbons – are carbons whose combustion generates the energy required to perform and/or support almost every economic activity in the developed world. Burning fossil fuels is also among the main driving factors for anthropogenic emissions of carbon in the atmosphere, leading to climate change, and bringing more disruptive extreme weather events around the world (IPCC 2014). Coal is present in solid form in seams, while oil and natural gas are available as fluids which are trapped underground in the form of wells, and often found in the same location: in those cases oil (liquid form) lies at the bottom of the gas which floats on the top of it. First discovered in the US in 1859, cheap oil found greatest global use after the discovery of the richest wells in the Persian Gulf in 1908 (Campbell 2013).

Understanding how much fossil fuel is available in the ground is notoriously difficult. Two measures are used, namely 'resources,' which estimate the total amount of the fossil fuel available anywhere in the world, and 'reserves,' which estimate the proportion of resources that are economic to recover. Data reliability in the estimation of 'resources' and 'reserves' is lacking, and institutions in the energy sector provide different accounting metrics for both 'conventional' and 'non-conventional' reserves (e.g. IEA; BP, OPEC). These represent major difficulties in the estimation of how and when production peaks (Campbell 2013; Höök et al. 2010). In the case OPEC countries, oil and gas reserves data is often a national secret. As production quotas are defined based on reserves data, the reporting is often ambiguous, influenced by political interests, and therefore not reliable (Bentley and Bentley 2015). On the other hand private companies, such as BP, tend to be conservative in their reporting (Campbell 2013; Bentley and Bentley 2015). In addition, while the discovery of additional reserves is now increasingly rare, data can change with time as new technology make the extraction of previously uneconomic resources more feasible. If the measure of resources was accurate then it should always decrease with use. Reserves will go up and down depending on the price of the fossil fuel (increased prices can make previously uneconomic reserves economic), technology, and discovery.

During 1960s, oil wells of the size of 50 billion barrels were discovered every year. Over the same period consumption was lower than 8 billion barrels per year globally. Since then, consumption has grown fast, reaching about 30 billion barrels per year today. Over 80% of all oil we consume today comes from oil fields discovered before 1970 (Wijkman and Rockström 2013). Today, the Middle East and North Africa account for about 75% of global reserves in crude oil. Saudi Arabia accounts for approximately 20% of global reserves, followed by Iran and Iraq with about 10% each. Despite demand for oil slightly decreasing in OECD countries, it is rapidly increasing in the growing economies of China, India, and Brazil. In order to fuel such a growth with oil, a dramatic increase in world production is required (Wijkman and Rockström 2013).

Despite such uncertainty in reserves data, production data is much more reliable. The production peak of several energy commodities has been experienced for various resources at national levels already. Among those coal depletion problems in the United Kingdom, Germany, and Japan that favoured oil adoption in Europe (Höök et al. 2010). Figure 3.3 shows the production data of coal in the UK (DBE IS 2018), and the Hubbert peak model that fit those data.

In the 1960s crude oil surpassed coal as the main source of energy to fuel the world's economy. In 2010, oil and oil derivatives supplied energy to 96% of the transportation sector globally (WEC 2011). According to IEA (2017a), total primary energy supply more than doubled globally between 1971 and 2015, but the dependency on fossil fuels only slightly changed from 86% to 82%. Oil is also fundamental for the production of fertilizers necessary to increase land productivity and boost agriculture production. It is estimated that every calorie of energy contained in our daily food requires seven or eight calories of energy from fossil fuels to be produced (Wijkman and Rockström 2013).

A common and important distinction among fossil fuels is between what are conventional and non-conventional reserves. In the most simplistic terms,

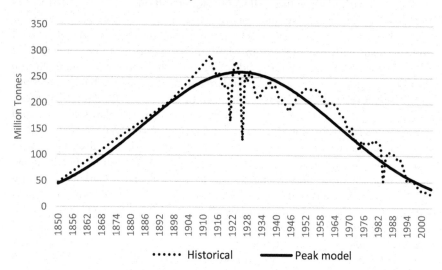

UK Coal production 1850–2000

•••••• Historical ——— Peak model

Figure 3.3 Historical peak in production of coal production in the UK

Source: UK Government Department of Business, Energy and Industrial Strategy (2018)

conventional reserves are the ones that are easy to extract and cheap to process after use, whereas the non-conventional reserves are found in areas that require larger investments to be extracted, and overall need specific and expensive processes to be converted for use.

While reserves get depleted they face the same problem encountered in dwindling mineral ores: extraction becomes more energy intensive. The ratio describing such a dynamic problem is the Energy Returned on Energy Invested (EROEI), i.e. the ratio of energy produced from a particular source during its useful life time to the energy spent to access such a source. Following a traditional economical approach, higher EROEI sources will be preferred to lower EROEI sources. In the extracting industry, easy sources will be depleted before deposits that are difficult to be reached, progressing from higher to lower EROEI. While EROEI decreases for a particular commodity, production growth slows down. In the case of crude oil, it maintained an EROEI between 50 and 100 for the most of 20th century. Today, the EROEI of oil has decreased to 15 to 20 (Bardi 2014; Wijkmann and Rockström 2013).

In the case of oil and gas, it is difficult to find agreement on the boundaries between conventional and non-conventional reserves. This is the case even between respected scientific journals such as the *Oil & Gas Journal* and the *World Oil*, as well as among countries such as Canada and Venezuela (Campbell 2013). The main metric for comparison among classes of oil is the American Petroleum

Institute (API) gravity index, which categorise oil in terms of its density in comparison to water. In particular it uses API 10° to refer to the density of water, implying oil with lower values will sink in water and oil with higher API values will float on it. The Association for the Study of Peak Oil (ASPO) and Gas, founded by Campbell in the year 2000 to raise awareness on the issue of peak oil and gas, deals with this problem in detail and considers oil to be conventional when API is above 17.5°. On the side of gas the definition is even more blurred. ASPO accounts for conventional gas relying on *condensate* (gas that becomes liquid at the pressure of Earth's surface and can be considered as oil for many uses), *natural gas liquids* (NGL) which are produced in dedicated plants, and *liquefied natural gas* (LNG) which is gas in liquid form when at very low temperatures.

According to Campbell (2013) the peak of conventional oil was passed in 2005. Other oil categories and derivatives are assumed to follow shortly. However, we are far from running out of oil, and it will find a market for several decades, both for energy and other material production. While conventional oil extraction has slowed down, natural gas has acquired more and more interest and space in the global energy mix. However, the high cost of transportation and technical problems with distribution currently confine gas to be mainly a regional source of energy. Gas is mainly transported and distributed through pipelines on land. Cryogenic liquefaction (obtaining liquefied natural gas – LNG) is necessary for gas transportation by sea, which makes it more expensive. Still local gas peaks are possible, such as the one in 1970 in the United States (Bardi 2014).

Non-conventional oil and gas includes eight further types that can be differentiated according to their level of distribution, level of extraction, and costs among others. These are (i) oil from coal, (ii) oil extracted from artificial fracturing of low permeability reservoirs (shale oil or tight oil), (iii) extra-heavy oil or tar sand (API lower than 10°) and bitumen, (iv) heavy oil (API between 10° and 17.5°), (v) deep water oil and gas (below 500 meters water depths), (vi) polar oil and gas, (vii) liquids from gas plants, and (viii) gas from coal. Non-conventional resources are known to be large, but extraction is normally difficult, costly and environmentally damaging, and above all, slow. The most commonly discussed options considered are extraction of oil and gas from shales (shale oil and shale gas), oil from tar sand, and oil converted from coal (Campbell 2013).

Shale gas allowed a return to high levels of production fuelling economic growth through natural gas, in particular in the US (Rockström and Klum 2012; Bardi 2014). Some experts claimed its potential to make 'peak oil' irrelevant, while others claimed this an exaggeration generated by the confusion between reserves and resources (Rockström and Klum 2012). Shale gas also increases the risk of methane leaching during fracking and extraction processes increasing pollution rates. Tar sand is a solid product of oil that has been exposed to the atmosphere for a long period, from which oil can be obtained. Tar sands deposits are large, in particular in Canada, but the extraction and processing of tar sand into oil involves EROEI ranging between 3 and 5. A similar problem exists in the conversion of coal to oil. At the current levels of technology, one barrel of oil can be obtained by processing about one ton of coal.

In a similar way to Campbell, Höök et al. (2010) (who is also a member of ASPO) analysed the problem of data reliability in the case of coal and proposed a possible generic forecast for the century. A comparison on data definitions among World Energy Council (WEC), German Federal Institute of Geoscience and Natural Resources (BGR), with additional data taken from United States Geological Survey (USGS), Energy Information Administration (EIA), British Petroleum (BP) Statistical Review and the International Energy Agency (IEA) has been performed highlighting a similar problematique as in the case of oil. A forecast was performed based on available reserve data and compared with a second, optimistic, forecast accounting for a doubling of reserves due to hypothetical discovery rate in the future. The two forecasts have a different peak in production of about 20 years. Figure 3.4 highlights the global peak of coal production which occurs between 2011 and 2016 (IEA 2017b). As the data show, after a major increase in production in Asia over the last 20 years, coal production started declining recently. This is due to a number of different factors, not least a major shift in China's policy to clean up atmospheric pollution in cities (BP 2017).

The price dynamics of the three energy resources (oil, coal, gas) discussed here is fundamental to the stability of economic growth. Figure 3.5 shows the changes in price for these commodities over the past five decades. As can be seen there is a tendency for the price of these resources to be relatively stable during 'normal' periods of economic activity. However, there are significant increases in prices in the 1970s and since the year 2000. As already highlighted, the 1970s saw politics between the Middle East and USA driving export restrictions which in turn led to sharp rises in oil prices and significant impacts on economies around the world. According to Campbell (2007) the increase in price since 2000 is due to the production peak of conventional oil although the increase in demand from Asia, and in particular China, is also a key driver. A price spike in the year 2008 is seen in oil, natural gas and coal. Real Natural gas and coal prices returned to their pre-2000 levels relatively quickly while oil price maintained a high cost for years, before decreasing in 2015. This high cost of oil was seen to facilitate the growth in non-conventional oil and gas exploration. Subsequent increases in global production have since seen a sharp decline in investments into these non-conventional sources following the decrease in prices.

Agriculture, food-energy nexus, and planetary boundaries

When the focus is on global sustainability analysis, agriculture is the most complex among economic sectors. Agriculture is the most vulnerable to and, when accounting for deforestation as a source of anthropogenic emissions, the first cause of, climate change. Agriculture is also the main source of wealth creation in the majority of undeveloped countries, employing above 40% of the global labour force, reducing food poverty while simultaneously satisfying the demand needs of a growing population expected to exceed nine billion people by 2050 (UN 2018). The complex interconnect of society and climate risk via agriculture has a major

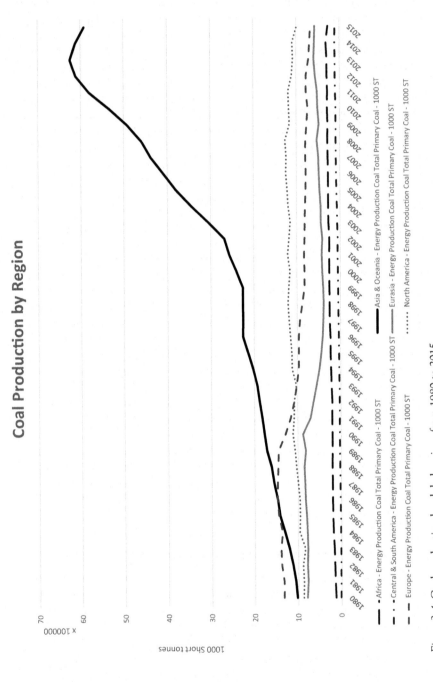

Figure 3.4 Coal production by global regions from 1980 to 2015

Source: IEA (2017b)

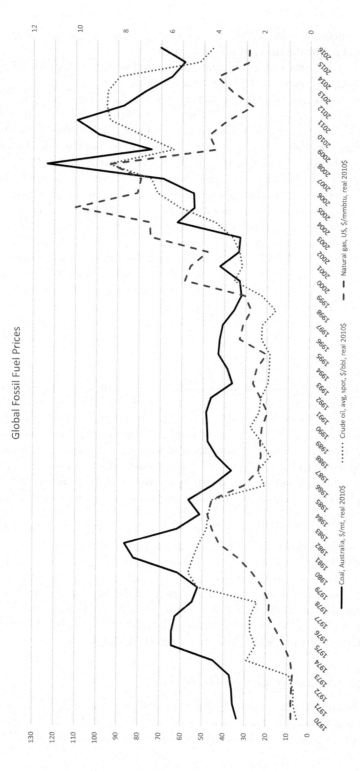

Figure 3.5 Real global prices of crude oil, coal, and natural gas from 1970 to 2016

Source: World Bank Global Economic Monitoring (2017)

impact on emigration from undeveloped to developed countries, increasing social pressures and political tension worldwide.

Everything that grows on land requires water and nutrients. Topsoil, able to retain both, is also essential. The sustainability of those inputs to agriculture is the most important factor affecting its persistence as economic sector in each country. No water means no food. The world is two-thirds covered with salty water, accounting for 97.5% of total water on Earth, and is thus unsuitable for agriculture purposes. The remaining 2.5% is called fresh water, and can be found in the form of ice (68.1%), underground water flows (30.1%), and surface water (1.2%) (Mekonnen and Hoekstra 2011). Green water refers to water dependent on rains, and blue water on the flows from which water can be withdrawn for various uses, including rivers, lakes, and ground water. Today, agriculture uses approximately 70% of total freshwater withdrawal for food production. The remaining goes 19% to industrial systems, and 11% to housing utilities. Approximately 90% of agriculture water use (both crops production and livestock) is in the form of green water, which, during times of drought and low rainfall, has to be substituted with blue water via irrigation (Mekonnen and Hoektstra 2010).

No nutrients means low quality of food and low productivity of land. Soil must contain various forms of nutrients to allow for plant growth. Bindraban et al. (2015) lists 14 nutrients essential for food production, including nitrogen (N), phosphorus (P), potassium (K), magnesium, calcium, copper, zinc, and nickel. NPK fertilizers offer an artificial input to increasing land productivity (IFA 2009). Following nutrients' natural cycle all of those are transferred back to soil after plants' death, or in the form of manure after being eaten by animals, or at the animal's death. In other words all nutrients of soil are naturally recyclable. However, the continuous demand for food and livestock, without a closed loop to return the nutrients to the soil, requires the use of other human-made sources to increase land productivity. However, the overuse of artificial inputs leads to other environmental issues such as eutrophication (Rockstrom et al. 2009).

Different climate and soil temperature characteristics would affect the ability of topsoil to produce food, leading to approximately 12 different types of topsoil in the world (USDA 2018). Shifts in climate patterns can impact food production (IPCC 2014). Sea level rise would impact ground water greatly, such drastically reducing the amount of arable land that can be used by farmers (IPCC 2014). Topsoil is also influenced negatively by erosion, due to wind and water flows on agricultural land which is made worse by deforestation and monoculture, largely affecting agriculture in hillslopes terrains (FAO 2019).

Food-energy nexus and balance of payments

Growing interest has been given to the relationship between food and oil, in particular due to the strong correlation between their price from 2006 onwards (Figure 3.6). Various economic factors, such US dollar volatility can affect such

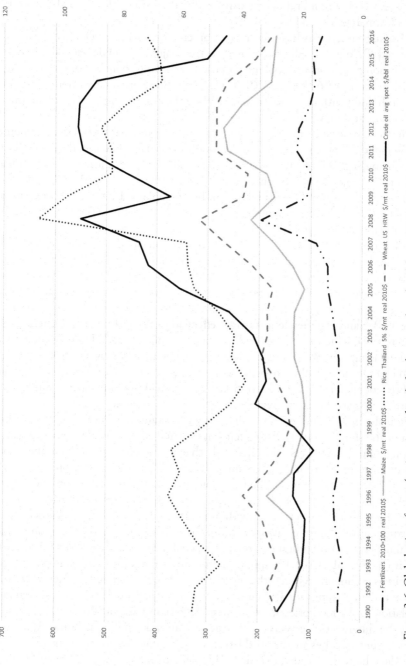

Global Crop and Crude Oil Prices

Figure 3.6 Global price of crops (maize, rice, wheat), fertilizers, and crude oil from 1990 to 2016

Source: World Bank Global Economic Monitoring (2017)

a relationship (Adam 2011). However, physical relationships and standard economic behaviours of supply demand given the substitutability of commodities between food output and energy can support the explanation of such a correlation (Armah et al. 2011).

Traditional biomass has been used as an energy source far before coal was discovered. Biomass is still widely used in the majority of undeveloped countries for in-house heating and cooking purposes, occupying about 9% of global energy production in 2016 (REN21 2016). However, those are used without appropriate in house ventilation, and remain among the major sources of death through indoor air pollution after HIV (UN 2019).

In the last decades, more emphasis has been given to the production of energy from modern biofuels and ethanol. In countries such as Thailand, Brazil, and US, producing vegetable oil (e.g. soy, palm oil) and crops (e.g. maize, sugar cane) has become a major source of energy production (OECD-FAO 2017) despite the efficiency of this process is still far from the one obtained with conventional fossil fuels (Arodudu 2017). However, biofuels only represent 0.8% of total energy production today (REN21 2016).

While farmers have the choice between producing food or fuel, market volatility and the rise in the price of oil can generate an increased shift of demand to biofuels, increasing their prices, and resulting in income opportunities to farmers and biofuel exporting countries. Despite the amount of energy produced from biofuels is relatively small at the global level, some countries (such as Brazil or the US) could experience a stronger effect from these dynamics. Others, such as Malaysia, which is a large producer of palm oil, increased biofuel production following market price increases, while damaging their ecosystems (OECD-FAO 2017). Environmental needs are often seen as economic constraints. Most importantly energy fluctuations can translate into agricultural fluctuations due to the current increased competitiveness of biofuels and ethanol.

On the other hand, energy is necessary to sustain industrial agriculture. This is not the simple case of fuelling machineries and equipment, but mostly for the production of fertilizers and chemicals that are given as input to arable land to increase productivity. It is estimated that 30% of the cost of production of crops is due to energy given the large amount of fertilizers used to produce those (IAASTD 2009). The NPK (nitrogen, phosphorus, potassium) fertilizers are a major source for productivity growth in land. The Haber Bosch process is used to separate ammonia from nitrogen. More than 70% of production of ammonia is still dependent on natural gas, relying on coal, heavy oil, or nuclear for the rest of it (Bicer et al. 2016). Phosphorus is currently largely obtained from phosphate rocks as a mineral. As such the more it is depleted the more the energy needed to extract it. Interesting dynamics on the control of phosphate rocks emerged in relation to the food price spike of 2006–2008 (Cordell et al. 2009, 2011). Based on the differences between an organic and an industrial agricultural system in three climate zones in the world (tropic, sub-tropic, temperate landscapes) to produce biofuels, Arodudu et al. (2017) demonstrated how changes in farming practice impact the amount of energy input and land required.

Climate change, agriculture and planetary boundaries

The climate system is nothing more than a manifestation of the amount, distribution, and net balance of energy at the Earth's surface (Steffen et al. 2015). Today's climate change is the increase of such energy, generating risks of imbalance in the climate system stability as well as distribution effects all over the Earth. Climate change (or global warming) is probably the most compelling environmental problem due to human activity visible by experts and non. It is mostly measured through the overall increase in global average temperature, and largely driven by the accumulation of anthropogenic greenhouse gas emissions in the atmosphere (IPCC 2014). Figure 3.7 shows data on carbon concentration in the atmosphere, and compares them with the temperature anomaly in land area (NASA 2019) presenting a strong relationship between the concentration of carbon dioxide (CO_2 equivalent) in the atmosphere and the average temperature. CO_2 is not the only greenhouse gas, but it is the largest fraction of gases that cause global warming. Others include methane, nitrous oxides, and water vapour. Greenhouse gases trap the heat that reaches the Earth from the Sun.

Climate change is not a new phenomenon for the Earth. There have been many different climate eras, from warmer periods to glacial ages, multiple times

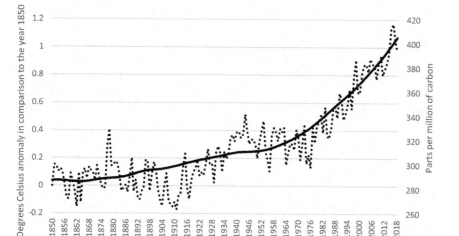

Figure 3.7 Correlation between CO_2 concentration and global average temperature
Source: NASA (2019)

over the Earth's history. Tectonic plate movement change ocean circulation and generate volcanos which erupt. The volcanic eruptions disperse in the atmosphere and can cause global cooling over the short term. If enough volcanic activity occurs, releasing carbon emissions, then they can also cause global warming. Soil absorbs carbon both directly as well as via plants and animals. Over thousands of years, carbon accumulates into the soil (buried), and temperature cools down. Glacial eras appear when temperature lowers below certain thresholds. These are characterised with a layer of ice and snow covering the majority of the Earth's surface, which reflects the irradiation from the sun, and keeps the surface cooler. Volcanos, carbon emissions from the ocean, and other elements of the carbon cycle can increase the temperature again and melt ice. Such a dynamic results in irregular climate cycles over and over between one era and the next. Rockström et al. (2009), shows how climate stabilised in the Holocene starting approximately 11,700 years ago. Emissions and absorption rates from the carbon sinks equilibrated together with the natural carbon cycle, allowing for the development of agriculture and society in the way we created it today (Rockstrom et al. 2009).

In the last two and a half centuries, human activity has led to an exponential increase in carbon emissions. Anthropogenic climate change is due to the emissions generated by exponential economic growth that has pushed humanity away from the stable era of the Holocene. The formal beginning of the Anthropocene is under debate by the academic community, likely to be chosen as the start of industrial revolution (Lewis and Maslin 2015). Agriculture (including deforestation), together with electricity and heat production represent the top sources of carbon emissions today, accounting for 24% and 25% respectively, followed by industry (21%), transportation (14 %), and housing (6.4%) (IPCC 2014).

The short-term impact of climate warming on temperate regions is likely to result in an increase in crop yields due to the higher levels of carbon concentration in the atmosphere, and a warmer and more humid climate. Cereals production such as wheat, rye, oats, and barley will be particularly influenced. However, yields might fall in the medium term due to increased disease infestation (Weijkman and Rockström 2013; IPCC 2014). In addition, shifts in weather patterns, extreme weather events, and sea level rise will have negative consequences for agriculture in the medium to long term. Changing weather patterns, such as delays in the monsoon season or droughts becoming more prevalent, will require assessments on which, where, and at what time crops are grown. Climate models predict a reduction in available water in several regions, including southern Europe, northern Africa, parts of western Africa, southern Africa, southern Australia, the north-eastern parts of Latin America, and parts of western North America. Extreme weather events, such as hurricanes, floods, or heat waves (Weijkman and Rockström 2013), are becoming more frequent and violent than in the past decades (e.g., typhoon Haiyan in the Philippines and hurricane Katrina in the USA). Alongside immediate losses in production, more disruptive weather events can accelerate land erosion (Stern 2006; IPCC 2014; Lloyd 2015).

Sea level rise is not only an issue due to the loss of land around coastal areas, islands that will disappear under the sea, or the need to develop infrastructure to avoid flooding cities in times of high tide. Its major impact is mostly due to the salinisation of ground water, which is often used to grow plants in agriculture, and represents the major source of blue water today. This will drastically reduce the amount of available arable land that can be allocated to produce food.

IPCC (2014) provides a comparison of future scenarios of global average temperature to 2100. Large uncertainties exist in performing this type of analysis, and the majority of scenarios range from a plus 2 degrees to a plus 5 degrees in comparison to pre-industrial levels. A minus 5 degrees in global average temperature below pre-industrial levels corresponds to the last glacial era (Sterman 2000). Scenarios above 2 degrees can have a significant impact on human society, ecosystems, and the ability of the climate to avoid tipping points (Steffen et al. 2018).

Aware of these issues, 196 country representatives met in Paris in 2015 at the 21st Conference of Parties (COP21), as part of the United Nations Framework Convention on Climate Change (UNFCCC) to set a climate target at +2 degrees Celsius of global temperature increase, and commit to implementing policies to achieve this goal. Such a target could be met by keeping the average carbon concentration in the atmosphere below 450 ppm (parts per million) of carbon. It is worth noting that such an objective would imply an 80% reduction in greenhouse gas emissions from their current level by 2050. If economic growth does not stop, the only solution is to decouple growth from environmental damage using technology improvements as well as social changes (Jackson 2009, 2016). Despite the challenge of achieving this target, requiring the synergy of legal, social, and technological innovation to be applied in every country in parallel, it is important to note that the +2 degree target is nothing more than a compromise between the scientific community and policy makers (Wijkman and Rockström 2013; IPCC 2014). Asserting that 450 ppm of carbon corresponds to +2 degrees average global level increase, is true to the level of confidence of 70% only (IPCC 2014). That is, even if a 450 ppm target is met, there exists a 30% possibility that consequences of climate change will be far worse than expected.

The +2 degrees threshold could be too high to allow for the climate to stabilise due to reinforcing feedback loops (Steffen et al. 2018). Among the most classic examples we find the reinforcing feedback mechanism between ocean acidification and vapour in the atmosphere. The ocean capacity of absorption, and thereby being a carbon sink, can saturate and then become a net carbon emitter. Water vapour on the other hand, is the strongest greenhouse gas in trapping the Sun's energy, and its quantity in the atmosphere is strongly affected by feedback mechanisms. The higher the greenhouse emissions, the higher the temperature, the higher the amount of vapour in the atmosphere because of evaporation. The more the vapour in the atmosphere, the greater the heat retained, allowing for more water to evaporate such bringing temperature even higher (IPCC 2014). This feedback loop has the power to bring the system away from stability increasing risks of extreme events and hot house pathways for the Earth (Steffen et al. 2018).

Climate change represents only one of the nine thresholds in ecological systems that could result in self-reinforcing feedback loops that have the potential to generate risk and negative impacts to the economy. The planetary boundaries were initially proposed in Rockstrom et al. (2009), and subsequently updated in Steffen et al. (2015). Both climate and ecosystems responses are normally non-linear. The feedback loops can reinforce dynamics that can bring systems to over-pass thresholds leading to unknown risk, collapsing ecosystems, and destabilising climate even further.

The planetary boundary framework arises from the scientific evidence that Earth is a single, complex, integrated system (Steffen et al. 2015). Not designed to be 'down-scaled' or 'disaggregated' to smaller levels, such as nations or local communities (Steffen et al. 2015), the framework gives an aggregate picture on the average state of the world. Thresholds are defined based on the maintenance of the Holocene-like state of the Earth system and on the level of human-driven change that could destabilise this state (Steffen et al. 2015). The correct management of human growth within planetary boundaries should aim to deal with all boundaries together, aiming at regulating the functioning of the biological systems, thus increasing Earth's resilience to future shocks and possible threshold effects. However, uncertainty lies in the way the self-regulating cycles and their complex interconnections can react.

With exception of the stratospheric ozone depletion, caused by emission of chlorofluorocarbons (that were banned after the Montreal Protocol in 1987), all other thresholds are linked directly and indirectly with agriculture. Five of those are regional in nature (biosphere integrity, land-system change, freshwater use, biochemical flows, and atmospheric aerosol loading). Climate change and ocean acidification are global in nature. According to the Stockholm group, genetic biodiversity, and phosphorus and nitrogen cycles have far passed the high risk threshold, and are now beyond the boundary. Land system change is close to it. Freshwater use is in safe space, even if Jaramillo and Destouni (2015) showed evidence that freshwater might be already beyond risk threshold.

In a world governed by exponential growth, the risks indicated by the planetary boundaries just get worse. IUCN (2007) showed that the current rate of species extinction is between 1000 and 10,000 times faster than the natural extinction rate. This is largely due to chemical substances and pesticides applied in industrial agriculture as well as accommodating increases in food demand through expanding agricultural land at the expenses of forests. Forests also represent one of the major carbon sinks mitigating climate change. According to IFA (2009) increasing the use of fertilizers is needed to reduce by three times the emissions of greenhouse gas in comparison to expanding land per unit of output. This is in contrast with the expanded view provided by the planetary boundaries. In fact, additional use of industrial fertilizers would worsen the disruption of nitrogen and phosphorus cycles. Among its major consequences we find leaching to aquatic ecosystem, and the eutrophication of algae poisoning that would affect fisheries negatively (Wijkman and Rockström 2013).

A different kind of thinking is required. The next section discusses the social dimension of the problem.

Food security, social unrest, migration, food waste, and growing population

The picture just presented is even worse when looking at population dynamics worldwide. Today's global population is approximately 7.6 billion people, expected to reach between 9.4 and 10.3 billion people by 2050 and between 9.6 and 13.2 billion by 2100 (UN 2018). Despite decreasing in the last years, one person out of ten is estimated to be undernourished, with 795 million people food unsecure worldwide, the vast majority of whom live in sub-Saharan and Eastern Africa, as well as Southern and Eastern Asia (FAO 2015). Most developed regions, accounting for approximately 1.8 billion people today, are expected to not increase significantly in terms of population over the century (Figure 3.8). Asian countries, that today account for about 4.5 billion people, are expected to grow significantly till mid-century, surpassing 5.2 billion people by 2050, and then slowly reduce their population till 2100. These include China and India having approximately 1.4 and 1.3 billion people respectively today, and expecting India to become the most populous country worldwide with about 1.6 billion people by 2050. The larger fraction of the increase in human population is in African countries, moving from today's 1.2 billion people to 2.8 billion in 2050 and above 4 billion by the end of the century, with Nigeria expected to become the third most populous country with above 400 million people by 2050.

The assumptions determining such a forecast are rooted in economic transition theory (Bloom 2011; Bongaarts 2009). In particular, countries that have reached a good per capita wealth where women are well educated, working, and participating in the economy at any level are assumed to have decreasing fertility rates. In these countries, birth rates remain below death rates bringing the entire population down over time, such as Japan (UN 2018). In China, population is increasing, but is assumed to reach a peak in population around 2050, following a pattern similar to current industrialised countries in the past. Important to note that a positive gap between economic and population growth rates in China for the next 30 years, is expected to bring another 300 million people into the highest income band of global population. This would generate increased demand for more expensive commodities, such as meat instead of rice. IAASTD (2009) estimated that by 2050 food demand will experience between a 70% increase to a doubling between 2000 and 2050, in turn demanding proportional increases of fertilizers and water consumption.

The long-term implication of such dynamics can be deleterious for the entire world economy. Among the greatest and unjust implications of climate change, is that it will affect the world differently in different parts of it. Tropical areas, which are largely populated by growing and poorer populations, and most often reliant on agriculture to sustain their economy, will be the most

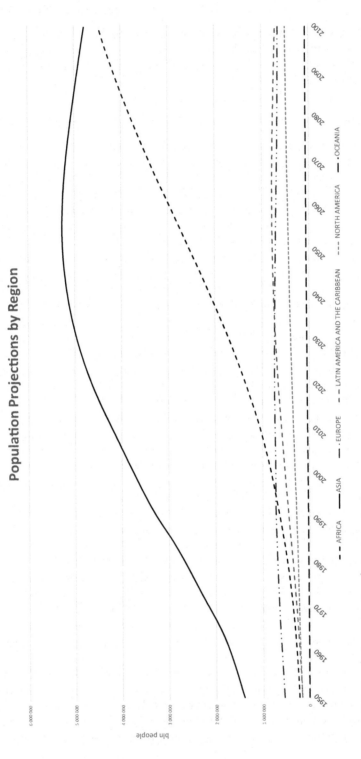

Population Projections by Region

bln people

5 000 000
5 000 000
4 000 000
3 000 000
2 000 000
1 000 000
0

1950 1960 1970 1980 1990 2000 2010 2020 2030 2040 2050 2060 2070 2080 2090 2100

- - AFRICA   ——ASIA   — · EUROPE   — — LATIN AMERICA AND THE CARIBBEAN   — — — NORTH AMERICA   — · ·OCEANIA

Figure 3.8 Population projections by region over time

negatively affected. For example, it is expected that rice harvest in Asia might fall by 25% due to ground-level ozone. Tropical regions are likely to suffer a 25% to 50% reduction of crop yields due to climate change (IIASTD 2009; IPCC 2014). Extreme weather events, such as droughts or floods, will also impact production and risk the continued access to cheap food (Jones and Phillips 2016). Without effective management and governance these dynamics will push people to migrate in search of more stable lands and access to food. These movements are already the cause of extremists and populist behaviours both around the world.

It is interesting to note that the problem of food security today is not a matter of the world capacity to produce enough food for everyone, but rather a matter of economic systems and supply chain inefficiency in distributing food output. In fact, today's supply chain wastes approximately 30% of the entire food product from land, 10% of which would be sufficient to satisfy the food demand of the poorest in the world (FAO 2011; Kummu et al. 2012). Additionally small changes in global diets, and less resource intensive food production have the potential to significantly reduce the problem (UN 2019).

The next section covers the pollution problem globally so completing the coverage of the World3 and the comparison with today's macro systems.

Pollution and waste

At the time of the World3, persistent pollution was the main concern generating the dynamics of collapse. Meadows et al. (1974) found these types of problems in nuclear radioactive waste, DDT, mercury, and other substances. In this section, we review the state of those particular systems and the continuous emissions of pollutants in ecosystems.

Nuclear solution

Since the 1950s nuclear energy was promoted as an alternative to energy shortages providing abundant and cheap energy for all (Bardi 2014). As Figure 3.9 shows, the concern of the Limits to Growth team of a continued exponential growth in nuclear can be seen starting in the 1970s (IAEA 2017). However, after a rapid increase and spread of the technology globally, the industry levelled off in the 1980s following on from the Chernobyl accident in April 1986. It has been estimated that after the Chernobyl plant explosion, more than 400 times the radioactivity of the Hiroshima atomic bomb was released (Baracca 2008). The continuous development of new technology, often led by military funding, started raising the possibility of safe nuclear energy, bringing the second generation plants (Chernobyl technology) to third and third+ (which are second generation with mechanical and electrical controls to apply auxiliary systems to improve security from disasters) by 2030 and 2040. However, the various minor accidents happening in Japan from 1990s (Baracca 2008), and the most recent Fukushima disaster in 2011 due to a tsunami hitting the nuclear plant, generated

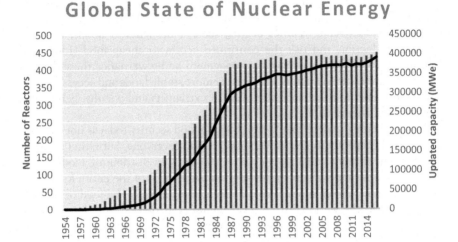

Figure 3.9 Number of nuclear reactors in operation and electricity capacity of those reactors

Source: IAEA (2017)

populistic concern all over the world, reducing the investment and growth in these plans going forward (IAEA 2017).

Other constraints to current nuclear technology include the dependence on uranium as a mineral. In particular as military expenditure on nuclear changes then the costs for uranium extraction need to be increasingly borne by the energy sector, as do the costs of cleaning and storing nuclear waste over the long term, making nuclear energy much more expensive and uneconomic (Bardi 2014).

Persistent organic pollutants, pesticides, and food security

Persistent organic pollutants (POP) are organic compounds that are resistant to environmental degradation and can persist in the environment from a time scale of years to millennia (SCPOP 2018). The vast majority of those are generated via industrial activity, and, as such, were considered among the planetary limits by the Limits to Growth team (Meadows et al. 1974).

Among the POP of interest, we find DDT. The formula of DDT earned the Nobel Prize for Muller (in 1948) because of its ability as an insecticide to control malaria. DDT has been widely used as a pesticide for the protection of agricultural production for decades, and was seen as a solution to food poverty worldwide. However, evidence built up in the literature of the negative effects of DDT on human health, most of those listed in Carson (1962). Starting in 1968, countries started banning the use of DDT for agricultural use, with United States applying the ban in 1972 (SCPOP 2018).

In 1995, the first conference of parties (COP) discussed POPs that could have similar effects to DDT on environment and health. A list of 12 was proposed and refined within the Stockholm Convention on POPs, and in 2004, 148 countries agreed to ban such compounds from the market and production. In 2018, the majority of countries agreed to the Stockholm convention, although still missing are some major economies including Israel, Italy, and the United States (SCPOP 2018).

Today, other types of pesticides are industrially in use, often associated with their ability to support the eradication of food poverty globally. Among the most famous is Roundup-Ready, patented and in use by Monsanto since 1970s (Robin 2010). The use of any type of pesticide is now often paired up with the Genetically Modified Organisms (GMOs) debate. The laboratory engineering of food gives it the characteristic to resist the pesticide produced in couple with it. This allows its application to the entire cultivated field killing all but the modified crop. However, the limited population of insects that are able to survive the pesticide, tend to multiply creating a new generation of insects that are no longer affected by the chemical. This results in continuous innovation by the chemical industry which, based on business principles, is forced to quickly introduce new pesticides in the field, without enough testing in all environmental conditions. The result is the leaching of those chemicals in the environment that cannot be easily assessed in terms of health and environmental impact (Robin 2010).

Air pollution

Another major concern within the Limits to Growth was the continuous growth of air pollution identified as non-persistent pollution, and most often correlated with the growth of industrial activity and transport. Areas that are particularly impacted are cities which have significant traffic, areas near large airports with thousands of take-offs and landings each day, power stations most likely based on coal plants, and other industrial plants. Today, air pollutants are identified as PM2.5 and PM10 as particulate matter of 2.5 and 10 micrometres of diameter respectively (UNECE 2016). Both cases can cause cancer and lung diseases by inhalation as well as enter the food chain via depositing on agricultural soil, as demonstrated in various studies (Liu et al. 2018; Shupler et al. 2018).

Globally the continuous industrial pressure of most countries and a shift in manufacturing towards the East has seen a growth in academic literature focusing on Chinese and Indian case studies (Wang et al. 2018; Zhang et al. 2018). In the most polluted cities such as Beijing, governments apply smart metering to monitor pollution levels and give warnings including the requirement to wear masks to provide protection from particulates in the air (Wu et al. 2018). Despite air pollution being predominantly a local issue a global assessment has been proposed by

Steffen et al. (2015). The dynamics appear to be in line with the limits to growth study and local policies are required to stop some of the World3 scenarios, even though their effects would be mostly local.

Waste, recycling, landfills, and ecosystems

In the World3, the problem of waste and recycling was viewed through the lens of resource availability. Still, industrial activity was assumed proportional to the amount of pollutants released in the environment as chemicals and poisoning substances (Meadows et al. 1972, 1974). In this section we review the state of industrial output after consumer use.

The issue with this type of waste today is not a matter of space but a matter of potential dispersion in ecosystems. The options for consumer waste are (i) landfill, (ii) recycled, (iii) dispersed in ecosystems as is, and (iv) incinerated in specific plants, normally storing the particulate emitted by the burning of waste (Bardi 2014). The recycling option is probably the most notable for the sustainable community, but given the inefficiency of household's recycling commitments, as well as the down-cycling of recycled material, recycling remains marginal in its utility. For example, according to the USGS (2017) no more than 50% of the totality of metals is recycled in the US.

An extreme case is the one of E-waste (waste of all electronic material worldwide, including computers and electrical appliances). Today, approximately 80% of the E-waste of the entire world is transported to Asia, and 90% of it is handled in China (Chen et al. 2010; Hicks et al. 2005; Ladou and Lovegrove 2008). A large fraction of that waste is landfilled in Guyin, the largest E-waste landfill in the world. Studies demonstrate that the burning of those appliances generated pollutants that were causing health problems including childhood mutations in the nearby population, due to inhalation and absorption in their food chains of those substances (Zhang 2017; Robinson 2009).

In the case of plastic, for example, Jambeck et al. (2015) estimated that approximately 8 million tonnes of plastics are released in the ocean every year. WEF et al. (2016), using the methodology of Jennings et al. (2008) for the estimation of fish population in the ocean, has shown that business as usual scenarios would bring greater quantities of plastic than fish in the ocean by 2050. In fact, today's global waste of plastic is 32% directly dispersed in the ecosystems (mostly via China and South East Asia), 40% landfilled, and 14% incinerated and used to generate energy. Of the 14 % destined for recycling, only 2% is estimated to be reintroduced for the same use (WEF et al. 2016; Jambeck 2015). Plastic accounts for 6% of oil consumption and 1% of the carbon budget, expected to grow in business as usual scenarios till 2050.

Today's solutions to those issue are often focused at the upstream of the supply chain around the design of processes which would enable the production of appliances that are more easily disassembled into their components after use and then directed back to the producer for manufacturing of new products. These types of solution take the name of closed-loop supply chains, or cradle to cradle, or circular economy. Still little legislation is in place today to compel companies to adopt such techniques. Of course the re-use culture of the customer will also play an important role (Bardi 2014).

Financial risk – the need for system policy science

Given the preceding picture, the complexity of a transition towards sustainability is shown to be a large-scale issue that requires a systems understanding of the dynamic interconnections among the sub-systems of society, the environment, and the economy. The financial system, through creating and allocating money, is intended as a control on many of the interconnections and its performance impacts the dynamics of the world system. Therefore, the financial system should be in a position to support leading the world system towards a global environmental transition (Silver 2017). In fact, the lack of a financial sector was among the criticisms of the Limits to Growth (Meadows 1982). Modelling financial and policy systems realistically is a key requirement for providing policy consultancy today (Keen 2017).

This section discusses the role of the financial system in terms of its financial risk function as intermediary between assets owners and the real and natural economy. It discusses the technological constraints of the green transition in terms of energy and agriculture showing the respective financial and policy requirements, and demonstrates how the current (market led) financial system alone cannot approach those requirements effectively without policy support. Top-down visions towards long-term sustainability need to be embedded in policy development, and regulation and policies have to be made to support such a vision. Models that can support approaching those issues are today more necessary than ever. The chapter concludes with a call on models, and introduces the rest of the book, which is the presentation of one of those models.

The role of the financial system and financial risk

The financial system, as every economic sector, has to create value and make profit to be economically viable. It does so via its activity of risk management in many forms. According to Silver (2017) there are four functions of the financial system:

1 Manage payments
2 Manage physical risk
3 Smooth long-term consumption
4 Allocate savings towards useful investments

While the management of payments is a very efficient social technology whose contribution to society is via enabling other economic activities, the direct value creation of the financial system is obtained via the other three functions, all of which can be reconnected to risk management. For the purpose of this book, 'risk' can be defined as the 'likelihood that expected plans would deviate from desired due to uncertain factors that are intrinsic in every future.' These factors might be human induced, systemically generated, or simply uncontrollable such as variations in the weather climate or a volcano eruption. It is important to note the connection between 'future' and 'risk.' As the financial system is in the position of creating and distributing money bearing interest, its role is to exchange current values with greater future values given certain parameters of risk of failure. Thus risk assessment, mitigation, and management are key requisites to support each economic activity towards growth and global value creation.

The three forms of risk just presented are the responsibility of different financial institutions. Managing physical risk is the duty of the insurance sector, whose business model consists in estimating the likelihood (risk) of certain events happening together with the damage caused by those events. The risk of the individual is mitigated via spreading it among the collective, imposing an interest premium to all insured to cover for the few affected by the unlucky events. The business model is sustainable as far as risks can be predicted with a certain degree of certainty, and falter when unpredictable events tend to increase in damage or frequency. Today, approximately 7% of global financial assets are owned by insurance industries (WB 2018).

Smoothing long-term activity is the work of the banking system via loans for assets purchase with both the purpose of household consumption (e.g. mortgage for a house), and investments for productive assets (e.g. capital investments and development). The liquidity generated for the loan emerges from household deposits in the banks or in the form of newly issued debt money. In this case, risk comes into play as the likelihood of the borrower to return their debt, resulting in an interest rate correspondent to the risk of failure in payments. The higher the interest rate the greater the profit, which is then distributed between depositor and banking system itself.

Allocating savings towards useful investments is the work of investment banks and asset management firms. According to Silver (2017) a distinction has to be made between cash deposits and savings. The first are short-term liquidity in banks available for withdrawal at any time, while the second are immobilised long-term liabilities supposed to be invested in long-term productive activities (e.g. pension funds). These types of assets have to be invested in low-risk activities to assure long-term return. Tower Watson (2014) published a report stating that global pensions are immobilised in equity (i.e. stocks of private companies) for 52%, public and private bonds for 29%, and other activities for 19%. If the pension funds are large enough then they can be exposed to the overall success of the global economy, and are often dubbed 'universal owners.' Assuring the long-term growth of nations and large firms becomes a strict requirement for wealthy pensions.

Despite being largely regulated by governments, free market still forms the basement of the financial system, which, within law, performs all activities seeking the highest return. Maxton and Randers (2016) criticise these activities, being short-term focused as imposed by the calculation justifying the feasibility of investments. Eq. 3.1 shows the calculation of the Net Present Value (NPV_N) of a sum of future cash flows (CF_n) from present time ($n = 0$) to a generic year (N). NPV is the most widely used formula for estimating the feasibility of an investment. Whatever discount rate or interest rate (measure of risk d) on future values, it always gives greater importance to short-term cash flows rather than long-term ones. In addition, continuous reward based on short-term gains is given to people working in finance, reinforcing the focus on short-term gains at the expense of long-term sustainable investments (Keen 2017).

Eq. 3.1 – Net present value

$$NPV_N = \sum\nolimits_{n=0}^{N} \frac{CF_n}{(1+d)^n}$$

The term 'sustainable or green finance' emerged to start addressing those issues and diverting the work of the financial system towards sustainability (Jones et al. 2013; Costanza et al. 2014; Battiston et al. 2017). Among its greatest challenges there is a need to estimate risks and implement policies without historical data to rely on. In fact, one of the greatest challenges of dealing with climate change is that no real data to estimate the possible impact of its effect on financial assets have been collected yet. In addition, free market led finance generates a strong path dependency in the socio-technological system as seen in the following section.

Market-driven path-dependent technologies and green transition

Path dependency is a term indicating the lock-in situation of a systems' states due to the initial path taken, resulting in strong inertia against allowing system change. Capital investments in physical assets are examples of path dependency. Physical assets can persist over a long time providing the money required to pay off any debts or interest on investments. Alongside which they can be a drag on knowledge creation and technology improvements, making it harder for other not mature techniques to diffuse. Free market and competition, with relatively limited support from governments, can often facilitate disentangling path dependencies. However, cases such as the energy and agricultural systems present hard challenges even with larger public support because of the scale and long-term nature of the investments required. Most important the financial system led by market principles has the effect of reinforcing these dynamics, making it even more difficult to create finance and opportunities for the emerging competitor technologies (i.e. solar and wind, and non-industrial food systems).

Nowadays, mature technologies and businesses have long developed to keep prices of output low and competitive, resulting in stable profits, ease of receiving loans and low interest rates. In turn, this facilitates their capabilities in improving technologies, such reducing prices even more and reinforcing their economic sustainability over time. On the other hand, a new entrant can find it difficult to compete on price, so not gain market share and recording unstable profits. From the financial sector this means higher risk, higher interest rates and low availability for loans. The high interest rates impact on higher price of output making the technology less competitive, weakening their economic sustainability, with lack of investments in research and development and slowing their penetration in the market. This results in lower desire for investment in those technologies giving larger attraction for the former one.

These dynamics are explained by the causal loop structure in Figure 3.10. The structure generating behaviour is formed by three reinforcing feedback loops (R1, R2, R3) acting in synergy. The difference among the two technologies is that in the first case the competitiveness generated by low price would reinforce the momentum via the three different channels to increase investments and lower price even further. In the second, the constrained competitiveness would activate the same reinforcing feedback structure in the opposite direction resulting in the new technology struggling. Reinforcing feedback loops are in fact at the heart of path dependency in complex systems (Sterman 2000).

Looking at the energy transition towards green energy this is exactly what is happening between finance and technology (Silver 2017). The ability of a global transition to oil in the early 1900s was due to an absolute superiority of its usability in comparison to coal (Maxton and Randers 2016). Today fossil fuels remain attractive technologies for investments. In a similar way, agriculture is

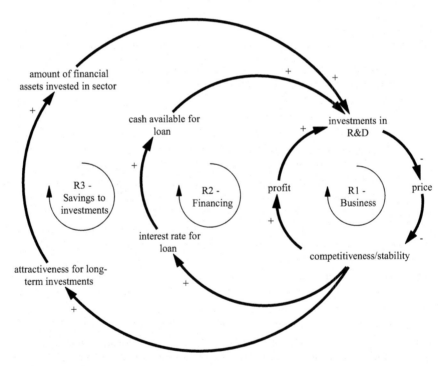

Figure 3.10 Reinforcing feedback loops from market forces generating technological path dependency

heavily reliant on oil, based on pesticides, industrial fertilizers and monoculture with over 80% of total agricultural land in use by multinational corporations (DB and EcoNexus 2013). Given that fossil fuels are the major cause of climate change, and agriculture a central cause of biodiversity loss and environmental pollution, demand for a global transition towards green energy and alternative farming techniques is growing. However, finance led by free market and growth, with no way to incorporate the external costs of these impacts, cannot cope with it alone. In the absence of de-growth, social practices and clean technologies will have to be developed and applied with the main aim to decouple growth from environmental limits in the next decades (Jackson 2016).

The following section explores the requirements of energy and agricultural systems towards a sustainable transition.

Green energy and energy efficiency

A fast energy transition to renewables is a must in order to contain the negative effects of climate change (IPCC 2014). Given today's state, such a transition presents technological challenges that are peculiar both by sector and technology.

Renewable energy can be categorised as:

- Hydroelectric
- Solar
- Wind
- Geothermal
- Bio-energy

Energy uses considered here are:

- Power generation and electricity
- Heating system and thermal processes in industry
- Transportation

Table 3.1 shows the share of energy consumption in terms of fossil fuels, renewables, and nuclear divided by the three sectors, and averaged globally based on IEA data (2017c).

Table 3.1 Share of energy consumption by sector and technology

Resource/sector	Electricity	Heating	Transportation	Global average
Fossil fuels	66.30%	72.70%	97%	**78.60%**
Renewables	23.10%	26.20%	3%	**18.90%**
Nuclear	10.60%	1.10%	-	**2.50%**
Fraction of final consumption (weight for average)	18%	53%	29%	100%

Data show that global energy consumption is 78.3% represented by fossil fuels, 2.5% by nuclear energy, and 19.2% by renewable sources. The net of energy losses in transformation and distribution processes starting from primary supply is approximately 38%. Electricity generation (power sector) accounts for 18% of total consumption, dominated by fossil fuels at 66.3% (mostly natural gas and coal), followed by renewables at 23% (mostly hydroelectric), and nuclear at 10.6%. Fifty-three percent of consumption relates to heating in households and industries as well as thermal processes in industry. Approximately one quarter of this energy comes from renewables, whereas 72% still depends on fossil fuels, and a small fraction on nuclear. The transportation sector consumes 29% of total energy output, 96% of which is fossil fuels (mostly oil), leaving a small fraction to renewables.

This section describes these data in detail showing the different challenges by sector and technology.

Electricity

Renewable electricity supply is currently largely represented by hydroelectric (70% of total), a mature technology greatly improved during the 20th century. Hydro is followed by wind with 15%, bio-energy with 8.4%, solar photovoltaic (PV) with 5%, and geothermal with 1.6% (IRENA 2018). In order to understand the electric market and possible development of renewables it is important to first look at the energy mix given the daily load demanded by the economy.

As Figure 3.11 shows the daily demand of electricity of urban and industrial areas follows peak curves that differ between summer and winter (with spring and autumn in the range between the two). Based on the amount of daylight available, and the time of the day in which people tend to be at home, in factories or in the office for work, the two curves show three levels of power demand: base load, intermediate, and peak. Considering today's power system lacks battery storage technology (that could allow the production of energy prior to consumption and deliver that on demand based on the time of the day), the current system has to constantly provide energy in order to assure demand is satisfied. A mismatch between the two would cause blackouts. In order to meet hourly demand, different power plants have to be activated at different times of the day. This is why no single type of energy can be used today to satisfy the demand of the entire electricity grid.

Coal technology is normally used in steam power plants. These are closed-cycle highly pressurised water pipeline that first increases water temperature to create steam in a boiler by burning coal, and secondly releases that same energy that is captured in large turbines to rotate a shaft. The resulting mechanical energy is transformed into electricity by means of an electricity generator, while the low energy cooled down steam is collected in a condenser and pushed back in the system, closing the cycle. Nuclear reactors have a much more complex technology to generate thermal energy and transform it to mechanical and electric, but in principle the final end remains the use of a turbine collecting the energy from

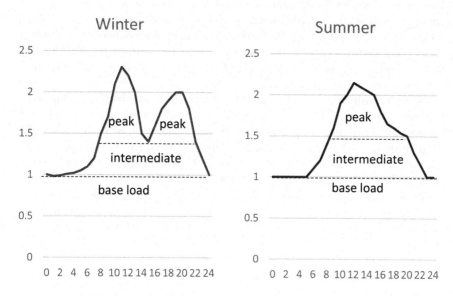

Figure 3.11 Power load of electric energy during winter and summer in a developed country

a flow to rotate a shaft, and generate electricity. Both types of plant are difficult to switch on and off and hard to control in terms of power generation requiring teams of engineers and preparation time to be set up. That is why coal and nuclear capacity can be used for the baseload only and is unsuitable for managing peaks.

Gas turbines, instead, have similar properties to the engines used to power modern airplanes. Gas turbines are fueled with petroleum derivatives and natural gas, and release about half the carbon content per unit of energy in comparison to coal. This results in them being the most flexible source of energy, suitable both for baseload (often in the combined cycle with double efficiency to average coal power plants, or single gas turbines), as well as intermediate load and hourly peaks management, able to be switched on and off quickly.

Hydroelectric power plants use the potential energy given by the difference in height between two water levels, with turbines placed at the bottom end ready to exploit such energy. Such technology relies on large (high) dams in the presence of rivers and lakes. Activating a hydroelectric plant consists in opening a valve to allow the water to stream from the water stock down to the valley. This means that the more the dam is full, the greater the amount of energy that can be provided. Using hydroelectricity as baseload is not possible unless the amount of rain or melting glaciers would match the outflow of water flowing down to the turbine every day. That is why hydroelectricity is used for managing peaks and intermediate loads during the day. In times of little rain, the dam could easily reduce its water level and reduce its efficiency in energy generation. The economic sustainability of hydroelectric plants is obtained by opening water flow, thus supplying energy, during the peak demand making a profit out of high energy prices, and using energy to pump the same water back upstream during the night, exploiting the base load when demand is low. Still hydroelectricity is constrained by space and geography.

Solar and wind are dependent on the weather. Without a battery storage technology, solar is available during daylight only making it suitable for peaks and intermediate in times of good weather. Wind capacity can be installed both on and off shore, with large wind farms away from urban areas. Wind is potentially suitable for the baseload, even though assuring such capacity at all times would require the use of large amounts of land or ocean area to install plants. Both solar and wind remain variable sources of electricity, requiring the use of hydroelectric (where possible) or gas turbines to respond to such variability. Electricity from geothermal requires the transformation of thermal energy from the ground into electricity, and represents a stable source of energy despite being constrained by location and efficiency. Bio-energy provides a good source of energy, but remains based on available land, and generates competition with land availability for agriculture.

When oil was discovered, its superiority and versatility gap in comparison to coal, coupled with a cheap price, have been the greatest factors supporting its penetration in the energy market and the energy transition toward oil (Maxton and Randers 2016). Figure 3.12 shows the comparison in terms of costs between conventional fossil fuels and the range of renewable resource technologies, as well as the trend in average cost between 2010 and 2017. The costs are based on

Change in Cost per Source and Comparison with Fossil Fuel Cost

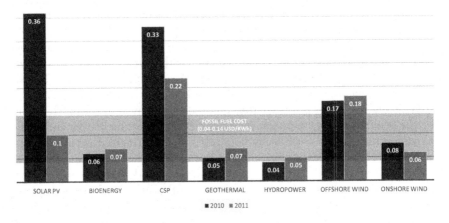

Figure 3.12 Costs comparison between sources of energy

Source: IRENA database (2017)

many factors including the depletion level in case of fossil fuels, the size of the plants, their location, and so on. Whereas bio-energy electricity cost per kilowatt-hour remained almost constant, it is interesting to note the trend in the other resources. In particular, geothermal and hydro cost shows an increase, most likely dependent on the increased investments deploying more plants in less favorable conditions than 2010. Capacity increased even though the technology did not achieve improvements in efficiency. Important decreases can be found in both solar and wind costs. The drastic decrease in solar photovoltaic to become competitive to fossil fuels is given both through improved technology and from the learning curve in positioning those plants in order to be more effective than in the past. Still large amount of solar plants are built in areas that are not economically competitive to fossil fuels. Wind farm technology improved in effectiveness and size both offshore and onshore, becoming today cheaper than fossil fuels in particular locations (REN 2018). In addition, constant depletion of oil and gas will increase costs of extraction of fossil fuels in the long term making renewables more and more competitive, supporting their market penetration over time.

There are two additional caveats to consider in addition to the costs of electricity generation. First, is the variability problem that characterises solar and wind. Being dependent on weather, their applicability will remain variable over time. This would mean two possibilities, both of which increase costs of production. One option would be overcapacity, assuring that while the wind does not blow sufficiently in one area it might do so in another, such satisfying the total demand. A second option, which is currently under research and development, requires the application of batteries able to store energy in times in which it is produced but not demanded, and release it when demand is higher than supply. Based on current technology levels, both solutions are not economic, bringing the technology out of the range of competitiveness. In addition they would generate additional pressures on mineral resources such as lithium, currently recyclable at 1% of consumption and assumed reaching peak of inland reserves by 2030. Therefore, the current option is to use gas turbines and hydro power to deal with solar and wind plant variability, and exploit geothermal and biofuels when that is possible.

Given these trends market forces alone seem unlikely to allow the green energy revolution to happen smoothly, and the speed of change is critical. Therefore, there is need for fossil fuels to remain in the ground to avoid further contributions to climate change despite their current market competitiveness. Policy input in the process is fundamental to stop climate change. A good example for a success story is Germany, able to produce 70% of total electricity demand using wind during the winter, and managing daily hours during summer with solar (Fraunhofer 2018).

Heating

Heating and cooling energy from renewables is the lowest technology intensive sector amongst the energy sectors being 90% dominated by bio-energy. In particular, about 18% of total heat consumption in 2015 was still in the form of traditional biomass and mostly in developing and undeveloped countries (IEA 2017c). According to the Sustainable Development Goals (UN 2019) indoor air pollution in low income countries due to inadequate ventilation for cooking and heating remains the second largest cause of death globally after HIV. Solar concentration thermal accounted for approximately 2.1% of total energy consumption from heating, finding applications in household heating at low temperatures, with the largest plant (above 1GW) in the Middle East for the evaporation of steam for the oil industry. Geothermal has been used in suitable areas accounting for 0.5% of the share of total heating consumption. Modern biomass generation was in use to the remaining 6.1% (REN21 2018).

Currently, research and development in biomass is dependent on the high price of oil, which makes it valuable for markets to invest in those types of alternative technologies. Solar concentration generation is still not able to generate high temperatures to support industrial processes such as steel and cement production. Heating buildings is possible, but the constraints of transportation of biomass would have a similar problem to coal, making it difficult to speak about a global market for biomass. Modern biofuels are improving, but the limitation on forests and land, and the competition for food production might not allow for a rapid expansion of renewables for heating. In addition, the overall efficiency of biomass, in particular for home purposes in developing countries, would have to be increased drastically.

One solution for the heating system is a shift in the burden towards electricity generation via improving electric heat pumps and boilers (REN21 2018). Electric pumps would be a good option, even though they would rely on minerals and metals for their production, making the energy system more reliable on mineral industry than it is already. As these minerals are currently abundant this should support a temporary solution to the heating problem in the next decades, favouring the transition towards sustainability. However, given the great challenges already in place to support an energy transition in the electric system, any attempt to use those resources to support heating generation as well would add to the burden. Still natural gas plants and investments in modern biofuels may represent a buffer of production to allow for the green transition to take place in the next decades. In other words, a balanced energy mix, aiming at exploiting all resources in the most effective way would be key, along with the transition towards renewables.

Other options to support the burden of the transition include retrofitting existing assets and improved energy efficiency of new investments. Better technologies and better management have the potential to reduce demand for energy from factories, housing, and devices. Improvements in energy efficiency include better insulation of housing, lighter vehicles for transportation, better efficiency in lighting, more efficient use of heat, and so on. In the short run, energy efficiency can help decrease economic costs of energy, and reduce the burden of fossil fuel depletion. A constraint stands in the cost necessary to update current assets. Another issue related to new technologies is referred to as 'Jevons Paradox' or 'rebound effect.' It has been recognised in the literature that the advantage gathered by the use of more efficient technologies and dependent decrease in cost in terms of energy, most often implies a larger exploitation of such a technology that compensate the initial energy saving (Freeman et al. 2016).

Transportation

The transportation sector is today run by fossil fuels (mostly oil), with only a 3% share for renewables divided in 2.85% for modern biofuels and about 0.15% on electric vehicles (IEA 2018). The entry points of renewables are different by the four uses of energy in transport that are road transport (76%), marine (12%), avionic (11%), and rail at 2% share (REN21 2018).

Road vehicles are dominated by internal combustion engine technology, about two thirds dependent on private vehicles and light use commercial vehicles, 5% shares on bus transport, 22% on heavy trucks and shipping and a small fraction of two- and three-wheels vehicles (REN21 2018). The options for renewables are ethanol and biodiesel, and electric vehicles relying on battery technology, largely transitioning through hybrid vehicles. Biofuels are normally blended 50–50 with traditional fuels derivate from petroleum. Bus systems have been electrified mainly in urban areas. However, private vehicles and combustion engine constraints remain in the high cost and efficiency of battery technology, which keeps transition to renewable energy difficult and uneconomic, as well as largely led by public subsidies (IEA 2018). In 2017, the record of one million electric cars sold was reached, although this represents 0.15% of the private vehicles on our roads (IEA 2018).

Marine and aviation, accounting for about 4% of total carbon emissions in the atmosphere, face greater challenges than road vehicles for the transition, given the high weight and low weight to power ratio necessary for aerospace sector. The first 100% renewable transportation ship has been produced in China, whereas renewables in aerospace have to rely on 50–50 blended fuels between biofuels and traditional ones. The rail sector is already 39% electrified globally, even though such electricity is mostly produced by fossil fuels (REN21 2018).

As in the case of the heating system, great hope in the green transition of the transportation sector lies in the electrification of its devices, shifting the burden towards the increase in electricity generation which is still reliant on fossil fuels. Biofuels can support the transition but still remain a limited source given the constraints of agriculture. Other support might emerge from social policies, including, for example, fleet management and car sharing, or the strong emphasis on public transport and cycling paths in urban areas. Still the complexity of the transition would have to be taken into account carefully, pushing transportation system relying fully on electric systems, and increasing pressures on agricultural and mineral sectors.

Is it a choice between energy transition and food security?

The requirements for green energy transition generates additional production pressures on agriculture. Similarly to the energy system, agriculture and fisheries

are driven by market forces, and as such are also subject to strong path dependencies. This can be simply demonstrated noting that the food that we produce
without significant industrial inputs is today called 'organic' food to be distinguished from the common food which is grown using additives such as pesticides
and industrial fertilizers. Such path dependency is reinforced by current industrial
technology, the need to maintain economies of scale to keep food cost low, supporting the eradication of food poverty for a growing global population while
keeping the entire food system in the hands of a few large corporations (DB and
EcoNexus 2013). As seen, the current agricultural system is not environmentally sustainable, requiring us to think of its capabilities to achieve sustainability,
resolving food poverty, and supporting an energy transition using biofuels.

Approximately 68% of agricultural land is devoted to pasture and meat production, 29% to arable land requiring crops to be replanted after harvested, and 3%
accounts for permanent crops, which after harvest do not need to be replanted.
Only 1.2% of arable land is today devoted to organic production (Willer et al.
2018), with a growing fraction (13% of total in 2017) devoted to genetically
modified crops (ISAAA 2017). In other words, the use of industrial fertilizers
and pesticides largely dominates global agriculture today, with a growing use of
GMO developed together with specific pesticides (WRI 2014). Thirty percent of
crop production is currently used to feed animals, with the remaining distributed
for human consumption, which due to supply chains and retail inefficiencies, is
lost at about 35% of the total while leaving almost 800 million people undernourished (FAO 2015). Without accounting for deforestation, WRI (2014) calculates that approximately 46% of total greenhouse emissions from agriculture
are produced by cattle and ruminants, with the rest being dependent on fertiliza-
tion (20%), energy use in machineries (17%), paddy rice production (10%), and
manure management (7%). Looking at total dietary requirements, about 16% of
proteins come from fisheries. With depleted oceans, wild fishing peaked in the
1990s, giving more and more importance to aquaculture, which is supposed to
become the main source of fish production, representing almost 50% of total fish
protein production today (OECD-FAO 2017).

A market-driven agriculture sector is highly unlikely to generate a shift towards
environmental sustainability in the next two decades. For example, looking at
China and the expected food demand given economic growth, approximately
300 million people will move from low the medium-high income, generating a
strong shift from crop consumption to meat consumption which is much more
environmentally expensive. According to OECD-FAO (2017) China alone is
already producing 60% of total fish catch in the world to accommodate such a
need for proteins. Looking at areas such as India and sub-Saharan Africa, which
are recording great rates of population growth, the choice will be between environmental feasibility or famine for the vast amount of people. In addition, every
shock to oil price and cost rise due to scarcity (that in the next two decades will
eventually show up) will boost demand for biofuels, increasing pressures even
further. WRI (2014) calculated that by burning the entire biomass of today's
global agricultural and forest land, the amount of energy obtained would reach

approximately 32% of the total energy consumption in 2014. Assuming increases in energy needs for the future, this clearly makes biofuels and biomass energy generation a marginal contribution to the energy transition. It will be important to realise what is the real priority of agriculture between people (feeding everyone), energy (producing energy), and environment (being sustainable in the long term).

Are there options for sustainable farming?

In order to support a more sustainable agricultural system there exists some key pathways. Under the assumption of not revolutionising the entire economic system in the next few decades and focusing on the environmental sustainability aspects, these are (i) making agriculture more efficient, (ii) support changing diets in the developed world towards more environmental friendly solutions, (iii) support a more evenly distributed global supply chain. Making the food system more efficient is possible simply because the food system is very inefficient in different ways.

Firstly, the food supply chain records between a 20% and 35% loss of output from farm to retailer and household (FAO 2015). The reason for the loss tend to be linked to inefficient storage in developing countries, and on the selection of food and waste on the demand end in the developed countries. Solutions in reducing food waste along the supply chain would benefit all three aspects of sustainable farming mentioned previously, supporting better nutrition, more availability of land for biofuels, and lower environmental load.

Fertilizers use is also largely wasted in the environment, via leaching from topsoil to dead coastal areas. The greater the capability of the farmer in handling the right amount of fertilizers to benefit harvesting the easier it would be for fertilizers to remain contained on arable land. On this side, the deployment of climate-smart agriculture, that is agriculture supported with the use of sensors and information technology could potentially play a greater role. Climate smart could also be helpful in the repopulation of fisheries in the ocean. For example, Pauli (2017) suggested that a little attention in avoiding depletion of wild fisheries such as 'not fishing pregnant fishes' could make a great difference. However, while this might not be simple task among wild fishes, the continuous development of aquaculture (that is a largely controlled areas of fishes), would make it easier with the appropriate technologies, to identify those 'mum-fishes,' and release them in the wild ocean before harvest.

Changing global diets would have a significant impact on the global footprint of agriculture. For example, WRI (2014) shows how the production of proteins via red meat is the most inefficient process per unit of output in the entire food chain. If households would switch demand from red meat to white meat, that could save 60 to 80% of emissions and resources allocated to meat production, as well as reducing the amount of crop and pasture land to feed those animals. The move towards vegetable proteins would have an even greater benefit.

Pauli (2017) also proposes the potential of moving from what he calls 2 dimensions to 3 dimensions (3D) farming to increase productivity of current practices

30-fold. 3D farming consists in producing food output via algae farming, developing specific platforms under the sea that would allow nutrients and minerals to grow in height rather than extension, with the potential to grow exponentially following a fractal growth structure. Despite this potentially not being a desirable solution to support the production of high quality food, the availability of nutrients might still be able satisfy food demand cheaply, and it presents the advantage of being resilient to sea level rise as well as weather events. In addition, given the diffusion of powdered food containing all necessary nutrients (see high performance athletics), such a solution might be more feasible than initially considered. Importantly the potential impact of those solutions for biofuel production, considering algae can be used for the production of oils with high calorific power, can be considered.

Targeting a fairer distribution of capacity globally relying on international trade regulations and investment is justified by the change in population growth which will bring Africa and India to unprecedented conditions in human history in terms of food produced per capita by areas. The current trends are already alarming northern countries and contribute to a rising populist sentiment against immigration. However, to achieve a sensitive balance of investments and costs, a top down view from international institutions will be necessary. Together with governments there is a need to rely on inclusive growth policies, particularly aiming at educating the workforce, achieving gender balance in every economic activity, and at the same time fighting against food poverty. The need for activating all populations against the problems of climate change, as well as aiming at reaching energy and food access for all, might become a positive source of development for countries that will face hard challenges in the future.

All these options remain uncertain and require careful planning and deployment of both technologies and systemic support from policy. Models capable of addressing those uncertainties are needed.

Activating and supporting solutions for global sustainability – the need for system policy science

Governments all over the world are already dealing with the problems of the Anthropocene and looking to find sustainable solutions for the long term. This is particularly shown given the Sustainable Development Goals (UN 2019), using 17 goals (and over 200 hundred indicators) to handle and envision a sustainable future fairer for everybody. The SDGs support the climate target agreement signed in COP21 in 2015. However, the SDGs show that the technical inefficiencies of the sustainable transition are still far from being tackled at current technology and commitment level, and present great challenges ahead. Every single government should not consider their sustainable strategy separately from other governments, requiring a synergic commitment with their citizens, investors, and technology developers. Most importantly, the role of SDGs is to provide balance in the world society by giving a big picture and a system representation of the issues at stake. Ideally, every organisation should approach all of the SDGs simultaneously, given that increasing the performance in one of those can often lead to performance loss in others.

Markets driven by finance, and supported by financial risk, generate strong path dependencies and lock in technology situations. The current lack of financial interest in investing in the transition technologies makes it a hard challenge for markets. A market without government structure is like a human body without bones. It would simply destroy itself creating large imbalances and resulting in strong revolts. Most important time is not on our side, requiring a global commitment to invert the direction of global emissions and environmental damage, within the time of one generation. Governments will have to apply policies and redirect investments with clear objectives to allow for the transition to happen. Their action will have to be controlled and monitored as well as assessed to provide feedback to ensure the optimal use of our resources. Instruments that allow for transparent management of the socio-political interconnectivity of sustainability are needed.

The objective of system policy science in the Anthropocene is to recognise the reality as a complex system, show those path dependencies, identify and quantify systemic risk, and sensitise the possible policy levers to support decision making towards an efficient global level transition. There is need to create synergies between market-driven forces and system policies, while recognising that market operation and financial risk assessments alone cannot solve the problem of keeping the planet within planetary limits. On the other hand, modelling the society without the environment and the environment without the society appears to be ineffective. We need system scientists able to represent both the economic structures, the planetary systems, and the social response in the same framework.

Summary

The picture that emerged from all the preceding reveals a state of the world that is both complex and in trouble. Starting from the Limits to Growth model, various issues have arisen from the modelling perspective of 1972. A description of the dynamics of growth have been proposed, looking at the drivers of growth today. Capitalism has been explained and the role of financial system has been shown, as well as the search for productivity growth and the political chaos that characterises such a system. The state of global resources was revisited. The dynamics of mineral resources while feeding a growing economy have been proposed followed by the state of fossil fuels. The agricultural system was presented as the core of the sustainability dilemma. Pollution, both persistent and non, has been revisited as in comparison to 1972.

It is worth noting that all the differences that emerged from the comparison between the real world and the expectation of the Limits to Growth team while developing the World3. Differences between models and reality are dependent on the knowledge available at the time the models are built, and not everything can be predicted a priori. For example, the rise of internet technologies, allowed for a different way of running the economy today that could not have been predicted.

However, the banning of DDT (through the setup of the Stockholm Convention on POP to develop legislation to stop their use globally) was included in the Limits to Growth scenarios. What we can say for sure is that the Limits to Growth contributed in clearly outlining the world's environmental limits, most likely avoiding some of the terrible scenarios as presented in 1972. However, today's problem are still global and dependent on a similar type culture of growth as in the 1970s.

After the comparison of environmental limits between model and reality, the role of the financial system was reintroduced aligned with the technical, political, and social problems of supporting an energy and agricultural transition towards long-term sustainability. Solutions to problems are uncertain and mostly weak, requiring the development of models that can assess future scenarios to help the transition to be as risk free as possible. System policy science should bridge the gap between policy, markets, and society with the use of system models, to help future assessment.

The work that follows is a step in this direction. The work is a global impact assessment model named ERRE (Economic Risk, Resources and Environment) connecting the financial system with the energy (both fossil fuels and green), agriculture and climate systems through the real economy, by means of feedback loops, time lags and non-linear, rationally bounded, decision-making processes. The model allows the testing of hypotheses and events such as climate shocks, productivity gaps, technology change for green energy to support the energy transition, agricultural limits constraints, monetary policies such as money creation and amends in interest change, subsidies and carbon taxes, among others. All of these options have to be addressed via simulation, compared to real available data, and assessed in terms of a meaningful structure that reflects the real processes of the economy and the natural system.

In particular, this book proposes a step forward in the development of models that employ system dynamics, system thinking, behavioral and economic-resource modelling as complex system methodologies for modelling the global economy and resource risks. In order to do so, we rely on the World3–03 model as proposed in in Meadows et al. (2003), and integrate this with the modelling framework proposed by Jay Forrester between the 1970s and 1980s, namely the System Dynamics National Model (Forrester 1980; Forrester et al. 1976). The National Model was a large project led at the MIT Labs by Jay Forrester with the help of various PhD students (Senge 1978; Forrester 1992; Sterman 1981; Mass 1975). Despite the structure of the entire model has never been made public, some of its applications could be consulted and amended for the purpose of this work. Among those, the one of John Sterman (1981), which consisted of a simplified representation of the National Model for the study of the Energy Transition of the United States after the 1980s, was considered particularly suitable as a base for the development of the ERRE.

With 40 years of evolution of the state-of-the-art, new data availability, as well as the review in this chapter, the model has been largely updated. Major edits include, the integration of the food and agriculture system (as in the World3–03) in the energy transition model of Sterman (1981), the review of technology and supply structures, the revisit of the financial structure of the model, in particular defaults structure, balance sheets, the full review of the savings-loans system, and a representation of both the public and financial sector (banking) as separate entities in the model. The final result is a fully stock and flow consistent (SFC) economic model that applies fossil fuels, agricultural, and climate limits as boundaries to a growing economy, and allows the assessment of global extreme risk uncertainties towards the end of the century in a consistent way with both resources and economic systems.

The next chapter describes the evolution of system policy science and economics as a science starting in 1776 till today addressing all principles and limitations among methodologies to find the synergies and constraints among those. In particular, the history of system dynamics and its evolution alongside the other economic modelling approaches has been explored in detail. This allows the introduction of a theoretical and methodological knowledge base to engage in the review of the ERRE model in Chapter 5. The data used to calibrate the model as a metric for statistical validation of its results, as well as the uncertainty and risk analysis via scenario simulation is presented in Chapter 6. Both chapters are accompanied with an online document proposing all equations and structures of the ERRE, and numerous validation and behavioral tests at the https://doi.org/10.25411/aru.10110710. The book concludes with reflections and further directions of this line of work as well as providing policy recommendations based on the finding of this work.

References

Adam, C. (2011). On the macroeconomic management of food price shocks in low-income countries. *Journal of African Economies, 20*(S1), 163–199.

Aly, G. (2007). *Hitler's beneficiaries: Plunder, racial war and the Nazi welfare state* (J. Chase, trans.). Henry Holt and Co., New York.

Armah, P., Archer, A., & Phillips, G. C. (2011). *Drivers leading to higher food prices: Biofuels are not the main factor biofuels* (pp. 19–36). Springer, Berlin, Germany.

Arodudu, O. T. (2017). *Sustainability assessment of agro-bioenergy systems using energy efficiency indicators.* Universität Potsdam, Mathematisch-Naturwissenschaftliche Fakultät, Postdam, Germany.

Arodudu, O. T., Helming, K., Wiggering, H., & Voinov, A. (2017). Towards a more holistic sustainability assessment framework for agro-bioenergy systems – a review. *Environmental Impact Assessment Review, 62*, 61–75.

Baracca, A. (2008). *L'Italia torna al nucleare? i costi, i rischi, le bugie* (Vol. 860). Editoriale Jaca Book, Milan, Italy.

Bardi, U. (2014). *Extracted: How the quest for mineral wealth is plundering the planet.* Chelsea Green Publishing, Vermont, US.

Bardi, U. (2015, January 26). *Global sustainability institute research conference: The interface between sustainability and research policy.* Anglia Ruskin University, Cambridge, UK.

Battiston, S., Mandel, A., Monasterolo, I., Schütze, F., & Visentin, G. (2017). A climate stress-test of the financial system. *Nature Climate Change, 7*(4), 283.

Baumeister, R. F., Vohs, K. D., Aaker, J. L., & Garbinsky, E. N. (2013). Some key differences between a happy life and a meaningful life. *The Journal of Positive Psychology, 8*(6), 505–516.

Bentley, R., & Bentley, Y. (2015). Explaining the price of oil 1971–2014: The need to use reliable data on oil discovery and to account for 'mid-point' peak. *Energy Policy*, 86, 880–890.

Berne Declaration (DB) and EcoNexus. (2013). *Agropoly – a handful of corporations control world food production*. Berne Declaration (DB) and EcoNexus, Zurich, Switzerland.

Bicer, Y., Dincer, I., Zamfirescu, C., Vezina, G., & Raso, F. (2016). Comparative life cycle assessment of various ammonia production methods. *Journal of Cleaner Production*, 135, 1379–1395.

Bindraban, P. S., Dimkpa, C., Nagarajan, L., Roy, A., & Rabbinge, R. (2015). Revisiting fertilisers and fertilisation strategies for improved nutrient uptake by plants. *Biology and Fertility of Soils*, 51(8), 897–911.

Bloom, D. E. (2011). *Population dynamics in India and implications for economic growth*. WDA-Forum, University of St. Gallen, St. Gallen, Switzerland.

Bongaarts, J. (2009). Human population growth and the demographic transition. *Philosophical Transactions of the Royal Society B: Biological Sciences*, 364(1532), 2985–2990.

British Geological Survey. (2012). *World mineral production 2008–2012*. Keyworth, Nottingham.

British Petroleum. (2017). *BP statistical review of world energy June 2017*. British Petroleum.

Brown, L. R. (2008). *Plan B 3.0: Mobilizing to save civilization (substantially revised)*. WW Norton & Company, New York, US.

Calvo, G., Valero, A., & Valero, A. (2017). Assessing maximum production peak and resource availability of non-fuel mineral resources: Analyzing the influence of extractable global resources. *Resources, Conservation and Recycling*, 125, 208–217.

Campbell, C. J. (2007). The general depletion picture. *The Association for the Study of Peak Oil and Gas Newsletter*, 76.

Campbell, C. J. (2015). Modelling oil and gas depletion. *The Oil Age*, 1(1), 9–33.

Campbell, C. J., & Wöstmann, A. (2013). *Campbell's atlas of oil and gas depletion*. Springer, Berlin, Germany.

Capra, F., & Luisi, P. (2016). *The systems way of life: An unifying vision*. Cambridge University Press, Cambridge, UK.

Carson, R. (1962). *Silent Spring*. Houghton Mifflin, Boston, Massachusetts, US.

Castells, M. (1996). *The information age: Economy, society and culture* (3 Vols.). Blackwell, Oxford, 1997, 1998.

Chen, A., Dietrich, K. N., Huo, X., & Ho, S.-M. (2010). Developmental neurotoxicants in e-waste: An emerging health concern. *Environmental Health Perspectives*, 119(4), 431–438.

Cordell, D., Drangert, J.-O., & White, S. (2009). The story of phosphorus: Global food security and food for thought. *Global Environmental Change*, 19(2), 292–305.

Cordell, D., Rosemarin, A., Schröder, J. J., & Smit, A. (2011). Towards global phosphorus security: A systems framework for phosphorus recovery and reuse options. *Chemosphere*, 84(6), 747–758.

Costanza, R., Kubiszewski, I., Giovannini, E., Lovins, H., McGlade, J., Pickett, K. E., . . . Wilkinson, R. (2014). Development: Time to leave GDP behind. *Nature News*, 505(7483), 283.

Credit Suisse. (2015). *Global wealth report 2015*. Credit Suisse Research Institute, Zurich, Switzerland.

Department of Business, Energy and Industrial Strategy (DBEIS). (2018). *Historical coal data*. Available online: www.gov.uk/government/organisations/department-for-business-energy-and-industrial-strategy (accessed May).

Drucker, P. (1968). *The age of discontinuity*. Harper & Row, New York.

Druckman, A., & Jackson, T. (2010). The bare necessities: How much household carbon do we really need? *Ecological Economics*, 69(9), 1794–1804.

Food Agriculture Organization (FAO). (2011). *Global food losses and food waste*. FAO, Rome, Italy.

Food and Agriculture Organization (FAO). (2015). *The state of food insecurity in the world – meeting the 2015 international hunger targets: Taking stock of uneven progress*. FAO, Rome, Italy.

Food and Agriculture Organization (FAO). (2019). *Soil erosion – the greatest challenge for sustainable soil management*. FAO, Rome, Italy.

Forrester, J. W. (1980). Information sources for modeling the national economy. *Journal of the American Statistical Association, 75*(371), 555–566.

Forrester, J. W. (1992). Policies, decisions and information sources for modeling. *European Journal of Operational Research, 59*(1), 42–63.

Forrester, J. W., Mass, N. J., & Ryan, C. J. (1976). The system dynamics national model: Understanding socio-economic behavior and policy alternatives. *Technological Forecasting and Social Change, 9*(1–2), 51–68.

Fraunhofer ISE. (2018). *Energy charts*. Available online: www.energy-charts.de/index.htm (accessed June 2018).

Freeman, R., Yearworth, M., & Preist, C. (2016). Revisiting Jevons' paradox with system dynamics: Systemic causes and potential cures. *Journal of Industrial Ecology, 20*(2), 341–353.

Graeber, D. (2014). *Debt: The first 5,000 years. 2011*. Melville House, Brooklyn, NY.

Hicks, C., Dietmar, R., & Eugster, M. (2005). The recycling and disposal of electrical and electronic waste in China – legislative and market responses. *Environmental Impact Assessment Review, 25*(5), 459–471.

Höök, M., Zittel, W., Schindler, J., & Aleklett, K. (2010). Global coal production outlooks based on a logistic model. *Fuel, 89*(11), 3546–3558. www.fao.org/docrep/014/mb060e/mb060e00.htm (accessed 9 May 2015).

Hubbert, M. K. (1956). *Nuclear energy and the fossil fuel*. Paper presented at the Drilling and production practice.

Hubbert, M. K. (1962). *Energy resources: A report to the committee on natural resources of the National Academy of Sciences-National Research Council* (No. PB-222401). National Academy of Sciences-National Research Council, Washington, DC, USA.

IEA (2018), *Global EV Outlook 2018: Towards cross-modal electrification*, IEA, Paris, https://doi.org/10.1787/9789264302365-en.

International Assessment of Agricultural knowledge, Science and Technology for Development (IAASTD). (2009). *Agriculture at the cross road – Global report*. IAASTD, Washington, DC.

International Atomic Energy Agency (IAEA). (2017). *Nuclear power reactors in the world, 2017 edition*. International Atomic Energy Agency, Vienna, Austria.

International Energy Agency (IEA). (2017a). *Statistics – renewables information 2017*. IEA, Paris.

International Energy Agency (IEA). (2017b). *Statistics – coal information 2017*. IEA, Paris.

International Energy Agency (IEA). (2017c). *Data and statistics*. Available online: www.iea.org/data-and-statistics (accessed September 2017).

International Fertilizer Industry Association (IFA). (2009). *Fertilizers, climate change and enhancing agricultural productivity sustainably*. IFA, Paris, France.

International Renewable Energy Agency (IRENA). (2018). *Data and statistics*. Available online: www.irena.org/Statistics (accessed June 2018).

International Service for the Acquisition of Agri-Biotech Applications (ISAAA). (2017). *Global status of commercialized biotech/GM crops in 2017: Biotech crop adoption surges as economic benefits accumulate in 22 years*. ISAAA Brief No. 53. ISAAA, Ithaca, NY.

International Union of Conservation of Nature. (2007). *IUCN red list of threatened species*. Available online: https://portals.iucn.org/library/node/9047.

IPCC. (1990). *Climate change: The IPCC scientific assessment*. Australian Government Publishing Service Canberra, Australia.

IPCC. (2014). Climate change 2014: Synthesis report. In R. Pachauri & L. Meyer (eds.), *Contribution of Working Groups I, II and III to the Fifth Assessment Report of the Intergovernmental Panel on Climate Change*. IPCC, Geneva, Switzerland, 151. ISBN: 978-92-9169-143-2.

Jackson, T. (2009). *Prosperity without growth: Economics for a finite planet*. Routledge, Oxford, UK.

Jackson, T. (2016). *Prosperity without growth: Foundations for the economy of tomorrow*. Routledge, Oxford, UK.

Jambeck, J. R., Geyer, R., Wilcox, C., Siegler, T. R., Perryman, M., Andrady, A., . . . Law, K. L. (2015). Plastic waste inputs from land into the ocean. *Science, 347*(6223), 768–771.

Jaramillo, F., & Destouni, G. (2015). Comment on 'Planetary boundaries: Guiding human development on a changing planet.' *Science, 348*(6240), 1217.

Jennings, D. E., Gruber, S. H., Franks, B. R., Kessel, S. T., & Robertson, A. L. (2008). Effects of large-scale anthropogenic development on juvenile lemon shark (Negaprion brevirostris) populations of Bimini, Bahamas. *Environmental Biology of Fishes, 83*(4), 369–377.

Jones, A., Allen, I., Silver, N., Cameron, C., Howarth, C., & Caldecott, B. (2013). *Resource constraints: Sharing a finite world, implications of limits to growth for the actuarial profession*. The Actuarial Profession, London and Anglia Ruskin University Global Sustainability Institute, Cambridge, UK.

Jones, A., & Phillips, A. (2016). Historic food production shocks: Quantifying the extremes. *Sustainability, 8*(5), 427.

Keen, S. (2017). *Can we avoid another financial crisis?* John Wiley & Sons, Hoboken, New Jersey, US.

Keynes, M. J. (1930). *Economic possibilities for our grandchildren*. Essays in Persuasion, New York: Norton & Co, New York US.

Keynes, J. M. (1936). *The general theory of employment, interest and money (1936)*. Kessinger Publishing, Whitefish Montana, US.

Krahmer, E. M., & Meadows, D. H. (unpublished). *Money flows – a beginner's guide to the international financial system and its role in sustainable – or unsustainable – development*. 1994 Annual Meeting of the Environmental Grantmakers Association.

Kummu, M., De Moel, H., Porkka, M., Siebert, S., Varis, O., & Ward, P. J. (2012). Lost food, wasted resources: Global food supply chain losses and their impacts on freshwater, cropland, and fertiliser use. *Science of the Total Environment, 438*, 477–489.

Ladou, J., & Lovegrove, S. (2008). Export of electronics equipment waste. *International Journal of Occupational and Environmental Health, 14*(1), 1–10.

Lewis, S. L., & Maslin, M. A. (2015). Defining the anthropocene. *Nature, 519*(7542), 171–180.

Liu, J., Chen, Y., Chao, S., Cao, H., Zhang, A., & Yang, Y. (2018). Emission control priority of PM2. 5-bound heavy metals in different seasons: A comprehensive analysis from health risk perspective. *Science of the Total Environment, 644*, 20–30.

Lloyd's Report. (2015). *Food system shock – the insurance impacts of acute disruption to global food supply*. Lloyd's Emerging Risk Report 2015, London.

Mancheri, N. A. (2015). World trade in rare earths, Chinese export restrictions, and implications. *Resources Policy, 46*, 262–271.

Marx, K. (1867). *Capital – a critique of political economy – volume I: The process of production of capital*. Progress Publishers, USSR, Moscow.

Marx, K. (1885). *Capital – a critique of political economy – volume II: The process of circulation of capital*. Progress Publishers, USSR, Moscow.

Marx, K. (1894). *Capital – a critique of political economy – volume III: The process of capitalist production as a whole*. International Publishers, New York.

Marx, K. (1905). *Theories of surplus-value volume IV of capital* (S. Ryazanskaya, Ed.). From Marx to Mao Digital Reprints, 2016.

Mass, N. J. (1975). *Generic feedback structures underlying economic fluctuations*. Massachusetts Institute of Technology, Cambridge, MA, US.

Maxton, G., & Randers, J. (2016). *Reinventing prosperity: Managing economic growth to reduce unemployment, inequality and climate change*. Greystone Books, Vancouver, Canada.

Meadows, D. L., Behrens, W. W., Meadows, D. H., Naill, R. F., Randers, J., & Zahn, E. (1974). *Dynamics of growth in a finite world*. Wright-Allen Press, Cambridge, MA.

Meadows, D. H., Meadows, D. L., Randers, J., & Behrens, J. (1972). *The limits to growth*; Universe Books, New York, NY, USA.

Meadows, D. H., Meadows, D. L., & Randers, J. (2003). *The limits to growth: The 30-year update*. Routledge, Oxford, UK.

Meadows, D. H., Richardson, J., & Bruckmann, G. (1982). *Groping in the dark: The first decade of global modelling*. John Wiley & Sons, Hoboken, New Jersey, US.

Mekonnen, M. M., & Hoekstra, A. Y. (2010). A global and high-resolution assessment of the green, blue and grey water footprint of wheat. *Hydrology and Earth System Sciences*, 14(7), 1259–1276.

Mekonnen, M. M., & Hoekstra, A. Y. (2011). *National water footprint accounts: The green blue and grey water footprint of production and consumption. Volume 1: Main report*. UNESCO-IHE Institute for Water Education, Delft, Netherlands.

NASA. (2019). *Data on carbon dioxide and temperature anomaly*. Available online: https://climate.nasa.gov/vital-signs/carbon-dioxide/ (accessed June 2019).

OECD, FAO. (2017). *OECD-FAO agricultural outlook 2017–2016 – special focus: South-East Asia*. Available online: http://dx.doi.org/10.1787/agr_outlook-2017-en. (accessed May 2018).

Pauli, G. (2017). *The third dimension 3D farming and 11 more unstoppable trends*. JJK Books, Santa Barbara, US.

Piketty, T. (2014). *Capital in the 21 century* (A. Goldhammer, trans.). Belknap Press, Harvard, MA, US.

Prior, T., Giurco, D., Mudd, G., Mason, L., & Behrisch, J. (2012). Resource depletion, peak minerals and the implications for sustainable resource management. *Global Environmental Change*, 22(3), 577–587.

Randers, J. (2012). *2052: A global forecast for the next forty years*. Chelsea Green Publishing, Vermont, US.

REN21. (2016). *Renewables 2016 global status report*. UNEP, Paris, France.

REN21. (2018). *Renewables 2018 global status report*. UNEP, Paris, France.

Ricardo, D. (1891). *Principles of political economy and taxation*. G. Bell Available online at https://socialsciences.mcmaster.ca/econ/ugcm/3ll3/ricardo/Principles.pdf

Rifkin, J. (2014). *The zero marginal cost society: The internet of things, the collaborative commons, and the eclipse of capitalism*. St. Martin's Press, New York, US.

Robin, M.-M. (2010). *The world according to Monsanto: Pollution, corruption, and the control of the world's food supply*. The New Press, New York, US.

Robinson, B. H. (2009). E-waste: An assessment of global production and environmental impacts. *Science of the Total Environment*, 408(2), 183–191.

Rockström, J., & Klum, M. (2012). *The human quest: Prospering within planetary boundaries*. Max Strom Publication, Stockholm, ISBN 10: 917126289X / ISBN 13: 9789171262899.

Rockstrom, J., Steffen, W., Noone, K., Persson, A., Chapin III, F. S., Lambin, E., . . . Schellnhuber, H. J. (2009). Planetary boundaries: Exploring the safe operating space for humanity. *Ecology and Society, 14*, 1–33.

Schwab, K. (2017). *The fourth industrial revolution.* Currency, Currency Penguin, UK.

Senge, P. M. (1978). *The system dynamics national model investment function: A comparison to the neoclassical investment function.* Massachusetts Institute of Technology, Cambridge, MA, US.

Shupler, M., Godwin, W., Frostad, J., Gustafson, P., Arku, R. E., & Brauer, M. (2018). Global estimation of exposure to fine particulate matter (PM2. 5) from household air pollution. *Environment International, 120*, 354–363.

Silver, N. (2017). *Finance, society and sustainability: How to make the financial system work for the economy, people and planet.* Springer, Berlin, Germany.

Smil, V. (2010). *Energy myths and realities.* AEI Press, Washington, DC.

Smith, A. (1776). *An inquiry into the nature and causes of the wealth of nations* (S. M. Soares, Ed.). Metalibri Digital Library. Available online at https://www.ibiblio.org/ml/libri/s/SmithA_WealthNations_p.pdf

Steffen, W., Richardson, K., Rockström, J., Cornell, S. E., Fetzer, I., Bennett, E. M., . . . De Wit, C. A. (2015). Planetary boundaries: Guiding human development on a changing planet. *Science, 347*(6223), 1259855.

Steffen, W., Rockström, J., Richardson, K., Lenton, T. M., Folke, C., Liverman, D., . . . Crucifix, M. (2018). Trajectories of the earth system in the anthropocene. *Proceedings of the National Academy of Sciences, 115*(33), 8252–8259.

Sterman, J. (1981). *The energy transition and the economy: A system dynamics approach* (2 Vols.). MIT Alfred P. Sloan School of Management, Cambridge, MA.

Sterman, J. (2000). *Business dynamics: Systems thinking and modeling for a complex world.* McGraw-Hill, New York, USA.

Stern, N. (2006). *Stern review on the economics of climate change, 2006.* Government of the United Kingdom, London.

Stiglitz, J. E. (2012). *The price of inequality: How today's divided society endangers our future.* W. W. Norton & Company, New York, US.

Stockholm Convention on Persistent Organic Pollutants (SCPOP). (2018). *History of the negotiations of the Stockholm convention.* Available online: http://chm.pops.int/The Convention/Overview/History/Overview/tabid/3549/Default.aspx (accessed May 2018).

Swain, J., & Mukherjee, I. (2007). *Fossil fuel use up again.* World-Watch Vital Signs, 36.

Towers Watson. (2014). *Global pension assets study 2014.* Available online: www.intermediachannel.it/wp-content/uploads/2014/02/Global-Pensions-Asset-Study-2014.pdf.

United Nations. (2019). *The sustainable development goals report 2019.* United Nations, Geneva, Switzerland.

United Nations Economic Commission for Europe (UNECE). (2016). *Towards cleaner air – scientific assessment report 2016.* UNECE, Geneva, Switzerland.

United Nations Population Division Report. *United Nations, department of economic and social affairs.* Available online: http://esa.un.org/unpd/wpp/unpp/panel_population.htm (accessed May 2018).

United States Department of Agriculture. (2018). *The twelve orders of soil taxonomy.* Available online: www.nrcs.usda.gov/wps/portal/nrcs/detail/soils/edu/?cid=nrcs142p2_053588 (accessed May 2018).

US Department of Energy (DOE). (2011, December). *Critical materials strategy.* DOE.

US Geological Survey. (2000). *Mineral commodity summaries 2000*. US Department of the Interior. Available online at https://www.usgs.gov/centers/nmic/mineral-commodity-summaries

US Geological Survey. (2001). *Mineral commodity summaries 2001*. US Department of the Interior. Available online at https://www.usgs.gov/centers/nmic/mineral-commodity-summaries

US Geological Survey. (2002). *Mineral commodity summaries 2002*. US Department of the Interior. Available online at https://www.usgs.gov/centers/nmic/mineral-commodity-summaries

US Geological Survey. (2003). *Mineral commodity summaries 2003*. US Department of the Interior. Available online at https://www.usgs.gov/centers/nmic/mineral-commodity-summaries

US Geological Survey. (2004). *Mineral commodity summaries 2004*. US Department of the Interior. Available online at https://www.usgs.gov/centers/nmic/mineral-commodity-summaries

US Geological Survey. (2005). *Mineral commodity summaries 2005*. US Department of the Interior. Available online at https://www.usgs.gov/centers/nmic/mineral-commodity-summaries

US Geological Survey. (2006). *Mineral commodity summaries 2006*. US Department of the Interior. Available online at https://www.usgs.gov/centers/nmic/mineral-commodity-summaries

US Geological Survey. (2007). *Mineral commodity summaries 2007*. US Department of the Interior. Available online at https://www.usgs.gov/centers/nmic/mineral-commodity-summaries

US Geological Survey. (2008). *Mineral commodity summaries 2008*. US Department of the Interior. Available online at https://www.usgs.gov/centers/nmic/mineral-commodity-summaries

US Geological Survey. (2009). *Mineral commodity summaries 2008*. US Department of the Interior. Available online at https://www.usgs.gov/centers/nmic/mineral-commodity-summaries

US Geological Survey. (2010). *Mineral commodity summaries 2010*. US Department of the Interior. Available online at https://www.usgs.gov/centers/nmic/mineral-commodity-summaries

US Geological Survey. (2011). *Mineral commodity summaries 2011*. US Department of the Interior. Available online at https://www.usgs.gov/centers/nmic/mineral-commodity-summaries

US Geological Survey. (2012). *Mineral commodity summaries 2012*. US Department of the Interior. Available online at https://www.usgs.gov/centers/nmic/mineral-commodity-summaries

US Geological Survey. (2013). *Mineral commodity summaries 2013*. US Department of the Interior. Available online at https://www.usgs.gov/centers/nmic/mineral-commodity-summaries

US Geological Survey. (2014). *Mineral commodity summaries 2014*. US Department of the Interior. Available online at https://www.usgs.gov/centers/nmic/mineral-commodity-summaries

US Geological Survey. (2015). *Mineral commodity summaries 2015*. US Department of the Interior. Available online at https://www.usgs.gov/centers/nmic/mineral-commodity-summaries

US Geological Survey. (2016). *Mineral commodity summaries 2016*. US Department of the Interior. Available online at https://www.usgs.gov/centers/nmic/mineral-commodity-summaries

US Geological Survey. (2017). *Mineral commodity summaries 2017*. US Department of the Interior. Available online at https://www.usgs.gov/centers/nmic/mineral-commodity-summaries

Wang, F., Zhou, Y., Meng, D., Han, M., & Jia, C. (2018). Heavy metal characteristics and health risk assessment of PM2. 5 in three residential homes during winter in Nanjing, China. *Building and Environment, 143*, 339–348.

Wijkman, A., & Rockström, J. (2013). *Bankrupting nature: Denying our planetary boundaries*. Routledge, Oxford, UK.

Willer, H., Lernoud, J., & Kemper, L. (2018). The world of organic agriculture 2018: Summary. In *The world of organic agriculture: Statistics and emerging trends 2018* (pp. 22–31). Research Institute of Organic Agriculture FiBL and IFOAM-Organics International.

World Bank Databank (WB). (2018). *Global economic monitoring database*. Available online: https://data.worldbank.org/ (accessed September 2017).

World Economic Forum (WEF), Ellen MacArthur Foundation and McKinsey & Company. (2016). *The new plastics economy – rethinking the future of plastics*. Available online: www.ellenmacarthurfoundation.org/publications.

World Energy Council (WEC). (2011). *Global transport scenarios 2050*. WEC, London.

World Resources Institute (WRI). (2014). *Creating a sustainable food future – a menu of solutions to sustainably feed more than 9 billion people by 2050*. World Resources Institute, Washington, DC.

World Trade Organization (WTO). (2017). *Annual report 2017*. Centre William Rappard, Geneva, Switzerland.

Wu, R., Zhong, L., Huang, X., Xu, H., Liu, S., Feng, B., . . . Wu, F. (2018). Temporal variations in ambient particulate matter reduction associated short-term mortality risks in Guangzhou, China: A time-series analysis (2006–2016). *Science of the Total Environment, 645*, 491–498.

Zhang, B., Huo, X., Xu, L., Cheng, Z., Cong, X., Lu, X., & Xu, X. (2017). Elevated lead levels from e-waste exposure are linked to decreased olfactory memory in children. *Environmental Pollution, 231*, 1112–1121.

Zhang, X., Yuan, Z., Li, W., Lau, A. K., Yu, J. Z., Fung, J. C., . . . Alfred, L. (2018). Eighteen-year trends of local and non-local impacts to ambient PM10 in Hong Kong based on chemical speciation and source apportionment. *Atmospheric Research, 214*, 1–9.

Part II

Economic Risk, Resources and Environment (ERRE) model

4 Economic thinking and system modelling

The previous chapter gave a snapshot on the use of system thinking and modelling of the world based on the top-down view characteristic of system dynamics. It highlighted the differences between the World3–03 model's scenarios, and the evolution of the state of the real world until present. In this chapter, we give further elucidation on the approach of complex system science in support of policy making, and introduce the methodology in use for the development of the Economic Risk, Resources and Environment (ERRE) model which is presented in this book.

For the purpose of this book, we define a 'complex system' as a set of elements mutually connected one to another that act towards a purpose and 'complex systems science' as the use of scientific approach to understand and study those systems. A useful classification of methodologies to address complex systems can be found in Mobus and Kalton (2015). Among those approaches they include:

- Social systems and economics (politics, governance, cultures)
- System dynamics (policy design)
- Network theory (interconnectivity and effect propagation)
- Information theory (effective messages, knowledge encoding, and communications)
- Cybernetics (error feedback and regulation)
- Psychology and neurobiology (brain architecture, behaviour adaptation, and learning)

With the term 'system policy science,' we refer here as the use of each of those approaches with the final aim of influencing policy making. Examples can be found in the literature (Keen 2011; Stermann 2000; Barabási 2013; Richardson 1991; Thaler and Ganser 2015). At the most fundamental level, they all make use of quantitative data and equations to develop models. However, depending on the purpose of the analysis and the research questions to be answered, every methodology can reveal gaps in understanding in comparison to the others. This section lists the predominant families and philosophies of modelling that are in use for influencing policy making today, describes their founding principles, and highlights overlaps between methodologies. The order in which these methods

DOI: 10.4324/9781315643182-6

are described was chosen to provide a structural understanding of the foundations of the modelling community.

Regardless of the preferences on techniques, and the modelling family to support policy making, it is important to first describe the role of economists, that have been the key professional figures aside from policy makers. Over the last 250 years, economics kept evolving as a science, while attempting to describe events happening in the real world. The next section describes the evolution of economic thinking, and it is placed as the foundation for describing the evolution of methodologies that follow in the chapter. These methodologies are:

1   Input-output analysis
2   Econometrics
3   Computable general equilibrium
4   Integrated assessment models
5   System dynamics
6   Agent-based modelling
7   Complex networks

Review of economic thought as base for system modelling

Today's economic theory is the result of a trial and error process of knowledge creation that has lasted at least 250 years. The classical theory represents the beginning of economics as a science, previously considered an outcome of political action (Toni and Bernardi 2009). Classical economics forms the foundation for economic thought today. It emerged from the assumption that free market, international trade and capitalism would positively impact human well-being over time as described in *The Wealth of Nations* (Smith 1776). Classical economics continuously developed with the first introduction on utilitarianism by Bentham (1789), the theory of international comparative advantage by David Ricardo (1891), and Marx (1867) findings on the limitations on free trade and capitalism in the creation of well-being for all classes in the society, among others.

Neoclassical economics emerged from the increased complexity of human society and the continuous elaboration of those theories during the second industrial revolution. Many of the neoclassical thinkers shaped the economy as we see it today. Walras (1877) was recognised as the father of the general equilibrium theory; Jevons (1871) is well known for his marginal theory on factor productivity explaining how improvements in technology efficiency could generate higher absolute consumption of resources via feedback effects; Pareto (1896), who, looking at income inequality curves, described the Pareto optimality theory within complex societies, more commonly known as 80/20 rule well used in managerial practices today; Schumpeter (1912) proposed the theory of destructive innovation and the role of entrepreneurs in economic development; and, focusing on government's role in free market economies, Keynes (1936) emerged as the father of the public economy. Other schools of thought of the time used to distinguish themselves from the mainstream because they did not share the same values and methodologies. Among those we find the school of Institutional Economics (Dewey 1910).

The great depression of 1929 increased pressure for developing national accounting systems. Among the major thinkers we find Simon Kuznet (1937), who proposed the GDP indicator as well as the well-known long-term growth theory described by the Kuznet curve. Research on international trade of the time was led by Wassily Leontief (1936) who proposed input-output tables as a mean for an accounting system to address and monitor the balance of import exports between firms, and subsequently among countries.

After the Bretton Woods Conference in 1944, Keynes' theories on the role of the public sector in managing international development took dominance, with neo-liberal thinking opposing in different ways. Among those we find Paul Samuelson (1956) who contributed formalising quantitative analysis of economic variables, and Milton Friedman (1956) with the Chicago School of Economics who represent the strongest institution in support of neo-liberals between 1950s and 1960s. One of the main contributions of the Chicago school was the quantitative theory of monetary growth as a key opposer to the Keynesian approach. In *The Methodology of Positive Economics*, Friedman (1953) lay down two of the most influential principles of today's economic theory: (i) the validity of any theory should be judged by its ability to predict and not at all by the reality of its assumptions and (ii) anytime two or more theories predict equally well, the simplest and the therefore more general is preferred. In other words, no matter how unrealistic models are, they should mainly be assessed by their mathematical ability to match aggregated data. Such an argument breaks the symmetry between prediction and explanation, thus legitimating the abstraction of the neoclassical school.

During those years, general equilibrium theory from Walras was formalised in mathematical terms by Arrow and Debreu (1956). In addition, growth theory was reinforced by the models of Solow (1956), and Modigliani and Miller (1958). The shift to neoclassical thinking as the leading economic paradigm to define policy consultancy was recorded in the early 1970s. Among the major events, US peak oil required the gold standard of the Bretton Woods to be substituted with the debt money system in the US, resulting in fluctuating exchange rates as we experience today. Due to the inability of the gold standard to be flexible enough to respond to changes in employment and growth in time of crisis, money creation was left unconstrained, supporting markets to adapt freely and efficiently to changes in economics.

Between the 1950s and 1970s three groups of thought that were opposed to the neoclassical thinking emerged: the post-Keynesian economists, the evolutionary economists and the ecological economists. Post-Keynesian (PK) economics focuses on the uneven growth rate of an economy or why it deviates from its long-term secular growth path as well as differences in growth rates between economies. The principles it relies on include (i) economies expand in the context of history, (ii) human expectations have significant effect on economic activity, (iii) institutions play an important role in shaping economic events, (iv) a focus on realism of systems rather than logic, and (v) the realisation that capitalism

creates inequality and classes that divide in the society. Among the major thinkers in this field we find Kalecki (1954), Kaldor (1957), Sraffa (1960), and Minsky (1957). In particular, Minsky is known for his research on the instability of
capitalism and in the financial system, concluding that a perfectly functioning
capitalist system would always lead to boom and bust dynamics and will somehow always lead to financial crashes (Minsky 1957). Kaldor (1957) focuses on
disequilibrium growth theory relying on increasing marginal returns in contrast
to Walras hypothesis. A synthesis of the PK approach can be found in Eichner
(1976, 1987), Eichner and Kregel (1975), Davidson (1981), and, more recently,
in Lavoie (2014).

Post-Keynesian economics share important assumptions with evolutionary economics that in turn draws from institutional economics (Radzicki 2003, 2005).
While neoclassical economics moved from the intellectual revolutions of Isaac
Newton, institutional and evolutionary economics draws their foundation from
the Darwinian evolutionary change theory (Hamilton 1953). To an institutional
economist there is no timeless, universal laws that exist in economics, and they
value policies based on understanding rather than prediction. They also believe
that cultural anthropology rather than physics provides the correct methodological foundation for economics, they rely on holism and emergent disequilibrium
processes as foundation of systems understanding, and believe that the power
of institutions play an important role in determining economic dynamics. The
opening of the Association for Evolutionary Economics welcomed institutional
economics contribution, which principles have formally been put together in
Gruchy et al. (1987).

The ecological economics community developed focusing on the environmental constraints as bounding systems to a growing economy. The criticism on
growth theory become obvious when seeing the world as a finite system, largely
driven by disequilibrium forces and reinforcing feedback loops (Costanza and
Daly 1992). Their main question remains whether or not the supply of ecological factors, such as finite resources in the world and the finite sinks for waste,
will ultimately limit economic activity. Ecological economists rely on a holistic
approach to problem solving (Costanza and King 1999), and share an evolutionary perspective of system irreversibility according to the second principle
of thermodynamics. The main argument is the social need of a paradigm shift
towards a steady state economy to avoid ecosystems damages or even collapse
of the economy, looking towards sustainable well-being for all in the indefinite
long term. Among the major exponent we find Herman Daly (1974) and Robert
Costanza (1991).

The presence of positive loops in the economy was also recognised by Krugman
(1979) while researching international trade between nations. The Krugman's
view demonstrated that two initially equivalent economies, because of their possibility to specialise, would still improve their chance to increase productivity
thus legitimating trade between the two. In traditional thinking, inequality was
driven by a difference among countries that would create the inability of some
countries to compete in the international market. In Krugman's view, a positive

feedback mechanism depending on specialisation and productivity growth would unbalance the international landscape of the economy, creating path dependencies which would rather cut some countries out of competition, and in turn generating unsustainable growth. Lucas (1972) formalised the theory of rational expectations of economic agents, thus assuming that economic agents could make optimal decisions based on rational expectations of their markets. In addition, the Lucas' critique on macroeconomic theory (Lucas 1976) made an important contribution to economic thinking, stating that macro-economic dynamics should be driven by microeconomic assumptions and not the other way around.

Rational expectation theory was challenged by cognitive economists since the 1950s and today's field of behavioural economics. Behavioural economics combines insights, theory, and methods from economics and psychology to identify how human decisions systematically deviate from neoclassical formulation, and explain the implication of less-than-optimal decision making from the economy as a whole. In the words of Herbert Simon (1957, p. 198): "the capacity of the human mind in formulating and solving complex problems is very small compared with the size of the problem whose solution is required for objectively rational behaviour in the real world or even for a reasonable approximation to such objective rationality." According to Thaler and Ganser (2015), despite Simon being awarded the Nobel Prize, he had little impact on the economic thinking of the time since bounded rationality was considered a true but 'unimportant' concept. In other words, if imperfect, adaptive, evolutionary processes of firms and households that survive and prosper are those who have acted as if they had made their decisions rationally, the process becomes irrelevant and thus can be ignored (Alchian 1950).

Simon's theory was expanded in Tversky and Kahneman (1974) demonstrating how the empirical evidence was overwhelming on how non-rational agents survive, thus influencing economic behaviour. According to Mullainathan and Thaler (2000) behavioural economics identified three main factors that cause human decision making to deviate from global rationality: (i) bounded rationality, that reflects the limited cognitive abilities and knowledge that constrains human problem solving, (ii) bounded will power, that explains why people sometimes make choices that are not in their long-term interest; and (iii) bounded self-interest, which explains why people often sacrifice their self-interest to help others. In fact, in order to break the assumption of perfect rationality it is sufficient to have one single decision maker that acts against the market (Keen 2017). In reality, in order to formulate meaningful predictive models, it should rely on the way the majority of economic agents behave, and these are generally not acting optimally (Thaler and Ganser 2015).

In the meantime growth theory kept developing, while ecological aspects of growth were evidently embedded in macroeconomic theory. Building on top of Lucas' work, Romer (1990) proposed endogenous growth theory, describing the innovation process within countries to determine growth. The theory recognises the presence of reinforcing feedback loops in an economy, with focus on those based on learning and research and development. Possible spillover effects towards the rest of the society are determinants of long-term growth. In the meantime, evidence was demonstrating the interaction between growth and climate change, as well as feedback from climate to economy (IPCC 1990). Nordhaus (1992) developed one of the first synthesis for climate economic models, with negative feedback from climate to growth. This work is one of the pioneers for integrated assessment models to study global emissions-economy interaction. Nordhaus (1992) kept his estimate of climate effects on the economy very conservative, far from the assessment provided today in the IPCC (2014), and was criticised thereafter for not respecting the principle of conservation of mass that should be common for models based on physical flows (Fiddaman 1997).

The major single event demonstrating the erroneous nature of the mainstream approach to economics was the global financial crisis in 2007–2008. It demonstrated the need to research alternative approaches that could break the fallacies of neoclassical thinking (Keen 2017; Lavoie 2014). Despite economic systems being recognised as complex systems since the beginning of time, the efforts of complex system science to understand the nature of economic behaviour has never been as strong (Cincotti and Raberto 2012a; Battiston et al. 2012, 2016b; Caldarelli et al. 2010; Gallegati and Kirman 2012; Monasterolo and Raberto 2018). Thus, Minsky's theories on the inherent instability of the capitalist system received attention again supported by the work of Keen (2013), and the continuous push for a change in the economic system towards meaning, sustainability, and prosperity entered the global policy agenda with Jackson (2009, 2016).

Based on this economic review, the next section describes and compares modelling methods in use today, and places the foundations for the approach adopted to develop the ERRE model.

Economic modelling methods

Based on the review of economic theory in the previous section, this section compares the modelling approaches that have been in use by the scientific community since early 1900. This review starts with the econometric and input-output tables, pioneers of quantitative economic analysis during 1930s, thus responding to the economic stability needs after the great recession of 1929. Computable general equilibrium (CGE) modelling is presented as the mainstream tool for policy assessment today. CGE is based on the assumed existence of general equilibrium stationary points in the economy, as well as optimal behaviour of economic agents. Integrated assessment models are then introduced relying on the integration of energy and climate modelling on the CGE framework, using similar basic assumptions. Despite widely being used for policy making today, these are widely criticised and considered misleading for the weaknesses they carry in their founding assumptions (Pindyck 2013).

System dynamics is then presented as an answer to those limitations. System dynamics (SD) modelling applied to the economy has been widely ignored or misused in economic policy (Radzicki 2005). SD models tend to neglect optimum and equilibrium hypotheses while relying on bounded rationality, non-linear behaviour, and disequilibrium at their core foundation. In SD, economic theory is substituted with knowledge of management practices as observed in businesses and large organisations (Lyneis 1980; Forrester 1961). Then, techniques that exploit improved computing power (complex networks and agent based modelling) are explored.

Input-output tables and analysis

Input-output tables represent an effective and simple instrument for analysing economic systems, as well as laying out the cross industry accounting structure of an economy. The origin of input-output analysis go back to the physiocrat Quesnay (1758) when he proposed the *Tableau of Economique* in order to manage land to define agricultural policy to distribute resources between workers and landowners. However, it is with Wassily Leontief (1936) that the first input-output analysis was proposed as a mean of structuring national accounting systems. Today, input-output tables are well established instruments often placed at the base of other modelling methodologies to address dynamic problems (Barker et al. 1987; Dixon and Jorgenson 2012; Pollitt et al. 2015).

At a given point in time, an input-output table of an economy consists of the collection of bilateral production flows from each industry to all the other industries as well as towards consumer sectors. In the resulting matrix, productive sectors are represented as rows, while the columns report the same sectors and their consumption, as well as the final consumers. Each cell of the table reports the amount of output generated by the sector in the row that is supplied to the sector reported as a column at a given time. The values can be expressed both in physical and monetary units. Reading the total amount of input to each sector gives an overview of the cost of production, while reading the sum of the rows, gives the estimate of the market potential for that sector (Leontief 1936).

The strength of the input-output table that generates value for the other modelling paradigms is in its accounting structure of the entire economy (Meadows 1980). The weakness is that data collected in different countries or in different industries can be reported in different ways, or can be lacking in information. Important assumptions have to be taken in order to assure the obtained matrix is bilateral (Timmer et al. 2015). As a result, discrepancies can arise in developing input-output tables from different communities analysing the same bilateral flows, generating sources of disagreement in the analysis.

After the bilateral matrix is complete it can be used for analysis purposes supporting strategic planning at industrial and national levels. Interestingly, one of the implications of input-output analysis is the extensive use of the so-called Leontief production function, initially proposed by Jevons and others before (Mishra 2007). The analysis consists of assuming an increase in demand of one particular item, tracing back the demand for all other items connected to that particular industry. For example, if the final consumption of one commodity A would rise by 10%, it is assumed that the demand for all industries producing the input for the industry producing commodity A would rise linearly by 10%.

Given that all those industries might require commodity A as input for production, the result would be an even larger increase in the demand for commodity A, and so on. Thus, the initial table can be rewritten addressing the amount of effective input necessary for each industry given an expected rise in demand. In order to address the independence of input factors in the economy the resulting matrix is inverted, thus reporting the total (direct and indirect) outputs from the row industry that is required for each unit of production from the column industry. This table can be used to assess the amount of total production of all intermediate and final goods that would be needed to satisfy any desired final demands. Reading down the column would give an idea of the industry's expenses on inputs (Meadows 1980).

Input-output analysis is based on the assumption of (i) linearity between input and output, (ii) continuity of system behaviour towards the future, and (iii) instantaneous adjustment of productive factors to obtain production. Therefore, its applicability remains limited for short-term analysis and giving an indication of the very next step in business and national planning. When looking at the aggregate level of the entire economy, or even the world level, in which available data can take years to be measured and reported, an input-output analysis would be worthless. As a result, most uses of input-output analysis for policy purposes are combined with other methodologies (Barker 1987; Trefler and Zhu 2010; Johnson and Noguera 2012; Koopman et al. 2014).

Timmer et al. (2016) developed an input output table of the world, addressing the state of those systems from the year 1999 to 2014. The world input-output tables have been formulated on the basis of supply and use tables, national input-output tables of planned economies, and UN Comtrade database (Dietzenbacher et al. 2013). Focusing on both national and international money, products and services flows, the world input-output table can be considered as a set of national input-output tables that are connected to each other via bilateral trade flows. WIOD (2019) released a version of its database in 2016 with data updated till 2014. It covers 43 countries, including all 28 EU countries, 15 other countries including US and BRICS, and aggregated the rest of the world as a single region. It provides details for 55 industries, including agriculture, mining, construction, utilities, 14 manufacturing industries, telecom, finance, business services, personal services, eight trade and transport services industries and three public services industries. Another of these approaches has been launched by Chatham House who provide the Resource Trade database (Chatham House 2019) for addressing the bilateral consistency between trade flows. Starting from UN Comtrade, and comparing its consistency with various sources, a bilateral trade matrix in both monetary and real values has been proposed for the majority of mineral, energy, and food commodities traded worldwide.

Dietzenbacher et al. (2013) warns against the use of the input-output tables without a consistent check on the methodologies used to generate the bilateral matrix. In particular, a database (the table) should not be seen as better than other databases, but rather suitable or not suitable for answering certain research questions. However, their rigorous assessment of input-output data makes it a valuable methodology in support of other modelling methods as demonstrated by the numerous application of econometric and computable general equilibrium models that place input-output tables at their core, and as described in the following section.

Econometrics

The modern meaning of the term 'econometrics' is due to the foundation of the journal *Econometrica* (Frisch 1933). Econometrics indicates the union of economic statistics, application of mathematics to economics, and validation of economic theory. It is worth noting that each of those applied separately from the others cannot be directly related to econometrics. Geweke et al. (2008) places econometrics as the branch of economics that aims at giving empirical content to economic relations for testing economic theories, forecasting, decision making, and for ex-post decision/policy evaluation.

Today, econometrics can be divided in two sub-fields: (i) econometric theory that concerns with tools, methods, and the study of properties of econometric approach, and (ii) applied econometrics that describes the development of quantitative economic models, and their application to validate theories (Hansen 2016). Therefore, econometrics supports developing the mathematical foundations that can feed the other economic modelling approaches, while supporting qualitative assessment of those theories using quantitative methods. Considering econometrics strongly focuses on explanation of possible future events, and that real validation of models can be truly recognised when those events happen in that future, it results that econometricians are subjected to trial and error improvement of their models over time. Among the most famous statisticians we find Box (1976). In Box and Draper (1987, p. 424) it is emphasised the humility of the econometric approach with the argument "All models are wrong, some of them are useful."

The dominating characteristics of the paradigm is its reliance on statistical verification of model structures and parameters, thus forcing modellers to firmly tie their work to statistical observations of real-world systems (Hansen 2016). In other words, each element in an econometric model must be observable, and sufficient historical data should exist to permit precise estimation of the relationships to other variables.

The most common statistical tools used for the estimation of parameters and structural relationships are ordinary least square (OLS) regression (Wooldridge 2006) and co-integration techniques (Granger 1986). These are methods that postulate general relationships between historic observations based on linear regression, coherence analysis between time series, analysis of variance, and develop measures for evaluating how good that fit is with various statistical tests (for example the R coefficient of correlation, the Fisher test, or the Durbin-Watson test). The required uniqueness of the solution requires relationships to be monotonic (Mercure et al. 2018). As a result, most relationships in an econometric model are linear or log-linear (Oxford Economics 2017). The resulting set of equations and structural parameters, is allowed to simulate for the next time step beyond observables, allowing testing of exogenous hypothesis based on important policy levers. The assumption an econometric forecast is built upon is that the underlying causal mechanism will hold in form, strength, or stochastic properties, from the historical time series to the simulated forecast (Meadows 1980).

Structural causation is one of the key concerns of econometric models. In particular, combining economic theoretical consistency with statistical evidence, few variables are assumed as being the root cause for the behaviour of others, thus allowing for the estimation of the coefficients that would inform the model forecast. When two-way causation appears, it can be either represented by means of simultaneous equations – that means solving the system of equations in order to assure a one way causation with time lag – or vector autoregression – that assures the variation of each explanatory variable does not co-vary with other variables, as well as being strictly independent from the error term.

Some econometric models can contain feedback through lagged endogenous variables, even though these will present a minimal part of the model itself. If variables that are required for developing a model do not exist, these are normally substituted with other variables used as a proxy by means of indirect hypothesis about the correlation with observed variables. Such an approach creates, in the long run, the pressures to improve and expand databases all over the world (IMF 2018; WB 2018).

The majority of econometricians are interested in questions that require precise, short-term values of economic variables. They find most of the concepts they need in the traditional economic theory, and even when looking at other disciplines their bias remain strictly linked to the social sciences. Despite many econometric models being dynamic, they often accept assumptions of optimum and equilibrium rather than dynamic phenomena (Oxford Economics 2017). The relatively short-term focus of many economic problems allows econometricians to neglect long-term feedback processes that are characteristics of other disciplines, such as geology, earth science, and physics, and allows them to define conclusions within the boundary of economic systems. Those effects can be considered as exogenous, and can be constrained with ranges that can be considered linear in the time frame of interest. In fact, in the very short time frame, the numerical coefficients calculated with linear approximation are likely to be still valid. Those model results, being very effective at addressing precise information about systems, are difficult to use in order to address policy changes of their entire system in the longer term, or in circumstances that have not been historically observed (Meadows 1980).

A great example of successful econometric model is given by Cambridge Econometrics and the E3ME work (Mercure et al. 2018; Pollitt and Barker 2009; Pollitt and Mercure 2018). The model is based on more than 40 years' experience in the econometric and policy consultancy field (Barker 1987). E3ME is an E3 (economy energy, and environment) model of the economy that employs a post-Keynesian structure of the economy rooted on supply-demand equality, and relies on input-output tables for the disaggregation of the economy in countries, and each country in industrial sectors. The model definition starts with the definition of demand, and uses it as the foundation for the definition of the relationships of the other variables of the economy. In order to define these relationships it employs co-integration analysis on historical time series to reveal relationships among variables, and uses linear regression for the definition of its structural equations. The dynamic behaviour of the system emerges from the iteration of the input-output table at the core of the system, thus generating growth over time. In so doing, the model is an out-of-equilibrium model, relying on historical data to extrapolate behaviours for the future (Cambridge Econometrics 2019). Recent developments of the E3ME proposed the integration of the money creation and distribution structure in line with post-Keynesian theory (Pollitt and Mercure 2018).

One of the application of the E3ME framework is for global analysis using the E3MG (Global) model. E3MG splits the world into 59 global regions, and 43 sectors in each region. An input-output table is employed thus linking all sectors via bilateral trade equations. Historical data cover the period 1970 to present and simulate 35 years into the future. Being aware of the limitation of the econometric approach for climate impact assessments, Mercure et al. (2018) integrates E3ME with FTT (Future Technology Transformation) and GENIE (Grid Enabled Integrated Earth) system model. These latter two are models of resources and technology choice that are highly non-linear models led by cost curves, depletion dynamics, and non-linear technology development, and an integrated carbon-cycle and climate simulation model (Holden et al. 2018). This allows the structuring of feedbacks between economy, energy, and climate system, thus allowing for a comprehensive analysis of economic policy using econometric method.

Despite E3ME representing one of the best examples of econometric analysis of economic systems, today policy makers employ the computable general equilibrium models and integrated assessment models for policy assessment. These are described in the following section.

Computable general equilibrium

The family of general equilibrium models relies on the assumption of market equilibrium as initially defined in Walras (1877), and mathematically formulated in Arrow and Debreu (1954). According to Dixon et al. (2013), the CGEM represents the ideal practical framework to address policy relevant questions while comparing effects of policy change based on a base line scenario. Shoven and Whalley (1992) assert that, despite the weaknesses of the methodology, there is no clearly superior alternative model available to policy makers to base their decisions upon. These include investment efficiency and distributional consequences of alternative policy changes, thus asserting that CGEMs provide normative content to address policy change in today's world. This book aims at demonstrating the weakness of such an argument in favour of disequilibrium methodologies such as system dynamics as proposed in the following sections. However, in this section we shall describe the functioning of CGE models and some examples of their applicability.

In its initial formulation, Arrow (1951) proposed two theorems of welfare economics stating that any competitive equilibrium is Pareto optimal, and that any Pareto optimal allocation can be supported as a competitive equilibrium with appropriate lump-sum transfers. The direct implication of these theorems is that government interventions in the economy that distorts relative commodity prices will have a social cost when analysed using a general equilibrium model. Policies such as taxes or tariffs will move the economy away from a Pareto optimal allocation therefore causing a long-term suboptimal loss to the economy (Shoven and Whalley 1992). Such a hypothesis would prevent governmental intervention while supporting the free market view on today's world.

The first CGEM for policy intervention was published by Johansen (1960), as a 22 sector study of economic growth for the Norwegian economy. In its standard formulation, as described in Arrow and Hahn (1971) and proposed in Shoven and Whalley (1992, p. 1, 9, 10), a CGEM is described as follows:

> A general equilibrium model of an economy can be best understood as one in which there are markets for each of N commodities, and consistent optimization occurs as part of equilibrium. The number of consumers in the model is specified. Each consumer has an initial endowment of the N commodities and a set of preferences, resulting in demand functions for each commodity. Market demands are the sum of each consumer's demands. Commodity markets depend on all prices, and are continuous, non-negative, homogeneous of degree zero, and satisfy Walras's law (i.e. that at any set of prices, the total value of consumer expenditures equals consumer incomes). On the production side, technology is described by either constant-return-to-scale production functions and the linear homogeneity of profits in prices (i.e. doubling all prices doubles money profits) imply that only relative prices are of any significance in such a model. The absolute price level has no impact on the equilibrium outcome. . . . In a pure exchange economy, consumers have endowments and demand functions (usually derived from utility maximization).

Thus, equilibrium is characterised by a set of prices and levels of production in each industry such that market demand equals supply for all commodities. In other words, equilibrium prices always clear markets. Walras' law remains a basic check on any equilibrium model. A system model that would violate such a law would represent some human error and incorrect distortion (Shoven and Whalley 1992). Velupillai (2005) argues that such a standard CGE formulation is neither computable not constructive in the strict mathematical sense. Considering that applying general equilibrium analysis to policy issues involves computing equilibria, the underlying assumption is that an equilibrium exists for a given model before attempting to compute it. Because they do not provide a technique to prove why the equilibria can be determined, the approach remains non-constructive. As a result existence per se has no policy significance, constraining the models in comparative policy use.

In the neoclassical school of thought which characterises CGEM, monetary policies have no effect on the real economy. As firms and consumers optimise resources instantaneously, a quantitative easing policy would generate a proportional increase in prices of all commodities, thus having no effect on the real economy. This is in contrast to the way reality works, as demonstrated with the money injection to the economy after the 2007–2008 financial crisis (Barker 2009). As a result the post-Keynesian school of thought, which aims at modelling the real effects on investments due to bounded rationality of agents, inclusive of the effect of endogenous money creation, provide a more realistic explanation on the functioning of real world systems (Pollitt and Mercure 2018).

Over time, more sophisticated general equilibrium models have been developed, named as Partial Equilibrium (PE) models and Dynamic Stochastic General Equilibrium (DSGE) models. PE consist in developing market models separated by industry, relying on micro-economic foundations in which firms equilibrate supply and demand as well optimise decision making via equilibrium prices. DSGE assume stochastic variability of parameters and equations in the long-term equilibrium of models, implying possibilities of market imperfections and risk assessment analysis. An example of partial equilibrium and stochastic analysis is given in FAPRI-UK model (Moss et al. 2011). FAPRI-UK, is a UK agricultural commodity model, disaggregating the regions of England, Wales, Scotland, and Northern Ireland, and covering dairy, beef, sheep, pigs, poultry, wheat, barley, oats, rapeseed, and biofuel sectors. The model is integrated in the FAPRI partial equilibrium model developed at the University of Missouri and generally used for policy assessment for US and Europe (Binfield et al. 2001).

CGE models assume the presence of dynamic equations generating the system behaviour, that is stocks (accumulations in the system such as capital) and flows (change in stocks such as capital investment and discard) are in use. Feedback mechanisms are introduced to handle stocks in the system. Despite their ability for accounting for feedbacks, the CGEM remain largely driven by linear relationships, where parameter specification is carried out using deterministic calibration, often to one year's data. Neglecting the long-term feedback processes emerging from the geophysical and environmental spheres, CGEMs assume that technology improvements will always assure capacity can respond to demand efficiently no matter resource constraints. In CGEMs agents are perfectly rational, therefore assuming all information about the market are available to decision makers at the time of taking decisions. Assuming optimality in decision making, they remain limited in answering questions in a consistent way with reality.

CGE historically rely on the neoclassical production function as formulated by Cobb-Douglas in 1928 (Mishra 2007). A more sophisticated version of the Cobb-Douglas was proposed in Arrow et al. (1961), as the Constant Elasticity of Substitution (CES) production function. CES allows for the inclusion of additional factors in the formulation for production beyond capital and labour, while assuring mathematical consistency. Further application of the CES involve Sato (1967), who proposed a generalisation of CES with a generic number of input factors, and Papageorgiou and Saam (2008), providing examples of a nested production function, which uses CES function as an input to another production function.

Dixon and Jorgenson (2013) explains the use of CGEM in most of its aspects. For example, the Monash style modelling approach (which is founded on Johansen (1960)) employs a single country model which uses bilateral input-output tables for the disaggregation in economic sectors. It employs linear relationships and optimisation to solve the model. Dixon is aware of the limitation and poor performance of CGEM and DSGE in forecasting. He argues that the most important characteristics for a modeller is the ability to communicate results effectively, thus laying down a methodology in four steps to better address clients' needs. In the Monash style, models are initialised on one single data point, and historical events are applied as exogenous inputs to the simulation in order to make the model to match historical data. The historical explanation is then decomposed among the factors influencing variables of interest with exogenous variables. Thus the simulation is used to perform a base run scenario, and multiple policies in the future are applied to allow clients to feel the effect of their policies, and support their decision making.

The output of the Monash model, as well as any model in general, are strongly dependent on the assumption of the input-output tables it relies on. Monash type models lay the foundation for the construction of the GTAP (Global Trade Analysis Project) which stands as a multi-decade investment for the construction of a input-output database of the world, extending the data as much as could be assessed. The aim of GTAP was to develop an input-output database to support the development of multiple modelling efforts. GTAP is not just a reconciled database bilateral trade flows for 113 countries, but also a collection of trade tariffs and preferences for trading between those countries (Hertel 2013).

Among the users of GTAP in the CGEM community we find GEM-E3 (Capros et al. 2013). GEM-E3 is a multiregional, multi-sectorial model of the world economy extensively used as a tool for policy analysis and impact assessment for the European Union. Its purpose is to model the economy, energy system, and GHG emissions. It accounts for 38 regions and 31 sectors interlinked via bilateral trade flows, using GTAP and UN Comtrade databases. Perfect competition between sectors is assumed as well as equilibrium unemployment. The production sectors optimise decisions and employ a CES production function for the generation of output. Energy resources are disaggregated between coal, gas and oil, and corresponding emissions and atmospheric pollutants are calculated. As in the standard approach, comparison with historical data is not considered. The model is initialised at the latest numerical data available, allowing the model to simulate towards the future. The use of GEM-E3 is normally simulated in line with other models in use at the European Commission, ranging from partial equilibrium (e.g. Primes) to integrated assessment models (e.g GAINS) as described in NTUA (2014). Each model covers a different part of the policy question, and provides output data as input to the other models in order to provide a final picture on policies of interest.

CGEM are largely criticised for their basic assumptions and low ability to predict future scenarios. As a result Oxford Economics (2017) provides an hybrid econometric-CGEM approach to overcome some of those limitations. In Oxford Economics (2017) co-integration is used as an instrument to define long-term relationships between variables, and uses those in order to define the structural coefficients of these relationships. The modular structure of the model is reflected in the input-output tables it gathers from private data, representing the world economy by interlinking 46 countries in detail, six regional blocks (OPEC, Eastern Europe, Africa, Latin America, rest of OECD, rest of the world) and the eurozone. The general equilibrium of the model adapts to exogenous time series, including population growth, total factor productivity and capital growth accumulation. The resulting econometric relationships obtained with a mix between vector autoregression and linear regression, form a backbone of the system to extrapolate short term (six months to a few years) into the future. These are coupled with economic general equilibrium theory to define long-term dynamics of the system towards the desired equilibrium. The model employs the Taylor rule to control interest rate, Phillips curve for the modelling of inflation, and opt for a Cobb-Douglas as a production function to link assets to supply. The final result is a model which allows the testing of short-term policy (Keynesian school) and market shocks (e.g. oil price spike), that would create short-term bumps that will return to the long-term equilibrium.

Despite the criticisms of CGEMs, their narrative tend to be more positive for policy makers, thus receiving more attention in the consultancy process. Today CGEM are taught in economics schools all over the world, thus reinforcing their dominance even further. The major world scale event revealing the weaknesses of those models was the financial crisis of 2007–2008. While CGEM were the main tool to support policy consultancy, the financial crisis revealed that the complexity of the real world was far beyond their potential.

Before presenting the system dynamics model as a potential solution to some of CGEM weaknesses, the next section explores the integrated assessment models, still based on neoclassical assumptions while embedding energy and climate in the economic equation, thus being an approximation for closing the feedback loop from environment to economy.

Integrated assessment models

Current integrated assessment models (IAM) are the result of the scientific effort to describe the interaction between human development and the natural environment in the last 50 years. The first IAMs emerged from the inclusion of carbon emissions in the energy models of 1970s and 1980s based on the neoclassical general equilibrium theory. Their input to economic modelling was to close the feedback loop from emissions to the economy using an uncertain damage function (Nordhaus 2013). The IPCC represents the greatest effort of IAM community in consulting policy making today, and represent the scientific consensus (or dispute) towards mitigation and adaptation of global society to climate change (IPCC 2014). Despite criticisms, their greatest success has been the exploration of possible paths for the abatement of carbon emissions in the attempt to slow down climate change.

IAMs aim at integrating the knowledge from different domains in the same framework. They include the geophysical system (resource depletion such as fossil fuels and phosphorus), land management (land use change and erosion), hydrology (water flow and scarcity), carbon cycles, ocean and atmospheric pollution, renewable energy and resources (fish stocks and over exploitation), political science, game theory, and economics. Differently from all domains emerging from the physical sciences, IAM provide monetary terms to variables such as capital assets and prices, thus shaping the framework necessary to apply and compare environmental policy (such as subsidies, carbon taxes and trade regulations) in the standard of CGEMs. The analysis must include capital, emissions, concentration, change in natural system, and natural systems impact back to the economy thus closing the loop. In simple words, the basic analysis consists in weighting the social costs of decreasing anthropogenic climate change against the damage caused by its effects (PBL 2014).

IPCC (2019) interrogated IAMs to assess the possible path the economy should take to increase their likelihood of remaining under 1.5 degrees Celsius, which is considered a threshold to dynamically activate natural processes that would unbalance planetary systems farther away from the Holocene (Steffen et al. 2018). Human activities are estimated to have increased global average atmospheric temperature to +1.0 degree Celsius from pre-industrial levels, and the current path of economic growth is on the trajectory to increase +2°C by 2030 and probably plus 3–4°C degrees by 2050. Unfortunately, the actions proposed in IPCC (2019) are unlikely to be met by the current proposed actions of governments.

Most IAM modellers (as system dynamicists do) have to deal with a trade-off between transparency of results and deep analysis to address policy questions (PBL 2014). A result based on a simple model useful for communication purposes, remain poorly formulated and lack sufficient detail to investigate important aspects of natural systems. In contrast, large and detailed models, developed to address the system detail at climate, land, or resource levels, remain often impenetrable to be modified by anyone who has not directly participated in the modelling process (PBL 2014; Nordhaus 2013). Detailed models are necessary because natural systems are complex. Still, data gathering remains an important limitation of those models and availability of public datasets for natural systems is lacking. That is why improvements in monitoring technologies are in demand in every IPCC report since 1990 (PBL 2014; IPCC 1990, 2014).

For example, the DICE (Dynamic Integrated Climate Economy) model was developed for the purpose of simplicity and communication of results. DICE is a neoclassical general equilibrium model of economic growth, which uses a longer time frame for simulating the effects (assumed non-linear but limited) of climate change. The initial version was composed of four endogenous stock variables, i.e. Capital, CO_2 in the atmosphere, Atmosphere and Upper Ocean Temperature, Deep Ocean Temperature. The dynamics of growth were driven exogenously by population and total factor productivity, both inputs in a Cobb-Douglas production function for the determination of economic output. This version has been updated over the years still maintaining the simplicity and small dimension, with the majority of changes reflecting the estimation of parameters and nature of equations rather than in size (Nordhaus 2008, 2017). The same model has been used as a regionalisation effort in the RICE (Regional Integrated Climate Economy) model, including 12 regions in order to test the results of non-cooperative games from countries on climate change among others. For a precise description of the model and its equations it is possible to consult the material published over the years (Nordhaus 1992, 2008, 2013, 2017). For the scope of this text we shall focus on the central node of the model, that is the climate damage function and its effect on the output. Eq. 4.1 shows the calculation of the output available $P(t)$ in the DICE model:

Eq. 4.1 – Damage function and production in DICE

$$P(t) = \pi(t) \times CB(K, L) \times (1 - SC(t)) \times \frac{1}{1 + \chi(t)}$$

Where $\pi(t)$ is an exogenous technology factor, $CB(K, L)$ is the Cobb-Douglas formulation of output, taking capital and population as input factors, $SC(t)$ is the social cost of carbon, and $\frac{1}{1 + \chi(t)}$ is the damage function. The important aspect is that both social cost of carbon and the damage function, have the effects of reducing output, allowing the user to simulate different input parameters depending on their estimates. Whereas $SC(t)$ is a non-linear function of relative GHG emission bounded at 1, $\chi(t)$ is a non-linear function (normally quadratic) of atmospheric and upper ocean temperature change. This equation can be tested by adding the effect of carbon concentration in the atmosphere and sea level rise in a similar way. DICE 1992 simulates from 1965 to the year 2300 with a base estimate of damage function influencing negatively GDP reaching minus 4% of output when atmospheric temperature exceeds +5°C.

On the other hand, a good example of a large model is the IMAGE 3.0 (Van Vuuren et al. 2015). Started in the 1980s as a globally aggregated model focused on carbon cycle and economy interlinkages, IMAGE is one of the first integrated assessment models (Van Vuuren et al. 2015). The model has been updated in great detail over the years (currently available in the third version), and used for policy assessment in many contexts, including IPCC (2014), UNEP (2007), OECD (2008, 2012), and IAASTD (2009). In order to maintain high complexity while at the same time assuring quality of results and sustainability of the modelling process over four decades, IMAGE relies of various research groups each responsible for the maintenance of specific components of the model. Each component can be seen as a stand-alone model itself, sometimes developed based on the aggregation of models of the past (Hildenrink et al. 2008). The model maintains the economy as relatively simplified, and includes important non-linear details in terms of modelling of agricultural systems, energy systems, and carbon cycles.

In particular, the model maintains population and technology change as well as preferences for resource consumption as exogenous. These inputs generate agricultural system and energy system demand, whose effects are captured by the MAGNET (partial equilibrium model of agriculture) and TIMER (optimal equilibrium energy depletion and carbon emissions model). MAGNET's outputs are inputs for TEM, which is a land use and land use change module to capture the shifts in land patterns. TIMER feeds into MAGICC to account for the carbon cycle and the interaction between atmosphere and oceans. Both MAGICC and TEM feeds into LPJ and IMAGE-N, which are designed to capture the impacts of agriculture shifts on the biosphere of land systems. The entire system feeds into GISMO (Global Integrated Sustainability Model) whose objective is to quantify the impacts of ecosystem services on human development. In Hildenrink et al. (2008), GISMO is described as the integration between two economic models that are based on partial equilibrium (International Futures – IF) and CGEM input-output tables (Dynamic Applied Regional Trade – DART). Despite the majority of modules of IMAGE 3.0 being highly non-linear, the core of the economy still remains neoclassical in nature while modelling optimal behaviours of their agents.

One of the major strengths of the IMAGE model is its spatial resolution in presenting its scenarios. Image 3.0 divides the world system in 26 regions based on their natural characteristics and quality of data. For each region, local data are also considered for land use, land cover, water treatment, and associated biophysical processes using grid modelling. Data consider 5×5 arcminutes (i.e. 10 square kilometres at the equator) for land use change, and 30×30 arcminutes for water treatment, carbon cycles, and plant growth (Van Vuuren et al. 2015). Data can be found in different websites such as FAOSTAT (2019) (land use change), University of Maryland (2019) (forest management), and NASA (2019) (population). In addition, linear algorithms based on the IPAT (Impact, Population, Affluence, Technology) and Kaya Identity (IPCC 2014) formulations have been developed to transform economic and carbon emission simulations at the level of regional aggregate scale to the spatial grid (Van Vuuren et al. 2007). This transformation allows the assessment of simulation runs in terms of local scale grids to identify areas at higher risk of climate change.

Whatever is the level of granularity, most IAMs follow similar underlying assumptions which are treated as weaknesses of the community. Most results from the IPCC work are obtained from optimisation models that, in line with CGEM, assume agents can optimise decisions based on perfect information (Nordhaus 2013). As a result, every response of an IAM model to policy inputs would generate a quick adaptation of input factors for production, and assume that economies would respond effectively and fast to every policy input. As a result, IAMs output tend to be more positive than the way reality could behave, neglecting information delays and feedback processes influencing decision making. In fact, despite the purpose of IAMs being normative, their structure implies nothing more than a descriptive theory of systems. For example, simulations that aim at representing carbon taxes (or social cost of carbon) and their effects on the environment-economy nexus, can be seen as no more than indicative.

Another major critique of IAMs is based on treatment of discount rates (Fiddaman 1997). Discount rates describe the willingness of the present generation to account for the well-being of future generations at the time they take decisions. Considering that climate change has major implications for the long-term future, every positive discount rate would assume a reduction in the welfare of future generations. This is a particularly dangerous assumption when analysing fat-tail event distribution and possible catastrophic consequences of climate change. Whereas certain exogenous variables can be framed between finite higher and lower levels of uncertainty (so-called thin-tailed distributions, including the pace of economic growth, change in technology factors, and the potential for renewable energy growth), a fat-tail indicates the possible consequences of very low probability events that can generate high negative impact for society. Fat-tail distribution are important for the analysis of risk and system resilience, including climate extreme events (Lloyd 2015), droughts (IPCC 2012), and interactions between ocean and climate (Steffen et al. 2018). These type of shocks, that society is not designed to respond to, can generate unexpected behaviours with difficulty for planning responsive actions to mitigate them. Most importantly, fat-tail distribution events rise in likelihood with the increase of temperature (IPCC 2012). As a result, accounting for positive discount rates would not just treat future generations asymmetrically from present ones but decrease their ability to deal with higher risks in comparison to today's world.

Today, integrated assessment models are largely dominant in supporting policy relevant climate questions in the IPCC report (2014). Other examples include RAINS (Kelly 2006), PAGE (Hope 2011), REMIND (Luderer et al. 2015), LEAP (Heaps 2008), MESSAGE (Rečka 2013), POLES (Keramidas et al. 2017), GLOBIOM and MIRAGE (Valin et al. 2013). These models tend to overlap each other in terms of scope, therefore requiring model comparison before being used for policy recommendation (IPCC 2014). In addition, considering they often share similar basic assumptions in terms of optimality and formulation of equations, various models tend to find agreement among themselves, making little practical utility of the comparison processes, if not to assure politicians that scientific community found consensus before taking action.

Due to these uncertain fundamental assumptions, IAMs have largely been discredited as reliable forecasting tools. For example, Pindyck (2013) argues that the assumptions and weaknesses of IAM make their policy analysis completely useless. IAM projections create a perception of knowledge and precision for stakeholders, despite that perception being illusory and misleading. In fact, Janse et al. (2015) argues that IAMs should never be used to forecast the future, but mainly to explore possible scenarios based on given policy inputs. In particular, no data exist today for the precise estimation of a damage function from climate to economy, and climate effects are assumed to have effects over longer time horizons than have been recorded yet. This is also why IAMs are employed mostly for very long-term scenarios, being simulated with time steps between one and five years, with time horizon of one century or more.

The next section aims at describing system dynamics as a possible approach that can respond to CGEM and IAM limitations while expanding their scope and improving their performances.

System dynamics

In its traditional form, system dynamics can be described as a pragmatic managerial approach to complex social systems. Differently from the previously described modelling methods, system dynamics does not rely on any specific theory of systems at its core. Rather, the professional system dynamicist approaches problems based on a few principles that can be summarised as follows:

1   The purpose of the model (the question to be answered) is the main determinant of the content of that model.
2   Holistic is the perspective in use to define the system boundaries around the model purpose. The modellers observe the system from the top, far enough away to allow approximating discrete events with flows of decisions thus justifying the continuous time modelling approach.
3   The system behaviour is dependent on the endogenous structure of the system. This places feedback loops at the core of the analysis. A feedback loop is a closed path between accumulations processes (described with stocks and flows), whose strength is modelled using non-linear relationships. Important to note that at least one stock must be present in each feedback loop.
4   Reinforcing (generating disequilibrium) and balancing (seeking equilibrium) feedback loops are the only two major forces generating dynamics in a system model.
5   Decision making has to be represented as it is, not as it should be. Thus decisions are placed at the core of feedback systems, and based on the principle of bounded rationality and non-linear decision rules that describe cognitive capabilities and behaviours of agents. Discovery of the decision rules people actually use requires empirical work, including field observation of decision making behaviour.
6   The presence of delays (both physical and information) in the system can significantly influence behaviour, thus these have to be carefully represented.
7   The model must be conform to physical laws such as the second principle of thermodynamics, and assure all structures remain consistent with real possibilities.
8   The solution to problems prioritises the definition of general rules which would allow the system to achieve the desired dynamic performance in the indefinite long term. As a result, the activity of using the model to match historical data on the point-to-point basis for the purpose of forecasting is seen as secondary, if not a waste of time. System dynamics seek tipping

points in the system and shifts in feedback loop dominance that would drastically change the trajectory of its variables from one behavioural pattern to
another.

9   Because of non-linearities, models cannot be solved analytically, but rather
by mean of simulation. System models are mostly used to assess scenarios, in
search of high leverage points that would have the power to change system
behaviours.

Mathematically, a system dynamics model is a set of non-linear differential equations solved in continuous time. Feedbacks are influences from one state variable
to a change in other state variables. Richardson (1991) presents a historical view
of the study of the feedback concept in the social sciences way before 'system
dynamics' was conceived. He shows the hidden contribution of feedback thinking in the theories of the major economists of the past, including Malthus, Smith,
Marx, and Keynes. For example, Adam Smith's idea of supply-demand formulation, and the presence of an invisible hand that equilibrates markets based on
such a relationship, is nothing more than a balancing feedback loop. Richardson
(1991) highlights how control engineering, mathematics, econometric, biology, cybernetics, and computer science made formal use of feedback concepts
since the late 17th century, and shows how social sciences formalised the use of
feedback between the 1930s and 1950s (Wiener 1948; Ashby 1956; Von Bertalanffy 1950; Kalecki 1935; Kaldor 1940; Phillips 1950; Goodwin 1951). However,
because of limited computing power, scientists used to rely on analytical solutions
of systems, thus assuming linearity and a relatively small size of models.

The first paper describing the method of 'system dynamics' was a critique to the
economic modelling approach and theory (Forrester 1957). Based on the experience in control engineering and servo-mechanics matured during World War
II, the advances in computing power, and the work in management consulting
at MIT, Forrester hired three electrical engineers to set up the field. A major difference to previous methods was the need of an infographic approach to visually
represent stocks and flows in the computer, therefore favouring system thinking
while modelling (the first example is the Dynamo compiler). With emphasis on
non-linear relationships that characterise industrial systems and decision making, models could be solved with simulation only. In turn, models could become
larger than the state-of-the-art of the time (Forrester 1961).

The approach was initially formalised as 'industrial dynamics' in Forrester
(1958), and subsequently in the first textbook of the field (Forrester 1961). The
following decade was characterised by a continuous application of the method
to corporate problems, leading to Principles of Systems (Forrester 1968). It did
not take long to realise that the method was suitable for complex problems far
beyond the boundaries of industrial systems. In 1969, Forrester was commissioned
to study the long-term 'urban dynamics' in the city of Boston (Forrester 1969).
In 1970s, Forrester attracted the attention of the Club of Rome while engaged
in approaching the 'Predicament of Mankind' (CoR 1970), leading to the first
world computer model, *World2*, as published in *World Dynamics* (Forrester 1971).

The major finding of the time was that social systems can have counterintuitive behaviours (Forrester 1971). While most economists and policy makers tend to make decisions based on short-term goals (one to five years), these decisions can have important negative implications for the longer term (beyond a ten-year time horizon). Recognising the scope of applications towards the social sciences, he renamed the approach 'system dynamics' (Forrester 1971). The first publication making use of *System Dynamics* as a field was the *Limits to Growth* work (Meadows et al. 1972) presenting the results of global modelling advances using the *World3* model.

Despite the tremendous impact of this line of work on global society, it was far from accepted by the economics profession. Probably the harshest criticism came from William Nordhaus. Although apparently misinterpreting many of its assumptions and fundamentals, Nordhaus (1973) provides a detailed review of *World2*. The major criticisms included (i) the lack of accounting for exponential growing technology that could remove all world limits, (ii) the 'too severe' damage functions in pollution and land systems sectors, and (iii) the assumption of resource limits as a possible scenario within 2100. Nordhaus (1973) removed those constraints, thus allowing the model to keep growing prosperously. 'System dynamics' was judged as a methodology far from a scientific method, highlighting the lack of communication abilities of its results and the insensitive approach of Forrester in proposing policies that were against humanity (Nordhaus 1973). The years that followed are characterised by a vivid contrast with the economic profession. The IIASA symposium in the 1976 is an example (Sterman 1988). The results of these frictions have been fully synthesised in Meadows et al. (1982) and Meadows (1980), with the basic conclusion that most economists disagree with the paradigm of 'system dynamics' because it was different from their own. Greenberg et al. (1976, p. 142) classified system dynamicists of the time as "boy economists." Casti (1981, pp. 418–419) in "some outrages in the name of modelling" categorised system dynamics as a "toy" and referred to it as "an illustration of the type of senile maundering and immature egocentricity . . . [that] infests the social sciences like maggots of an organically-grown peach."

Concerned with the global pressures highlighted in World Dynamics, Forrester, with colleagues at the MIT, spent most of 1970s formalising a System Dynamics National Model (SDNM) of the US economy (Forrester et al. 1976; Forrester 1977, 1979, 1980). Various PhD students were involved in the development and improvement of its structure based on the comparison with neoclassical economic theory (Mass 1975; Senge 1978; Sterman 1981). In particular, Mass (1975) analysed short to medium term business cycles emerging from inventory-labour force interaction and the presence of perception and material delays in the system. Mass (1975) also demonstrated that random perturbation can activate business cycles perpetually in the long term. Senge (1978) focuses on the SDNM investment function and comparison with the neoclassical formulation. The SDNM assumes the presence of inventories, backlogs, stock of capital, and delivery delays among others. If a series of equilibrium assumptions in the parameters controlling the investment function are made, it could be reduced to the standard neoclassical formulation. Senge used econometric techniques to estimate the parameters of the SDNM investment function and compared it with historical data in various industrial sectors of the US economy, resulting in an improvement in fitting historical data. Sterman (1981) was interested in long-term energy transition from conventional (cheap) non-renewable resources to non-conventional (more expensive) resources after US peak oil. Sterman's purpose was to run scenarios for the analysis of energy price overshoot and oscillation dynamics, and relative effects on inflation and stability in the US economy in the long term. Sterman removed short-term structures from the national model, and embedded various characteristics of the energy system, including capital retrofit of energy efficiency, resource depletion, and pricing strategies from the OPEC sector (this model will be described in detail in the following chapter).

Forrester et al. (1976), Forrester (1977), and Forrester (1979) provide preliminary findings and overarching structures of the model. The SDNM aimed at describing in detail the dynamics of an economy, composed of public sector, banks, firms, households. Firms are represented with a similar structure, and can be adapted with its parameters to replicate the dynamics of different services, manufacturing, and agricultural firms, including knowledge production and insurance sectors. The firms were represented in both real and financial aspects, having knowledge of prices at the core of the system. Each firm was responsible for the management of its own debt, that could be both long and short term, labour force, and capital investments adapted to meet demand generated endogenously by the other sectors, managing short-term vacancy creation and modelling in detail the short-term dynamics of backlog of orders of capital. On the side of supplier an inventory was introduced, so capturing the famous cyclical short-term dynamics generated by interaction of labour and inventory internal to each firm. The banking system was represented in detail in the model, and was responsible for providing interest bearing money to the productive sectors, as well as to the household sector. The interest rate dynamics were linked with an overall inflation level measured by the GNP deflator.

In 1980, Forrester was asked to provide an overview of the SDNM to open a discussion with the economic community. Forrester (1980) presents the overarching method in developing the SDNM. Emphasis was given on the mental information base of policy and decision makers within business, showing little attention on statistical estimation of parameters. Equations were not presented since the model was a work in progress at its 67th version. Debate was put forward in Zellner (1980) and Stolwijk (1980). According to Zellner (1980), the innovations Forrester claimed to bring to economic modelling were actually already covered in the available body of knowledge. Econometricians used to combine their mathematics with an institutional economic approach, thus estimating parameters based on human judgement. In addition, Bayesian statistics was already well developed to analyse uncertainty of output and human factors in decision making. The lack of point-to-point prediction as well as no presence of any stochastic component to the simulation was seen as a weaknesses in the Forrester's approach. Stolwijk (1980) criticised the SDNM from the perspective of the servo-mechanic engineers that find it difficult to get consistent conclusions for policy consultancy the larger the models become. Forrester (1980) replied saying that an alternative approach on system analysis based on simulation and non-linearities was useful to open new ways towards the future. He rejected the need to use stochastic components in simulation, rather suggesting to shift the focus on the deterministic system structure of the national economy to design systems with improved performance. Most important he rejected the option of providing point-to-point forecast since that type of prediction is actually not possible in general, as demonstrated analytically in Forrester (1961, Appendix K, L and N).

Although the relationship with the economic profession was far from smooth, the strength of 'system dynamics' was evident in the approach to complex corporate problems and project management in general. Roberts (1978) provides collections of papers showing market penetration of new products, research and development studies, marketing policies, aging management, and resource management, whereas Lyneis (1980) shows examples of labour stability, financial control and accounting, dynamics of price setting, and responses. This allowed Meadows (1980) to start distinguishing modelling projects between 'general understanding' and 'implementation stage' projects. The first, are process oriented, generally involving clients in the modelling process, aiming at influencing their mental models. These tend to remain limited in size, and aim at defining new concepts and theories (e.g. World3). The second are product oriented, that is they aim at developing models that can be used again and again to define specific predictions with the aim of giving precise instructions. As a result, they tend to be large, rarely involving clients in the modelling process, and impenetrable to non-experts (e.g. Roberts 1978; Lyneis 1980). The following two decades represented the golden age of system dynamics, in which the community expanded in many directions and consolidated the work of Forrester in various fields. Many more applications to corporate issues and more are presented in Sterman (2000), whereas Ford (1999) demonstrates the ability of the method to modelling environment and ecological issues. Other examples are proposed in Morecroft (2007) and Warren (2008) looking at organisation behaviours and strategy consulting.

Formal statistical methods and algorithms were developed and embedded in new software. Among the major ones we find Peterson and Schweppe (1974), Peterson (1975), Peterson (1980) who, based on electronic engineering techniques and Kalman filtering (as previously applied by Schweppe 1964, 1965a, 1965b, 1973), developed the FIMLOF (Full Information Maximum Likelihood via Optimal Filtering) algorithm. FIMLOF is particularly useful for model calibration to historical data, and parameter estimation for policy optimisation thus making a step forward to respond to criticism from the economic profession. However, a match between historical data and model simulation remained a very limited test from a system dynamicist' point of view who prioritises the understanding of the system before all. Senge and Forrester (1980) provide a list of 21 tests for supporting confidence in building models, including extreme scenario, sensitivity analysis, and family type tests. In Sterman (2000), emphasis is given to the econometric method, suggesting that the integration of formal econometric techniques to estimate parameters can be of value to the field of 'system dynamics.' He also proposes Theil Statistics (Theil 1966) as a statistical econometric test in addition to the other proposed in Senge and Forrester (1980), to support empirical evidence on the distribution of error between models and data.

Barlas (1989, 1990, 1996) discusses the meaning of model validity, formal aspect of model validation, epistemologies of science behind the possibility of validation, and the relationship between the model purpose and the ability of that model to fulfil that purpose. Sterman (2002) summarises the same concept arguing that the word 'validation' should be removed from the vocabulary of the modellers. Since all models remain abstractions from the real world, infinitely different from the world the aim at representing, expecting a sense of 'validity' or 'truth' of that model, is a non-sense. Because "all models are wrong," models should rather be evaluated for their ability of being useful in solving issues. We all use models (mental or formal) to solve problems, and we rely on the best model we can to deal with that problem. Even when models fail to help in solving problems, 'system dynamics' focuses on the modelling process as an activity to elucidate problems and build confidence and skills in the modellers. Thus (even if partially) all models are useful (Forrester 1985).

In the meantime, a major effort was spent in defining boundaries and overlaps between 'system dynamics' and economic theory. Morecroft (1983, 1985) made explicit the overlap existing between traditional system dynamics method in modelling corporations and the concepts of information theory, bounded rationality and decision rules as more common in the Carnegie School of Economics. The Carnegie School has roots on the work of Herbert Simon (1957), Cyert and March (1963), and others who pioneered the study of human decision making within firms. Their work shows how the behaviour of complex organisations can be understood only by taking into account the psychological and cognitive limitations of human factors. In line with 'system dynamics,' feedback was placed as the foundation for adaptive behaviour within organisations. Sterman (2000) describes five of the modelling fundamentals of decision making in system dynamics as follows:

1   The inputs to all decision rules in models must be restricted to information actually available to the real decision makers (the so-called Baker criterion, who served US President Nixon as senator in the 1970s).
2   The decision rules and rules of thumb in a model should conform to managerial practice.
3   Desired and actual conditions should be distinguished in the model.
4   Decision rules should be reproduce realistic behaviour under extreme conditions.
5   Equilibrium should not be assumed. Equilibrium and stability may or may not emerge from the interaction of the elements of the system.

Simon (1957, 1979, 1982) advocated that ideal perfect rationality is not possible in human organisation, who are rather characterised by decision rules based on a small amount of information that could better be described as intended rationality. Morecroft (1983) focused on the flow of information within firms, the quantity and quality of information that is under judgement to managers while taking decisions, their ability to process and measure data from the firm, their decision rules and rules of thumb necessary to make decisions based on those information, and the functional form and department division within firms. Similar studies include Sterman (1989), Paich and Sterman (1993), Diehl and Sterman (1995); Kampmann and Sterman (1998). Differently from Forrester, these studies adopted relatively small models keeping synthesis and transparency at the core of their success.

Over the years, Forrester kept working on the economic synthesis based using his SDNM, which full structures has never been published to date (Forrester 1992, 2003). Further work had been carried out with Hynes (1987) conducting his PhD to improve the structure of the interest rate formulation and monetary policy of the national model. In the last publication on the SDNM, Forrester (2003, pp. 29–30) argued:

> The system dynamics economic model has been developed over several decades. Initially it was to have been much larger than the current simplified model, which now has somewhat over 200 levels and 1400 auxiliary equations. . . . Some people have questioned the need for such a large and complex model. Indeed, many applications in education and in policy design might be better handled with a collection of far simpler models. But I have felt that it is important to have a model in which the major modes of economic behaviours exist simultaneously for examining how the different modes may interact. . . . After the larger system is understood, it will be desirable to revert to much simpler special purpose models.

The aim was to develop a national economic theory that could be adapted to any country. The key advantages of the model were to provide a high degree of modularity that could be targeted to different economies and sectors, and could deal with different levels of aggregation. However, given the comparison purpose to neoclassical theory, the SDNM always shared some neoclassical and standard economic formulations (Radzicki 2011).

Radzicki focused his entire career on demonstrating overlaps between 'system dynamics' method and the economic modelling approach that did not share neoclassical assumptions. This process culminated with Radzicki (2005), in which he suggests that post-Keynesian, institutional economics, and system dynamics should join forces as three strands of heterodox evolutionary economic modelling approaches. In fact they share the same basic principles around pragmatism and attempt to model the real world as it is, in contrast to neoclassical approach that relies on an atomistic Newtonian view of the economy and logic consistency based on economic theory. Radzicki (1990) lays down the characteristics of institutional economics (Dewey 1910) arguing these are the same of the 'system dynamics.' Institutional economists employ pattern modelling approach to investigate system, that is acting as detectives who find clues that allow them to develop general structures and theories to form the culture of the field. This is exactly the same of 'system dynamics,' in developing archetypes (fundamental models structures) emerging from the modelling consultancy process. The main difference between the two schools is that Institutional economists lack formal modelling procedures in their analysis toolkit, making system dynamics a perfect companion.

In Radzicki and Sterman (1994) foundation has been placed between 'system dynamics' and evolutionary economic modelling. In particular, evolutionary economic models tend to possess one or more of the following traits: (i) path dependency, (ii) the ability to self-organise, (iii) multiple equilibria, (iv) chaotic behaviour. The typical 'floating goal' structure as well as the non-linear feedback processes which are characteristic of 'system dynamics' tend alone to determine all four characteristics of evolutionary modelling. In addition, Forrester (1985) emphasises the importance of the modelling process, as a never ending process that should always be assessed for the ability of models to replicate reality. This process is evolutionary by definition. Radzicki (2003) provides a synthesis of system dynamics within the overall economic modelling map, and lays the historical connections between system dynamics, evolutionary economics, and post-Keynesian economics, among others. Some of the sharing principles of the three schools: (i) the economy is in a perpetual state of disequilibrium, (ii) use of a holistic approach, (iii) focus on historical analysis of events, (iv) reliance on behavioural and bounded rationality of agents, and (v) macro-economic behaviour is the result of micro-economic structures.

Radzicki (2005) provides an overview of his post-Keynesian-institutionalist-system dynamics model. The model focuses on a national economy and is composed of eight sectors structured in systems. At the top level the economy is composed of fiscal authority, monetary authority, banking, households, mega-corp, competitive firms, underground economy, and environment. Each of those sectors is structured in sub-components. For example, mega-corp is composed of capital producing, energy producing, goods producing, and service producing sub-sectors, whereas the competitive firms contains raw materials producing and agricultural production sub-sectors. Each of these sub-sectors is described by various sub-components themselves. For example, the goods producing sub-sector of the mega-corp consists of 13 interacting units including: capital, R&D, productivity, inventory-backlog, long & short run expected orders, pricing & inflation, and accounting strategy. The entire model neglects neoclassical formulations, rather using the principles outlined in post-Keynesian, institutionalist and evolutionary economics literature.

On the side of ecological modelling, ecological economists supported the use of system dynamics as mean to embed social development within ecological constraints (Costanza 1989) since the pioneering work of the Limits to Growth (Meadows et al. 1972, 1974). Ecological economics embed the detailed study of energy systems, energy transition, and depletion as proposed by Naill (1977, 1992). Examples of system dynamics models applied to the ecological question can be found in Ford (1999), Ruth (1995), Jørgensen (1994), Maxwell and Costanza (1994), Bergh and Straaten (1994), Bergh (1993), Costanza and Daly (1992), and Bergh and Nijkamp (1991). Interesting work on this line of thought has also been performed recently by Sverdrup et al. (2018) on the basis of the *World3* model, proposing a larger and integrated global resource model named *World6*.

The continuous work of the community was found of value for organisations beyond the mere modelling application. Senge (1990) relies on his expertise in the field to define managerial practices to support organisation in developing better performance. He did so relying on the concept of archetype. The archetypes are recognisable structures of systems often common between different systems that can be of use in different situations. Senge listed nine major archetypes: (i) balancing process with delays, (ii) limits to growth, (iii) shifting the burden, (iv) eroding goals, (v) escalation, (vi) success to the successful, (vii) tragedy of the commons, (viii) fixes that fail, and (ix) growth and underinvestment. These archetypes are generally applied to all sorts of ecological, evolutionary and growth models that can be formalised in the computer. An important application in the social science, was the adoption of group model development or participatory modelling. For example, Videira et al. (2012) relies on use of causal loop diagrams and shared understanding of stakeholders to develop mind maps and shared understanding between participants. However, this process rarely involves the development of formal computer models behind it. This allows participants to decision making to develop a shared vision, and inform decisions together. Often this approach is aligned to toolkits of management practices, such as information systems and data tools.

Another example of a successful modelling organisation supporting national planning and participatory modelling is represented by the Millennium Institute developing their Threshold21 model (Millennium Institute 2007; Bassi et al. 2011; Millennium Institute 2014). Taking example from the limits to growth and integrating the thinking of more mainstream economic models, they developed an integrated assessment model of a generic nation at the threshold between developing and underdeveloped world. The model has been improved and applied to policy relevant questions one country at a time since 1990s, accounting for more than 40 consultancy projects worldwide (Millennium Institute 2007). The Threshold 21 model is used to allow policy makers to see the difference between short-term budgetary allocation decisions on the medium- to long-term time horizon at the national level. A global version of the model has been proposed in Bassi et al. (2011) to show how green policy investments can help lead the world towards sustainable development. Similarly to the SDNM, Threshold21 shares some fundamental structure and equations in line with neoclassical thinking (Radzicki 2011).

In addition, 'system dynamics' models and theories can be made more effective via the creation of learning environments to embrace the needs of policy makers and managers in receiving lessons from models. This approach was named 'flight simulator' with the first applications in Fish Banks (Meadows et al. 1993), People Express (Sterman and Morrison 1988), and Oil Producers Microworld (1988). Today, flight simulators are used to dispel complex problems in simple scenarios that can allow policy makers to compare the expectations on their policy outcomes (mental models) to the actual results of their policies. For example, Sterman et al. (2013) describes the application of flight simulators linked to role playing negotiation games to support learning. Sterman et al. (2012) and Sterman (2014) describe C-Roads and En-Roads models and the approach used to support decision makers in favour of global climate and energy transition. Also recent work of the Millennium Institute aiming at presenting the interaction between economic growth and the sustainable development goals (SDGs) relies on flight simulators to allow users to assess synergies and divergences in their policies in the attempt to achieve the SDGs (Millennium Institute 2018).

As it is possible to see from this review, 'system dynamics' can both be seen as a disciplined modelling method based on specific managerial principles, an integration method for stakeholder engagement and management practices, as well as a translation tool from economic theory into stocks, flows and feedback loops. When the methodology is exploited at its root foundations, system dynamics can be used to model structures that include ecological, evolutionary, neoclassical, behavioural, and post-Keynesian economics. As a result it can replicate the assumption and structures of every integrated assessment and general equilibrium model developed to date, and has the potential to expand on those (Radzicki 2011).

Probably the major weakness of the method is that it is easy for a 'system dynamics' modeller to embed assumptions from economic schools without realising they are using them. The Indian fable of the Blind Men and the Matter of the Elephant might allow to better explain what 'system dynamics' really is (Meadows 2008). Each man, approaching the elephant from a different position (school of thought) can conclude they are touching something different, easily generating disagreement among each other. However, it is just by appreciating the big picture, that an answer can be given. A system dynamics model can easily include assumptions that can generate contrast between school of thoughts, or rather embedding theories that overlap to some schools while neglecting others. As a result, comparing system dynamics and economic modelling cannot be made a priory relying on the system dynamics method. It is rather the responsibility of the modellers to describe where their assumptions overlap with economic thinking and where they do not, thus demonstrating the formal consistency of their theories in an integrated economic-environment framework, in the attempt to create deeper understanding of systems.

The ERRE model is one of those which integrates economic thought into a system dynamics framework. Before presenting its characteristics in detail, it is important to conclude in this chapter by describing the modelling method emerging from increased computing power and a recognition of complexity in the economy.

Modelling exploiting increased computing power and interconnectivity

As shown in the previous section, although 'system dynamics' could provide benefits over integrated assessment and computable general equilibrium models, the latter two, aligned with econometric study of new data, remain the main paradigm in policy consultancy since the 1950s. It was the financial crisis in 2007–2008 that gave evidence to policy makers of their weakness, thus looking for new solutions in the computer and social science disciplines that embrace complexity at their deepest level. This section briefly describes agent-based modelling and complex networks.

Agent-based modelling

Agent-based models (ABM) study macro-behaviour of systems as an emergent property from the micro-structure characterised by interacting heterogenous agents. According to Tesfatsion (2001), agents are modelled with very simple rules and behaviours. However, while interacting among each other and with the surrounding environment, disequilibrium behaviours of the entire system and complex macrostructures can emerge. As a result, ABM can be employed to assess how global regularities can emerge from the interaction between individual agents without any need of a top-down control, and determine which alternative structures can be influenced from the bottom-up perspective. The power of ABM allows problems that go far beyond what economic theories are accustomed to, to be approached. For example, Natalini et al. (2015) introduced a new indicator for political fragility in order to measure political risk linked with resource scarcity. In Natalini et al. (2019) an analysis is proposed in order to show how political fragility can spread in global trade networks based on this new metric. Today, the use of agent based modelling found application in fields that require complex system thinking including biology, medicine, social sciences, economics, and finance.

One of the key areas of research with ABM involves the understanding of learning processes and adaptation, following an Evolutionary type modelling philosophy. Among the leading authors in the field we find Bryan Arthur, who directed the Santa Fe Institute of Complexity research. Arthur (1994) presents the formal computer model demonstration of the theories of Kaldor (1957) on increasing marginal returns, showing how technology led clusters of firms (e.g. Silicon Valley) can run increasing marginal returns on their investments, thus supporting the view of reinforcing loop dominance against the general equilibrium economy led perspective. ABMs can be highly path dependent models. Arthur (1994), Arthur et al. (1996), Arthur (1999) demonstrated how relatively small changes in the policy can lead to qualitatively different outcomes in technology diffusion in the long run, leading to technology 'lock-in.' As a result, one single technology can come to dominate a particular sector, with highly non-linear outcomes. Interestingly, the first publication of Arthur on the topic was supported by Kenneth Arrow, the Nobel economist who formalised in mathematical terms the Walras theorem of general equilibrium in Arrow and Debreu (1954). As a foreword to Arthur (1994, pp. IX–X), Arrow writes:

> The concept of increasing returns has had a long but uneasy presence in economic analysis. The opening chapters of Adam Smith's 'Wealth of Nations' put great emphasis on increasing returns to explain both specialization and economic growth. Yet the object to study moves quickly to a competitive system and a cost-of-production theory of value, which cannot be made rigorous except by assuming constant returns. . . . Increasing returns have more than one source. Arthur shows how the transmission of information based on experience may serve as a reinforcement for early leading positions and so act in a manner parallel to more standard forms of increasing returns. . . . It is clear that Arthur's papers, are an important part of the modern movement toward using positive feedback mechanisms to explain economic growth." Arrow concludes with "I must emphasise the importance of these variant approaches, particularly in areas where conventional tools simply fail.

One interesting model used by the ABM community study economic dynamics and bottom up interaction of firms while being governed by central authorities are Eurace and Symphony (Cincotti et al. 2012b; Raberto et al. 2019). In those models, ABM allows the replication of reality in much higher granularity in comparison to system dynamics as well as the other economic modelling approaches. For example, Eurace models central banks, commercial and investment banks, goods producer sectors, capital sectors, households and various other economic agents. All of those 'sectors' are populations of agents interacting one to another while simulating the functioning of an economic ecosystem. ABM is also used to address technology evolution models in the political economy. Dosi et al. (2010) addresses the theoretical assumption of Schumpeter (1912) on entrepreneurial destruction and innovation after one century, and the synergies that could be obtained by embedding in the same model centralised Keynesian public policies and innovative firms.

Among the weaknesses of ABM is the requirements of large populations of agents to generate behaviour. In addition, because ABMs are fundamentally stochastic models, their use implies multirun simulation with different random numbers. Large models simulates thousands of agents (best practices assume that 10,000 agents is a minimum number to analyse systems) with hundreds of multiple seeds, thus requiring consistent computing power. For example, a single Eurace simulation with 200 seeds and about 7000 agents, would require about two hours on an ordinary machine. Larger simulation would require computers in series, or even supercomputers to reach results in sensible times (Raberto et al. 2016).

Another weakness of ABM models stands on the side of validation techniques and difficulty in matching simulations with real data. In fact most economic data tend to be aggregated, whereas the agents-behaviour tend to be intuitively defined by the modeller. As a result, it is difficult to build client confidence in assessing specific economic behaviours in the policy consultancy process. The advocates of ABM remain the ones interested in explaining system complexity, aiming at reaching the detail of the real world phenomena. Current techniques for modelling agents include reinforcement learning algorithms, neural networks, Q-Learning, and genetic algorithms (Tesfatsion 2002).

Similarly to system dynamics modelling, the use of agent-based modelling does not exclude the categorisation of models in any specific economic school. Econometric estimates of equations, optimum assumption in decision making, general equilibrium, or limits to growth assumptions can be embedded in each agent. The literature already shows integrated assessment ABM models (Lamperti et al. 2018; Dosi et al. 2017), the advantage of ABM on general equilibrium (Gallegati 2016), and gives potential to develop hybrid system dynamics agent-based models (Rahmandad and Sterman 2008). In fact, Scholl (2001) outlined strengths and weaknesses of both SD and ABM and highlighted how they can complement each other.

Complex networks

Due to the high range of applicability in computer and social science complex networks has received large investments all over the world for its development (Caldarelli 2007; Barabasi 2016). Its roots are in graphs theory and decision trees as first applied by the mathematician Euler in 1735. The components of a network are nodes (or vertices) and links (or edges). The main difference between a decision tree and a complex network is the presence of closed paths that can lead a node towards itself passing towards other nodes via links (Caldarelli 2007).

Complex networks can present fixed or variables nodes, with fixed or variable connections with the other nodes of a system. The relationship with agent-based modelling, system dynamics, and the other forms of dynamic modelling is strong. Agents can be represented as nodes with specific behaviour, and their interaction with other agents can be made via links. In fact, complex networks can be seen as the foundation for the analysis of agent based modelling (Tesfatsion 2002), presenting common structural indicators used as typology tests, such as betweenness and centrality. In the case of system dynamics, integrated assessment, and computable general equilibrium models, they can be seen as networks composed of fixed nodes and fixed links. In particular, each variable is a node, and every equation represent the weight of the influence between one node and another through links.

However, network analysis provides additional features and strengths in the analysis of complexity that are not common tools in the other modelling schools presented so far. For example, the power law distribution addresses the distribution of the degree of interconnection between nodes in the network. From the network perspective, the Pareto distribution curve (Pareto 1896) is recognised as the first power law, in which few wealthy individuals tend to have more connections among themselves, whereas the large majority of the population used to have fewer connections while earning little income (Barabasi 2016). A network whose degree of distribution follows a power law is named scale-free network (Caldarelli 2007). Other inequality measures can be found applying network percolation, which allows to define the change in network structure based on the connectivity among sub-networks.

Currently, complex networks found effective application in economics in the study of systemic risk in financial networks (Scala et al. 2016), climate stress tests (Battiston et al. 2017), analysis of interbanking (Petrone and Latora 2018; Battiston et al. 2016b), evaluation of system complexity in financial networks (Battiston et al. 2016a), assessment of corporate leadership and inequality (Glattfelder 2013; Battiston 2004), game theory (Cimini 2017), and asymmetric theories (Barucca et al. 2018). Among those application we find the Debt Rank whose objective has been to study the possible shocks and default on banks and implication for the network of banks and mutual cascading effects (Bardoscia et al. 2016). Battiston et al. (2017) shows an example of the Climate Stress tests using the Debt Rank algorithm. Assuming exogenous shocks as loss of value in the assets of one bank as stranded assets, the algorithm allows the addressing of the propagation of that shock through the network of banks, thus resulting in measures of risk for the entire economy. Complex networks applied to financial system took more dominant since the 2008 financial crisis. In particular, challenging the too big (or too central or too interconnected) to fail via systemic risk analysis and cascading effects (Battiston et al. 2012).

Complex networks found also application for sentiment analysis in the study of social networks and information in the internet in general (Del Vicario et al. 2017a, 2017b). For example, Del Vicario et al. (2017b) shows how political sentiment recorded in social networks could have predicted election results using social network analysis. Similar analysis have been performed in the analysis of stock exchange to address the change in price of commodities while trading (Bonanno et al. 2004).

Summary

This chapter has provided a review of the economic theory, and contextualised the development of economic modelling methods in the last century. Whereas Chapter 1 and 2 contextualised the Limits to Growth study as the statement of a world problem, and Chapter 3 highlighted the differences between that model and the state of the world we are at today, Chapter 4 aimed at presenting the science that is required to engage in such political questions today. As seen, economics has evolved as a trial and error process over the last 250 years. Together with economic thought, and supported by computing power, methodologies have been developed to sustain the economic argument. Interestingly, despite many of the theories being developed before the 1950s, it was only with the advent of computers that these theories could be formalised and tested thus supporting further development of the theory itself.

In this review, the Limits to Growth work and system dynamics in general have been placed aside econometrics, input-output analysis, general equilibrium, integrated assessment, agent-based modelling and complex networks. As system dynamics was not accepted by the mainstream economic profession since the very beginning, many of the system dynamics modellers provided the analytical foundation and discipline of the field, allowing it to become stronger and more resilient in the face of the same questions from the past. In this book we argue, that because of the peculiar approach of system dynamics method to economic questions, it would be important to define the boundaries of the model in term of that economic school to avoid misinterpretation of results.

The following chapter shows the model developed in this study, Economic Risk, Resources and Environment (ERRE).

References

Alchian, A. A. (1950). Uncertainty, evolution, and economic theory. *Journal of Political Economy*, 58(3), 211–221.

Arrow, J. J. (1951). *Social choice and individual values*. John Wiley & Sons, Inc. New York; Chapman & Hall, Limited, London.

Arrow, K. J., Chenery, H. B., Minhas, B. S., & Solow, R. M. (1961). Capital-labor substitution and economic efficiency. *The Review of Economics and Statistics*, 43(3), 225–250.

Arrow, K. J., & Debreu, G. (1954). Existence of an equilibrium for a competitive economy. *Econometrica: Journal of the Econometric Society*, 265–290.

Arrow, K. J., & Hahn, F. H. (1971). *General competitive analysis* (vol. 12). Advanced Textbooks in Economics. North-Holland Publishing Co., Amsterdam, The Netherlands.

Arthur, W. B. (1994). *Increasing returns and path dependence in the economy*. University of Michigan Press, Ann Arbor, Michigan, US.

Arthur, W. B. (1999). Complexity and the economy. *Science*, 284(5411), 107–109.

Arthur, W. B., Holland, J. H., LeBaron, B., Palmer, R., & Tayler, P. (1996). Asset pricing under endogenous expectations in an artificial stock market. *The Economy as an Evolving Complex System II*, 27.

Ashby, W. R. (1956). *Introduction to cybernetics*. John Wiley & Son, Hoboken, New Jersey, US.

Barabási, A.-L. (2013). Network science. *Philosophical Transactions of the Royal Society A: Mathematical, Physical and Engineering Sciences*, 371(1987).

Barabási, A.-L. (2016). *Network science*. Cambridge University Press, Cambridge, United Kingdom.

Bardoscia, M., Caccioli, F., Perotti, J. I., Vivaldo, G., & Caldarelli, G. (2016). Distress propagation in complex networks: The case of non-linear debtrank. *PloS One*, 11(10), e0163825.Barker, T. (2009). *Understanding and resolving the big crunch*. Paper presented at the a conference on "The Big Crunch," Cambridge. Available online: www.new economicthinking. org/downloads/Big_Crunch.

Barker, T., Peterson, W., & Peterson, W. A. (1987). *The Cambridge multisectoral dynamic model* (Vol. 5). Cambridge University Press, Cambridge, UK.

Barlas, Y. (1989). Multiple tests for validation of system dynamics type of simulation models. *European Journal of Operational Research*, 42(1), 59–87.

Barlas, Y. (1996). Formal aspects of model validity and validation in system dynamics. *System Dynamics Review: The Journal of the System Dynamics Society*, 12(3), 183–210.

Barlas, Y., & Carpenter, S. (1990). Philosophical roots of model validation: Two paradigms. *System Dynamics Review*, 6(2), 148–166.

Barucca, P., Caldarelli, G., & Squartini, T. (2018). Tackling information asymmetry in networks: A new entropy-based ranking index. *Journal of Statistical Physics*, 173(3–4), 1028–1044.

Bassi, A. M., Ansah, J. P., Tan, Z., & Pedercini, M. (2011). Modelling global green investment scenarios: Supporting the transition to a global green economy. *Towards a green economy: Pathways to sustainable development and poverty eradication*. Available online: www.unep.org (accessed July 2015).

Battiston, S. (2004). Inner structure of capital control networks. *Physica A: Statistical Mechanics and Its Applications*, 338(1–2), 107–112.

Battiston, S., Caldarelli, G., May, R. M., Roukny, T., & Stiglitz, J. E. (2016a). The price of complexity in financial networks. *Proceedings of the National Academy of Sciences*, 113(36), 10031–10036.

Battiston, S., Farmer, J. D., Flache, A., Garlaschelli, D., Haldane, A. G., Heesterbeek, H., . . . Scheffer, M. (2016b). Complexity theory and financial regulation. *Science*, 351(6275), 818–819.

Battiston, S., Mandel, A., Monasterolo, I., Schütze, F., & Visentin, G. (2017). A climate stress-test of the financial system. *Nature Climate Change*, 7(4), 283.

Battiston, S., Puliga, M., Kaushik, R., Tasca, P., & Caldarelli, G. (2012). Debtrank: Too central to fail? financial networks, the fed and systemic risk. *Scientific Reports*, 2, 541.

Bentham, J. (1789). *An introduction to the principles of morals*. Athlone. Available online at https://www.earlymoderntexts.com/assets/pdfs/bentham1780.pdf

Bergh, J. (1993). A framework for modelling economy-environment-development relationships based on dynamic carrying capacity and sustainable development feedback. *Environmental & Resource Economics*, 3(4), 395–412.

Bergh, J. C. J. M. van den, & Nijkamp, P. (1991). Operationalizing; sustainable development: Dynamic ecological-economic models. *Ecological Economics*, 4, 11–33.

Bergh, J. C. J. M van den, & Straaten, J. van der (eds.) (1994). *Towards sustainable development: Concepts, methods, and policy*. Island Press, Washington, DC, US.

Binfield, J., Donnellan, T., Hanrahan, K. F., McQuinn, K., Westhoff, P. C., & Young, R. E. (2001). *FAPRI-Ireland 2001 EU baseline briefing book*. Available online: https://core.ac.uk/download/pdf/62758479.pdf (accessed June 2019).

Bonanno, G., Caldarelli, G., Lillo, F., Micciche, S., Vandewalle, N., & Mantegna, R. N. (2004). Networks of equities in financial markets. *The European Physical Journal B*, 38(2), 363–371.

Box, G. E. (1976). Science and statistics. *Journal of the American Statistical Association*, 71(356), 791–799.

Box, G. E., & Draper, N. R. (1987). *Empirical model-building and response surfaces* (Vol. 424). John Wiley and Sons, Hoboken, New Jersey, US.

Caldarelli, G. (2007). *Scale-free networks: Complex webs in nature and technology*. Oxford University Press, Cambridge, UK.

Caldarelli, G., Chessa, A., Pammolli, F., Gabrielli, A., & Puliga, M. (2013). Reconstructing a credit network. *Nature Physics*, 9(3), 125.

Cambridge Econometrics. (2014). *E3ME technical manual v6.1*. Available online: www.e3me.com/wp-content/uploads/2019/09/E3ME-Technical-Manual-v6.1-onlineSML.pdf (accessed December 2019).

Capros, P., Van Regemorter, D., Paroussos, L., Karkatsoulis, P., Fragkiadakis, C., Tsani, S., . . . Revesz, T. (2013). GEM-E3 model documentation. *JRC Scientific and*

Policy Reports, 26034. Available online at https://ec.europa.eu/jrc/en/publication/eur-scientific-and-technical-research-reports/gem-e3-model-documentation

Casti, J. (1981). Systemism, system theory and social system modeling. *Regional Science and Urban Economics, 11*(3), 405–424.

Chatham House. (2019). *Resource earth database.* Available online: https://resourcetrade.earth/data (accessed June 2019).

Cimini, G. (2017). Evolutionary network games: Equilibria from imitation and best response dynamics. *Complexity. 2017,* Article ID 7259032. https://doi.org/10.1155/2017/7259032.

Cincotti, S., Raberto, M., & Teglio, A. (2012a). *The Eurace macroeconomic model and simulator.* Paper presented at the Agent-based Dynamics, Norms, and Corporate Governance. The Proceedings of the 16-th World Congress of the International Economic Association, Palgrave, London, UK.

Cincotti, S., Raberto, M., & Teglio, A. (2012b). Macroprudential policies in an agent-based artificial economy. *Revue de l'OFCE, 5,* 205–234.

Club of Rome (1970). *The predicament of mankind: A quest for structured responses to growing world-wide complexities and uncertanties.* Proposal to the Club of Rome Geneva, Switzerland.

Costanza, R. (1989). What is ecological economics. *Ecological Economics, 6*(1), 1–7.

Costanza, R. (1991). The ecological economics of sustainability. In *Environmentally sustainable economic development: Building on Brundtland* (pp. 83–90). UNESCO, Paris.

Costanza, R., & Daly, H. E. (1992). Natural capital and sustainable development. *Conservation Biology, 6*(1), 37–46.

Costanza, R., & King, J. (1999). The first decade of ecological economics. *Ecological Economics, 28*(1), 1–9.

Cyert, R. M., & March, J. G. (1963). *A behavioral theory of the firm* (2nd Ed., pp. 169–187). Prentice-Hall, Englewood Cliffs, New Jersey, US.

Daly, H. (1974). The economics of the steady state. *American Economic Review,* 15–21.

Davidson, P. (1981). Chapter 10: Post Keynesian economics: Solving the crisis in economic theory. *The Crisis in Economic Theory,* 151–173.

De Toni, A. F., & Bernardi, E. (2009). *Il pianeta degli agenti: teoria e simulazione ad agenti per cogliere l'economia complessa.* UTET università, Turin, Italy.

Del Vicario, M., Scala, A., Caldarelli, G., Stanley, H. E., & Quattrociocchi, W. (2017a). Modeling confirmation bias and polarization. *Scientific Reports, 7,* 40391.

Del Vicario, M., Zollo, F., Caldarelli, G., Scala, A., & Quattrociocchi, W. (2017b). Mapping social dynamics on Facebook: The Brexit debate. *Social Networks, 50,* 6–16.

Dewey, J. (1910). *How we think.* D.C. Heath, Boston, MA.

Diehl, E., & Sterman, J. D. (1995). Effects of feedback complexity on dynamic decision making. *Organizational Behavior and Human Decision Processes, 62*(2), 198–215.

Dietzenbacher, E., Los, B., Stehrer, R., Timmer, M., & De Vries, G. (2013). The construction of world input – output tables in the WIOD project. *Economic Systems Research, 25*(1), 71–98.

Dixon, P. B., & Jorgenson, D. W. (2012). *Handbook of computable general equilibrium modeling.* Newnes. Available online at https://econpapers.repec.org/bookchap/eeehacgem/1.htm

Dixon, P. B., & Jorgenson, D. W. (2013). *Handbook of CGE modelling* (Vol. 1) SET. ISSN:2211-6885. http://dx.doi.org/10.1016/B978-0-444-59568-3.00001-8.

Dixon, P. B., Koopman, R. B., & Rimmer, M. T. (2013). The MONASH style of computable general equilibrium modeling: A framework for practical policy analysis. In *Handbook of computable general equilibrium modeling* (Vol. 1, pp. 23–103). Elsevier. Available online at https://econpapers.repec.org/bookchap/eeehacgem/1.htm

Dosi, G., Fagiolo, G., & Roventini, A. (2010). Schumpeter meeting Keynes: A policy-friendly model of endogenous growth and business cycles. *Journal of Economic Dynamics and Control*, 34(9), 1748–1767.

Dosi, G., Napoletano, M., Roventini, A., & Treibich, T. (2017). Micro and macro policies in the Keynes+ Schumpeter evolutionary models. *Journal of Evolutionary Economics*, 27(1), 63–90.

Eichner, A. S. (1976). *The megacorp and oligopoly*. Cambridge University Press, Cambridge, UK.

Eichner, A. S. (1987). *The Macrodynamics of advanced market economies*. ME Sharpe Inc, Armonk, New York, US.

Eichner, A. S., & Kregel, J. A. (1975). An essay on post-Keynesian theory: A new paradigm in economics. *Journal of Economic Literature*, 13(4), 1293–1314.

FAOSTAT. (2019). Available online: www.fao.org/faostat/en/#data (accessed June 2019).

Fiddaman, T. S. (1997). *Feedback complexity in integrated climate-economy models*. Massachusetts Institute of Technology, Cambridge, MA, US.

Ford, A. (1999). *Modeling the environment: An introduction to system dynamics models of environmental systems*. Island Press, Washington, DC, US.

Forrester, J. (1957). *Dynamic models of economic systems and industrial organizations*. System Dynamics Group Memo D-0. Massachusetts Institute of Technology. Available online: http://www.systemdynamics.org/

Forrester, J. W. (1958). Industrial dynamics: A major breakthrough for decision makers. *Harvard Business Review*, 36(4), 37–66.

Forrester, J. W. (1961). *Industrial dynamics*. Pegasus Communications, Waltham, MA, US.

Forrester, J. W. (1968). *Principles of systems* (Vol. 1, p. 51). Wright-Allen Press, Inc., Cambridge, MA, US.

Forrester, J. W. (1969). *Urban dynamics*. Pegasus Communications, Waltham, MA, US.

Forrester, J. W. (1971). Counterintuitive behavior of social systems. *Technological Forecasting and Social Change*, 3, 1–22.

Forrester, J. W. (1977). Growth cycles. *De Economist*, 125(4), 525–543.

Forrester, J. W. (1979) An alternative approach to economic policy: Macrobehavior from microstructure. In Kamrany, N & Day, R. (eds.), *Economic issues of the eighties* (pp. 80–108). Johns Hopkins University Press, Baltimore, MD.

Forrester, J. W. (1980). Information-sources for modeling the national-economy-rejoinder. *Journal of the American Statistical Association*, 75(371), 572–574.

Forrester, J. W. (1985). The model versus a modeling process. *System Dynamics Review*, 1(1), 133–134.

Forrester, J. W. (1992). Policies, decisions and information sources for modeling. *European Journal of Operational Research*, 59(1), 42–63.

Forrester, J. W. (2003). Economic theory for the new millennium. *System Dynamics Review*, 29(1), 26–41.

Forrester, J. W., Mass, N. J., & Ryan, C. J. (1976). The system dynamics national model: Understanding socio-economic behavior and policy alternatives. *Technological Forecasting and Social Change*, 9(1–2), 51–68.

Friedman, M. (1953). The methodology of positive economics. *Essays in Positive Economics*, 3(3), 145–178.

Friedman, M. (1956). The quantity theory of money: A restatement. *Studies in the Quantity Theory of Money*, 5.

Frisch, R. (1933): Editorial. *Econometrica*, 1, 1–4.

Gallegati, M. (2016). Beyond econophysics (not to mention mainstream economics). *The European Physical Journal Special Topics*, 225(17–18), 3179–3185.

Gallegati, M., & Kirman, A. (2012). Reconstructing economics: Agent based models and complexity. *Complexity Economics*, 1(1), 5–31.

Geweke, J., Horowitz, J. L., & Pesaran, M. H. (2008). *Econometrics*. The New Palgrave Dictionary of Economics, Second Edition. Edited by Durlauf, S. N. & Blume, L.E. Available online: https://webcache.googleusercontent.com/search?q=cache:jHe9iWRcY McJ:https://opus.lib.uts.edu.au/bitstream/10453/17610/1/2008008226.pdf+&cd=2&hl=it&ct=clnk&gl=uk (accessed July 2019).

Glattfelder, J. B. (2013). *Backbone of complex networks of corporations: The flow of control decoding complexity* (pp. 67–93). Springer, Berlin, Germany.

Goodwin, R. M. (1951). The nonlinear accelerator and the persistence of business cycles. *Econometrica: Journal of the Econometric Society*, 1–17.

Granger, C. J. (1986). Developments in the study of cointegrated economic variables. *Oxford Bulletin of Economics and Statistics*, 48(3), 213–228.

Greenberg, M., Crenson, M. A., & Crissey, B. L. (1976). *Models in the policy process*. Russel Sage Foundation, New York, US.

Gruchy, A. G., Stabile, D. R., & Dodge, N. T. (1987). *The reconstruction of economics: An analysis of the fundamentals of institutional economics*. Greenwood Press, New York, US.

Hamilton, D. B. (1953). *Newtonian classicism and Darwinian institutionalism: A study of change in economic theory*. University of New Mexico Press, Albuquerque, New Mexico, US.

Hansen, B. E. (2016). *Econometrics*. University of Wisconsin, Department of Economics, Madison, US.

Heaps, C. (2008). *An introduction to LEAP* (pp. 1–16). Stockholm Environment Institute Stockholm, Sweden. Avaialble online at https://www.energycommunity.org/documents/LEAPIntro.pdf

Hertel, T. (2013). *Global applied general equilibrium analysis using the global trade analysis project framework* (Vol. 1). Chapter 12 from Handbook of CGE Modelling. SET. ISSN:2211-6885. http://dx.doi.org/10.1016/B978-0-444-59568-3.00012-2.

Hilderink, H., Lucas, P., Ten Hove, A., Kok, M., De Vos, M., Janssen, P., Meijer, J., Faber, A., Ignaciuk, A., Petersen, A., & De Vries, B. (2008). *Towards a global integrated sustainability model – GISMO 1.0 status report*. Available online: www.pbl.nl/en/publications/Towards-a-Global-Integrated-Sustainability-Model-GISMO1.0-status-report (accessed July 2018).

Hines, J. H. (1987). *Essays in behavioral economic modeling*. PhD thesis, Massachusetts Institute of Technology. Sloan School of Management, Cambridge, MA, US.

Holden, P. B., Edwards, N. R., Ridgwell, A., Wilkinson, R., Fraedrich, K., Lunkeit, F., . . . Lam, A. (2018). Climate – carbon cycle uncertainties and the Paris agreement. *Nature Climate Change*, 8(7), 609.

Hope, C. (2011). *The PAGE09 integrated assessment model*. A Technical Description. Available online: www.jbs.cam.ac.uk/fileadmin/user_upload/research/workingpapers/wp1104.pdf; www.czp.cuni.cz/ekonomie/MESSAGE%20description_CUNI.pdf (accessed July 2018).

IAASTD. (2009). *International assessment of agricultural science and technology for development*, Global Report. Island Press, Washington, DC, US.

International Monetary Fund (IMF). (2018). *IMF data*. Available online: www.imf.org/en/Data (accessed September 2018).

IPCC. (1990). *Climate change: The IPCC scientific assessment*. Australian Government Publishing Service Caniberra, Australia.

IPCC. (2012). Managing the risks of extreme events and disasters to advance climate change adaptation. In: *A special report of working groups I and II of the intergovernmental panel on climate change* [Field, C. B., Barros, V., Stocker, T. F., Qin, D., Dokken, D. J.,

Ebi, K. L., Mastrandrea, M. D., Mach, K. J., Plattner, G.-K., Allen, S. K., Tignor, M. & Midgley, P. M. (eds.)] (p. 582). Cambridge University Press, Cambridge, UK, and New York, NY, USA.

IPCC. (2014). *Climate change 2014: Synthesis report*. In Pachauri,R. & Meyer,L. (eds.), *Contribution of Working Groups I, II and III to the Fifth Assessment Report of the Intergovernmental Panel on Climate Change* (p. 151). IPCC, Geneva, Switzerland. ISBN: 978-92-9169-143-2.

IPCC. (2018). Summary for policymakers. In Masson-Delmotte, V., Zhai, P., Pörtner, H.-O., Roberts, D., Skea, J., Shukla, P.R., Pirani, A., Moufouma-Okia, W., Péan, C., Pidcock, R., Connors, S., Matthews, J. B. R., Chen, Y., Zhou, X., Gomis, M. I., Lonnoy, E., Maycock, T., Tignor, M., & Waterfield, T. (eds.), *Global warming of 1.5°C. An IPCC special report on the impacts of global warming of 1.5°C above pre-industrial levels and related global greenhouse gas emission pathways, in the context of strengthening the global response to the threat of climate change, sustainable development, and efforts to eradicate poverty* (p. 32). World Meteorological Organization, Geneva, Switzerland.

Jackson, T. (2009). *Prosperity without growth: Economics for a finite planet*. Routledge, Oxford, UK.

Jackson, T. (2016). *Prosperity without growth: Foundations for the economy of tomorrow*. Routledge, Oxford, UK.

Janse, J. H., Kuiper, J. J., Weijters, M. J., Westerbeek, E. P., Jeuken, M. H. J. L., Bakkenes, M., . . . Verhoeven, J. T. A. (2015). GLOBIO-Aquatic, a global model of human impact on the biodiversity of inland aquatic ecosystems. *Environmental Science & Policy, 48*, 99–114.

Jevons, W. S. (1871). *The theory of political economy*. Augustus M. Kelley, New York, US.

Johansen, L. (1960). *A multi-sectoral study of economic growth* (Vol. 82). North-Holland, Amsterdam.

Johnson, R. C., & Noguera, G. (2012). Accounting for intermediates: Production sharing and trade in value added. *Journal of International Economics, 86*(2), 224–236.

Jørgensen, S. (1994). Review and comparison of goal functions in system ecology. *Vie et milieu, 44*(1), 11–20.

Kaldor, N. (1940). A model of the trade cycle. *The Economic Journal*, 78–92.

Kaldor, N. (1957). A model of economic growth. *The Economic Journal, 67*(268), 591–624.

Kalecki, M. (1935). A macrodynamic theory of business cycles. *Econometrica, Journal of the Econometric Society*, 327–344.

Kalecki, M. (1954). *Theory of economic dynamics*. George Allen, London.

Kampmann, C., & Sterman, J. D. (1998). *Feedback complexity, bounded rationality, and market dynamics*. Memo D-4802, System Dynamics Group. Massachusetts Institute of Technology, Cambridge, MA, US.

Keen, S. (2011). *Debunking economics*. ZED Books Limited, London, UK.

Keen, S. (2013). A monetary Minsky model of the great moderation and the great recession. *Journal of Economic Behavior & Organization, 86*, 221–235.

Keen, S. (2017). *Can we avoid another financial crisis?* John Wiley & Sons, Hoboken, New Jersey, US.

Kelly, J. A. (2006). An overview of the RAINS model – environmental research centre report. Available online: https://epa.ie/pubs/reports/research/air/EPA_overview_of_rains_model_ERC4.pdf (accessed July 2018).

Keramidas, K., Kitous, A., Despres, J., & Schmitz, A. (2017). *Poles-JRC model documentation. JRC technical reports, European commission*. Available online: https://publications.jrc.ec.europa.eu/repository/bitstream/JRC107387/kjna28728enn.pdf (accessed July 2016).

Keynes, J. M. (1936). *The general theory of employment, interest and money.* Kessinger Publishing, Whitefish Montana, US.

Koopman, R., Wang, Z., & Wei, S.-J. (2014). Tracing value-added and double counting in gross exports. *American Economic Review, 104*(2), 459–494.

Krugman, P. R. (1979). Increasing returns, monopolistic competition, and international trade. *Journal of International Economics, 9*(4), 469–479.

Kuznets, S. (1937). *National income and capital formation, 1919–1935.* National Bureau of Economic Research, Chicago, US.

Lamperti, F., Dosi, G., Napoletano, M., Roventini, A., & Sapio, A. (2018). Faraway, so close: Coupled climate and economic dynamics in an agent-based integrated assessment model. *Ecological Economics, 150,* 315–339.

Lavoie, M. (2014). *Post-Keynesian economics: New foundations.* Edward Elgar Publishing.

Leontief, W. W. (1936). Quantitative input and output relations in the economic systems of the United States. *The Review of Economic Statistics,* 105–125.

Lloyd's Emerging Risk Report. (2015). *Food system shock – The insurance impacts of acute disruption to global food supply.* Lloyd's Emerging Risk Report, London.

Lucas Jr, R. E. (1972). Expectations and the neutrality of money. *Journal of Economic Theory, 4*(2), 103–124.

Lucas, R. E. (1976, January). *Econometric policy evaluation: A critique.* In Carnegie-Rochester conference series on public policy (Vol. 1, No. 1, pp. 19–46).

Luderer, G., Leimbach, M., Bauer, N., Kriegler, E., Baumstark, L., Bertram, C., Giannousakis, A., Hilaire, J., Klein, D., Levesque, A., Mouratiadou, I., Pehl, M., Pietzcker, R., Piontek, F., Roming, N., Schultes, A., Schwanitz, V., & Strefler, J. (2015). *Description of the Remind model (version 1.6).* Available online: www.pik-potsdam.de/research/transformation-pathways/models/remind/remind16_description_2015_11_30_final (accessed June 2017).

Lyneis, J. M. (1980). *Corporate planning and policy design: A system dynamics approach.* Massachusetts Institute of Technology, Cambridge, MA, US.

Marx, K. (1867). *Capital – a critique of political economy – volume I: The process of production of capital.* Progress Publishers, USSR, Moscow.

Mass, N. J. (1975). *Generic feedback structures underlying economic fluctuations.* Massachusetts Institute of Technology, Cambridge, MA, US.

Maxwell, T., & Costanza, R. (1994). Spatial ecosystem modeling in a distributed computational environment. In *Toward sustainable development: Concepts, methods, and policy* (pp. 111–138). Island Press, Washington, DC.

Meadows, D. H. (1980). The unavoidable a priori. *Elements of the System Dynamics Method,* 23–57.

Meadows, D. H. (2008). *Thinking in systems: A primer.* Chelsea Green Publishing, Vermont, US.

Meadows, D. L., Behrens, W. W., Meadows, D. H., Naill, R. F., Randers, J., & Zahn, E. (1974). *Dynamics of growth in a finite world.* Wright-Allen Press, Cambridge, MA.

Meadows, D. L., Fiddaman, T., & Shannon, D. (1986). Fish Banks, Ltd. Laboratory for Interactive Learning. University of New Hampshire, Durham, New Hampshire, US.

Meadows, D. H., Meadows, D. L., Randers, J., & Behrens, J. (1972). *The limits to growth.* Universe Books, New York, NY, USA.

Meadows, D. L., Fiddaman, T., & Shannon, D. (1993). *Fish Banks, Ltd. A micro-computer assisted group simulation that teaches principles of sustainable management of renewable natural resources* (3rd ed.) Laboratory for Interactive Learning, University of New Hampshire, Durham, NH.

Mercure, J.-F., Pollitt, H., Edwards, N. R., Holden, P. B., Chewpreecha, U., Salas, P., . . . Vinuales, J. E. (2018). Environmental impact assessment for climate change policy with the simulation-based integrated assessment model E3ME-FTT-GENIE. *Energy Strategy Reviews, 20,* 195–208.

Millennium Institute. (2007). *Technical documentation for the Threshold21 starting framework model.* Available online: www.cepal.org/ilpes/noticias/paginas/2/40352/t21sfdocu mentation.pdf (accessed June 2018).

Millennium Institute. (2014). *T21-Kenya agriculture, food and nutrition security, and rural poverty scenarios: Scenario analysis and policy recommendations.* Millennium Institute, Washington, DC.

Millennium Institute. (2018). *iSDG integrated simulation tool.* Available online: www. millennium-institute.org/isdg (accessed June 2018).

Minsky, H. P. (1957). Central banking and money market changes. *The Quarterly Journal of Economics, 71*(2), 171–187.

Mishra, S. K. (2007). *A brief history of production functions.* doi:10.2139/ssrn.1020577.

Mobus, G. E., & Kalton, M. C. (2015). *Principles of systems science.* Springer, Berlin, Germany.

Modigliani, F., & Miller, M. H. (1958). The cost of capital, corporation finance and the theory of investment. *The American, 1,* 3.

Monasterolo, I., & Raberto, M. (2018). The EIRIN flow-of-funds behavioural model of green fiscal policies and green sovereign bonds. *Ecological Economics, 144,* 228–243.

Morecroft, J. D. (1983). System dynamics: Portraying bounded rationality. *Omega, 11*(2), 131–142.

Morecroft, J. D. (1985). The feedback view of business policy and strategy. *System Dynamics Review, 1*(1), 4–19.

Morecroft, J. D. (1988). System dynamics and microworlds for policymakers. *European Journal of Operational Research, 35*(3), 301–320.

Morecroft, J. S. M. (2007). *Business dynamics A feedback systems approach.* John Wiley & Sons Ltd, Hoboken, New Jersey, US.

Moss, J., Patton, M., Zhang, L., & Kim, I. S. (2011). *Fapri-UK model documentation,* June. Available online at www.afbini.gov.uk/publications/fapri-uk-model-documentation (accessed May 2018).

Mullainathan, S., & Thaler, R. H. (2000). *Behavioral economics.* National Bureau of Economic Research (NBER), Working Paper 7948.

Murray, V., & Ebi, K. L. (2012). *IPCC special report on managing the risks of extreme events and disasters to advance climate change adaptation (SREX).* BMJ Publishing Group Ltd.

Naill, R. F. (1977). *Managing the energy transition: A system dynamics search for alternatives to oil and gas.* COAL2 Model, United States.

Naill, R. F. (1992). A system dynamics model for national energy policy planning. *System Dynamics Review, 8*(1), 1–19.

NASA. (2019). *Socio economic data and application center (SEDAC).* Available online: https://sedac.ciesin.columbia.edu/data/sets/browse (accessed June 2019).

Natalini, D., Bravo, G., & Jones, A. W. (2019). Global food security and food riots – an agent-based modelling approach. *Food Security, 11*(5), 1153–1173.

Natalini, D., Jones, A., & Bravo, G. (2015). Quantitative assessment of political fragility indices and food prices as indicators of food riots in countries. *Sustainability, 7*(4), 4360–4385.

National Technical University of Athens – NTUA. (2014). *Primes model 2013–2014 Detailed model description.* Available online: https://ec.europa.eu/clima/sites/clima/

files/strategies/analysis/models/docs/primes_model_2013-2014_en.pdf   (accessed July 2016).

Nordhaus, W. D. (1973). World dynamics: Measurement without data. *The Economic Journal*, 83(332), 1156–1183.

Nordhaus, W. D. (1992). *The 'dice' model: Background and structure of a dynamic integrated climate-economy model of the economics of global warming* (No. 1009). Cowles Foundation for Research in Economics, Yale University, New Haven, CT, US.

Nordhaus, W. D. (2008). *A question of balance: Economic modeling of global warming.* Yale University Press, New Haven, CT, US.

Nordhaus, W. D. (2013). *Integrated economic and climate modelling* (Vol. 1). Chapter 16 from Handbook of CGE Modelling. SET. ISSN:2211-6885. http://dx.doi.org/10.1016/B978-0-444-59568-3.00016-X.

Nordhaus, W. D. (2017). *Evolution of Assessments of the Economics of Global Warming: Changes in the DICE model, 1992–2017* (No. w23319). National Bureau of Economic Research.

Nordhaus, W. D., & Sztorc, P. (2013). *DICE 2013R: Introduction and user's manual*, November. Available online: http://www.econ.yale.edu/~nordhaus/homepage/homepage/documents/DICE_Manual_100413r1.pdf (accessed June 2019).

OECD. (2008). *OECD environmental outlook to 2030.* Organisation for Economic Co-Operation and Development, Paris.

OECD. (2012). *OECD environmental outlook to 2050.* Organisation for Economic Co-Operation and Development, Paris.

Oxford Economics. (2017). *The Oxford global economic model August 2017.* Available online: www.oxfordeconomics.com/global-economic-model (accessed May 2018).

Paich, M., & Sterman, J. D. (1993). Boom, bust, and failures to learn in experimental markets. *Management Science*, 39(12), 1439–1458.

Papageorgiou, C., & Saam, M. (2008). Two-level CES production technology in the Solow and Diamond growth models. *Scandinavian Journal of Economics*, 110(1), 119–143.

Pareto, V. (1896). *Course of political economy.* Lausanne, switzerland.

PBL Netherland Environmental Assessment Agency. (2014). *Integrated assessment of global environmental change with IMAGE 3.0: Model description and policy application.* Available online: www.pbl.nl/sites/default/files/downloads/pbl-2014-integrated_assessment_of_global_environmental_change_with_image30_735.pdf (accessed December 2019).

Peterson, D. W. (1975). *Hypothesis, estimation, and validation of dynamic social models: Energy demand modeling.* Massachusetts Institute of Technology.

Peterson, D. W. (1980). Statistical tools for system dynamics. *Elements of the System Dynamics Method*, 224–241.

Peterson, D. W., & Schweppe, F. (1974). Code for a general purpose system identifier and evaluator (GPSIE). *IEEE Transactions on Automatic Control*, 19(6), 852–854.

Petrone, D. W., & Latora, V. (2018). A dynamic approach merging network theory and credit risk techniques to assess systemic risk in financial networks. *Scientific Reports*, 8(1), 5561.

Phillips, A. W. (1950). *Mechanical models in economic dynamics.* London School of Economics and Political Science, London, UK.

Pindyck, R. S. (2013). Climate change policy: What do the models tell us? *Journal of Economic Literature*, 51(3), 860–872.

Pollitt, H., & Barker, T. (2009). Modeling the financial crisis with the global, econometric E3MG model. *IUP Journal of Applied Economics*, 8.

Pollitt, H., & Mercure, J.-F. (2018). The role of money and the financial sector in energy-economy models used for assessing climate and energy policy. *Climate Policy*, *18*(2), 184–197.

Pollitt, H., Summerton, P., & Klaassen, G. (2015). A model-based assessment of first-mover advantage and climate policy. *Environmental Economics and Policy Studies*, *17*(2), 299–312.

Quesnay, F. (1894). *Tableau Oeconomiqueh [microform]: First Printed in 1758 and now reproduced in facsimile for the British economic association.* Palgrave Macmillan, London UK.

Raberto, M., Ozel, B., Ponta, L., Teglio, A., & Cincotti, S. (2019). From financial instability to green finance: The role of banking and credit market regulation in the Eurace model. *Journal of Evolutionary Economics*, *29*(1), 429–465.

Radzicki, M. J. (1990). Institutional dynamics, deterministic chaos, and self-organizing systems. *Journal of Economic Issues*, *24*(1), 57–102.

Radzicki, M. J. (2003). Mr. Hamilton, Mr. Forrester, and a foundation for evolutionary economics. *Journal of Economic Issues*, *37*(1), 133–173.

Radzicki, M. J. (2005). Institutional economics, post Keynesian economics, and system dynamics: Three strands of a heterodox economics braid. *Economics (ICAPE)*, *5*, 7.

Radzicki, M. J. (2011). System dynamics and its contribution to economics and economic modeling. *Complex Systems in Finance and Econometrics*, 727–737.

Radzicki, M. J., & Sterman, J. D. (1994). Evolutionary economics and system dynamics. *Evolutionary Concepts in Contemporary Economics*, 61–89.

Rahmandad, H., & Sterman, J. (2008). Heterogeneity and network structure in the dynamics of diffusion: Comparing agent-based and differential equation models. *Management Science*, *54*(5), 998–1014.

Rečka, L. (2013). *The message model description.* Available online: http://www.czp.cuni.cz/ekonomie/MESSAGE%20description_CUNI.pdf (accessed June 2018).

Ricardo, D. (1891). *Principles of political economy and taxation.* G. Bell. Available online at https://political-economy.com/david-ricardo-on-the-principles-of-political-economy-and-taxation/

Richardson, G. P. (1991). *Feedback thought in social science and systems theory.* Pegasus Communications, Waltham, MA.

Roberts, E. B. (1978). *Managerial applications of system dynamics.* Massachusetts Institute of Technology, Cambridge, MA, US.

Romer, P. M. (1990). Endogenous technological change. *Journal of Political Economy*, *98*(5, Part 2), S71–S102.

Ruth, M. (1995). Information, order and knowledge in economic and ecological systems: Implications for material and energy use. *Ecological Economics*, *13*(2), 99–114.

Samuelson, P. A. (1956). Social indifference curves. *The Quarterly Journal of Economics*, *70*(1), 1–22.

Sato, K. (1967). A two-level constant-elasticity-of-substitution production function. *The Review of Economic Studies*, *34*(2), 201–218.

Scala, A., Zlatić, V., Caldarelli, G., & D'Agostino, G. (2016). Mitigating cascades in sandpile models: An immunization strategy for systemic risk? *The European Physical Journal Special Topics*, *225*(10), 2017–2023.

Scholl, H. J. (2001). *Agent-based and system dynamics modeling: A call for cross study and joint research.* In Proceedings of the 34th annual Hawaii international conference on system sciences (pp. 8-pp). IEEE.

Schumpeter, J. A. (1912). *Theorie der Wirtschaftlichen Entwicklung: The theory of economic development.* Dunker & Humblot, Leipzig, Germany.

Schweppe, F. C. (1965a). Evaluation of likelihood functions for Gaussian signals. *IEEE Transactions on Information Theory, 11*(1), 61–70.

Schweppe, Fred C. (1965b). *Algorithms for estimating a re-entry body's position, velocity, and ballistic coefficient in real time or for post flight analysis. 1964–1964.* Massachusetts Institute of Technology, Lincoln Laboratory, Lexington, MA.

Schweppe, F. C. (1973). *Uncertain dynamic systems.* Prentice Hall, Upper Saddle River, New Jersey, US.

Senge, P. (1990). *The fifth discipline: The Art & Practice of Learning Organization.* Doupleday Currence, New York, US.

Senge, P. M. (1978). *The system dynamics national model investment function: A comparison to the neoclassical investment function.* Massachusetts Institute of Technology, Cambridge, MA, US.

Senge, P. M. (1997). The fifth discipline. *Measuring Business Excellence, 1*(3), 46–51.

Senge, P. M., & Forrester, J. W. (1980). Tests for building confidence in system dynamics models. *System Dynamics, TIMS Studies in Management Sciences, 14*, 209–228.

Shoven, J. B., & Whalley, J. (1992). *Applying general equilibrium.* Cambridge University Press, Cambridge, UK.

Simon, H. A. (1957). *A behavioral model of rational choice, in models of man, social and rational: Mathematical essays on rational human behavior in a social setting.* John Wiley and Sons, Hoboken, New Jersey, US.

Simon, H. A. (1979). Rational decision making in business organizations. *The American Economic Review, 69*(4), 493–513.

Simon, H. A. (1982). *Models of bounded rationality. Vol. 2, behavioral economics and business organization.* Massachusetts Institute of Technology, Cambridge, MA, US.

Smith, A. (1776). *An inquiry into the nature and causes of the wealth of nations* (S.M. Soares, Ed.). Metalibri Digital Library. Available online at https://www.ibiblio.org/ml/libri/s/SmithA_WealthNations_p.pdf

Solow, R. M. (1956). A contribution to the theory of economic growth. *The Quarterly Journal of Economics, 70*(1), 65–94.

Sraffa, P. (1960). *Produzione di merci a mezzo di merci: premesse a una critica della teoria economica.* G. Einaudi, Turin, Italy.

Steffen, W., Rockström, J., Richardson, K., Lenton, T. M., Folke, C., Liverman, D., . . . Crucifix, M. (2018). Trajectories of the earth system in the anthropocene. *Proceedings of the National Academy of Sciences, 115*(33), 8252–8259.

Sterman, J. D. (1981). *The energy transition and the economy: A system dynamics approach* (2 Vols.). MIT Alfred P. Sloan School of Management, Cambridge, MA.

Sterman, J. (1988). A skeptic's guide to computer models. In: L. Grant(ed.), *Foresight and national decisions* (pp. 133–169). University Press of America, Lanham, MD.

Sterman, J. D. (1989). Modeling managerial behavior: Misperceptions of feedback in a dynamic decision making experiment. *Management Science, 35*(3), 321–339.

Stermann, J. D. (2000). *Business dynamics: Systems thinking and modeling for a complex world.* McGraw-Hill, New York, USA.

Sterman, J. D. (2002). All models are wrong: Reflections on becoming a systems scientist. *System Dynamics Review: The Journal of the System Dynamics Society, 18*(4), 501–531.

Sterman, J. D. (2014). Interactive web-based simulations for strategy and sustainability: The MIT sloan learning edge management flight simulators, part I. *System Dynamics Review, 30*(1–2), 89–121.

Sterman, J. D., Fiddaman, T., Franck, T., Jones, A., McCauley, S., Rice, P., . . . Siegel, L. (2012). Climate interactive: The C-ROADS climate policy model. *System Dynamics Review, 28*, 295–305.

Sterman, J. D., Fiddaman, T., Franck, T., Jones, A., McCauley, S., Rice, P., . . . Siegel, L. (2013). Management flight simulators to support climate negotiations. *Environmental Modelling & Software, 44*, 122–135.

Sterman, J. D., & Morrison, B. (1988). *People express management flight simulator: Software and Briefing Book. Available from the author, Sloan School of Management, MIT, Cambridge, MA 02142. See web.mit.edu/jsterman*

Stolwijk, J. A. (1980). Information sources for modeling the national economy: Comment. *Journal of the American Statistical Association,* 569–572.

Sverdrup, H. U., Olafsdottir, A. H., Ragnarsdottir, K. V., & Koca, D. (2018). *Developing the world6 integrated global model; causally linking natural resource use, energy use, commodities, population dynamics, health impacts, governance dynamics and the economy.* 36nd International Conference of the System Dynamics Society, System Dynamics Society, Reykjavik.

Tesfatsion, L. (2001). Introduction to the special issue on agent-based computational economics. *Journal of Economic Dynamics and Control, 25*(3–4), 281–293.

Tesfatsion, L. (2002). Agent-based computational economics: Growing economies from the bottom up. *Artificial Life, 8*(1), 55–82.

Thaler, R. H., & Ganser, L. (2015). *Misbehaving: The making of behavioral economics.* W. W. Norton, New York.

Theil, H. (1966). *Applied economic forecasting.* North Holland Publishing Company, Amsterdam.

Timmer, M. P., Dietzenbacher, E., Los, B., Stehrer, R., & De Vries, G. J. (2015). An illustrated user guide to the world input – output database: The case of global automotive production. *Review of International Economics, 23*(3), 575–605.

Timmer, M. P., Los, B., Stehrer, R., & de Vries, G. (2016). *An anatomy of the global trade slowdown based on the WIOD 2016 release* (No. GD-162). Groningen Growth and Development Centre, University of Groningen, Groningen, the Netherlands.

Trefler, D., & Zhu, S. C. (2010). The structure of factor content predictions. *Journal of International Economics, 82*(2), 195–207.

Tversky, A., & Kahneman, D. (1974). Judgment under uncertainty: Heuristics and biases. *Science, 185*(4157), 1124–1131.

UNEP. (2007). *Global environment outlook 4.* United Nations Environment Programme, Nairobi.

University of Maryland. (2019). *Global forest change database.* Available online: https://earthenginepartners.appspot.com/science-2013-global-forest (accessed June 2019).

Valin, H., Havlík, P., Forsell, N., Frank, S., Mosnier, A., Peters, D., . . . van den Berg, M. (2013). Description of the GLOBIOM (IIASA) model and comparison with the MIRAGE-BioF (IFPRI) model. *Crops, 8*(3.1).

Van den Bergh, J. C., & Nijkamp, P. (1991). Operationalizing sustainable development: Dynamic ecological economic models. *Ecological Economics, 4*(1), 11–33.

van den Bergh, J. C., van der Straaten, J., & Koskoff, S. (1994). *Toward sustainable development: Concepts, methods, and policy.* Island Press, Washington, DC, US.

van Vuuren, D. P., Kok, M., Lucas, P. L., Prins, A. G., Alkemade, R., van den Berg, M., . . . Kram, T. (2015). Pathways to achieve a set of ambitious global sustainability objectives by 2050: Explorations using the IMAGE integrated assessment model. *Technological Forecasting and Social Change, 98*, 303–323.

van Vuuren, D. P., Lucas, P. L., & Hilderink, H. (2007). Downscaling drivers of global environmental change: Enabling use of global SRES scenarios at the national and grid levels. *Global Environmental Change, 17*(1), 114–130.

Velupillai, K. V. (2005). The unreasonable in effectiveness of mathematics in economics. *Cambridge Journal of Economics*, 29(6), 849–872.

Videira, N., Antunes, P., Santos, R., & Lopes, R. (2010). A participatory modelling approach to support integrated sustainability assessment processes. *Systems Research and Behavioral Science*, 27(4), 446–460.

Von Bertalanffy, L. (1950). The theory of open systems in physics and biology. *Science*, 111(2872), 23–29.

Walras, L. (1877). *Éléments dÉconomie Politique Pure ou Théorie de la Richesse Sociale* (2nd. part). Corbaz, Laussane, Switzerland.

Warren, K. (2008). *Strategic management dynamics*. John Wiley & Sons, Hoboken, New Jersey, US.

Wiener, N. (1948). *Cybernetics or control and communication in the animal and the machine*. MIT Press, Cambridge, MA, US.

Wooldridge, J. M. (2006). *Econometrics: A modern approach*. South-Western College Publishing, Mason, OH, US.

World Bank Databank (WB). *Global economic monitoring database*. Available online: https://data.worldbank.org/ (accessed September 2018).

World Input Output Database (WIOD). *World input output database*. Available online: www.wiod.org/home (accessed June 2019).

Zellner, A. (1980). Information sources for modeling the national economy: Comment. *Journal of the American Statistical Association*, 75(371), 567–569.

5   System structure and theory

In this chapter we present the Economic Risk, Resources and Environment (ERRE) model. The focus is on the top level architecture of the system, highlighting cross-systems structure, major feedback loops generating behaviour, and the sectors the form the ERRE. In addition, a comparison to economic theory is provided in order to translate this work in the standard of economic thinking, and improve the effectiveness to influence policy. This chapter is accompanied with an online appendix where all equations, system structures and details of the model are provided alongside the computer version of the model. This involves behavioural tests and demonstrations of why the model fits in a certain theory as explained in this chapter. The appendix is available at https://doi.org/10.25411/aru.10110710.

Purpose, boundaries, and theory

Economic Risk, Resources and Environment (ERRE) is a system dynamics model whose purpose is to analyse the financial pressures emerging from global economic growth while coping with natural limits in both energy and agricultural systems. A major feature of the model is to integrate in the same framework both the dynamic evolution of long-term phenomena (e.g. energy transition, climate effects) and the short- to medium-term structures that are more relevant to the policy agenda of decision making (e.g. extreme weather events, or short-term shocks). The ultimate goal is to bring understanding of the sustainability transition closer to the needs of decision makers, and build resilience in economic systems. While the model belongs to the family of E3 models (Economy, Energy, Environment), it is possible to introduce the term R3 model (Resources, Risk and Resilience) thus shifting the analysis towards the short term, including variables such as prices of natural resources, interest rates, debt, and many others.

The founding principles that we embrace in the development of ERRE are:

1   Global in scale: the model has to aggregate economic and resource variables from public databases in order to address the general dynamics of growth in the global economy.

DOI: 10.4324/9781315643182-7

2   Ecologically limited: the model has to explicitly represent resource limits around agriculture and energy. These include (i) finite resource constraints and limited substitutability of resources for both agriculture and energy systems, and (ii) risk of climate emissions and negative consequences for food output.

3   Focused on risk variables: the model has to endogenously represent the dynamics of resource prices and interest rates. The aim is to address the possible implication of resource constraints on the financial system, as well as the feedback from the financial system to economic activity.

4   Integration of Micro and Macroeconomic aspects of growth: the model should rely on the micro-economic structure of supply chains and industrial processes to generate the macroeconomic behaviour of national accounting systems, and integrate these with the macroeconomic perspective typical of banking and public systems.

5   Bounded rationality: the model should represent economic agents based on principles of bounded rationality, perception delay of information feedback, and non-linear adaptive behaviour of decision makers based on that information.

6   Driven by population dynamics: demand should be driven by population growth, while economic sectors have to employ workers to perform production. Thus firms should offer wages for their services, while labour can decide the sectors to work for, or be (voluntarily) unemployed.

7   Consistent structure for a closed loop economy: the model has to explicitly model households and their role in the financial system. This includes savings accumulation decisions, consumption decisions, receiving income from firms, as well as their relationships with banking and government.

8   Stock and flow consistency: the model must correctly represent a national accounting system, and respect the stock-and-flow consistency of their cash flows. This has to be true for every economic sector and for the economy as a whole.

9   Policy relevant: Represent explicitly the public sector and policy levers that can impact the complex dynamics between natural resources, growth and finance. These include carbon tax, subsidies, and monetary policies in general.

10 Suitable to test short-term shocks: allow for the eventual representation of environmental shocks in the system, as short-term unexpected events that can disrupt the system thus addressing resilience in the economy.

In order to address such a scope of work, the model draws from various school of economics with particular emphasis to behavioural, evolutionary, ecological, post-Keynesian, and partially neoclassical economic schools (Radzicki 2005). In detail:

• Solow growth models – the model includes equations which are characteristic of the neoclassical school, including Constant Elasticity of Substitution production function (Arrow et al. 1961; Sato 1967) and assumes technology development as exogenous input to production (Solow 1956). As a result, the current model does not reject the neoclassical approach, rather, it aims at enriching such a theory with improved model structures.

- Evolutionary school – the model includes various structures that represent path dependencies and disequilibrium in the system rather than assuming equilibrium as a fixed point at the foundation of its dynamics. These involve price structures, energy retrofit and capital formulation structures, among others. Our model does not reject the hypothesis of equilibrium in the econ-omy, but rather it allows one to be found in the case that it exists rather than assuming it a priory.
- Carnegie and behavioural schools – the model formally embeds informa-tion feedback from the system state to decision makers, delays in collecting information, and imperfection of action when taking decisions that impact the system. These structures aim to represent human decision making as bounded rational and based on cognitive decision rules (normally non-linear) as empirically demonstrated in the Carnegie school and Behavioural economics since the 1950s (Simon 1957, 1979; Tversky and Kahneman 1974; Thaler and Ganser 2015).
- Post-Keynesian – the aspects that are common to a post-Keynesian school include (i) the behaviour of money creation policies, and (ii) Stock and Flow consistency property of the economy. Given the inability of the agents to optimise based on increased availability of liquidity, and path depend-encies generated by human behaviour, money creation policies propagate their effects to the real economy. In addition, the ERRE uses a balance sheet approach for the modelling of financial stocks and flows, thus assuring con-sistency of financial transactions across all sectors of the economy in line with accounting principles.
- Ecological school – an important objective of our work is to look at the eco-logical constraints to growth (e.g. climate change, or resource depletion) to find possible implications for finance and the real economy.

The two models that more than others inspired the development of the ERRE are *World3–03* (Meadows et al. 2003) and *The Energy Transition and the Econ-omy* (Sterman 1981). These models have been reviewed in the previous chapters both pragmatically and following a comparative approach within an econom-ics frame. All these critiques have been taken into account, and used to update the final model in many of its structures. It is important to note that the ERRE model is a global model whereas Sterman (1981) is a national model of the US economy. Due to the change in scale, some variables available in Sterman (1981) can be found to have real world counterpart whether others cannot. For exam-ple, the model can calculate GDP as measure of economic development through aggregating the GDPs of every country in the world, whereas a global figure for interest rates does not exist, thus generating little meaning in the attempt of cali-brating such variable. These characteristics have strong implications in terms of policy analysis. However, the proposed model aims at being an economic theory foundation for the development of lower scale system models (such as national) (Forrester et al. 1979; Forrester 2003). Further work can be applied to regionalise the model following the same methodology described in this chapter.

The next section describes the two models used as the starting framework for developing ERRE.

The starting frameworks

The purpose of models is a major aspect to consider when using existing frameworks as foundation for novel work (Sterman 2000). The ERRE model started with the specific purpose of sustainability and risk analysis in the global economy, under the assumptions of environmental limits and economic growth. Therefore, the model is both required to capture long-term dynamics that are typical of an economic transition, and, at the same time, short-term behaviours of firms, with the possibility to model exogenous inputs such as policies or environmental shocks to the economy.

The two models that have been used as foundation for this work are the World3–03 model (Meadows et al. 2003) and the Energy Transition and the Economy (ETE) model (Sterman 1981). Both models have a long-term focus, thus capturing the general dynamics of the economic system over decades.

In particular, the World3–03 model purpose is:

> to capture the general dynamics of economic growth in a finite planet (Meadows et al. 1974).

The model simulates global dynamics from 1900 to 2100, neglecting the overall short-term dynamics of the economy. The model is composed of about 250 element, 13 stock variables, and 14 major non-linear relationships. The financial sector, prices, and technology are implicit in the structural relationships of the real economy.

Figure 5.1 shows the sectors of World3 as published in Meadows et al. (1974). In particular the model represents a fully integrated theory of human development (including demographic and economic transitions) in a finite world, with major implications for possible catastrophic long-term dynamics dependent on growth overshooting natural limits. The model demonstrated that assuming various constraints in the real world (resources, pollution, land), and slow adaptation of people in dealing with such constraints, even if growth could have been able to address some limits it would always have grown further and hit other limits.

In Sterman (1981, p. 2), the model purpose is to "evaluate the effects of depletion and rising energy prices on economic growth, inflation, and other key economic and energy indicators." The model builds on and contributes to the work developed on the System Dynamics National Model (SDNM) at the MIT, which is the result of the work of many over the years under the supervision of Forrester. Mass (1975) focused on the modelling of the industrial supply structures that are responsible for business cycles and fluctuation in the economy. In

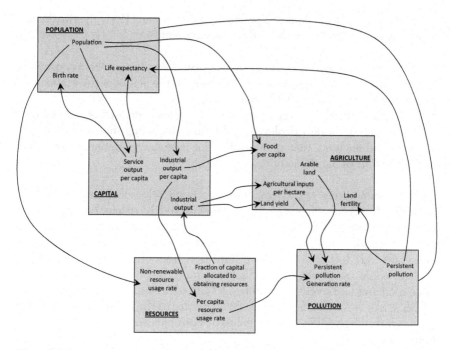

Figure 5.1 Interactions among the five basic economic sectors of World3
Source: Meadows et al. (1974)

particular, the structures describing the interaction between wages, prices, perception of demand and supply capacity for production have been made explicit. Senge (1978) focused on the modelling of the capital investment function in such a framework. He adopted econometric estimate and simulation techniques to compare the SDNM investment function with the one generally used in neoclassical theory, demonstrating improvements of fit on the latter. Other work after Sterman (1981) include Hines (1987) who analysed the structures of the financial sector, in particular around interest rate and money supply. The SDNM has not been published to date and Forrester kept working on it as a general national economic theory using system dynamics (Forrester 2003).

Sterman (1981) used the general economic structure of the SDNM to analyse the impact of peak oil on the US economy. Structures representative of short-term dynamics (e.g. labour-inventory business cycles or short-term debt creation) were neglected. The model simulates from 1900 to 2050, a suitable time frame to capture the possible turning points for the energy transition from cheap conventional energy to more expensive non-conventional energy resources.

In exploring such an issue, the economic model is grounded on energy modelling. The model details the structures to capture the dynamics of energy retrofits in every sector of the economy using putty-clay capital addition structures, and includes the oil pricing strategies of OPEC as source of energy import in case of an energy shortage from domestic production. In Sterman (1981) the two domestic energy productive sectors have the following definition:

- Conventional energy: cheap fossil fuels assumed to have reserve constraints nationally, and a limits to growth feedback on the ability of the economy of discover more of those with available capacity.
- Non-conventional energy: a small energy sector composed of technologies that were not widely deployed at the time (including shale oil, shale gas, solar and nuclear), that is assumed to not have energy resource constraints in the time of the simulation.

Energy commodities are assumed to be completely substitutable for one another. However, conventional resources would have reached a peak in production due to depletion in the time frame of the simulation, whereas non-conventional resources could have been assumed to keep growing. Most important, due to the delay in the transition from one source to the other, demand could overshoot supply, thus generating important implications for price increases and overall inflation. To address the full market dynamic, the OPEC sector was included as a possible importer to the US economy in times of energy shortage. OPEC is assumed to be both importer of capital and goods from the US economy, owner of US financial debt, and exporter of energy when dynamics are in overshoot. Several strategies of OPEC in defining oil export prices were considered.

Figure 5.2 shows the five producing sectors as in Sterman (1981). The model assumes bounded rationality of agents and adaptive adjustments of capacity to demand via both perception delays in obtaining information for capital investment, and physical delays such as capital formation. All sectors are modelled as an integrated supply chain, with households driving consumption growth. While firms order capital, consume energy, and hire labour based on expected demand and available capacity, households are assumed to generate demand based on population growth and keeping individual consumption with a positive trend based on past behaviour. The model integrates real and financial flows in the same framework, generating demand for money based on private sector asset growth. Thus government and financial sectors are represented in simplified form. While government is responsible for collecting taxes and generating expenditure, the financial sector endogenously applies monetary policies in terms of changes in the money supply and changes in interest rate as a function of available cash in the economy and inflation. The model exogenously assumes labour productivity growth based on historical data in line with the Solow growth model (1956). Population growth was also an exogenous input based on the National Bureau Forecasts on population.

In comparison to the World3–03, the ETE model is much larger, accounting for approximately 250 stock variables and above 3500 total elements between non-linear relationships, auxiliary variables, and parameters.

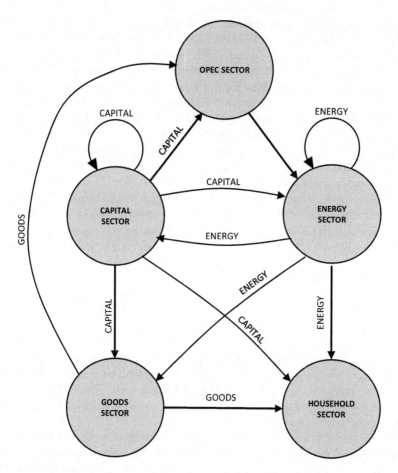

Figure 5.2 Physical flows in the energy transition and the economy model

Source: Sterman (1981)

Integrating existing frameworks and further development

Both models can be considered as the sum of various sub-structures that describe some specific systems of the real world. For example, World3 was composed of 11 sub-sectors including demographics, industrial capital, and non-renewable resources. As a result, the creation of ERRE was based on the choice of some of these sub-structures from both models, and use of those as a starting point. In addition to modelling the interaction between existing structures, it is important to note that both models are relatively outdated in the formulation of the economic theory for the purpose of ERRE. Thus, after merging the structures, the final model was compared to today's state of the art, calibrated to available data and re-formulated accordingly.

In ERRE the sectorial and modular perspective as taken in Sterman (1981) took dominance. With the objective of modelling the effects of fossil fuel depletion on fossil fuel prices, with relative cascade effect on food price, the supply chain structure adopted in Sterman (1981) was used and enhanced with the agriculture sector. In particular, the 'conventional' and 'unconventional' energy sectors in ETE were used as a base for the 'fossil fuel' and 'renewables and nuclear' sectors in ERRE. The OPEC sector in ETE is embedded into the fossil fuel of the ERRE. In addition, the agriculture sector is included in ERRE as responsible for both the production of biofuels, thus competing for an energy market share to meet energy demand, and the generation of food output. This latter is assumed to respond to food demand, that is dependent on households as a result of increasing population and disposable income. Based on the World3–03 structure for the land sector, agriculture includes the limits to growth given the maximum amount of potentially arable land convertible to agricultural land for the scope of production. The sub-sector of Arable Land of the World3–03 is taken and enhanced with the wider economic theory as in Sterman (1981). Banks and public sector are based on Sterman (1981) but updated based on today's state of the art. These remain simplifications of the structures of the real world with the main roles of providing fiscal and monetary policies to the real economy.

The resulting framework was updated both theoretically and structurally. In particular, the structure of the economy connecting household savings deposits with banks balance sheet, and the debt of every firm in the model was completely restructured giving more emphasis on the debt money system as the instrument for running today's economy. Banks were represented as a general aggregated sector, represented in terms of the Basel III framework. Thus, a balance sheet approach is employed for every economic agent to assure stock-and-flow consistency in the economy as a whole.

The increased focus in the financial risk structures, required additional improvements in the structure of interest rates and defaulted capital, thus requiring improved details in the financial and real structures of capital assets. The structures that were not necessary for the purpose of Sterman (1981) became fundamental for ERRE in particular when addressing the dynamics of short-term climate shocks. Structures devoted to capture the dynamics of shipments and inventory-workforce were reintroduced.

In addition to both models, the climate system was also represented in very simplistic form. A generic structure of emissions accumulation and cycles with ocean and soil was developed in order to run scenarios of limits associated with the negative impact of climate on the food system. Modelling climate can require models composed of many variables. A simple model developed by the system dynamics community (Fiddaman 1997) and used as base for C-Road (Sterman et al. 2012) accounts for approximately 400 variables. The climate model ESCIMO (Randers et al. 2019) includes above 1000 elements. The climate dimension in ERRE is a simple one, with three stocks replicating the possible dynamics of the hot house effect (Steffen et al. 2018). In a similar way to DICE, the climate dimension of ERRE aims at testing the hypotheses of negative feedback of climate on food,

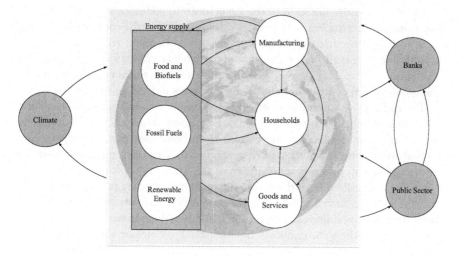

Figure 5.3 ERRE model sector overview

testing both damage functions as defined in the IPCC report, and more severe ones. The ERRE climate structure is modelled to allow testing uncertain conditions such as the hypothesis of hot house Earth (Steffen et al. 2018), and the possible damaging impact of climate on food loss. Figure 5.3 shows the sectorial perspective of ERRE.

In terms of model structure, further minor amends have been performed with the objective of homogenising the larger edits in a consistent purposeful global framework. All data used to calibrate and run the model have been taken from public sources (World Bank, United Nations Population Division, Food and Agriculture Organization, Energy and Information Administration) and aggregated at the global level. The resulting dataset required further edits on the structures of the model that were not be able to be calibrated on today's data. For example, the energy market and the energy retrofit structures were revised in the attempt of calibrating the model to the historical data.

The final result is a novel global system dynamics model that can serve both as a stand-alone application for generic run scenario comparisons, and as base for further development towards more sophisticated lower scale solutions such as regional or national models. All mistakes in ERRE remain the full responsibility of the authors of this work.

The economy within limits – model architecture

The ERRE model is a general disequilibrium model of the world economy bounded by environmental limits. In ERRE, growth can be generated both endogenously in the financial behaviour of firms and households, and exogenously via the application of population and technology growth curves that underpin the model for the entire duration of the simulation. In addition, exogenous money creation and government debt policies can be applied in the calibration process. It is worth noting that the application of both endogenous and exogenous disequilibrium factors allows for a good fit of the model to historical data during the calibration phase. This supports the evolutionary hypothesis of an economy in disequilibrium in contrast to mainstream economic modelling approaches.

The rest of the economy is governed by the reinforcing and balancing feedback loops that are characteristic of a capitalist economy. These include endogenous money creation, production and consumption behaviour, physical structure of capital and labour. Adaptation of the economy to limits are endogenously modelled, and system pressures emerging from the interaction between growth and limits are transmitted from the real to financial economy via prices, income and interest rates. In such a framework, exogenous policy inputs can be given both from the public and financial sectors, and additional environmental shocks can be applied to address the implication for financial risk measures. Figure 5.4 shows the top level view of the ERRE model, highlighting the sources of exogenous inputs to the model as well as some major interactions among component sectors.

As a system of systems, the architecture can be viewed in terms of its hierarchical structure as depicted in Figure 5.5. At the top level of the economy, the relationships between households, banks, government, climate, and firms define the core structure of the ERRE, consisting of a first level network among systems. At the second network level firms and households interact via real and financial flows in a fully functioning supply chain. At this level, firms generate demand for inputs to the rest of the economy, that is monitored and supplied by the interested producing firm. However, while some productive sectors are assumed to have no competition, and represent the entire market for those particular commodities, the energy market is assumed to have three competing suppliers for the entire economy, represented in Figure 5.5 as the third network level within the ERRE.

Given that population and labour productivity change have been considered outside the boundaries of the research question presented here, they have been both taken as exogenous input to the model. Population is applied as a time series using the UN Population Division forecast for the whole duration of the simulation. Labour productivity is formulated as the amount of real output (GDP) produced by every employed person (Jackson 2016). As a result of major differences across economic sectors, labour productivity is estimated exogenously for each sector while calibrating the model. Therefore, labour productivity can range from the Solow growth model that assumes exponential growth over the decades, to the stagnation scenario as proposed by Jackson and Victor (2015). Both inputs are provided in the following chapter.

While the economy grows, the dynamics of economic activity accumulate depletion and scarcity of natural resources, in turn generating pressures that propagate from the real economy to the financial system. In particular, the land system presents one of the limits by non-linearly increasing the cost of land development the more land is depleted. Such a structure is adapted from the Limits to Growth.

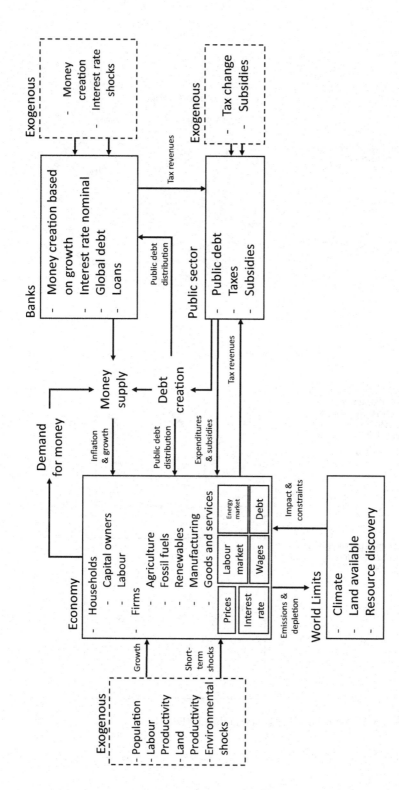

Figure 5.4 ERRE model architecture

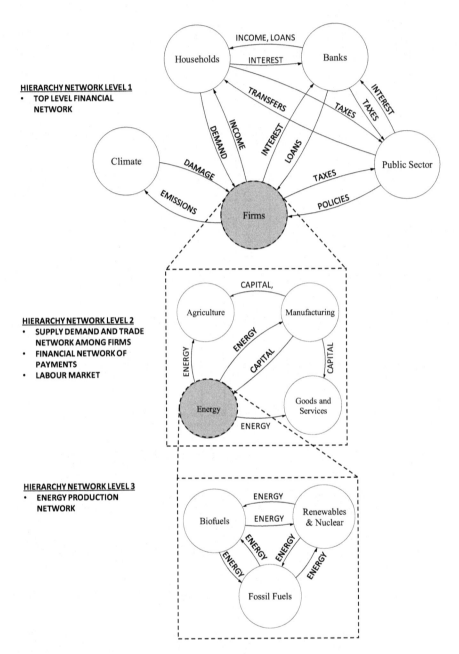

Figure 5.5 Hierarchical network view of the ERRE model

However, given the ERRE model is not designed to look at the dynamics of population growth and collapse, food output is treated as a normal commodity whose dynamics are governed by prices and demand. In addition, resource depletion and discovery dynamics are similar to the one depicted in Sterman (1981), generating dynamics of a production peak in the fossil fuel industry, systemic pressures on the rise of fossil fuel prices, and subsequent growth in the market share for alternative energy resources. Finally, the climate system accumulates emissions that above certain thresholds can have negative consequences on food output. All of these factors play a role in simultaneously affecting financial risk.

In such a context, the financial sector has the role of printing money and controlling the interest rate for the whole economy. The government collects taxes from every economic activity and gives back the income via government transfer to households. Options for applying subsidies and tax changes are also considered.

In this section, we cover the major high level feedback loops, and reveal the top level system architecture that allows to keep the economy together. This includes:

- The role of households between government, banks and firms;
- The stock and flow consistent structure of the economy, inclusive of the economy balance sheet matrix and the financial flows across sectors;
- The production and utility functions, and their role in determining the structure of the closed loop supply chain;
- The role of capital charge rate formulation and net present value formulation as a base for investment formulation; and
- The high level feedback structure interlinking the resources constraints and shocks to financial risk of firms, and relative balancing feedback loop from finance to stabilise the system.

Due to the size of the model, a full analytical description of the equations and system structures that form the ERRE model was not possible here. Rather, this chapter is accompanied by an online appendix that contains the set of equations and behavioural assumptions in fine detail. In particular, the online appendix reports the ERRE model sector by sector, starting from the top level view on the model. It reveals the mathematical formulation and decision feedback in each sector, and the use of non-linear relationships to model human decision making in line with the behavioural economic school. The ERRE is a highly modular system model, aiming to use the same structures as elements of different economic sectors. This allows to model financial, real and natural systems in each firm sector and the interconnection among those. In addition, it reveals the long-term limits to growth structures in the fossil fuels, agricultural land, and climate system formulation. The structure of the online appendix involves:

1 Government

    a   GDP and national income accounts
    b   Government balance sheet

2   Financial sector

    a   Balance sheet
    b   Money creation and lending
    c   Interest rate nominal

3   Firms and households

    a   Balance sheets and financial decisions
    b   Defaults and interest rates
    c   Borrowing and debt
    d   Savings propensity
    e   Prices (both rational and irrational structures)
    f   Production, demand and utility
    g   Depletion of fossil fuels (Limits to Growth)
    h   Energy returned on energy investment (EROEI)
    i   Energy market
    j   Real assets and capacity
    k   Agricultural and forest land
    l   Energy requirements of assets
    m   Assets value
    n   Depreciation
    o   Return on investments
    p   Labour market
    q   Wages
    r   Voluntarily unemployed
    s   Dividends

4   Climate limits

    a   Temperature anomaly above pre-industrial levels
    b   Hot house effect

The structure of the ERRE model is presented and made publicly available in order to welcome criticism from the academic and practitioner communities. Despite not being fundamental while reading this book, it is recommended to consult this documentation together with the computer model, and a summary of behavioural tests of the ERRE to grasp the best out of it. Both documents are available at https://doi.org/10.25411/aru.10110710.

Economic structure around households

The households and banking sectors are at the heart of the ERRE model. As explained in the following section, the financial relationships between those, as well as the firms and the government, generate the structure that controls growth in the model.

Households, banks, and firms

Figure 5.6 shows the set of relationships connecting household savings, the correspondent behaviour of banks and the growth aspect generated in the business sector. The income of households increases the net savings which are stored in banks, thus allowing for additional lending and loans to the real economy. From the private sector perspective (both household and firms), borrowing rises liquidity, that allows for greater payments to labour, distribution of dividends, as well as the servicing of loans. The sum of these three components become income, thus closing the reinforcing feedback R1.

Under business as usual conditions, R1 is further reinforced by the forces generating growth in the business sector R2. In fact, given the availability of liquidity to firms, greater investments can be allocated to increase the stock of capital (and productive assets), which generate demand for further loans. Under the assumption of growth, additional investments would be greater than debt redemption thus generating additional demand for money to be injected in the system from the financial sector. Increased lending would boost liquidity even further thus supporting the growth of the economy given reinforcing feedback mechanisms. Despite the origin of the banking system as providing interest bearing cash using household savings (Yamaguchi 2013), the model shows how the reality of money creation emerges from loans demand in the private sector in line with Jackson (2016). As today's economic system is based on debt, the banks have the ability to print money based on a set of borrowers' requirements.

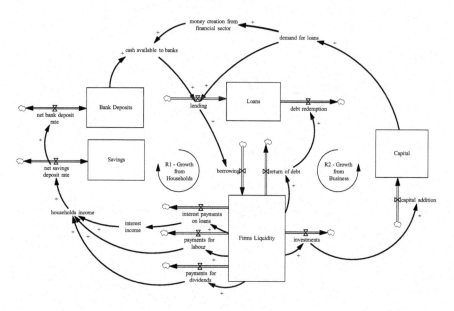

Figure 5.6 Reinforcing feedback loops in the financial dimension of savings deposits

Figure 5.6 depicts an abstraction from the ERRE model looking at the top level structural relationships in the economy between households, banks, and firms. However, as shown in the next sections of this chapter, the ERRE model disaggregates firms in sectors. While the stocks indicating savings, banks deposits and loans are correctly represented as single entities in the model, the stocks of firms' liquidity and capital are instead representative of the sum of the corresponding stocks in every sector of the economy.

Households, banks, and government

The second important aspect of households and banks is that they are the only two sectors in the economy that are allowed to own government debt. Government debt (securities) can be created only if there is a buyer for them. In the model it is assumed that both banking and household sector purchase a fraction of government debt each (Figure 5.7). When securities expire, their sum corresponds to the government retirement of debt, thus providing additional liquidity to both households and banks. Most importantly, government must service loans from the private sector, thus generating income to households and the financial sector proportional to the fraction of securities held.

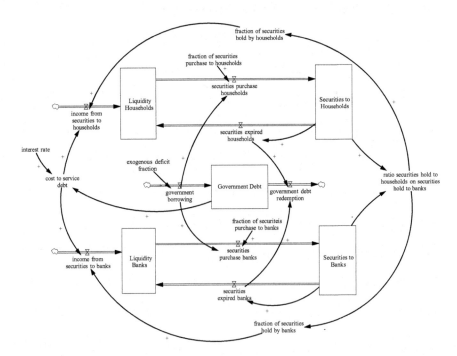

Figure 5.7 Distribution of government debt between households and financial sector

Stock and flow consistent economy

One of the objectives of the ERRE model is to be a suitable tool for policy support. The presence of feedback loops describing the interaction between economic and resource systems is a major strength of the model. However, it is by assuring stock and flow consistency of financial flows that those feedbacks can be translated into the language of policy makers. State of the art contains several modelling examples of income statements, balance sheets, and cash flow statements (Cincotti et al. 2012; Raberto et al. 2019; Lamperti et al. 2018; Jackson et al. 2016). In the representation of the modelling of ERRE we integrate the structures already present in Sterman (1981) with the one proposed in Yamaguchi (2013). In particular, the concept of balance sheet is introduced and the double-entry rule as principle for accounting system modelling has been used.

In so doing, every flow of cash that represents an outflow from one sector, has to become an inflow in another sector in the economy. In addition, respecting the double-entry rule facilitates the accounting of those flows within every sector, assuring they are reported on both the assets and liabilities sides of their balance sheets. Such an approach allows the balance of flows both in each sector, and in the entire economy. In the case of a closed loop economy (as it is in this case) the sum of all assets must always be equal to the sum of liabilities for the entire economy (Jackson 2016).

In order to assure the stock and flow consistency of the ERRE model, two conditions have to be met:

1   The balance sheet matrix of the economy must be consistent.
2   The outflows of cash from every sector must be an inflow to some other sector in the economy.

Table 5.1 shows the balance sheet consistency in the ERRE economy. The table reveals a common structure between the balance sheets of the firms. In particular, the general structure imposes a representation between assets and liabilities for each entity. On the assets side we find stocks of cash Λ and capital assets A. On the side of liabilities, a stock of debt D, that is proportional to the available capital assets A, and an equity ϵ, that is calculated to balance out assets and liabilities. As differences to the standard case, non-renewable resources account for the proven reserves PR as part of their assets, whereas the agriculture sector must account for the agricultural land AL.

The balance between government, households, banks and firms is obtained calculating the values that equilibrate the economy in both household and banking sectors. In particular, the government sector is assumed to have a null stock of liquidity Λ_{GOV} – i.e. all cash in is transferred instantaneously to the economy – and its debt D_{GOV} is balanced by the negative equity ϵ_{GOV}. Government debt is distributed as assets to households and banks.

In the case of the household sector, assets are represented by liquidity Λ_H, physical assets (A_H as capital and G_H as goods), government securities held Sec_H,

Table 5.1 Balance sheet matrix of the closed system economy

Assets/Liabilities	Variable	Capital (K)	Non-Renewables(N)	Renewables & Nuclear (R)	Agriculture(F)	Goods & Services(GS)	Households (H)	Government (GOV)	Banks(B)
Assets	Liquidity (Λ)	Λ_K	Λ_N	Λ_R	Λ_F	Λ_{GS}	Λ_H	$\Lambda_{GOV}=0$	$\Lambda_B=(LN_B+Sec_B)\times l/(1-l)\times(1-\tau)$
	Value of Capital (A)	A_K	A_N	A_R	A_F	A_{GS}	A_H	-	-
	Value of Durable Goods(G)	-	-	-	-	-	G_H	-	-
	Value of Agricultural Land (ALL)	-	-	-	AL_F	-	-	-	-
	Value of Proven Reserves(PR)	-	PR_N	-	-	-	-	-	-
	Securities Hold(Sec)	-	-	-	-	-	$Sec_H=\mu\times D_{GOV}$	-	$Sec_B=(1-\mu)\times D_{GOV}$
	Savings(S)	-	-	-	-	-	$S_H=(LN_B+Sec_B)\times l/(1-l)\times(1-\tau)$ $-\Lambda_K-\Lambda_N-\Lambda_R-\Lambda_F-$ $\Lambda_G-\Lambda_H-\Lambda_B-Res_B$	-	-
	Loans(LN)	-	-	-	-	-	-	-	$LN_B=D_C+D_N+D_E$ $+D_F+D_G+D_H$
	Monetary Reserves(Res)	-	-	-	-	-	-	-	$Res_B=(LN_B+Sec_B)\times$ $\tau/(1-\tau)$
Liabilities	Debt(D)	$D_K=\delta_c\times A_K$	$D_N=\delta_N\times(A_N+PR_N)$	$D_R=\delta_R\times A_R$	$D_F=\delta_F\times(A_F+AL_F)$	$D_{GS}=\delta_{GS}\times A_{GS}$	D_H	D_{GOV}	-
	Equity(ϵ)	$\epsilon_K=\Lambda_K+A_K-D_K$	$\epsilon_N=\Lambda_N+A_N+PR_N-D_N$	$\epsilon_R=\Lambda_R+A_R-D_R$	$\epsilon_F=\Lambda_F+K_F+AL_F-D_F$	$\epsilon_{GS}=\Lambda_{GS}+K_{GS}$ $-D_{GS}$	$\epsilon_H=\Lambda_H+K_H$ $+G_H+Sec_H+S_H-D_H$	$\epsilon_{Gov}=-D_{Gov}$	-
	Deposits(S)	-	-	-	-	-	-	-	$S_B=S_H$
	Debt Money(DM)	-	-	-	-	-	-	-	$DM_B=\Lambda_K+\Lambda_N+\Lambda_R$ $+\Lambda_F+\Lambda_G+\Lambda_H+\Lambda_B+Res_B$
	Total Assets-Total Liabilities	0	0	0	0	0	0	0	0

and savings S_H. In the ERRE, household's debt D_H is assumed to be initialised with available data (IIF 2018), whereas equity ϵ_H balances out the sector. Finally, bank deposits S_B and household savings S_H have to be balanced together and equilibrate the rest of the economy. On the side of banks' assets, loans LN_B are assumed to be equal to the sum of debt in the private sector. Liquidity Λ_B and reserves Res_B of banks are calculated based on loans and on the structure of Basel III regulations which aim to keep banks solvent. This includes an average fraction of reserves r and liquidity l to be held in their vaults. On the liabilities side, banks have to keep household's savings in the form of bank deposits S_B, and debt money DM_B. This latter represent the time deposits of the firm sector in banks, which has to correspond to the sum of all cash of every sector (i.e. the money supply). As a result, household's savings S_H can be calculated to balance the entire economy (see Table 5.1). It is worth noting that the entire structure of the closed loop economy relies on the amount of capital assets in the economy (i.e. savings are dependent on loans, that are dependent on debt, that relies on physical assets).

Table 5.2 shows the total amount of cash flows between sectors in the ERRE model. Reading the table from left to right, it presents the eight sectors of the economy and the destination of their outflows toward the other sectors. Further details on the calculation of these flows is depicted in the following section.

Households receive government transfers (expenditures), expiring securities and interest payments from the government, payments from firms in terms of wages and dividends, and from banks both as dividends and wages as well as interest received from loans from the private sector. Thus government receives tax income and can borrow money from the economy, then flowing all cash available into households and as subsidies to firms. Banks behave as a sovereign institution in the model lending money and retiring debt from each sector, as well as controlling a nominal interest rate to change inflation and dampen oscillation in the financial system. Finally, in order to sustain growth, the bank has to inject and withdraw money based on the state of the economy. Thus whatever imbalance remains is controlled by the bank, which is capable of printing money out of nothing thus keeping the entire economy in balance.

From stock and flow consistent to closed loop supply chain consistency

The stock and flow consistency of the financial flows of the model requires a balance in all cash flows in the systems among sectors. Given the ERRE model is a multi-layer model, capable of representing both financial and real flows, the financial architecture must be consistent with the real architecture of the system. In so doing, an important role is played by the production functions in the model, the initialisation structure of the system, and important assumptions that link costs and prices in the model. It is important to realise that the basic architecture of the ERRE model is neoclassical and consistent with the general equilibrium modelling framework (i.e. firms capable of production with neoclassical

Table 5.2 Summary of financial flows in the model

from \ to	Inflows							
	Capital	Non-renewables	Renewables	Agriculture	Goods	Households	Government	Banks
Capital	- Payments for capital - Payments for capital from defaults to firms	- Payments for energy	- Payments for energy	- Payments for energy		- Dividends - Wages	- Taxes	- Interest payments - Return of debt - Payments for capital from defaults to banks
Non-Renewables	- Payments for capital	- Payments for energy - Payments for capital from defaults to firms	- Payments for energy	- Payments for energy		- Dividends - Wages	- Taxes	- Interest payments - Return of debt - Payments for capital from defaults to banks
Renewables (Outflows)	- Payments for capital	- Payments for energy	- Payments for energy - Payments for capital from defaults to firms	- Payments for energy		- Dividends - Wages	- Taxes	- Interest payments - Return of debt - Payments for capital from defaults to banks
Agriculture	- Payments for capital - Payments for agricultural land developemnt	- Payments for energy	- Payments for energy	- Payments for energy - Payments for capital from defaults to firms - Payments for Agricultural Land from defaults to firms		- Dividends - Wages	- Taxes	- Interest payments - Return of debt - Payments for capital from defaults to banks - Payments for agricultural land from defaults to banks
Goods	- Payments for capital	- Payments for energy	- Payments for energy	- Payments for energy	- Payments for capital from defaults to firms	- Dividends - Wages	- Taxes	- Interest payments - Return of debt - Payments for capital from defaults to banks

| | Inflows | | | | | | | |
from \ to	Capital	Non-renewables	Renewables	Agriculture	Goods	Households	Government	Banks
Households	- Payments for capital	- Payments for energy	- Payments for energy	- Payments for energy - Payments for food	- Payments for Goods	- Payments for capital from defaults to households - Payments for goods from defaults to households	- Taxes - Purchase securities	- Interest payments - Return of debt - Savings deposit - Savings withdrawal - Payments for capital from defaults to banks - Payments for goods from defaults to banks
Outflows — Government	-	-	-	-	-	- Government transfers - Interest payments - Cash from securities expired		- Interest payments - Cash from securities expired
Banks	- Lending / Borrowing	- Lending / Borrowing	- Lending / Borrowing	- Lending /Borrowing	- Lending / Borrowing	- Lending /Borrowing - Dividends - Wages - Interest payments	- Taxes - Purchase securities	- Money creation - Money withdrawl

formulation, and households driving demand led by a utility function). Such a formulation is then enhanced with system dynamic disequilibrium structures that aim at improving the equilibrium theory with more realistic assumptions.

This section first provides the explanation of the why's of this choice. First, general considerations on production and utility functions from economic theory are made. Secondly, the production and utility functions, and their systemic variations as used in the ERRE are presented. Third, we show the implications of those structures for modelling a closed loop supply chain among various sectors, as depicted in ERRE.

Considerations on production and utility functions

The objective of a production function is to define a structural relationship between inputs to production and output. The production function in use in Sterman (1981) is a variation on a two level constant-elasticity of substitution (CES) production, which integrates energy and capital at the first level, and nests the results with labour using a Cobb-Douglas function on the second level (Sato 1967; Arrow et al. 1961). Variations on the standard formulation include the exogenous application of technology growth, inclusion of delays in ordering decisions as well as non-linear adaptation from energy availability to output thus constraining supply in time of energy shortages (Sterman 1981).

A similar approach is used to calculate utility in the households sector as the driver for demand in the entire model. In fact households consume both goods and capital, that in turn consume energy to operate. In addition, utility (as a measure of satisfaction derived from consumption) is assumed to receive positive effects from the voluntary unemployed. Therefore, the utility function employees a two level CES production function, where the first level includes the integration of capital and energy and the integration of goods and energy, whereas the second level nests together these results with the effects from the voluntary unemployed (Sterman 1981).

In the ERRE model, the same approach is used for the productive sectors and variations on this are applied for the production of agriculture output and household utility. However, production functions have been an important topic of discussion, and require justification for such a choice.

Nowadays, the two standard forms of production function used in dynamic economic modelling are:

1   Cobb-Douglas production function
2   Leontief input-output production function

The Cobb-Douglas is an equation which takes the following form:
   Eq. 5.1 – Cobb-Douglas production function

$$P = P_0 \times \left(\frac{K}{K_0} \right)^{\varepsilon} \times \left(\frac{L}{L_0} \right)^{1-\varepsilon}$$

Where P is production, K is the capital, K_0 is the capital at the beginning of the simulation, L is the labour, L_0 is the labour at the beginning of the simulation, and ε is a parameter between 0 and 1 representing the elasticity of substitution between labour and capital to obtain production. This formulation is continuous for every value of K, L, ε thus allowing for the calculation of the marginal productivity of every input factor thus deriving P based on each input factor. For example the marginal productivity of capital would be:

Eq. 5.2 – Marginal productivity in Cobb-Douglas production function

$$\frac{\partial P}{\partial C} = P_0 \times \varepsilon \times \left(\frac{K}{K_0}\right)^{\varepsilon-1} \times \left(\frac{L}{L_0}\right)^{1-\varepsilon} \times \left(\frac{1}{K_0}\right) = \varepsilon \times \frac{P}{K}$$

Such a property allows for the calculation of the investment function, while assuming optimal capability of firms in understanding the exact amount of capital that is necessary to reach desired production. Under the assumption of increases in demand, and no change in productivity, the formulation would result in growth of labour and capital proportional to demand change.

An important property that can be seen as a weakness of such a formulation is the possible implication of shortages of one or other productive factor. For example, when keeping the elasticity of substitution constant, a forced perturbation that would not allow the adjustment of capital to desired levels (e.g. hurricane shock) would generate pressure to reach production by increasing labour, thus assuring the perfect substitutability of one productive factor for the other. Such a condition would not be representative of the real world for the majority of capital intensive industries. Thus, variants on this formulation allows the elasticity to vary, or assumes decreasing marginal productivity (i.e. the exponents of labour and capital would sum to less than 1) (Cincotti et al. 2012). In addition, Shaikh (1974) argued that such a formulation should not even be called a production function, simply because its properties would allow the equation to match to whatever pattern of historical data, making it unsuitable for the purpose it is supposed to fulfil.

The CES production function is a more sophisticated formulation than the Cobb-Douglas, but implications for neoclassical theory would hold (Arrow et al. 1961). In the case of labour and capital it takes the following form:

Eq. 5.3 – Constant elasticity of substitution production function

$$P = P_0 \times \left(\varepsilon \times \frac{K}{K_0} + (1-\varepsilon) \times \frac{L}{L_0}^{-\rho} \right)^{-\frac{1}{\rho}}$$

Where ε represents the value share of capital, $(1-\varepsilon)$ represents the value share of labour on total production, and the ρ the elasticity of substitution between capital and labour. The equation does not solve for $\rho = 0$; however, it is possible to demonstrate that calculating the limit of the equation with ρ tending to zero, the final result would be exactly the Cobb-Douglas Formulation of Eq. 5.1.

On the other hand, the Leontief production function, under the assumption of labour and capital as input to production, would have the following formulation:

Eq. 5.4 – Leontief production function

$$P = min\left(P_K, P_L\right) = min\left(K \times \pi_K, L \times \pi_L\right)$$

Where P is production, P_K is the maximum production reachable from capital, P_L the maximum production with available labour, K is capital, L is labour, π_K is the productivity of one unit of capital, and π_L is the productivity of every worker. The standard formulation of the Leontief production function assumes no substitutability between the two production factors, thus providing less flexibility than Cobb-Douglas in allowing the equation to match historical data. The Leontief is well understood in the general industrial production context of an assembly line to produce one unit of product. For example, if the production of one car would require four wheels and one steering wheel, the productivity of each wheel could be calculated as ¼ whereas the productivity of one steering wheel as 1/1. In sum, the production of ten cars, can be achieved if and only if 40 wheels and ten steering wheels are available for assembly. Such a formulation would allow the calculation of the amount of desired capacity for each productive factor simply dividing the desired production by their productivity, thus allocating investments and costs.

Thus, a Leontief production function would be more suitable for low-scale dynamic systems, such the decision making of a single firm. Useful application of this thinking has been found in the agent-based modelling community (Cincotti et al. 2012), which simulate thousands of companies competing against one another, while observing behaviour emerging from their complex interactions. The Leontief production function is, in fact, not continuous in the presence of significant delays in ordering capital and hiring labour. While maximum production of labour and maximum production of capital oscillate, the resulting output would be a discontinuous function, which would be representative for small-scale systems but not at the aggregated level of the entire economy.

It is worth remembering that the system dynamics view requires to look at systems from the top, imagining looking at the world from far enough that discrete decisions of managers in day to day activity can be approximated as continuous flows of decisions (Richardson 1991). In fact, the system dynamics view is suitable for the perspective of a high level manager or a policy maker. In ERRE, the required level of aggregation is the one of the entire world. From this perspective, every economic sector is representative of the entire group of firms in the world which operates in that market, both in the small scale and crossing boundaries of countries with different legislation and constraints.

For the purpose of the ERRE model, the main interest is in the understanding of the dynamics of growth within world limits and capturing the pressures that emerge in the financial sector due to the interaction between growth and environmental limits. Given such a purpose, the application of neoclassical theory and production function represents an even greater demonstration of the fallacies of the current economic system and paradigm.

Thus the production function formulation used in Sterman (1981) is considered suitable for the purpose of the ERRE model. Even if the ERRE model can be used as a general theory for country level economies, it is advised that the more regional the scale, the more sophisticated the production function would have to be. Using Leontief and variants on it would be a possibility, or alternatively using an original labour productivity growth theory developed ad-hoc for the purpose for the model. It is important to recognise that, despite the ERRE model being devised in the light of the application of exogenous shocks in the economy, the application of shocks that are too severe would result in less meaningful behaviours from the economic system due to the neoclassical theory underpinning it.

The ERRE production and utility function

GENERIC BUSINESS SECTOR

Figure 5.8 shows the modelling of production in a generic business sector in ERRE. At the first level of the production function, capital and energy are nested together in a CES equation to obtain effective capital, whereas labour is adjusted by labour productivity to obtain effective labour. Those calculations are input to the Cobb-Douglas at the second level of the production function, thus obtaining

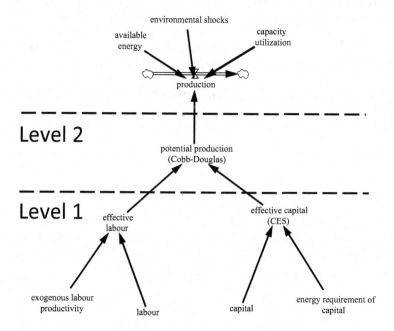

Figure 5.8 Production function in the business sector of ERRE

potential production for that sector. The effective production is a flow of commodities, and is further affected by other variables such as available energy, environmental constraints, and capacity utilisation.

In particular, effective capital K^{eff} is calculated as:

Eq. 5.5 – Effective capital in ERRE

$$K^{\text{eff}} = K_0 \times \left(\varepsilon_{\text{CES}} \times \frac{K}{K_0} + \left(1 - \varepsilon_{\text{CES}}\right) \times \frac{E}{E_0}^{-\rho} \right)^{-\frac{1}{\rho}}$$

Where K_0 is the capital at initial time in the simulation, ε_{CES} is the value share of capital as a fraction between the value of capital and the sum of capital and energy, $\frac{K}{K_0}$ represents the normalised increase in capital over time, $\frac{E}{E_0}$ is the normalised increase of energy requirement of capital over time, and ρ is the constant elasticity of substitution between capital and energy.

Effective labour L^{eff} is calculated as:

Eq. 5.6 – Effective labour in ERRE

$$L^{\text{eff}} = L \times \pi_L(t)$$

Where L is the labour and $\pi_L(t)$ the exogenous factor for labour productivity growth over time applied in line with the Solow growth model. The three options available here include (i) ramp growth, (ii) exponential growth, or (iii) decreasing marginal returns to productivity stagnation. Given the aggregated level of the economy and the real data the ramp growth is preferred, simply because it shows how the level of growth in labour productivity decreased over time (Jackson 2016).

At the second level, potential production P, is calculated with the Cobb-Douglas formulation as:

Eq. 5.7 – Second level CES production function in ERRE

$$P = P_0 \times \left(\frac{K^{\text{eff}}}{\text{eff}_0} \right)^{\varepsilon_{\text{CB}}} \times \left(\frac{L^{\text{eff}}}{L^{\text{eff}}_0} \right)^{1-\varepsilon_{\text{CB}}}$$

Where ε_{CB} is the elasticity of substitution between labour and capital.

The resulting equation is used for the calculation of potential production for the sectors of capital, goods, non-renewable energy, and renewable energy, with variants for the non-renewable sector, in relation to depletion.

AGRICULTURE

In the case of agriculture, the approach assumes the addition of land as the third production factor (Figure 5.9). Thus, at the first level of the production function

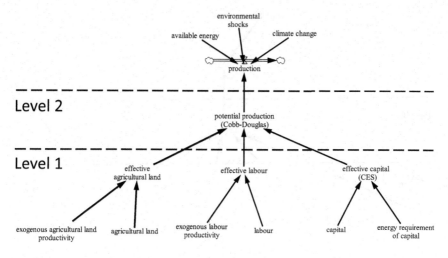

Figure 5.9 Production function in the agriculture sector

the effective agricultural land AL^{eff} is introduced in a similar way to labour productivity as:

Eq. 5.8 – Effective agricultural land

$$AL^{eff} = AL \times \pi_{AL}(t)$$

Where AL is the stock of agricultural land, $\pi_{AL}(t)$ the exogenous curve addressing productivity of every hectare of land.

Thus at the second level of the production function, agricultural output is
calculated in the following way:

Eq. 5.9 – Second level CES production function in agriculture

$$P_F = P_{F_0} \times \left(\frac{AL^{eff}}{AL_0} \right)^{\varepsilon_{ALF}} \times \left(\frac{K^*}{K^*_0} \right)^{\varepsilon_{KF}} \times \left(\frac{L^*}{L^*_0} \right)^{1-\varepsilon_{ALF}-\varepsilon_{KF}}$$

P_F represents the food output from the agricultural sector, P_{F_0} the food output
at the initial time in the simulation, ε_{AL_F} represents the value share of agricultural land on total production, and ε_{K_F} the value share of capital on total
production. As a condition for the Cobb-Douglas production function, the sum
$\varepsilon_{ALF} + \varepsilon_{KF} < 1$.

HOUSEHOLDS

In the ERRE model, the households are assumed to treat food, voluntary unemployed,
goods and services and capital as indistinguishable as indistinguishable factors

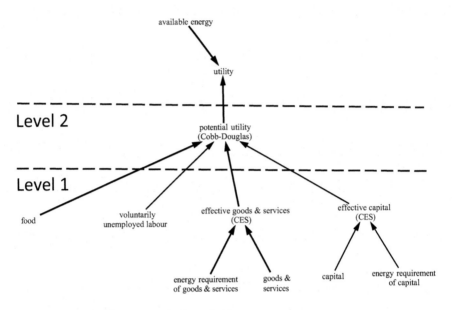

Figure 5.10 Utility function in the household sector

generating utility, and assessing them for their economic value in terms of their input to utility. The potential utility function is a two level Cobb-Douglas and CES function, filtering by available energy for the calculation of utility (Figure 5.10).

Thus, effective goods and services and effective capital are calculated in the equivalent way as if it were the productive sector (Eq. 5.10). Voluntary unemployed and food output are assumed to generate utility without any input of energy or technology. The resulting equation for potential utility *PU* becomes as follows:

Eq. 5.10 – Utility function in households

$$PU = PU_0 \times \left(\frac{F}{F_0}\right)^{\varepsilon_{F_H}} \times \left(\frac{K^{\text{eff}}}{K^{\text{eff}}_0}\right)^{\varepsilon_{K_H}} \times \left(\frac{GS^{\text{eff}}}{GS^{\text{eff}}_0}\right)^{\varepsilon_{GS_H}} \times \left(\frac{L}{L_0}\right)^{1-\varepsilon_{F_H}-\varepsilon_{K_H}-\varepsilon_{G_H}}$$

Where PU_0 is the potential utility at the beginning of the simulation, ε_{F_H}, ε_{K_H}, ε_{GS_H}, are the value shares of food, capital, and goods and services respectively, and F, K^{eff}, GS^{eff}, and L are the amount of food, capital, goods and services, and labour providing utility to households.

The production function and the closed loop supply chain

The equations of the production and utility functions have major implications for the structures underpinning the entire supply chain of the model. In particular, the ERRE model represents an economy composed of five productive sectors, each supplying output based on the need of the others. In a closed-loop supply chain in perfect balance, the real demand for each sector should match their supply capacity. This is not a compulsory condition for the model to run. In fact feedback processes underpinning the entire model would quickly match each other in the disequilibrium dynamics of the system. However, for the scope of this work, and possible further work development, we satisfy the ideal condition of initial supply chain balance. It is important to consider that we start the simulation from the year 2000, in which most data of interest are available.

Table 5.3 shows the type of output that each productive sector supplies to the other sectors of the economy. As it is possible to see, the goods and services sector supplies households only, thus representing consumption. The capital sector is assumed to be both industrial and construction capital, as well as provider for all goods and services that are consumed by each sector for productive activities. The energy sector is composed of non-renewables, renewables and nuclear, and agriculture, thus assuming that agriculture can allocate resources both for the production of food to deliver to households and biofuels which compete in the energy market. Table 5.3 provides the foundation of the real economy for the financial flows as depicted in Table 5.2. The entire structure of payments is dependent on the following description, and summarised in Table 5.4 at the end of this section.

In the backbone structure of ERRE model, firms are assumed to set prices in order to fulfil the cost of production while impacted from irrational market behaviour and market forces. In the case of the generic productive sector with capital, energy and labour as production inputs their value shares on the total cost of production would determine their relative productivity and composition of price structure. In mathematical terms:

Eq. 5.11 – Relation between costs and price

$$p = \frac{ucl \times L + uck \times K + uce \times E}{P}$$

Table 5.3 Type of output that each productive sector supplies to every other sector

From – > to	Goods and services	Capital	Agriculture	Non-renewables	Renewables	Households
Goods and Services	-	-	-	-	-	-Goods and Services
Capital	-Capital	-Capital	-Capital - Land development	-Capital	-Capital	-Capital
Agriculture	-Energy	-Energy	-Energy	-Energy	-Energy	-Food -Energy
Non-renewables	-Energy	-Energy	-Energy	-Energy	-Energy	-Energy
Renewables and Nuclear	-Energy	-Energy	-Energy	-Energy	-Energy	-Energy

Table 5.4 Supply chain equilibrium system of equation

Sector	Inputs to production and utility			
	Capital	Goods and services	Energy	Food
Goods and services	$\dfrac{\varepsilon_{K_{GS}} \times p_{GS} \times P_{GS}}{kcr_{GS} \times p_{K_{GS}}} \times \delta_{KG}$	-	$\dfrac{\varepsilon_{E_{GS}} \times p_{GS} \times P_{GS}}{p_E}$	-
Capital	$\dfrac{\varepsilon_{K_K} \times p_K \times P_K}{kcr_K \times p_K} \times \delta_{KK}$	-	$\dfrac{\varepsilon_{E_K} \times p_K \times P_K}{p_E}$	-
Agriculture	$\dfrac{\varepsilon_{K_F} \times p_F \times \left(P_F + \dfrac{P_{Fe}}{\tau}\right)}{kcr_F \times p_K} \times \delta_{KF} + \dfrac{\varepsilon_{AL_F} \times p_F \times \left(P_F + \dfrac{P_{Fe}}{\tau}\right)}{alcr_F \times p_{AL}} \times \delta_{AL}$	-	$\dfrac{\varepsilon_{E_F} \times p_F \times \left(P_F + \dfrac{P_{Fe}}{\tau}\right)}{p_E}$	-
Renewables	$\dfrac{\varepsilon_{K_R} \times p_R \times P_R}{kcr_R \times p_K} \times \delta_{KR}$	-	$\dfrac{\varepsilon_{E_R} p_R \times P_R}{p_E}$	-
Non-renewables	$\dfrac{\varepsilon_{K_N} \times p_N \times P_N}{kcr_N \times p_K} \times \delta_{KN}$	-	$\dfrac{\varepsilon_{E_N} \times p_N \times P_N}{p_E}$	-
Households	$\dfrac{\varepsilon_{K_H} \times VU_H}{kcr_H \times p_K} \times \delta_{KH}$	$\dfrac{\varepsilon_{GS_H} \times VU_H}{gscr_H \times p_{GS}} \times \delta_{GSH}$	$\dfrac{\varepsilon_{E_H} \times VU_H}{p_E}$	
Sum	P_k	P_{GS}	$P_E = P_{Fe} + P_N + P_R$	P_F

Where p is the price of output; P is the production of the sector; L, K, and E are labour, capital, and energy requirements; and ucl, uck, and uce are the unit costs of labour, capital, and energy respectively.

Thus, assuming the relative contribution of costs of the three components to production as the value shares ε_c for the capital, ε_E for the energy, and ε_L for the labour and assuring the Cobb-Douglas condition as:

Eq. 5.12 – Cobb-Douglas condition of exponents

$$\varepsilon_K + \varepsilon_E + \varepsilon_L = 1$$

assuring that the value share of capital to energy ε_{KE}, is calculated as follows:

Eq. 5.13 – Value share of energy in capital

$$\varepsilon_{KE} = \frac{\varepsilon_E}{\varepsilon_K + \varepsilon_E}$$

Combining Eq. 5.11, Eq. 5.12 and Eq. 5.13, it is possible to demonstrate that:

Eq. 5.14 – Value share of capital

$$\varepsilon_K = \frac{uck \times K}{P}$$

Eq. 5.15 – Value share of energy

$$\varepsilon_E = \frac{uce \times E}{P}$$

Eq. 5.16 – Value share of labour

$$\varepsilon_L = \frac{ucl \times L}{P}$$

In addition, it is possible to assume that the unit cost of energy uce corresponds to the price of energy p_E as:

Eq. 5.17 – Unit cost of energy

$$uce = p_E$$

The unitarian cost of labour ucl is wages w as:

Eq. 5.18 – Unit cost of labour

$$ucl = w$$

It is possible to calculate the cost of capital as proportional to the value of the capital at the time of purchase, as a function of interest, taxes, as well as average lifetime of capital itself, such that:

Eq. 5.19 – Unit cost of capital

$$uck = p_k \times kcr\left(i, \tau, \delta\right)$$

Where *kcr* is the capital charge rate of capital at current price p_k, *i* is the interest rate at the time of purchase, τ the tax rate, and δ the discard rate of real capital.

The same rationale can be extended to the case of food, households, and their additional production factors. In so doing, by combining the equations Eq. 5.7, Eq. 5.9, Eq. 5.11, Eq. 5.14, Eq. 5.15, Eq. 5.16, Eq. 5.17, Eq. 5.18, and Eq. 5.19, it is possible to calculate the reference values of each productive factor at the start year of the simulation to obtain balance.

However, while food and energy consumption are flows, thus requiring a perfect match between production and consumption, the case of capital and agricultural land, being stocks, is different. The values for the required capital and agricultural land additions to keep the stock in perfect balance must equal the discard of those stocks (which is a flow).

For example, in the case of agriculture the amount of capital production to balance the stock of agricultural capital is:

Eq. 5.20 – Amount of capital production to balance agriculture stock

$$KDR = \frac{\varepsilon_{K_F} \times p_F \left(P_F + \dfrac{P_{Fe}}{\omega} \right)}{kcr_F \times p_k} \times \delta_{kF}$$

Where *KDR* is the capital development rate, ε_{K_F} is the value share of capital for agricultural production, p_F is the price per unit of agricultural output, P_F is the amount of agricultural output devoted to food, P_{Fe} is the amount of agricultural output devoted to energy use in energy units, ω is the constant transformation from energy units in food units, kcr_F is the capital charge rate in agriculture, p_k is the price of capital units, and δ_{kF} is the capital discard per year.

This rationale, extended to all production and consumption sectors in the model, allows for the quantification of the flows that are necessary to balance the supply-demand network of the model. As Table 5.4 shows, the assurance of the solution of these equalities would generate the balance of the system at the initial condition, ceteris paribus on different exogenous factors (such as population growth and technology change). In other words, the entire structure of payments is dependent on the equations presented in Table 5.2 (real flows between sectors) and the prices of output from each sector.

A major implication of the solution of the system of equations presented in Table 5.2 is the way the ERRE model applies real data to define the real asset stocks and assure balance sheet consistency in the model. Each of the flows presented in Table 5.4 would allow the calculation of the relative stocks of production, that in turn would be used to calculate the stocks of financial value used to assure the balance sheet matrix relies on the correct set of data, while keeping the system in equilibrium.

It is very important to distinguish here the difference in terminology between equilibrium assumptions in the system dynamics term, and the one intended in the Computable General Equilibrium models. In CGEM, equilibrium states that there exists a value between supply and demand which would always bring the model to equilibrium, neglecting any external factor to markets, such as resource depletion or climate change. In the terms of system dynamics modelling, the concept of equilibrium indicates the reaching of the state of perfect balance between inflows and outflows from every single stock variable in the model. This condition, is not a formal requirements for the testing of simulation models in general, but it demonstrates the mathematical precision underpinning the model, in particular for assuring the condition of stock and flow consistency in the entire economy. For example, the Sterman (1981) approach to the problem was for the solution of the entire system of equations to move towards equilibrium, and voluntarily neglect some of these factors (small ones) in order to leave the system in precarious imbalance at the initial time of the simulation. Such an assumption, together with technology change, population growth, and depletion of resources, support the dynamics of disequilibrium in the US economy. In the case of the ERRE model, instead, real-world data on production variables have been used to initialise the model to a stable condition, and the resulting system of equations have been solved.

CAPITAL CHARGE RATE FORMULATION

In order to conclude the explanation of the basic architecture of the model, the equation defining capital (and agricultural land) charge rate, has to be defined. The formulation for capital charge rate in the ERRE model follows the same approach as in Sterman (1981), which is by proposing a variant on the neoclassical theory of optimal capital accumulation as described in Hall and Jorgenson (1967) and Hall and Jorgenson (1969). In particular, Sterman (1981) breaks the optimality condition of input to the equations, despite maintaining it as foundation for the structure of the business model. For the purpose of ERRE, particular attention has to be given to such an equation given the implications for the stock and flow consistency requirements of the firm sector of the model as requisite for national accounting systems today.

Both studies apply the resulting equations and theory to address the change in taxes on capital towards the gradual deregulation that happened in the US between 1954 to 1967. These changes involved (i) adoption of accelerator method for computing depreciation for tax purposes, (ii) adoption of investment tax credit, and (iii) adoption of fair value accounting for depreciation in the investment functions. Hall and Jorgenson (1967, 1969) demonstrated the good fit of the equation to historical data involving various industrial sectors in the US economy, including manufacturing, goods, and food industry.

For the purpose of ERRE, these three factors have been neglected since ERRE does not aim to reach precise estimates for tax policy data in capital accounting structures. Thus, ERRE uses an equation relying on two fundamental principles of business accounting as normal practice today:

- The long-term behaviour of firms to seek balance between revenue, the cost of capital and labour structure, given taxes, interest rates, discount rates and capital discard rate.
- The behaviour of firms in using net present value practices in discounting future values of assets giving more importance to short-term return on investment.

While providing the business structure with such short-term behaviour, ERRE's aim is to demonstrate the possible consequences of limits in a world which runs along business as usual principles.

Neglecting the factors of accelerated capital depreciation, fair value of accounting and investment tax credit, the equation for capital charge rate takes the following form:

Eq. 5.21 – Capital charge rate formulation

$$
kcr = \frac{(d+\delta)}{(1-\tau)} \times \left(1 - \frac{\tau \times \delta}{(d+\delta)} \times \left(1 - e^{-\frac{(d+\delta)}{\delta}} \right) \right)
$$

Where d is the discount rate, δ is the capital depreciation rate, τ represents the corporate tax rate.

Whereas depreciation δ and tax rate τ are exogenous parameters and inputs for exogenous policy shocks, the discount rate d is endogenously calculated, and representative of the rate of profit necessary for investors to engage in business activity. Thus it has to pay for the real cost of servicing debt, and a risk factor of expected returns.

Thus the discount rate d is represented in the following form:

Eq. 5.22 – Discount rate in the capital charge rate formulation

$$
d = i + \frac{\psi}{(1-\tau)} - \gamma
$$

Where i is the nominal interest rate at the time of capital purchase Eq. 5.24, γ is the inflation rate, τ is the tax rate, and ψ is the risk factor rate assumed to be constant and average across sectors, representing the amount of expected revenue on assets from capital owners.

The combined effects of Eq. 5.19, Eq. 5.21, and Eq. 5.22 are twofold:

1   Generate all the set of balancing feedback loops which constrains investments functions of firms when capital price and interest rates rise (this dynamics is fully explained in the firm section of this chapter).
2   Provides the foundation for the structure generating stock and flow consistency in the model. This allows balance between capital costs accounting for tax payments, interest payments, and dividends.

On this latter point, it is important to highlight the role of the ψ (risk premium before tax) parameter in the dynamics of the model. Given that capital owners' profit is dependent on the marginal revenue on top of interest and taxes, the larger this number is, the larger the amount of cash is devoted to those who own the capital rather than those who provide labour. Most important, it quantifies how sensitive a particular sector is to variations of interest rate and financial risk. Future versions of the ERRE model could apply sensitivity analysis on this parameter, to determine dynamics of inequality between classes of the society. The next section describes how financial risk is influenced by natural shocks and how resource limits can influence the real economy via financial variables.

From resource limits to financial risk

Looking at the system from the bottom-up perspective, this section describes the set of feedback loops that interlink resource limits and interest rates that are used as a measure for financial risk. Interest rates are input to investment decisions in the private sector (see preceding): the higher the interest the lower the investment as capital is more expensive.

In the ERRE model, the interest rate (i_{rp}) is modelled on three levels.

- Base interest rate for policy (i_b)
- Nominal interest rate (i_n)
- Interest rate with risk premium (i_{rp})

The base interest rate i_b is a constant value, with the possibility for exogenous change to test policies based on user requirements. The nominal interest rate i_n builds on the former adding a component dependent on inflation γ, and a non-linear effect of money demand to supply ratio. The interest rate with risk premium i_{rp} is different for each sector. It accounts for the interest rate nominal i_n summed up with a non-linear effect of the rate of default on debt $\lambda(\nabla_D)$ specific for every sector. Eq. 5.23 and Eq. 5.24 show the mathematical form of the interest rate. A deeper review of this structure can be found at https://doi.org/10.25411/aru.10110710.

Eq. 5.23 – Nominal interest rate

$$i_n = i_b + \lambda\left(\gamma, \frac{money\ available\ for\ lending}{money\ demand}\right)$$

Eq. 5.24 – Interest rate with risk premium

$$i_{rp} = i_n + \lambda(\nabla_D)$$

Figure 5.11 shows the reinforcing feedback loop governing such a dynamic behaviour. Available liquidity of one sector is assumed to decrease the average amount of defaults for that sector. An increase in defaults generates a response from the financial sector by raising the risk premium. Risk factors add to the nominal interest rate imposed from the banking system thus constituting the overall interest rate used for loans. The higher the interest, the higher the cost to service loans and the higher the total cost of operating capital which decreases liquidity itself. The feedback loop is positive. The more the liquidity grows (as described in a business as usual growing economy in Figure 5.11), the lower the cost of loans and, as such, sustaining availability of cash in the economy. It is important to note that the dynamics of reinforcing feedback loops plays a crucial role in real system economic models. When cash grows, the interest rate sustains the accumulation of further wealth while decreasing costs. However, if cash happens to decrease (maybe due to an exogenous shock), the reinforcing loop would act in the opposite direction, therefore increasing defaults and interest rates, which would increase costs and reduce liquidity. In such a case, the recovery of the sector would be driven by the balancing feedback loops as described in Figure 5.11.

Figure 5.12 expands the picture with two balancing feedback loops involving liquidity, capital accumulation, and debt for each sector as modelled in ERRE. In particular, the higher the liquidity, the higher is the push for higher investments which accumulates in production capacity. However, the higher the capacity, the higher the cost of operations (including labour and energy), thus increasing cash outflows (balancing loop B1). The same dynamics are also reinforced by

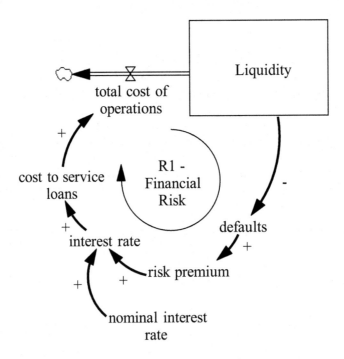

Figure 5.11 Reinforcing feedback loop from cash availability to interest rate in the private sector

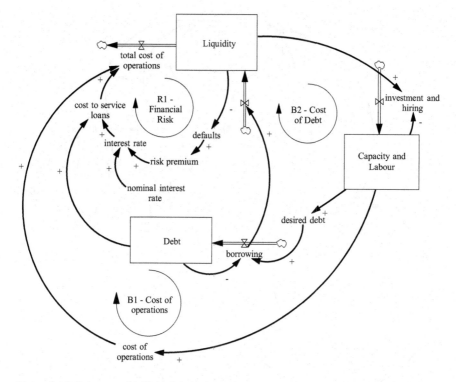

Figure 5.12 Balancing feedback loops counterbalancing interest rate within firm

the balancing feedback loop B2. In ERRE, it is assumed that managers would maintain a proportional relationship between debt and assets to manage risks while growing. Increased debt would generate higher cost of loans, thus balancing liquidity even further.

Figure 5.13 shows the expanded picture linking the impact of resources and environmental constraints (hexagon) to the dynamics of interest rate via real production flows. In particular, two reinforcing feedback loops emerging between the dynamics of price, production, and revenue are shown together with the balancing effect of demand from the supply chain, and adjustment of capacity to demand. Capital and labour increase production capacity, which in turn allows for larger sales and revenue, which supports liquidity accumulation and further investments (R2).

Price represents one of the most important variables for every productive sector since it lies at the core of both balancing and reinforcing feedback loops connecting demand and capacity adaptation. On the side of demand, increases in price have a balancing effect (B3). The higher the price, the lower the demand for commodities. The inventory have lower sales, thus reducing the desired inventory, which acts as a reduction on prices, therefore stabilising demand. On

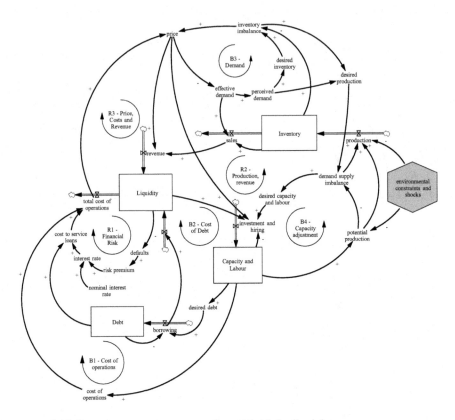

Figure 5.13 From resource constraints to financial risk feedback loop structure

the side of production, the major effect is reinforcing as captured in the dynamics of R3. The higher the price the higher are the revenue and inflow to liquidity, which enable higher investments. On the other side, greater price generates a short-term increase in investments, thus simulating the interest of the business sector to increase capacity to increase profits. This impact generates the forces which increase accumulated assets and debt, and therefore total costs of operations. However, as cost is a fundamental component of price, producers have embedded costs increases within the final price of outputs. This has implications for inflation rise and growth in the economy of ERRE. Finally, B4 shows the subsequent adjustment of capacity to imbalances between current production and demand.

Given such a dynamic interplay of both reinforcing and balancing feedback loops, captured between the dynamics of growth of business in both real and financial terms, environmental constraints and shocks can generate pressures that move the system from growth to instability and oscillation. In particular, environmental constraints have mostly negative effect on production (such as a short-term resource shocks) and potential production (long-term resource constraints given depletion or a rise in the cost of land).

A constraint to production would firstly require increases in the pressure to rise investments and capital to match desired production. While sales would not be instantaneously affected the first imbalance would be seen in the inventory due to the inability of capacity to meet desired production. As the inventory is lower than desired the price would start rising, thus reinforcing the effects on investments and costs. Supply would generate unbalancing pressures that would keep costs high thus reducing available liquidity. The lower the liquidity the higher the interest rates which would rise costs even further. This dynamic collapse of the sector would cease only when the effect on price was large enough so that demand drops below production levels. Due to the delays in capital formation and perceptions of economic variables, the dynamic would generate important oscillations, rises in interest rates with an increased rate of default in the economy, with implications for job loss and economic instability.

All these dynamics represent the fundamental structure that governs the ERRE model dynamics, and helps explain the behaviour of the scenarios presented in the next chapter. In particular, both climate and resource depletion provide negative feedback forces that, ultimately, reduce production. These can be tested alongside monetary policies and different technology growth scenarios, all of which, would impact production and demand for each productive factor in different ways. Each sector responds individually to the imbalance caused by environmental limits, cascading toward the other sectors due to the interconnectivity inherent in the ERRE. This allows the testing of specific scenarios such as the limits to the energy transition, the effect of carbon taxes or an alternative monetary policy. The online appendix at https://doi.org/10.25411/aru.10110710 goes deeper in the description of the ERRE model, and provides the behavioural tests that are fundamental for the understanding of the model calibration, and interpretation of model results.

Summary

In this chapter, the ERRE model was presented. After framing the ERRE in the context of model requirements and economic theory, the chapter has presented the two system models that more than others have influenced the structure of the ERRE. These are the Limits to Growth World3–03 model (Meadows et al. 2003) and the Energy Transition and the Economy model (Sterman 1981). The problems arising from the integration of existing models in relation to the ERRE model purpose are identified and briefly discussed. Most important, structures that were not present in both models, but highlighted as fundamental for the scope of global modelling today (i.e. climate, financial system, and defaults structure – see Chapter 3) have been explicitly integrated in the ERRE model framework.

Thus the model architecture has been made explicit, focusing on a multi-layer network structure underpinning nine systems interconnected one to another. The model has been presented at the top level view of this architecture, revealing how households, government, banks and firms, play a role in the interaction towards a growing economy. The model's basic characteristics, such as the financial stock and flow condition and closed loop supply chain condition, were explained in detail. This is linked to an analysis of the production and utility functions used in the model, which, connected to a neoclassical theory of optimality, structure the fundamental architecture necessary to both initialise and put all sectors together. Finally, a set of feedback loops interlinking resources constraints and financial risk have been made explicit, a fundamental element to give interpretation to the results that follow in Chapter 6.

It is worth noting that the content of this chapter is encouraged to be reviewed alongside the online appendix available at https://doi.org/10.25411/aru.10110710, where all system equations are described in fine detail. This includes behavioural tests to support system understanding, and the computer model itself.

References

Arrow, K. J., Chenery, H. B., Minhas, B. S., & Solow, R. M. (1961). Capital-labor substitution and economic efficiency. *The Review of Economics and Statistics, 43*(3), 225–250.

Bassi, A. M., Pedercini, M., Ansah, J. P., & Tan, Z. (2011). Modelling global green investment scenarios: Supporting the transition to a global green economy. In *Towards a green economy: Pathways to sustainable development and poverty eradication.* Available online: www.unep.org (accessed July 2015).

Cincotti, S., Raberto, M., & Teglio, A. (2012). *The Eurace macroeconomic model and simulator.* Paper presented at the Agent-based Dynamics, Norms, and Corporate Governance. The Proceedings of the 16-th World Congress of the International Economic Association, Palgrave, London, UK.

Fiddaman, T. S. (1997). *Feedback complexity in integrated climate-economy models.* Massachusetts Institute of Technology, Cambridge, MA, US.

Forrester, J. W. (1979). An alternative approach to economic policy: Macrobehavior from microstructure. In Kamrany, N. and R. Day (eds.), *Economic Issues of the Eighties* (pp. 80–108). Johns Hopkins University Press, Baltimore, MD.

Forrester, J. W. (2003). Economic theory for the new millennium. *System Dynamics Review, 29*(1), 26–41.

Forrester, J. W., Mass, N. J., & Ryan, C. J. (1976). The system dynamics national model: Understanding socio-economic behavior and policy alternatives. *Technological Forecasting and Social Change, 9*(1–2), 51–68.

Hall, R. E., & Jorgenson, D. W. (1967). Tax policy and investment behavior. *American Economic Review, 57*(3), 391–414.

Hall, R. E., & Jorgenson, D. W. (1969). Tax policy and investment behavior: Reply and further results. *The American Economic Review, 59*(3), 388–401.

Hines, J. H. (1987). *Essays in behavioral economic modeling.* Massachusetts Institute of Technology, Cambridge, MA, US.

Institute of International Finance (IIF). (2018). Available online: www.iif.com/ (accessed June 2018).

Jackson, T. (2016). *Prosperity without growth: Foundations for the economy of tomorrow.* Routledge, Oxford, UK.

Jackson, T., & Victor, P. A. (2015). Does credit create a 'growth imperative'? A quasi-stationary economy with interest-bearing debt. *Ecological Economics, 120*, 32–48.

Jackson, T., Victor, P. A., & Naqvi, A. (2016). *Towards a stock-flow consistent ecological macroeconomics.* WWW for Europe Working Paper, No. 114, WWW for Europe, Vienna.

Lamperti, F., Dosi, G., Napoletano, M., Roventini, A., & Sapio, A. (2018). Faraway, so close: Coupled climate and economic dynamics in an agent-based integrated assessment model. *Ecological Economics, 150,* 315–339.

Mass, N. J. (1975). *Generic feedback structures underlying economic fluctuations.* Massachusetts Institute of Technology, Cambridge, MA, US.

Meadows, D. L., Behrens, W. W., Meadows, D. H., Naill, R. F., Randers, J., & Zahn, E. (1974). *Dynamics of growth in a finite world.* Wright-Allen Press, Cambridge, MA.

Meadows, D. H., Meadows, D. L., & Randers, J. (2003). *The limits to growth: The 30-year update.* Routledge, Oxford, UK.

Raberto, M., Ozel, B., Ponta, L., Teglio, A., & Cincotti, S. (2019). From financial instability to green finance: The role of banking and credit market regulation in the Eurace model. *Journal of Evolutionary Economics, 29*(1), 429–465.

Radzicki, M. J. (2005). Institutional economics, post Keynesian economics, and system dynamics: Three strands of a heterodox economics braid. *Economics (ICAPE), 5,* 7.

Randers, J., Rockström, J., Stoknes, P.-E., Goluke, U., Collste, D., Cornell, S. E., & Donges, J. (2019). Achieving the 17 sustainable development goals within 9 planetary boundaries. *Global Sustainability, 2.*

Richardson, G. P. (1991). *Feedback thought in social science and systems theory.* University of Pennsylvania Press, Philadelphia, Pennsylvania, US.

Sato, K. (1967). A two-level constant-elasticity-of-substitution production function. *The Review of Economic Studies, 34*(2), 201–218.

Senge, P. M. (1978). *The system dynamics national model investment function: A comparison to the neoclassical investment function.* Massachusetts Institute of Technology, Cambridge, MA, US.

Shaikh, A. (1974). Laws of production and laws of algebra: The humbug production function. *The Review of Economics and Statistics,* 115–120.

Simon, H. A. (1957). *A behavioral model of rational choice, in models of man, social and rational: Mathematical essays on rational human behavior in a social setting.* Wiley, New York.

Simon, H. A. (1979). Rational decision making in business organizations. *The American Economic Review, 69*(4), 493–513.

Solow, R. M. (1956). A contribution to the theory of economic growth. *The Quarterly Journal of Economics, 70*(1), 65–94.

Steffen, W., Rockström, J., Richardson, K., Lenton, T. M., Folke, C., Liverman, D., . . . Crucifix, M. (2018). Trajectories of the earth system in the anthropocene. *Proceedings of the National Academy of Sciences, 115*(33), 8252–8259.

Sterman, J. (1981). *The energy transition and the economy: A system dynamics approach* (2 Vols.). MIT Alfred P. Sloan School of Management, Cambridge, MA.

Sterman, J. D. (2000). *Business dynamics: Systems thinking and modeling for a complex world.* McGraw-Hill, New York, USA.

Sterman, J., Fiddaman, T., Franck, T., Jones, A., McCauley, S., Rice, P., . . . Siegel, L. (2012). Climate interactive: The C-ROADS climate policy model. *System Dynamics Review, 28,* 295–305.

Thaler, R. H., & Ganser, L. (2015). *Misbehaving: The making of behavioral economics.* W. W. Norton, New York.

Tversky, A., & Kahneman, D. (1974). Judgment under uncertainty: Heuristics and biases. *Science, 185*(4157), 1124–1131.

Yamaguchi, K. (2013). *Money and macroeconomic dynamics: Accounting system dynamics approach.* Japan Futures Research Center, Awaji Island, Japan.

6   Data, statistics, and scenario analysis

In the previous chapter the ERRE model has been presented, both in terms of overarching architecture, major feedback loops and comparison to economic theory. The resulting system is composed of both reinforcing and balancing feedback loops, disequilibrium forces and non-linear relationships. Two major reinforcing feedback loops (i.e. population growth, technology change) have been substituted with exogenous inputs, leaving the ERRE dynamics to be mostly led by the balancing feedbacks. Such an hypothesis is often typical of a computable general equilibrium model (CGEM). However, we argue that the ERRE model is explicitly a disequilibrium model, mostly driven by endogenous disequilibrium behaviours contrasting to the mainstream school. Simulations and tests in support of such an argument can be found at https://doi.org/10.25411/aru.10110710.

In this chapter, we discuss the type of data used to develop the ERRE model, describe the database used as a mean for comparison with real data, and provide a statistical validation test as a metric of assessment of the goodness of fit of the model to available data. The disequilibrium inputs that allowed for the model calibration are shown. Finally, short-term scenarios used for the shock resilience analysis, and long-term fat-tail stress tests are applied to evaluate the possible uncertain futures. These latter relate to the world economy interacting with climate change (including hot house effect), resource depletion, and assessing the limits of a green energy revolution and carbon taxes by the end of the century.

Database definition, data inputs, and calibration

The data used to construct and as a measure for comparison with the real world belong to a variety of domains. For simplicity, in this section we will call these Data 1, Data 2, Data 3, and Data 4. Data 1 can be considered as implicit in the structure of the ERRE model, such as the network of causal relationships, every single equation, the shape of the non-linear relationship, or the value of every single parameter. Data 2 can be considered as the initialisation value of the stock variables, and the numerical values used as comparison to the real world indicators, as a mean of historical analysis and model calibration. Data 3 are all the external shocks and intelligence that are not captured by the endogenous structure of the model, which can impact its ability to explain history. Data 4 is the set

DOI: 10.4324/9781315643182-8

of behavioural analysis and output that the model can generate, each requiring additional statistical analysis to link between model inputs and output.

This is a very different approach from an average econometric or general equilibrium model. In fact, these normally ignore decision making via non-linear feedback structures in the model, and often build models based on the output data (Data 2 in our case), thus generating the set of parameters and relationships (Data 1) automatically based on the solution of regression models and simultaneous equations. As a result the approach adopted in ERRE requires stronger emphasis on data validation, that can be achieved only when exposing the model to system experts, such as businesses managers and practitioners involved in day to day activities within the system we aim at modelling. For example, the decision making processes described in Chapter 5, would require a database of information often available within large corporates, or while interviewing managers working in those organisations. Because such a type of validation was not possible for the scope of this work, most of these relationships have been taken from the literature or rely on the common sense of the modeller while conceptualising and testing the ERRE model.

Data 3, including the type of exogenous shocks that influenced the dynamic of the system, such as production shocks or the financial crisis, could not be addressed without a full engagement with businesses and practitioners as well. Finally, Data 4 was performed manually as described in this chapter, due to technological limits in developing automated calibration and batch simulation techniques, to simplify the management of output and testing of the model based on model inputs.

As a result, in this section we describe the approach of Data 2 only. This included the comparison of the model output to the real world indicators via statistical analysis, initialisation of the stock variables to the real data, and sensitivity analysis of key leverage parameters and non-linear relationships within a range of uncertainty considered acceptable for the purpose of the model. Further work can be applied to test these relationships with the use of historical event analysis, interviews with practitioners, and use of micro level databases describing the actual operational decisions of the companies which operate in the markets modelled in the ERRE.

The analysis of data, the data ingestion in the ERRE model, and the calibration to data have been a primary task for the development of ERRE. While collecting and analysing data, various structures of the earlier versions of the model resulted in being not consistent with reality, and thus were changed. As Sterman (2000) argues, modelling is an iterative process involving formulation of a dynamic hypothesis, the conceptualisation of structures, the testing via simulation, and the comparison between model output and the real world data. As far as the model appears not capable of explaining the data sufficiently well, its system boundaries have to be altered towards a more meaningful explanation (possibly simpler) of that dynamic phenomena.

Despite the comparison between model output and real data being considered a relatively unimportant test among the behaviour reproducibility tests described in Forrester and Senge (1980), we believe that a correct match between model output and historical data is fundamental when aiming at policy influence. This is also due to the larger availability of aggregated indicators in public databases since the early 2000s, and for the scope of policy influence for short-term shock scenarios towards system change. Differently from a standard econometric model, often focused on the precise estimate of parameters while missing the system view on the dynamic to capture, we employ a calibration as an attempt to capture the scale of the system at stake in all of its parts, in search of a correct interaction and a meaningful system theory among those. A set of 24 time series applied on the various leverage points in the ERRE model has been used as a metric for comparison with the general dynamic of the system. Among the most important we find real GDP, government debt, money supply, GDP deflator, food and energy prices, food and energy production, and total employment (see Table 6.1). After sensitivity tests have been considered complete, the resulting calibration was performed and compared with historical data with standard statistical metrics such as R square coefficient of correlation, mean absolute percent error (MAPE) to measure the actual fractional distance between historical data and model output, and Theil inequality statistics to decompose such distance between the components of average, cycles, and noise in capturing these data.

It is worth noting, that starting from equilibrium conditions it was not possible to capture any historical data, and often addressing some of those was not sufficient to approach the others. However, while applying all the disequilibrium elements as shown in the behavioural testing appendix available online at https://doi.org/10.25411/aru.10110710, a meaningful match between historical data and model output could be achieved. These can be considered as the minimal set of disequilibrium factors to be applied simultaneously to achieve a good fit between historical data and model output. This suggests an evolutionary hypothesis of economy in disequilibrium.

In this section we first describe the dataset used as input and metric of comparison for ERRE model behaviour, then we describe the initialisation and estimate of key parameters in the model, we show the disequilibrium factors and tables (both exogenous and endogenous) used to calibrate the model, and we perform a statistical analysis for addressing the match between historical data and model behaviour. The calibration is used in the following section as a base for base run formulation, scenarios analysis, stress testing, and policy analysis.

Data 2 – Output database

The variables that have been included as a metric of comparison for the model behaviour approached various aspects of the world economy, and come from different sources.

The public databases used for this study are:

1   World Bank development indicators – general economic variables
2   World Bank commodity prices – food price index
3   EIA energy statistics – energy production and price data
4   FAOSTAT – agriculture and emissions data

Table 6.1 Time series used to calibrate the ERRE model

Variable name	Source	Source variables used for calculation	Frequency	Extension	Comparative variable in the ERRE
Food Price Index	Global Economic Monitor Commodities World Bank 2018	- Agr: Food, 2010 = 100, nominal$	Monthly	Jan 2000-Oct 2017	Food price index 2000 = 1
Fossil fuel price	US Energy Information Administration 2019	- Europe Brent Spot Price (USD)	Monthly	Jan 2000-Apr 2019	N price of output after tax monthly
GDP deflator	Calculated from World Bank 2018	- GDP (constant 2010 US$) - GDP (current US$)	Yearly	2000-2016	Global GDP deflator
Real GDP	World Bank 2018	- GDP (constant 2010 US$)	Yearly	2000-2016	Global real GDP
Employment	Calculated from ILO 2018 and World Bank 2018	- Employment to population ratio, 15+, total (%) (modelled ILO estimate) - population between 15 and 65 years old - population above 65	Yearly	2000-2016	Global total employed
Nominal GDP	World Bank 2018	- GDP (current US$)	Yearly	2000-2016	Global GDP
Tax revenues	World Bank 2018	- Tax revenue (% of GDP) - GDP (current US$)	Yearly	2000-2016	Gov tax revenues
Government spending	World Bank 2018	- General government final consumption expenditure (current US$)	Yearly	2000-2016	Gov spending from general revenues
Money supply	Calculated from World Bank 2018	- GDP (current US$) - Broad money (% of GDP)	Yearly	2000-2016	B money supply
Government debt	Institute of International Finance 2019	- Government Debt	Yearly	2000-2018	Gov debt
Household debt	Institute of International Finance 2019	- Household Debt	Yearly	2000-2018	H debt
Employment in agriculture	Calculated from ILO 2018	- Employment in agriculture (% of total employment) (modeled ILO estimate) - Employment to population ratio, 15+, total (%) (modeled ILO estimate) - population between 15 and 65 years old - population above 65	Yearly	2000-2018	F labour

(Continued)

Table 6.1 (Continued)

Variable name	Source	Source variables used for calculation	Frequency	Extension	Comparative variable in the ERRE
Agricultural nominal output	World Bank 2018	- Agriculture, Forestry, and fishing value added (current USD)	Yearly	2000-2016	F revenue from savings
Biofuels production	Calculated from EIA 2018	- Fuel Ethanol Production (annual) (1000 bbl/d) - Biodiesel Production (annual) (1000 bbl/d)	Yearly	2000-2015	F shipment rate for biofuels in btu
Fossil Fuel Production	Calculated from EIA 2018	- Total Primary Coal Production (annual) (1000 ST) - Dry Natural Gas Production (annual) (Bcf) - Total Petroleum and Other Liquids Production (annual) (1000 bbl/d)	Yearly	2000-2016	N shipment rate
Renewables production	EIA 2018	- Electricity generation - Nuclear, renewables and others	Yearly	2000-2018	R production
Agricultural land	Calculated from World Bank 2018	- Agricultural land (sq. km)	Yearly	2000-2015	F total agricultural land
Forest land	Calculated from World Bank 2018	- Forest land (sq. km)	Yearly	2000-2015	F total forest land
Deforestation	FAOSTAT (2018)	- Net forest conversion (sq. km)	Yearly	2000-2015	F deforestation
Carbon from deforestation	Federici et al. (2015)	- Net forest conversion: annual total Co2 emissions	Yearly	2000-2012	Ghg deforestation
Carbon concentration	NOAA/ESRL 2018	- CO2 concentration (parts per million)	Yearly	2000-2017	Ghg co2eq concentration
Carbon from fossil fuel production	World Bank 2018 and FAOSTAT. (2015)	- Total CO2 emissions (kt)	Yearly	2000-2012	Ghg fossil fuel production
Carbon from agricultural production	FAOSTAT (2018)	- Net Emissions from AFOLU (kt) - Net Emissions from AFOLU (kt)	Yearly	2000-2016	Ghg agriculture production
Temperature anomaly	Met Office Hadley Centre 2019	- Temperature anomaly median	Yearly	2000-2017	Ghg temperature anomaly to pre-industrial levels

5   IRENA – renewables costs and price
6   Institute of International Finance – government and household debt
7   National Oceanic and Atmospheric Administration Earth Systems Research Laboratory and Met Office and Hadley Centre – climate related variables

In addition, academic papers (e.g. Federici et al. 2015) and the International Panel of Climate Change (2014) have been used to integrate additional data that could be not found in the public databases. Table 6.1 shows the database of output comparison used to construct the ERRE model, listing the source, the indicators used to calculate the variable, frequency, and extension of the time series and the ERRE variable used as metric of comparison.

The time series proposed in Table 6.1 required a little translation based on the consideration of the way these data are reported and the way the software used to develop the ERRE would interpret those data in the short term. In fact, despite different data sources adopting a similar representation to assign a certain year to a certain value that measure had been taken (for example two data sources adopt the year 2005 as the year to catch a certain variable), they often mismatch in the sense they consider a measure representing the beginning, the end or any time in between the two extremes as reference for the entire year. For example, the production GDP data in the World Bank database for the year 2005 are measures taken at the 31st December 2005 (the end of the year). For the software perspective, this is a relevant issue for calibrating a model, in particular when interested in dealing with short-term dynamics.

The software used to develop the ERRE model (Vensim DSS v7.2 from Ventana Systems Inc.) represents the beginning of each year as a integer number, while all values within a year are a represented as a fraction. For example, the 1st of January 2005 is represented with the number 2005, while the 1st of July 2005 correspond to the 2005.5. Table 6.2 shows the correspondence between the beginning of a month and the relative time used in the software for the year 2005.

Table 6.2 Accounting for time in Vensim software

Actual date	Software correspondence
1st January 2005	2005
1st February 2005	2005.083
1st March 2005	2005.167
1st April 2005	2005.25
1st May 2005	2005.333
1st June 2005	2005.417
1st July 2005	2005.5
1st August 2005	2005.583
1st September 2005	2005.667
1st October 2005	2005.75
1st November 2005	2005.833
1st December 2005	2005.917
1st January 2006	2006

Table 6.3 Exponents on production functions

Sector	Exponent capital	Exponent energy	Exponent labour	Exponent agricultural land
Capital	0.235	0.018	0.747	-
Goods and services	0.237	0.018	0.745	-
Agriculture	0.237	0.1	0.563	0.1
Fossil fuels	0.5	0.02	0.48	-
Renewables	0.5	0.05	0.45	-

Such a consideration resulted in the translation of all those time series whose value was taken at mid or end year, to assure the value were aligned with the software interpretation of that same time.

Each of the variables of the database formed the base for the initialisation of the relative comparative variable in the model. In addition, data from IRENA (2018) were included to estimate the initial price of both biofuels and renewables at the beginning of the simulation (see Figure 3.12).

Due to the neoclassical formulation of production function in the ERRE model, exponents of input factors were estimated accordingly. Given that the scale of the model is global, it was not possible to estimate these parameters econometrically. Thus they were formed on the basis of previous estimation for the US in Sterman (1981), and altered during simulation and calibration. The final set of exponents for each productive factor is proposed in Table 6.3. As it is possible to see, the labour force always accounts for the larger fraction of the value in the production of output for all sectors. Capital represents a large fraction of value for the production of energy, whereas agriculture is assumed to account for 10% of its value in the ownership of land.

Based on the initialisation rule presented in Chapter 5, the exponents and the production of each sector allowed the initialisation of the relative stocks of those production factors, including capital, energy intensity, and wages for each sector. This formed the foundation for the equilibrium assumption and the beginning of the testing and calibration of the ERRE model.

Calibration

In order to generate the dynamic behaviour necessary to catch the historical data, the database was used to initialise key variables, and all disequilibrium seen in the previous section were applied to the model in synergy, remaining careful to assure that the values of each parameter and element of disequilibrium remained within realistic ranges (see structural validation tests). An interesting observation emerging from the calibration of the model to the historical data, is that, unless taking all the exogenous and endogenous disequilibrium factors together (i.e. population, energy efficiency, money creation and government debt and technology growth, dividend and savings behaviours) it was not possible to generate a dynamic behaviour able to catch variables such as inflation, GDP and money supply at the same time. This supports the hypothesis of an economy in disequilibrium with endogenous element generating growth in the world economy.

According to Lyneis (1980), the calibration process is to be done by hand rather than using any automatic algorithm. This approach is particularly effective when developing large models such as the ERRE model. In those cases, starting the model development from the observation of historical data is the most efficient way to generate a good match between model and data. In Chapter 2 of this book, a semi-automated calibration was applied in the analysis of the World3–03-Edited (Pasqualino et al. 2015). It is worth noting that such an approach was possible because of the long-term perspective of the model, the smaller size, and the relatively low number of feedback loops. In the case of the ERRE model, an automatic approach was not possible at current technology level due to the large number of parameters and feedback loops in the system and the large presence of time delays that generate oscillation in the system. As a result, an approach as proposed in Lyneis (1980) was preferred for the calibration of the ERRE.

However, starting from previously existing frameworks rather than a database of time series, the result of model fitting remained more difficult. Despite the process being an iterative loop, composed of (i) change in disequilibrium factors, (ii) observance of model behaviour, and (iii) amends to the model, in this section we present the final outcome of this process. It is worth noting that in this phase, the simulation time has been kept to the time frame of interest of the historical data (2000 to 2030). Thus long-term effects such as depletion and climate change implications could have been omitted. These are reintroduced in the context of extreme scenario and policy analysis.

Exogenous inputs

Figure 6.1 shows the UN population division forecast from 2000 to 2100 used as input for all scenarios in the model. In this case, no additional sensitivity had been added to the model, assuming such a scenario as the most plausible.

Figure 6.2 and Figure 6.3 show the actual money creation non-linear inputs representing the total amount of cash generated exogenously by central banks and the amount of cash generated via debt creation from the government. Both tables required a careful interpretation of the input, and at the same time supporting a good fit between model output and the variables government debt and money supply among others.

As Figure 6.2 and Figure 6.3 show, it appears that the period in which most money was created by both institutions was prior and during the 2007–2008 financial crisis, with a slow decline after the year 2010. The monetary school of economics focused on monetary policy to support growth and wealth creation with money creation policies, unfortunately leading to the credit crunch

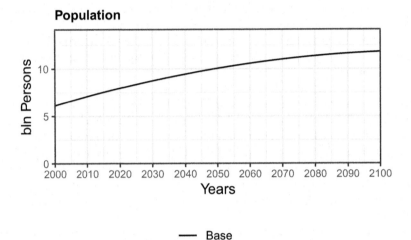

Figure 6.1 Population growth as input to the model

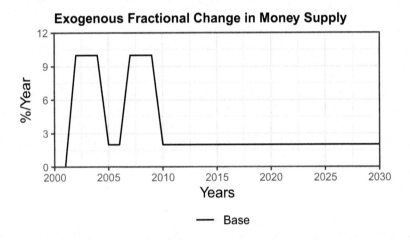

Figure 6.2 Exogenous money creation from central bank

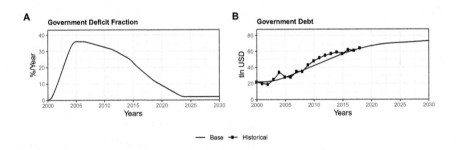

Figure 6.3 Exogenous government deficit and government debt as input for money creation

of 2007–2008. According to Figure 6.3, governmental deficit also rose over this time, with accelerating government debt. After the year 2012, lower money creation is shown in historical data. The future of the simulation is assumed to have an average of +2% increase in the money supply from banks and a +2% increase in the government deficit until the end of the simulation. Policies changing those values for the predictive behaviour policies could support analysis over the longer term, but are not considered for the purpose of this study.

Figure 6.4 shows the technology curves adopted to model the labour and land productivity in each sector of the ERRE model. Historical data show a decline in real GDP growth (WB 2018), thus leading us to neglect the hypothesis of exponential growing technology curves for those sector that represent the larger part of the economy, thus setting the economic growth trend (goods and services and capital sector). Therefore, ramp growth of +3% per year for the capital sector, +2.5% ramp growth for the goods and services sector, +2% labour productivity ramp growth for the agriculture sector were adopted. The fossil fuel sector was not assumed to have any overall technology productivity improvement due to the actual registered decrease in its EROEI in the last 20 years (Rye and Jackson 2018). In addition, a marginally decreasing growth rate with cap of +5% was adopted for the productivity of agricultural land, and a +3% exponentially increasing labour productivity for the renewables sector were considered for calibration and base run. It is worth noting that until the year 2030 agricultural land productivity is assumed to have the largest productivity growth mostly due to the expansion of fertilizer inputs and pesticides in the available agricultural land, and supporting the calibration of the agricultural land variable. However, this is assumed to have a cap and asymptote over the long term thus being surpassed by all other curves by mid-century. While the ramp growth of capital, goods and services, and agricultural labour would

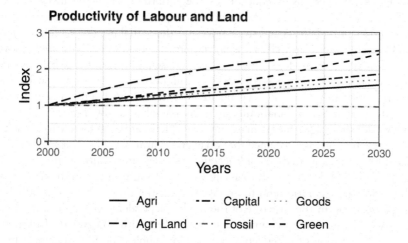

Figure 6.4 Technology change for every sector in the model

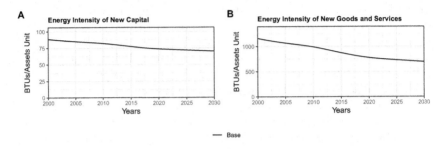

Figure 6.5 Energy intensity of new capital and goods for the household sector

keep going linearly over the longer term, renewables productivity will grow exponentially approximately doubling every 20 years. As we will see later, the exponential growth of the green energy sector is the major source of hope for a successful energy transition and climate impact reduction during the second half of this century.

Figure 6.5 shows the application of the energy intensity of new capital and goods in the household sector. It is worth noting that, for the productive sectors, every increase in labour productivity would assure an increase in their output with the same amount of energy. This effect lowers the ratio between energy consumption and real GDP as recorded in historical data globally (IEA 2017).

Endogenous inputs

Table 6.4 shows the list of endogenous disequilibrium parameters used to unbalance the model towards growth. In addition, it provides the values used to address the impact of both costs and stock prices on the actual prices for both the food and fossil fuel sector, as well as the global normal default rate. As the table shows, the normal propensity for savings has been chosen as if the average behaviour of household would tend towards a higher consumption of their income, rather than their attempt to save money to generate investments. Such a result is indicative as a disequilibrium explanation of an economy taken at the aggregated level of the world, showing there are many more people with the tendency to consume. On a second note, it is assumed that on average, firms would keep approximately 10% of their income in their bank accounts as a measure to mitigate risk of default and keep a high level of cash to assure expenses can be made. In the real world, dividend pay-outs ratio tend to be much lower than the 90% of income. This indicates a gap in the structure of the model, dependent on the need to model equity exchange and stock markets to generate wealth and growth. In fact the financial sector, has the tendency to generate bubbles and high income returns just by trading stocks and securities in the financial market, and such a structure

Table 6.4 Sensitivities of key parameters for model calibration

Parameter	Influence in the model	Value in lower stress condition	Value for calibration
Normal propensity for savings	Propensity for savings and consumption in comparison to equilibrium level. If 1, all income is spent in consumption, thus accumulating the growth rate in the economy.	1	0.75
Normal dividend pay-out ratio for each sector	Dividend pay-out ratio as fraction of total net income. If 1, all income is distributed as dividends.	1	0.9
Sensitivity of energy price on traders	Influence of stock price on market price. If 1, the price is determined just by cost of production. If 0, the price is determined mostly by stock price.	1	0.36
Sensitivity of food price on trade	Influence of stock price on market price. If 1, the price is determined just by cost of production. If 0, the price is determined mostly by stock price.	1	0.7
Global normal default rate	Constant fraction of firms defaulting. If 0 defaults are not considered.	0	0.005

is not present in the ERRE. As a result, the model calibrates well when most of income is redistributed to households, who, together with a high propensity to spend their income, generate growth in the economy via consumption.

Interestingly, the assumption of energy and food price as only determined by their cost was not sufficient to determine the dynamics of historical data characterised by boom and bust in the time frame considered. In both cases, a stock trade effect was modelled, demonstrating high sensitivity to the dynamics of prices. According to the value obtained, it appears, that the determinant of energy price is mostly market conditions (supply-demand pressures) and amplifications in the financial market. The influence of cost in the price is approximately 36% of total. On the side of food production, it appears that their market is less volatile in terms of stock (70% is determined by cost, and 30% by traders volatility). However, the calibration was also considered finished when approaching the lower bound of the price oscillations, thus not capturing most of its oscillation (see Figure 6.7). Additional analysis could support the hypothesis of a strong influence of the traders price than what is proposed here. Finally the parameter global normal default rate was considered as an additional disequilibrium factor. Despite presenting low sensitivity with respect to the model output, this parameter remains important for the understanding of default risk and dynamics of interest rates.

In addition to those, many more parameters have been included in the sensitivity analysis, but not presented here due to their lower impact on the sensitivity of the model in representing historical data. In system models of this kind, the

80/20 rule, or Pareto rule, applies well when differentiating the 20% of parameters that account for the 80% of the performance, and the 80% of parameters accounting for the 20% of behaviour. In the same way, and for the scope of this work, we prioritised the explanation of the high leverage elements in the system.

Statistical analysis of output

Table 6.5 shows the main descriptive statistics indicating the differences between model output and relative time series over the time frame captured by the time series. Additional indicators can be found in the online version of the model. For each variable, the mean absolute percent error (MAPE) has been reported as a simple measure for addressing the coefficient of fit obtained between the model and the data, or alternatively the ability of the model to capture the data. The coefficient of Pearson (R square) has been used as a metric to explain the correlation between model output and data, or rather the explanatory capability of the model output in explaining changes in data. Differently from the MAPE, R square addresses if the variables do vary following a similar pattern, rather than addressing how close they travel together. Ideally MAPE should obtain values that are as close as possible to 0, whereas R square should be as close as possible to 1.

As a third element we use the Theil's inequality statistics whose role is, when R square and MAPE do not perform well, to decompose the error between noise and systematic components. The three elements U_m (unequal mean), U_s (unequal variation), and U_c (unequal covariation) always sum together as 1, and help define where most of the error distribute. A high U_m represents a systematic error in the ability of the model output in capturing the same average of the data. A high U_s, represents a systematic error in the ability of the model to capture cycles and amplitude of variance in the model. The third element, U_c, represent the noise, that is the part of the data that the model finds hard to capture. Ideally, U_m and U_s should be as close to zero as possible, leaving all the error accumulating in U_c.

As Table 6.5 shows the model captures the historical data with a level of significance of +90% in the majority of cases (MAPE is around 10% in most variables), and captures the trend of most variables relatively well (R square above 90% for most variables). However, some outliers are present both on the positive and negative side as discussed later.

In particular, the model captures very well the real GDP (significance of 97.8% for percent error and 97.7% in the trend explanation), government debt (significance of 91.8% for percent error and 95% of trend explanation), fossil fuel production (91.3% for percent error and 98.2% in terms of trend), government tax revenues (90.8 % in terms of percent error and 96.5% in terms of trend), food value added (91.5% in terms of percentage error, and 91.5% in terms of trend explanation), and GDP deflator (92.2% in terms of percentage error, and 91.1% in terms of trend explanation). Some of these variables are compared to historical data in the base run formulation in Figure 6.7.

Table 6.5 Statistical comparison of model output to real data

Variable name	Comparative variable in the ERRE	MAPE (coefficient of fit)	R Square (correlation)	U_m (average)	U_s (trend and cycle)	U_c (noise)
Food Price Index	Food price index 2000 = 1	0.149	0.789	0.536	0.248	0.215
Fossil fuel price	N price of output after tax monthly	0.252	0.675	0.187	0.002	0.811
GDP deflator	Global gdp deflator	0.078	0.911	0.573	0.077	0.35
Real GDP	Global real gdp	0.022	0.977	0.35	0.015	0.635
Global employment	Global total employed	0.017	0.879	0.254	0.067	0.68
Nominal GDP	Global GDP	0.089	0.895	0.001	0.113	0.886
Tax revenues	Gov tax revenues	0.092	0.965	0.511	0.203	0.286
Government spending	Gov spending from general revenues	0.089	0.895	0.001	0.113	0.886
Money supply	B money supply	0.101	0.976	0.346	0.56	0.093
Government debt	Gov debt	0.082	0.95	0.264	0.135	0.601
Household debt	H debt	0.175	0.862	0.145	0.404	0.451
Employment in agriculture	F labour	0.11	0.735	0.477	0.089	0.435
Agriculture nominal output	F revenue from savings	0.095	0.915	0.379	0.305	0.317
Biofuels production	F shipment rate for biofuels in btu	1.97	0.731	0.609	0.372	0.019
Fossil fuel production	N shipment rate	0.087	0.982	0.729	0.257	0.013
Renewables production	R production	0.097	0.902	0.77	0.08	0.15
Agriculturalland	F total agricultural land	0.002	0.814	0.279	0.719	0.002
Forest land	F total forest land	0.008	0.267	0.757	0.228	0.014
Deforestation	F deforestation	0.932	0.473	0.888	0.039	0.073
Carbon from deforestation	Ghg deforestation	0.935	0.231	0.904	0.035	0.061
Carbon concentration	Ghg co2eq concentration	0.094	0.998	0.745	0.255	0.001
Carbon from fossil fuel production	Ghg fossil fuel production	0.121	0.658	0.633	0.041	0.326
Carbon from agricultural production	Ghg agriculture production	0.065	0.509	0.505	0.192	0.304
Temperature anomaly	Ghg temperature anomaly to pre-industrial levels	0.105	0.552	0.567	0.075	0.359

Two variables that are important for the scope of the ERRE but more difficult to calibrate are the food and energy prices. As it is possible to see, their score decreases for MAPE (85.1% fit for food, and 74.8% fit for the fossil fuel price) as well as for their correlation (R square) with historical data (78.9% significance for food price, and 67.5% significance for fossil fuel price). Both data streams are shown in Figure 6.7 for a visual comparison. As it is possible to see, the model is focused on capturing the second bump in the price of fossil fuel (2010 to 2014), and stays at the lower bound of the oscillation in the case of the food price. In both cases, the first peak in prices that occurs around the time of the financial crisis, was ignored by the model output. The model dynamics are rather focused in capturing the business cycle emerging from the interaction between price, capacity building and demand adaptation for both sectors. The ERRE model could potentially be altered such as to improve the fit to the data, but such an attempt would result in an overfit of the model to the data, with little real value for the simulation that follows. The structure representative of the financial crisis (or indeed any speculation present in food or energy prices prior to the financial crisis) were not considered in the ERRE, and thus no attempt was made to improve the fit further. This explains the lower scores in fitting the model to data for these two variables. It is worth observing the Theil's statistics for both time series. In particular, it is shown how the fit of the energy price is much greater, with high fit to the oscillation of price bump (only 0.2%), and most of the error represented by the noise component (81.1%). The story is a bit different for the food price in which most error is dependent on the fit to the averages (53.6% of the systematic error) and missing the intensity of the oscillation (24.8% of the systematic error).

One variable that is particularly out of fit is the biofuel production with a mean absolute percentage error of 197%, despite the good ability to explain the trend at 73.1%. The reason for this mismatch reveals an issue with the initial conditions at which the energy sector has been initialised. In fact the energy demand is dependent on the installed capacity of capital across all sectors and the goods in the household sector. In Sterman (1981), the capital production structure was formulated such that at the beginning of the simulation (1900), most energy was produced via conventional energy, and no further detail was necessary to capture the initial condition of energy production for alternative energy. The dynamic of interest (the energy transition) was emerging over 100 years in the simulation, thus the capital sector was constructed without paying attention to the initial condition and starting trend for production. In the ERRE model, starting the simulation in the year 2000 revealed a systematic error in the initialisation of the capital sector, and subsequently in the demand for energy, which triggers systematic issues in the initial trend of fossil fuels, renewables, and biofuels. While fossil fuels and renewables are already quite developed at the beginning of the simulation, the effect of this dynamic has little impact on their statistics. However, because biofuels represents a fraction below the 0.1% of total energy production, it appears to slowly catch the high production rate in biofuels necessary at the beginning of the century. Despite being delayed, the energy demand increases thus capturing the trend over time (73.1% significance), and improves for longer-term runs as seen in the simulations that follow in the chapter. For the purpose of this model and understanding of the general system dynamics and interaction between food and energy, improving this structure was considered not necessary, despite the low fit in the initial data. If this relationship would be studied further, amends to the capital structure and initialisation of the model would be necessary.

Three variables that perform particularly badly are Forest Land, Deforestation, and Carbon from Deforestation. Despite agricultural land fitting data pretty well (99.8% significance in data match, and 81.4% significance in trend explanation), forest land has a poor match with the actual trend in historical data (26.7% significance), with a 75.7% systematic error in capturing the average of this trend. This is linked with poor performance in capturing deforestation (7.8% for actual deforestation, and 6.5% carbon emissions from deforestation significance to match the data) and low R square (47.3% and 23.1% respectively). Such a poor performance reveals a system boundaries fallacy in the agricultural land structure of the ERRE as well as in the World3–03 model (where this structure was taken from and assuming the potentially arable land corresponds to forest land in ERRE) and it appears that the reality of forest land turned out to be worse than captured in the Limits to Growth.

Figure 6.6 shows a visual representation of the mismatch between historical data and simulated behaviour for forest land. As anticipated, the assumption of no-regeneration of agricultural land after erosion (in agreement with the structure of the World3–03) was confirmed to assure a general reduction in the absolute value of total agricultural land as revealed by historical data (FAOSTAT 2019). Due to the high cost curve and increase in land productivity, farmers have lower propensity for increasing production levels using agricultural land, preferring to employ more people and adding more capital and

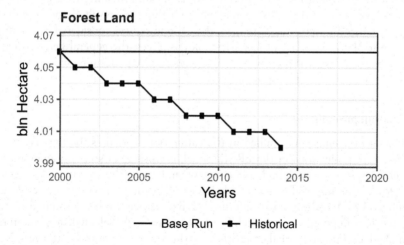

Figure 6.6 Forest land comparison between historical and simulated behaviour

energy intensity inputs to achieve the same purpose. As a result, the structure of the model assumes that no forest land is actually withdrawn (no deforestation), thus preserving conservation of forest ecosystems. In reality, forest land has also decreased over time (Figure 6.6) and deforestation has increased. The correct structure for agricultural land should account for an addition outflow from the stock of forest land towards fallow land (land without a specific use), probably supported by the inclusion of exogenous shocks such as fires in the Amazon (FAO 2019). Such an edit was not included in the ERRE since it is considered not relevant for the modelling the relationships between food and energy prices, economic growth and climate change. Improved models should include these dynamics in detail.

The weakness of the ERRE in capturing the dynamics of deforestation contributes to the performance in capturing emissions from fossil fuels and agriculture, and the relative temperature anomaly on pre-industrial levels. In fact, while their MAPE is quite good (87.9% for fossil fuels carbon, 93.5% for food carbon, and 89.5% for temperature anomaly) their correlation coefficient R square performs pretty low (65.8% for fossil fuels, 50.9% for food carbon, and 55.2% for temperature anomaly), with an important contribution of systematic error on missing their average (63.3% for fossil fuels, 50.5% for food carbon, and 56.7% for temperature anomaly). As Figure 6.7 shows, the actual model performance in capturing the temperature anomaly is below average, and does not capture any oscillation. This is due to two elements. The first is the capital structure (as explained for the poor match in the biofuels production data). In fact, such an effect implies a lower production of carbon at the beginning of the simulation for fossil fuels as well, and a partial effect on a reduction in agricultural output due to slow take-over of the capital sector. The second is not accounting for the deforestation element, which contributes for a large part to the emissions from agriculture. The result is that the final model performance is to minimise the effect of carbon emissions in comparison to real data, thus providing scenarios that are more positive than they could actually be in reality. As a result, despite the lower performance in capturing those data, the calibration was considered sufficient to move to the next phase of scenarios analysis, given the general behaviour was captured correctly for the variables of interest, while performing more positively on the negative effects of growth.

Base run formulation

The set of assumptions applied in the calibration is used as the foundation for the future projections in the ERRE model, consisting of scenario analysis, risk scenarios, stress testing, and policy recommendation. The base run (or Scenario 0) forms the first of the so-called behavioural prediction tests in Forrester and Senge (1980), stating how the future behaviours need to be plausible based on conditions imposed in the model. Figure 6.7 shows eight selected variables in the model base run, and visual comparison to the historical data from the year 2000 to 2030.

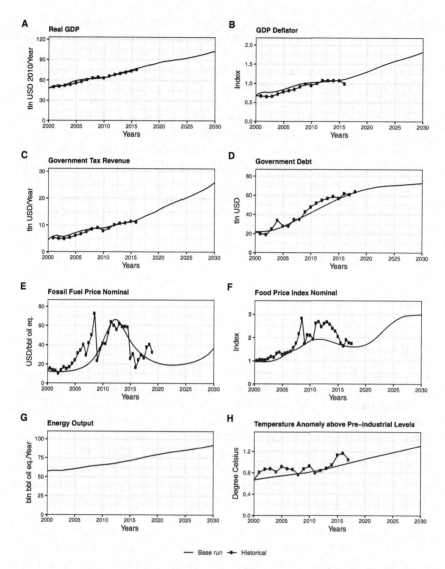

Figure 6.7 Selected variables in the base run of the ERRE model

As it is possible to see, the exogenous elements such as population growth, technology change, money creation, and government deficit creation, as defined in the previous section, generate growth in the model in almost every area of it. In particular, it is possible to see how real GDP growth, as well as energy output, and temperature anomaly all rise steadily during the simulation. It is worth noting how technology growth and population growth are major elements forming the foundation real economic growth. On top of that, monetary policies and firm behaviour in controlling their prices also support the inflation growth over time, leading to increasing GDP deflator, and a good match in the tax revenues. This last element interacts with the exogenous government deficit, thus providing a good match with the government debt. It is worth noting how the real data showed the large increase in debt during the early 2000s, and how fundamental the calibration with actual government debt was to explain such an input. The assumption of +2% growth in government debt after the year 2018 is reflected in the slower growth rate in the government debt for the future of the simulation.

While the economy is relatively stable in growth, fossil fuels and agriculture are affected by price fluctuations, mostly due to their importance and mutual influence in the system. As discussed, their dynamic is strongly affected by business cycles, as shown in the energy price (the cycle start increasing after the year 2025), and food price, where the cycle is stronger while being still affected by inflation growth due to household income directly impacting on their price in the model. As discussed in the previous section, the dynamics of temperature anomaly results in underestimating the real data for the time frame taken in consideration. This should be considered in the next phase of scenario analysis and stress testing.

Future making and risk – shock response, stress test scenarios, and policy

The resulting base run (or Scenario 0) is used as the foundation for the scenario analysis and stress testing. In this section we demonstrate the most important behaviour and model responses in the context of global risks. These include both short-term shocks, such as a fossil fuel production loss, or an extreme weather event impacting agriculture capacity (2000 to 2030 time frame), and long-term risks such as climate change, fossil fuel depletion, green growth and carbon taxes (2000 to 2100 time horizon). As in Forrester and Senge (1980) these scenarios belong to what we can consider extreme behavioural scenario tests (short-term shocks and long-term limits), extreme policy tests (carbon taxes), and system improvement test (solution to limits scenarios).

In this analysis, the short-term shocks are applied separately based on the base run scenario, and thus can be considered as a potential application and analysis using the ERRE model in the context of resilience and risk. On the other hand, the long-term scenarios build one on another to provide a series of uncertainty scenarios, each stress testing the behaviour of the previous one. Such an approach helps demonstrate the most important elements and sensitivities to inform society towards a global sustainability transition, and should be considered as indicative in the context of global policy.

Ideally, in order to provide a fully consistent analysis of risk and support a precise global long-term strategy driven by policy making and technology improvements, a set of probability distributions associated with each sensitivity analysis would be necessary. However, such probabilities are not possible in the context of global systems, and limited by the resources employed in this project. Rather our approach gives validity to the capabilities of the model in developing a better understanding of the global system as it moves towards the future on our finite planet. As far as new data will be available, and the pattern of the real world changes, the ERRE model is capable of being updated through its data inputs to reassess futures every time that is required.

Short-term risk scenarios and system resilience

The short-term (ST) risk scenarios consist in testing one short-term shock in the year 2020, and revealing the pattern of the model until the year 2030. The two scenarios considered are:

1   ST Risk Scenario 1 – a 10% fossil fuel production loss starting 1st January 2019, with one year peak from the 1st January 2020 to 31st December 2020, and shock mitigation with return to normality on 31st December 2021. The shock demonstrates the impact of an energy shock on food as well as on prices, interest rates, inflation, and economic growth.
2   ST Risk Scenario 2 – a 5 to 15% sudden shock in agriculture output most characteristic of an extreme weather, disease, or other disruptive event. The scenario shows the impact on food and energy price, overall sensitivity of the entire economy, inflation, and interest rates.

Fossil fuel policy shock

Figure 6.8 and Table 6.6 show the input applied to run the fossil fuel shock resilience scenario. The scenario simulates the impact of a loss of fossil fuel shipments

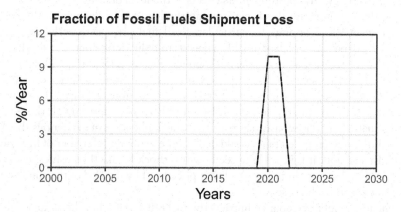

Figure 6.8 ST Scenario 1 – Input: Fossil fuel production shock

Table 6.6 ST Scenario 1 – Input parameter: Fossil fuel production shock

Short-term fossil fuel shipment loss	Parameter	Value
−10% production shock in 2020–2021 and ×10 sensitivity on ordinary production	Production shock loss Sensitivity of price change	+10% ×10
−10% production shock in 2020–2021 and ×20 sensitivity on ordinary production	Production shock loss Sensitivity of price change	+10% ×20
−10% production shock in 2020–2021 and ×30 sensitivity on ordinary production	Production shock loss Sensitivity of price change	+10% ×30

proportional to 10% of global production. A sensitivity analysis of 10 to 30 times larger effect of the impact of lost delivery to the economy in comparison to the traditional effect of supply demand on prices in the capital and goods and services sectors is used. In the ERRE model, energy availability is fundamental for the functioning of every other sector, and a sudden shock would directly impact output, thus demonstrating the sensitivity of each sector to energy production.

Figure 6.9 shows the impact of such a shock on selected variables in the ERRE model.

As Figure 6.9 shows, the shock demonstrates a direct influence of the fossil fuel output on the rest of the economy, and proportional impact on real GDP reduction. This is due to the inability of capital and goods sectors to produce and deliver output in the absence of energy. It is important to remember that the inventory of output in these two sectors have not been considered, thus they respond to such a shock with a sudden black-out to their production lines. The energy sector priorities itself and the household sector to assure the right availability of energy, thus pushing all its effects at the level of firms.

Oscillation after the shock persists, mostly due to its influence on the other variables of the economy. In particular, fossil fuel price is directly impacted. While demand cannot adapt quickly a persistent reduction in output capacity has the effect of creating a price spike corresponding to the shock. Depending on the sensitivity of markets to such a shortage, the nominal fossil fuel price can generate different types of fluctuations. The historical data from 2018 to 2019 show an increase in the nominal price of oil. Despite ERRE not capturing all these type of fluctuations endogenously, it seems that the application of exogenous shocks, such as the one proposed here, could explain the dynamic behaviour of historical data. In addition, it is possible to see how this shock breaks the business cycle of the fossil fuel sector, dropping to a lower price level by the end of the simulation in comparison to the base run.

The fossil fuel price change impacts the real price of food in the simulation by altering its business cycle. Differently from all the other sectors in the economy, it is assumed that the income growth in the household sector is capable of pushing demand up, thus generating relative inflation in the agricultural sector. Due

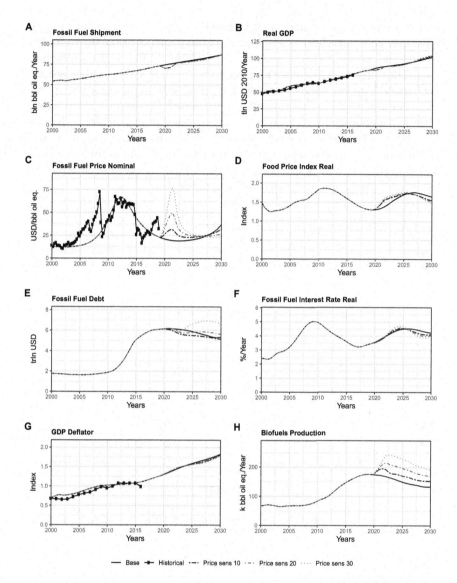

Figure 6.9 ST Scenario 1 – Output: Impact of fossil fuel production shock on selected variables

to the slow time delay in building capacity, the pressure from demand generates a cycle. Fossil fuel price increase thus has the effect of rising food price at a time when it is lower, and the higher the sensitivity of fossil price, the higher the impact on food output price. Another example of this methodology can be found in Pasqualino et al. (2019).

In ERRE, it is assumed that the higher the price of output, the higher is the propensity of one particular sector to build up capacity to respond to market profitability. As a result, the fossil fuel sector has the tendency to increase capacity and finance it through increased debt, as shown in the oscillation proposed here. The different possibilities for price increase, show direct consequences for debt creation and demand for money. The response from the bank is to increase the real interest rate to that particular sector, mostly due to the high increase in their demand for lending. The real interest rate increases its oscillation based on the fossil fuel price cycle and inflation perturbed by the shock. The effect on the global economy is partially mitigated by the shift in demand to the other energy sectors of the economy. There is increased biofuel production, used as a proxy for alternative energy resources in general, due to the shock.

Agricultural land shock and impact of an extreme climate event

Figure 6.10 and Table 6.7 show the application of a 5%, 10%, and 15% assets loss (both land and agricultural inputs) in the agriculture sector, simulating the possible disruption effect of a an extreme weather event.

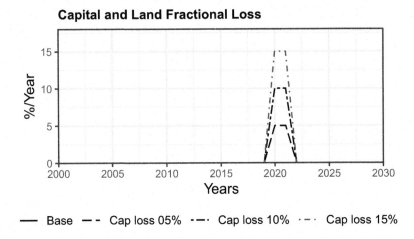

Figure 6.10 ST Scenario 2 – Input: Agricultural capacity shock

Table 6.7 ST Scenario 2 Input parameters: Agricultural capacity shock

Short-term food production loss	*Parameter*	*Value*
–5% assets loss in agriculture	Capital shock loss	+5%
	Agricultural land shock loss	+5%
–10% assets loss in agriculture	Capital shock loss	+10%
	Agricultural land shock loss	+10%
–5% assets loss in agriculture	Capital shock loss	+15%
	Agricultural land shock loss	+15%

Figure 6.11 shows the impact of this shock on selected variables.

As Figure 6.11 shows, the impact is dramatic on several aspects of the agricultural sector. First of all the large shock accumulates as land in default, reducing the availability of agricultural land for production. With a certain time delay, defaulted land is recovered and reintroduced as productive land but does not achieve the level of the base run at the end of this simulation. The direct consequence is a reduction in the production and inventory, thus generating oscillation

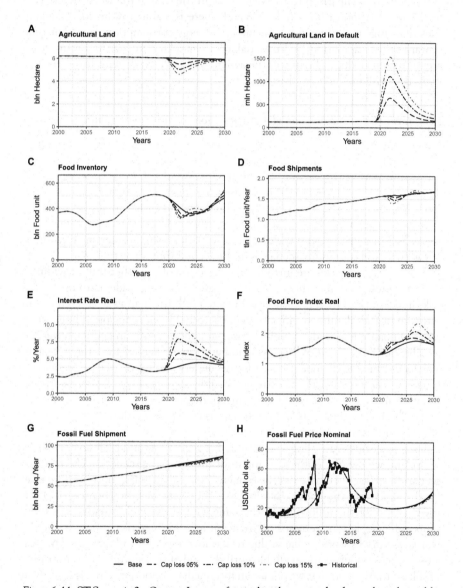

Figure 6.11 ST Scenario 2 – Output: Impact of agricultural capacity shock on selected variables

at the level of capacity to overcome the initial inefficiency. Shipments automatically reduce, both as an outcome of lower inventory and higher prices which reduce household demand. The more agricultural land is reintroduced in the system, the more the production will increase with oscillation due to the built capacity from the rest of the sector during the shock.

Real interest rates rise sharply as a direct consequences of capital defaulting. Real price impact the cycle pushing its increase to approximately 2.4 times the price index in comparison to the year 2000, in the case of the worst shock. Due to the formulation of household demand, there is a shift toward food demand thus reducing goods demand. This impacts energy consumption from that time onward in the simulation, and thus reduces demand for energy. As a result fossil fuel shipments reduce, the higher the agricultural land shock, with little sensitivity to the fossil fuel price in this simulation.

Long-term risk scenarios and global transition toward sustainability

In the long-term (LT) risk scenarios we project a base run simulation toward the year 2100, and gradually perform sensitivity analysis on the most pressing ecosystem issues of this century one by one. In a similar way, we assess sensitivity and stress tests in relation to the most discussed approaches to solving these long-term risks, such as the green energy technology and carbon taxes. In total, we simulate six scenarios, where, starting from a no-limits case, we apply climate and resource depletion limits for the first three scenarios, and consider green technology growth and carbon tax scenarios in the second three cases.

The LT risk scenarios are introduced one on top of the other thus providing a narrow representation of those plausible futures that we consider extreme fat-tail risks in a regime of high uncertainty. In fact, a full risk analysis would require an estimate of the likelihood of each scenario to hold true, thus providing a final range of possibilities under which to base our policies. Such an approach was not possible due to the limit of this research, but it can be applied for future research. We focus the ERRE model towards the understanding of highly unpleasant futures as the range of those extreme possible scenarios, which represent high negative impacts to our world economy, and thus require particular attention by policy makers. Figure 6.12 provides a visual representation of the scenarios adopted in this risk analysis.

Each scenario is run using a sensitivity between a low and high level risk scenario, and we use one of those as input for the following scenario. The first two scenarios consist of climate risks assessment, considered as the most pressing issue for the analysis of the ERRE. In both cases the worst scenario (highest risk) was used as base for the following. In the same way, Scenario 3 provides sensitivity on possible depletion scenarios on the fossil fuel side, ceteris paribus. While the worst case drives world collapse due to too low reserves available, and the best case assumes resources are available until the end of the century without causing problems to the economy, we opt for an intermediate option which has scarcity in the second half of this century. Thus, Scenario 4 and 5 apply the option of green

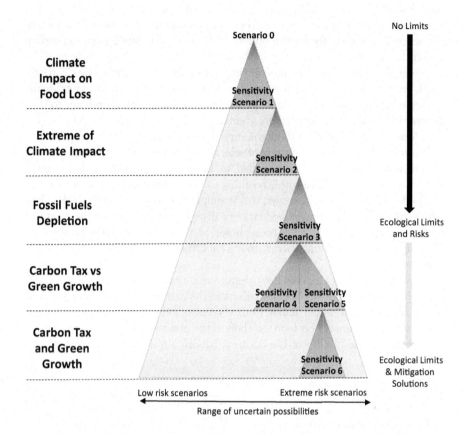

Figure 6.12 Decision tree for uncertain extreme risk analysis of long-term scenarios

growth sensitivity and carbon taxes sensitivity on Scenario 3, demonstrating the different impact of technology growth vs transition policy shocks. Thus the most favourable case for Scenario 5 (carbon tax) is used to introduce the inputs applied in Scenario 6, thus demonstrating how combined solutions can lead to better outcomes. This section shows these scenarios in detail, and concludes with regards to possible implications of these results.

Scenario 1 – Long-term hot house scenario

In the long-term scenarios, we assess the hot house effect (Steffen et al 2018) on food output on the top of a base run scenario. In this case we assume the IPCC (2014) low risk curve for impact of a temperature anomaly on food loss, with a -15% reduction in food output corresponding to a +5 degrees of temperature increase on pre-industrial levels. The four scenarios gradually introduce more pressing limits from climate change. Starting from the base run, we test how the model would behave when assuming that climate can generate food loss while the ocean behaves as a perfect absorber over the duration of the simulation. In the second case we consider the option of the ocean gradually stopping carbon absorption starting the year 2020. In the third, we assume the hypothesis of ocean stopping absorption and starting emitting carbon beyond a certain sink capacity level. In the fourth case we assume that temperature anomaly could gradually decrease ocean carbon capacity to –80% of maximum in correspondence to a +6 degrees increase in the temperature anomaly.

Figure 6.13 and Table 6.8 show the inputs to this scenario.

Figure 6.14 shows the sensitivity of selected variables to this scenario.

The way the climate was modelled in ERRE appears to provide marginal impact to the economy as a whole resulting in similar production emissions across all the four sensitivities. However, this is simply due to the fact the model gives little consideration of climate feedback as a disruption to any part of the economy apart from agriculture. This has been chosen to allow the exploration of the relationship between food and energy, above all. Other effects can be considered for future research.

This scenario demonstrates how, despite the same emissions from the economy, the effects on climate accumulations in the carbon cycle can have very different repercussions. In particular, in the base run and in the first scenario of this analysis (climate impact on food), carbon in the atmosphere remains (relatively) low since the high ability of the ocean to absorb a fraction of it. Carbon from

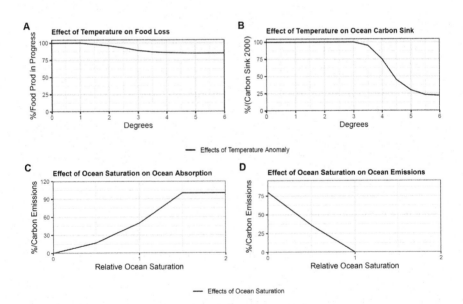

Figure 6.13 LT Scenario 1 – Input: Impact of climate on food production and hot house effect

Table 6.8 LT Scenario 1 – Input switches: Impact of climate on food production and hot house effect

Long-term food production loss and climate (IPCC low risk scenario)	Parameter	Value
Impact of Climate on Food	Switch Climate Effect on Food	ON
	Switch Stop Absorption	OFF
	Switch Ocean emissions	OFF
	Switch Temperature anomaly on ocean carbon sink	OFF
Impact of Stop Absorption from Ocean to Atmosphere	Switch Climate Effect on Food	ON
	Switch Stop Absorption	ON
	Switch Ocean emissions	OFF
	Switch Temperature anomaly on ocean carbon sink	OFF
Impact of Ocean Emissions to Atmosphere	Switch Climate Effect on Food	ON
	Switch Stop Absorption	ON
	Switch Ocean emissions	ON
	Switch Temperature anomaly on ocean carbon sink	OFF
Impact of Hot House Effect	Switch Climate Effect on Food	ON
	Switch Stop Absorption	ON
	Switch Ocean emissions	ON
	Switch Temperature anomaly on ocean carbon sink	ON

the atmosphere to the ocean keeps increasing, and no emissions from ocean to the atmosphere are considered. However, Scenarios 2 and 3 (stop absorption and emissions from ocean), present a very different dynamic behaviour. In particular, because the ocean reduces its absorption capacity from the year 2020, more carbon from global emissions is maintained in the atmosphere. When considering the hot house effect there is a reduction in the ocean absorption capability, maintaining a similar absorption capacity to the previous case reaching a peak around the year 2050. The carbon stock in the ocean then starts decreasing, emissions rise abruptly, and more and more carbon remain in the atmosphere.

This last variable is directly modelled as causing the temperature rise. In the case of the ocean behaving as a perfect absorber, it is assumed that the temperature increase will be approximately +3.5 degrees Celsius above pre-industrial levels by the end of this century. However, in case of ocean stopping absorption but not emitting carbon, the temperature rise could increase to +7 degrees Celsius. While assuming the gradual reduction in the capacity of the ocean to act as a sink leading to it becoming a net emitter of carbon, the temperature anomaly can reach +9 degrees Celsius by the end of the century. Despite this high increase in temperature the effect on food loss is contained with a –15% production loss on total output. As a result, food production loss increases, pushing real prices up due to the increased cost of agricultural inputs to generate the desired output based on demand from population based on their income.

All these scenarios are assumed to have an initial carbon sink in the ocean approximately 3.3 times higher than the current carbon in the atmosphere at

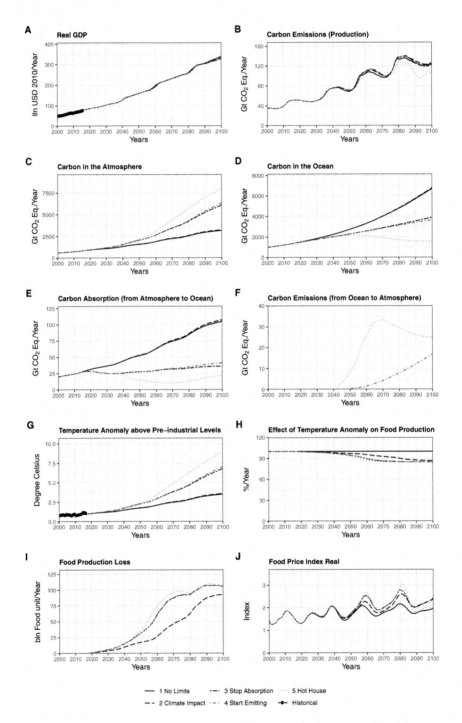

Figure 6.14 LT Scenario 1 – Output: Impact of climate on food system and Real GDP

the beginning of the simulation. The non-linear effects of carbon are determined such that the ocean reaches the tipping point due to saturation around the year 2020. Despite the difficulty of measuring these threshold, the aim of this section is not to provide a precise forecast, rather to show the sensitivity of the model to these inputs. Further work can be performed to better estimate the shape of these curves as soon as data become available.

Scenario 2 – Long-term climate impact assessment

Figure 6.15 and Table 6.9 show the inputs to the ERRE model in the case of a worse climate disruptive effect on food loss in addition to the previous scenario which explored temperature sensitivity. Here we test the models sensitivity to a range of food production losses associated with a given rise in temperature. The first case represents the loss of 15% of food production as in Scenario 1. We also test the sensitivity in the ERRE output by considering a high risk average food

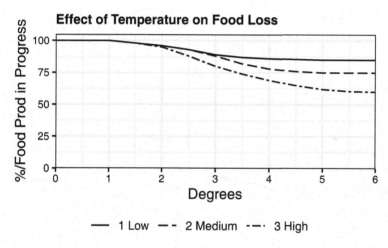

Figure 6.15 LT Scenario 2 – Input: High risk scenarios of climate impact on food

Table 6.9 LT Scenario 2 – Input switch: High risk scenarios of climate impact on food

Short-term food production loss	Parameter	Value
IPCC Low Risk Case (15% food loss at +5 degrees)	Impact curve case	1
IPCC High Risk Case (25% food loss at +5 degrees)	Impact curve case	2
Higher Risk Case (40% food loss at +6 degrees)	Impact curve case	3

loss based on IPCC (2014) (approximately 25% food loss globally) estimate, and a worse case estimate of an extreme risk in food loss of –40% of total output when temperature increase reaches the +6 degrees on pre-industrial levels. This latter is equivalent to a high risk scenario without mitigation policies as if the entire world would be impacted in the same way as the tropical areas (IPCC 2014).

Figure 6.16 shows the sensitivity of selected variables for Scenario 2.

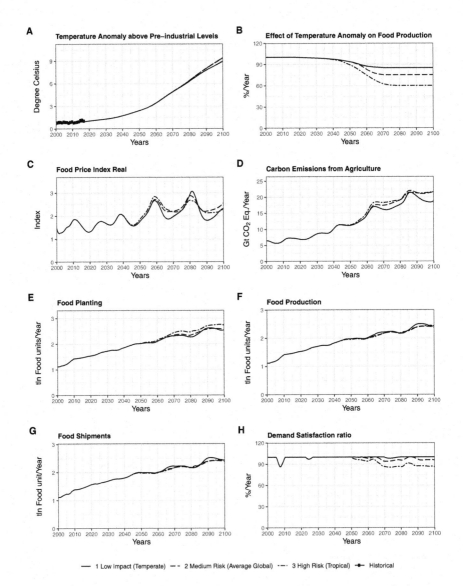

Figure 6.16 LT Scenario 2 – Output: High risk scenario of climate impact on food

While the temperature anomaly remains the same in each case, its impact on food loss increases in the three scenarios. This is reflected in the relative increase in the real food price index, despite a large fraction of its effect being mitigated by the balancing effect of the agricultural sector increasing capacity to respond to changes in demand. In fact, agriculture finds itself in the position of increasing planting and thereby increasing carbon emissions from agriculture. Despite the larger capacity, the impact of food loss offsets the investment increase, thus reducing actual production and shipment rate, also reduced by the price increase. Most important the stress imposed generates an important struggle for the agricultural sector which appear to reduce its ability to respond to demand, and ends in the position of satisfying no more than 85% of total demand by the end of this century.

A scenario of this type would likely trigger riots and other social responses to balance the disequilibrium. However, the ERRE model accounts for the merely production structure of the agricultural sector and therefore any societal response to this extreme condition is not modelled. Other models should be built to address the social response of such a scenario.

The most extreme case of food loss is considered as base for Scenario 3, adding the possibility of resource constraints to the economy.

Scenario 3 – Long-term climate and fossil fuel depletion risk

Figure 6.17 and Table 6.10 show the sensitivity inputs to address the fossil fuel resource depletion, tested in Scenario 3.

Figure 6.18, Figure 6.19, and Figure 6.20 show the impact of the depletion on the selected variables in ERRE, relative to the economy, energy sector, prices, and climate change.

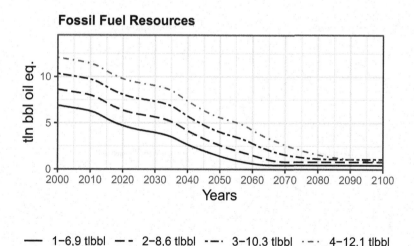

Figure 6.17 LT Scenario 3 – Input: Resource availability initial condition

Table 6.10 LT Scenario 3 – Input parameter: Resource availability initial condition

Long-term depletion risk	Parameter	Value
Resources available are scarce to allow the energy transition to happen smoothly with severe consequences for economic activity	Reference resources at year 2000	6.9 tln bbl
Resources available are scarce to allow the energy transition to happen smoothly with mostly severe consequences for economic activity	Reference resources at year 2000	8.6 tln bb
Resources available are scarce and allow the energy transition to happen smoothly with some negative consequences for economic activity	Reference resources at year 2000	10.3 tln bbl
Resources available are scarce but do allow the energy transition to happen smoothly without severe consequences for economic activity	Reference resources at year 2000	12.1 tln bbl

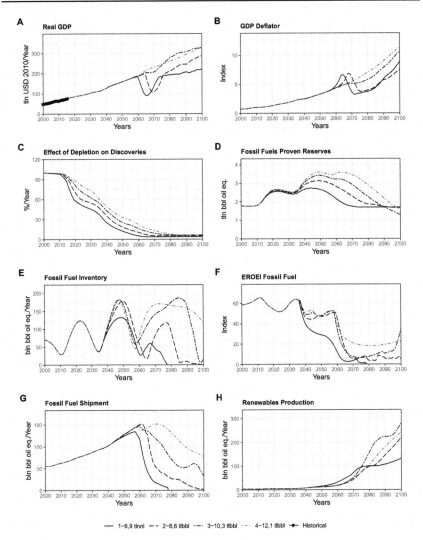

— 1–6,9 tlnnl — — 2–8,6 tlbbl —·— 3–10,3 tlbbl ·—· 4–12,1 tlbbl —•— Historical

Figure 6.18 LT Scenario 3 – Output (1/3): Impact of resource depletion on economic activity and energy transition

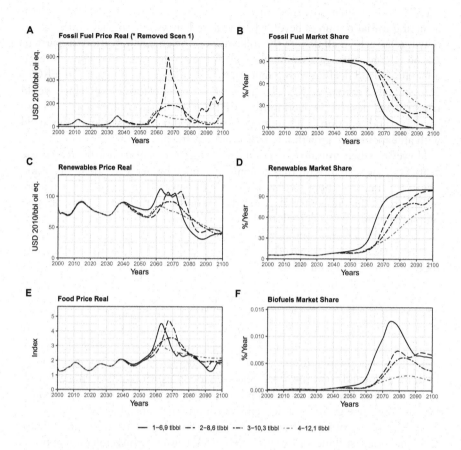

Figure 6.19 LT Scenario 3 – Output (2/3): Impact of resource depletion on energy prices and market shares

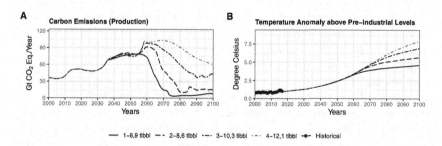

Figure 6.20 LT Scenario 3 – Output (3/3): Impact of resource depletion on carbon emissions and temperature anomaly

Figure 6.18 shows the possible repercussions of a scarcity of resources starting in the year 2010, with repercussion effects after mid-century, and assuming a constant +3% exponential growth in the renewable resources sector.

While resources deplete, difficulty in extraction increases such that fossil fuel demand is not met. The hit on demand due to lack on reserves occurs at different times in the simulation depending on the resources initially available. When assuming initial resources beyond 10.3 trillion barrels, the impact on the economy is relatively small despite the influence on the energy transition. In particular, no energy shortage is assumed to affect the economy, proven reserves reach a maximum and decline with a reduction in extraction from 2050. The EROEI of fossil fuels a drop after 2060, but it never decreases below a level which would trigger lower desired production from the fossil fuel sector. Shipments decrease smoothly and renewables have time to take over the energy system of the world with an exponential growth rate that is not too steep.

However, when initial resources decrease to 8.6 or 6.9 trillion barrels in the year 2000, the scenarios hit the economy in a much harder way. Energy depletion negatively impacts the economy before the renewable energy sector is mature enough to avoid a relative collapse in the economy. In the first case, the drop in output decreases from its peak to the output recorded 20 years before the drop. In the second case, real output drops to the level of 50 years before the collapse occurs. Thanks to the renewable energy increases after 2070, growth starts again, together with decreased levels of inflation. While in the first case, inventory reduces output, in the second, inventory goes to zero in the 2070s, thus stopping shipments. With no firms investing any energy on extraction, EROEI drops to zero as well.

Figure 6.19 shows the implications of this sensitivity test for resource scarcity on the market share and prices for fossil fuels, renewables, and biofuels (food price index). As it is possible to see, the worst case depletion has strong implications both for price and the transition. The scenario consisting of 6.9 trillion barrels of resources equivalent in the ground has been removed from the graph simply because the price grows exponentially becoming incomparable with the others. However, in case of 8.6 trillion barrels of resource equivalent in the ground, the fossil fuel prices still increase to very high levels triggering high inflation in prices of food and renewables. The worst the option, the faster the transition towards renewables. Biofuels market share increases in line with the peak in price, but decreases over time, due to the take-over of the renewable energy sector in providing energy to the rest of the economy. When considering higher levels of fossil fuel in the ground, the transition is smoother, prices do not increase beyond sustainable levels, and renewables increase in production is reflected in the low prices of energy towards the end of the century.

Figure 6.20 shows the impact of energy depletion on the temperature anomaly and emissions. Despite the depletion having significant implications for the economy, it appears that lower fossil fuels in the ground can generate lower emissions and keep the temperature anomaly to lower levels. In all cases the temperature anomaly would remain below the +9 degrees, with +8 degrees, +7.2 degrees, when fossil fuels are abundant, and +6 and +4.5 degrees in case of economic downturn due to low level of resource in the ground.

In this scenario, no technology is assumed to support the lower emissions of both agriculture and fossil fuels sectors, such as carbon capture technology or better farming techniques. In those cases, a more positive outcome could be reached.

For the next round of sensitivity we would employ the scenario in which initial resources are 8.6 trillion barrels at the beginning of the simulation, which triggers a downturn in the economy around 2070, and starts growth again around 2080.

Scenario 4 – Green growth solution

Figure 6.21 and Table 6.11 show the input of Scenario 4, providing a test for the sensitivity to green energy productivity growth under the assumption of high level climate impact on food system and the effect of fossil fuel depletion. In the ERRE model, the energy sector of interest for this scenario is the renewables and

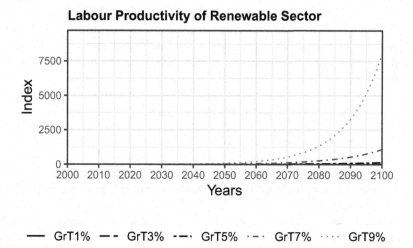

Figure 6.21 LT Scenario 4 – Input: Green technology productivity exponential growth

Table 6.11 LT Scenario 4 – Input parameter: Green technology productivity exponential growth

Green labour productivity growth	Parameter	Value	Productivity at year 2100 in comparison to year 2000
+1% green labour productivity growth from 2000	Exponential growth in green sector labour productivity	+1%	× 2.72
+3% green labour productivity growth from 2000	Exponential growth in green sector labour productivity	+3%	× 20.09
+5% green labour productivity growth from 2000	Exponential growth in green sector labour productivity	+5%	× 148.41
+7% green labour productivity growth from 2000	Exponential growth in green sector labour productivity	+7%	× 1096.63
+9% green labour productivity growth from 2000	Exponential growth in green sector labour productivity	+9%	× 8103.08

nuclear sector. While we are not expecting important take over for nuclear technology, this scenarios tests the hypothesis of increased productivity in renewables, and thus, the green energy sector.

The green energy sector is the only sector where we test the hypothesis of exponential growth in the productivity of labour. While every other scenario assumes a +3% labour productivity growth rate throughout the century, in this scenario we compare the options of lower growth rate +1%, and higher growth rates +5%, +7%, and +9% per year until 2100. For the sake of clarity, Table 6.11 shows the resulting productivity of labour at the year 2100 for each of these cases. In particular, the standard case of +3% growth assumes a ×20 increase in productivity in one century of technology development, which is an appropriate starting point for the analysis under an uncertain future. However there exist a large difference between the five cases since a +1% growth rate would result in only ×2.7 productivity increase over the century, while +5% accounts for approximately ×150 times by the end of the century, +7% corresponds to ×1096 increase in productivity, and +9% consists in a ×8103 increase in productivity by the end of the century. Despite all positive expectations on the possible evolution on technology these last two scenarios appear to be highly unlikely at the current level of knowledge, without thinking about a new (currently unknown) disruptive technology. However, it is important to test these hypothesis in order to show the fundamental functioning of the model as well as the limits of a possible energy transition given ecological limits assumptions.

Figure 6.22, Figure 6.23, and Figure 6.24 show the implications of this sensitivity on selected variables in the model, being economy, energy sector and ecological limits respectively.

One of the most alarming results of this test is that, at current levels of technology, and assuming that fossil fuel energy will not last until the end of the century, a slow take-over of green energy technology can push the economy toward global collapse. This is mostly due to the inability of the industrial sector (capital) to produce sufficient output for the rest of the economy and itself. Given that the capital sector does not prioritise one sector over another, the capital orders in the renewable sector remain lower than that which is necessary to support the economy to grow. The dynamic behaviour of this transition is constrained to collapse. In a similar way to the Limits to Growth (Meadows et al. 2003), the economy can collapse for a lack of resources, and despite highlighting the issue of growth and collapse, the model cannot deal with a post-growth economy simply because such elements have not been included in the dynamics of the system. For example, we did not consider the hypothesis of additional money creation policies at the time of difficulty, keeping the monetary and government growth rate at a +2% per year respectively. Alternatively, all sectors require capital and energy to produce, and no assumption on a substantial value change within the human system has been considered, such as the attempt to generate growth via human based output with little input from material capital.

As an advance on Meadows et al. (2003), we can describe in greater detail the possible dynamics of collapse in comparison to the Limits to Growth. In

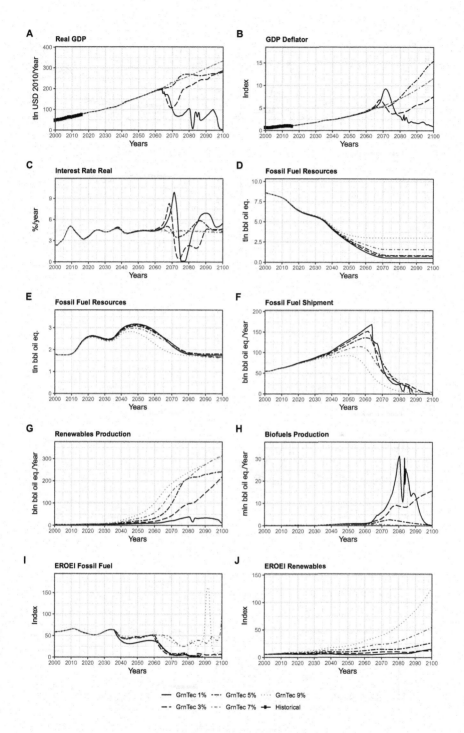

Figure 6.22 LT Scenario 4 – Output (1/3): Impact of green technology growth on selected variables

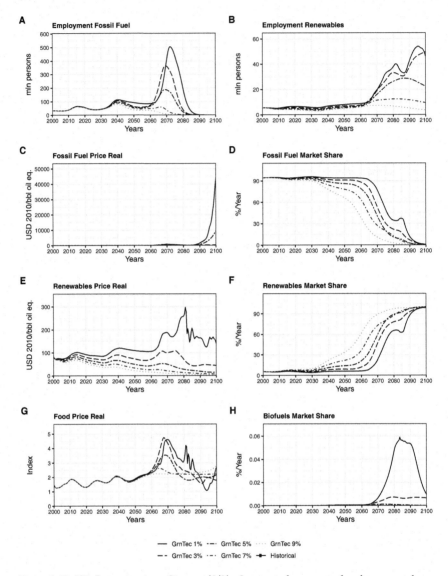

Figure 6.23 LT Scenario 4 – Output (2/3): Impact of green technology growth on employment, market shares, and prices

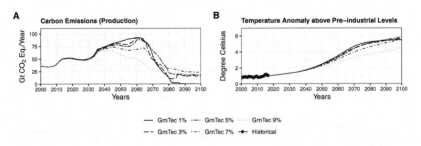

Figure 6.24 LT Scenario 4 – Output (3/3): Impact of green technology growth on temperature anomaly

particular, the ERRE model shows a period of high inflation during the peak of fossil fuel production, followed by lower demand and deflation until the end of the simulation. As a result, interest rates would first increase and then drop aiming to generate a recovery in the economic system. This interest rate is intended as the interest necessary by banks to be solvent. A negative interest rate would not be possible in this case, while more options could be addressed such as the negative interest rates for household, pushing them to invest more rather than saving. In this scenario, the energy shift to renewables is not successful, and a large fraction of the pressure is put on the biofuel industry, which collapses not far before the end of the century due to a lack in energy, capital, and demand.

An interesting result of the collapse is in the dynamics of employment in the energy sector. In fact, while the fossil fuel sector lowers its EROEI and productivity due to depletion, more capital and more people are necessary to extract additional resources. Employment thus rises pulling people away from the other sectors of the economy. This is the same case for renewables, However with a collapse by the end of the century leaving most people out of job. The energy market share at the end of the simulation is mostly composed of renewables despite the lower demand of a de-industrialised economy. Despite the economic collapse, enough carbon was burned to increase global average temperature to +5 degrees in comparison to pre-industrial levels, thus reducing the ability of farmers to produce food.

All other scenarios provide drastic improvements on the base simulation. In each scenario the negative effects are lower and lower, almost disappearing when green growth is above +7%. The general dynamic is to speed up the transition toward renewables, decrease renewables prices, avoid volatility and price peaks, and almost avoid the biofuel industry engaging in the transition. Real food price still increases due to the effect of household income growth on demand. Employment in the fossil fuel industry smoothly approaches zero, while the employment in renewables lowers due the high ability of each worker to produce more output. It is worth noting that the EROEI of the renewable sector does not follow the same pattern as labour productivity, achieving approximately 120 when labour productivity grows at +9% growth rate. This is due to the fact, that EROEI is calculated as the ratio between the energy produced and the energy that the sector is willing to employ to generate such an output. As a result, labour productivity is not a direct influence on the capital productivity and relative energy efficiency. This also explains the peak in EROEI of the fossil fuel industry around 2080 when simulating the best case of green energy productivity scenario. In fact, when the desired energy consumption of EROEI approaches zero, the EROEI can increase despite a low availability of resources.

Another interesting result of this scenario is that, even assuming a very high growth rate in labour productivity for the green sector, no guarantee can be given on the side of emissions and global temperature rise. In the best case scenario, temperature would still increase above +4 degrees on pre-industrial levels, as well as leaving more resources in the ground as stranded assets. The next scenario shows the same case when considering the hypothesis of carbon tax.

Scenario 5 – Carbon tax solution

Based on Scenario 3, in Scenario 5 we provide a sensitivity on the application of a carbon tax on fossil fuel industry to support the energy transition while keeping labour productivity growth of the green sector at +3%. In ERRE, the carbon tax is modelled in the same way as proposed in Sterman (1981). In particular, the fossil fuel industry calculates a market price, and the carbon tax is applied as a multiplier on top of such a price thus generating the fossil fuel price after tax. Because the price is then higher than in the free market hypothesis, the other energy suppliers find an advantage of cost, and the market shifts towards them more quickly. The market share of the fossil fuel sector and relative revenue is then split between what was the component of the tax and that which can stay in the industry. The relative tax revenue for the government is redistributed across all sectors of the economy as a tax break. In the first scenario we provide a sensitivity of applying a carbon tax to fossil fuels starting in 2030 and increasing to full application in 2033. The three levels considered are +50%, +150%, and +250% fossil fuel prices increase on market value. In a second round of the analysis we compare the case of +250% price increase when applied in 2030 or in 2020, thus demonstrating the importance of the time for action. Figure 6.25 and Table 6.12 show the input to the model to generating such a sensitivity.

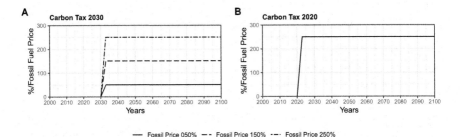

Figure 6.25 LT Scenario 5 – Input: Carbon tax on fossil fuels

Table 6.12 LT Scenario 5 – Input parameters: Carbon tax on fossil fuels

Carbon tax on fossil price	Parameter	Value
+50% fossil price increase in 2030, with relative income distributed used as tax relief for the economy	Carbon Tax 2030	+50% in 2030
+150% fossil price increase in 2030, with relative income distributed used as tax relief for the economy	Carbon Tax 2030	+150% in 2030
+250% fossil price increase in 2030, with relative income distributed used as tax relief for the economy	Carbon Tax 2030	+250% in 2030
+250% fossil price increase, with relative income distributed used as tax relief for the economy	Carbon Tax 2020	+250% in 2020

Figure 6.26 and Figure 6.27 show the sensitivity of output to a 2030 tax for selected variables.

In a similar way to the green energy labour productivity growth scenario, a carbon tax can have the effect of speeding the energy transition towards green energy, increasing the volume of stranded assets left in the ground, reducing carbon in the atmosphere and the negative impact of climate change. However, the

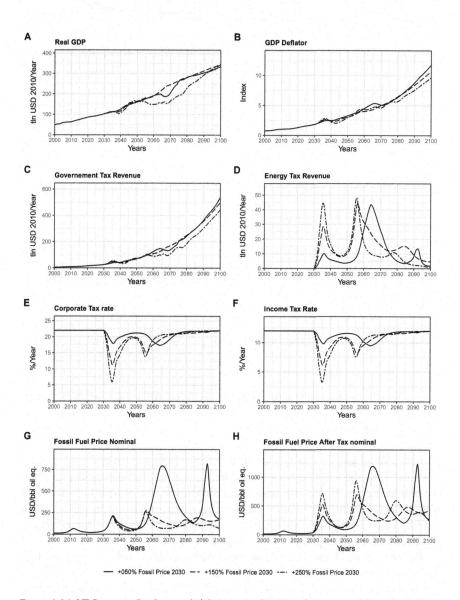

Figure 6.26 LT Scenario 5 – Output (1/4): Impact of 2030 carbon tax on selected variables

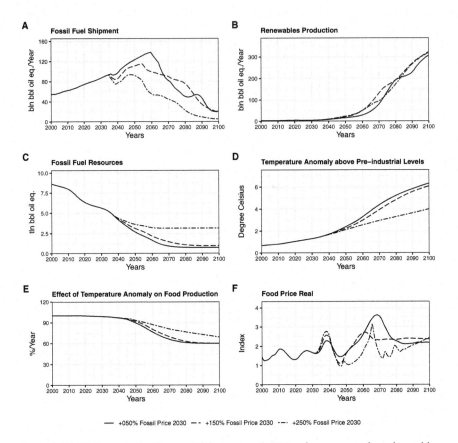

Figure 6.27 LT Scenario 5 – Output (2/4): Impact of 2030 carbon tax on selected variables

means to achieve this result is very different with potential negative consequences for the economy. In fact, a too strong carbon tax applied in 2030 can have the effect of destabilising the general dynamic of the economy. As Figure 6.26 shows, the year 2030 represents the beginning of a price increase during the business cycle the fossil fuel industry is part of. When the carbon tax hits the market, the price spike to the actual economy is so strong that it can generate higher prices (inflation increases) and reduce demand for the other commodities, thus pushing the economy in a general dynamic of persistent recession. In particular the +250% carbon tax policy appears to generate a deeper recession reducing general real output for the majority of the century.

Figure 6.28 and Figure 6.29 show the consequences of applying the same high leverage policy one decade earlier.

Applying the tax in 2020 as opposed to 2030 results in a much smoother transition, providing little impact on the overall economy, increasing tax income, decreasing

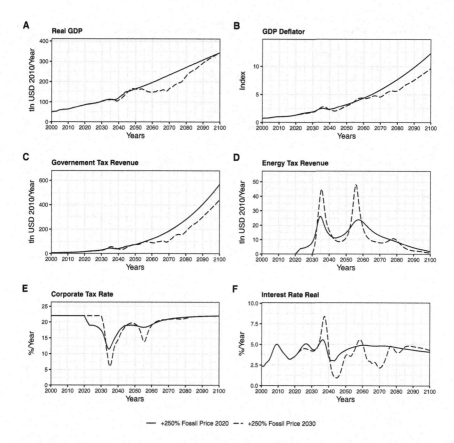

Figure 6.28 LT Scenario 5 – Output (3/4): Impact of 2020 carbon tax on selected variables

instability and prices in the energy market, and overall reducing the income generated from carbon tax itself. Interest rates remains much more stable, as well as inflation.

An interesting result is that because the 2020 carbon tax is applied one decade earlier, the downturn in the market price at that time makes it less effective in reducing carbon emissions than applying it one decade after. This might be possibly caused by the approach adopted in modelling the carbon tax as directly impacting the price of output of the fossil fuel sector, and different techniques to model carbon tax might provide different behaviours. However, the results of this scenario comparison suggest that the timing of application of the carbon tax, if synergic to the time in which the fossil fuel industry is more fragile (peak in the oscillation) can be a significant determinant of its effectiveness.

While aiming at a more efficient economy, we adopt this last, smoother, scenario as base for Scenario 6, where we test the combination of carbon tax in 2020 and green labour productivity growth.

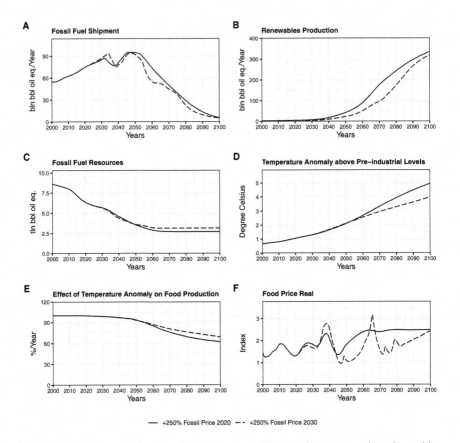

Figure 6.29 LT Scenario 5 – Output (4/4): Impact of 2020 carbon tax on selected variables

Scenario 6 – combined green growth and carbon tax solution

Figure 6.30 and Table 6.13 show the inputs applied to test the option of a combined effect of a carbon tax and a high growth in technology development of the green sector. The purpose of this analysis is to address the possible limits of an energy transition while applying both tax and investment policies to speed up the transition, under the hypothesis of hot house effect (Steffen et al. 2018). In addition to a +250% increase in fossil fuel price carbon tax in the year 2020, we compare the options of green labour productivity exponential growth at +3%, +6%, and +9%. Table 6.13 shows the relative productivity value in the three cases, being approximately ×20, ×400, and ×8100 by the end of the century respectively.

Figure 6.31 and Figure 6.32 show the sensitivity analysis on selected variables in the model.

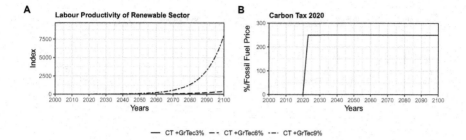

Figure 6.30 LT Scenario 6 – Input: Combined effects of green growth and carbon tax

Table 6.13 LT Scenario 6 – Input parameter: Combined effects of green growth and carbon tax

Green labour productivity growth	Parameter	Value	Productivity at year 2100 in comparison to year 2000
+3% green labour productivity growth from 2000	Exponential growth in green sector labour productivity	+3%	×20.09
+6% green labour productivity growth from 2000	Exponential growth in green sector labour productivity	+6%	×403.42
+9% green labour productivity growth from 2000	Exponential growth in green sector labour productivity	+9%	×8103.08

Figure 6.31 shows the impact of increasing productivity in the green sector on the functioning of the economy as well as on the energy transition. In particular, it is possible to see how, the instability in real GDP growth rate generated by the depletion case can be offset assuming improved green energy productivity. It is worth noting how the real growth decreases over time due to the assumed technology growth rate in goods and capital sectors, assumed to be ramp linear rather than exponential, setting the trend for the entire global economy. In all cases inflation results in not being particularly affected. Improvements in green energy technology can smooth the transition, pushing more fossil fuel resources to be stranded assets, increasing the output from renewables and supporting a faster transition. Renewables EROEI which starts at approximately 6, ends at 12 in case of +3% growth, 40 in case of +6% green growth, and 130 in case of +9% green growth. With green energy taking over the market before fossil fuel depletion hits the economy, energy prices do not rise as much, thus reducing the impact of the carbon tax, both in terms of revenue and tax relief to the rest of the economy.

Figure 6.32 shows the impact of green growth on energy prices, temperature anomaly, and agriculture. In particular, in the case of +3% growth, renewables

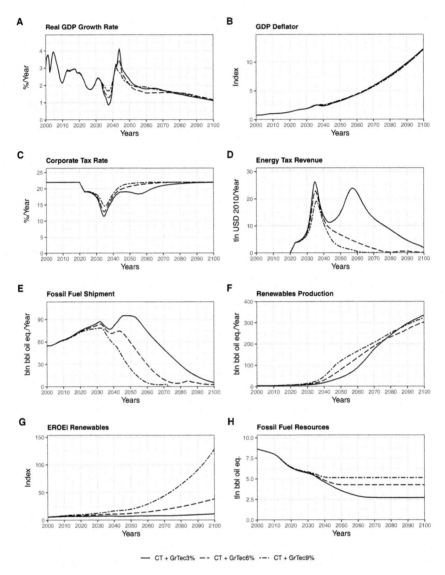

Figure 6.31 LT Scenario 6 – Output (1/2): impact of combined effects of green growth and carbon tax on selected variables

take time to reduce costs, thus, average energy prices remains dominated by increased costs in the fossil fuel energy sector, while no alternative exists for the majority of the 21st century. Temperature anomaly rises to +5 degrees, with a negative impact on food output. Real price of food increases to 2.5 index level and remains stable from 2050 onwards. The more green growth technology

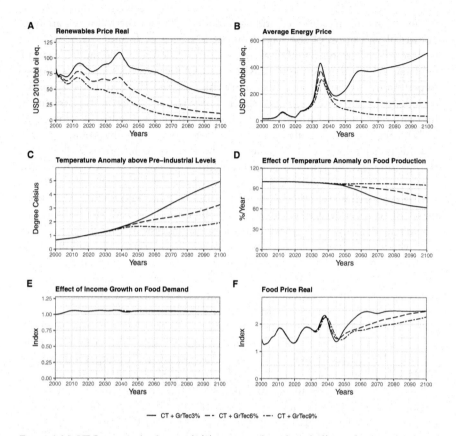

Figure 6.32 LT Scenario 6 – Output (2/2): impact of combined effects of green growth and carbon tax on selected variables

improves, the more the costs of energy decreases, thus avoiding the rise in the energy prices despite a period of relatively high prices between 2030s and 2040s. Because the transition is successful at keeping fossil fuel resources in the ground, the temperature rises reaches +3.5 degrees in case of +6% exponential growth in green energy productivity, and +2 degrees (COP21 target), in case of +9% productivity growth. In this case the impact on food loss remains contained to −5% production loss per year. Real food output keeps increasing in real terms, mostly due to the effect of household income growth on food demand, which pushes prices up above average inflation level.

Summary

In this chapter, the ERRE model has been used for risk and resilience scenario analysis in the context of global resources, dynamics of growth, and financial risk.

Based on a dataset of 24 time series coming from different public sources, the model has been calibrated and used as a base run for the following analysis. Statistical validation of the model output has been performed, demonstrating both sources of strength and weaknesses in the structure of the model, that are fundamental for considering the ERRE as a tool for policy advice. This allowed to perform stress testing and uncertainty risk analysis. The considered scenarios include both short-term resilience shocks analysis and long-term stress testing in line with the Limits to Growth approach to present model results (Meadows et al. 2003). Each scenario is built on top of another, providing analysis of uncertainty towards possible long-term extreme fat tails of world evolution, as well as stress testing to reveal the limits of possible solutions to ecological constraints in the next 80 years.

The results show that, without the hypothesis of hot house effect (i.e. ocean behaving as a perfect carbon absorber for the entire century), temperature rise would remain below +3 degrees Celsius above pre-industrial levels by 2100. However, when considering the hot house hypothesis and a high risk tail of impact of climate on food production, the situation becomes much less desirable. In this latter case, the management of global ecosystems, in line with resource depletion hypothesis, remains a very complex task, apparently leaving little hope for social and technological policies to avoid collapse of the economy.

To avoid a collapse requires an (potentially) unrealistic set of parameters (+7% or +9% growth rate in green technology and +250% price increase in fossil fuel form 2020). This scenario leads the world towards the policy target indicated by COP21.

Simulations and tests appear to demonstrate that in any type of climate scenario, real food price will increase in comparison to the case in which no climate change is considered. The strong correlation between food and energy prices appears to not be confirmed by the ERRE model, despite its structure showing that the oscillation in the price of one of the sectors could significantly impact the prices of the other. In addition, the effect of energy price shocks on food price can be stronger than the impact of a food price shock on the energy price.

This chapter is accompanied with an online appendix available at https://doi. org/10.25411/aru.10110710. The appendix provides additional experiments used as an assessment in terms of model behaviour, which underpin both strengths and weaknesses of the ERRE model. These include both exogenous and endogenous disequilibrium tests, supporting the view of a world economy in disequilibrium, in contrast with the general equilibrium view of computable mainstream economic models. This allowed the framing of the model within academic and economic literature, among both evolutionary, behavioural, and institutional type of models.

Weaknesses of the analysis include not considering any type of technology which can reduce the impact of production emissions. These might include changes in diet to reduce the carbon footprint of the household sector via agriculture, and use of carbon capture storage (CCS) technology to avoid carbon emissions from energy. On the other hand, no impact of climate change has been considered beyond the merely food production loss. More complex feedback solutions could be considered such as sea level rise, disruption of industrial and energy capital via extreme event shocks, and relative cascade impact to the rest of the economy. Thus we argue that the development of ERRE forms the perfect foundation for additional development and analysis to address the complexity of real-world phenomena with particular focus on systemic risk and uncertainty analysis.

References

FAO (2019). *Forest and water programme.* Available online: http://www.fao.org/in-action/forest-and-water-programme/news/news-detail/en/c/1207788/. (accessed september 2019).

FAOSTAT. (2019). Available online: www.fao.org/faostat/en/#data (accessed June 2019).

Federici, S., Tubiello, F. N., Salvatore, M., Jacobs, H., & Schmidhuber, J. (2015). New estimates of CO_2 forest emissions and removals: 1990–2015. *Forest Ecology and Management, 352,* 89–98.

International Energy Agency (IEA). (2017). *Data and statistics.* Available online: www.iea.org/data-and-statistics (accessed September 2017).

IPCC. (2014). Climate change 2014: Synthesis report. In R. Pachauri and L. Meyer (eds.), *Contribution of Working Groups I, II and III to the Fifth Assessment Report of the Intergovernmental Panel on Climate Change* (p. 151). IPCC, Geneva, Switzerland. ISBN: 978-92-9169-143-2.

International Renewable Energy Agency (IRENA). (2018). *Data and statistics.* Available online: www.irena.org/Statistics (accessed June 2018).

Lyneis, J. M. (1980). *Corporate planning and policy design: A system dynamics approach.* Massachusetts Institute of Technology, Cambridge, MA, US.

Meadows, D. H., Meadows, D. L., & Randers, J. (2003). *The limits to growth: The 30-year update.* Routledge, Oxford, UK.

Meadows, D., & Randers, J. (2012). *The limits to growth: The 30-year update.* Routledge.

Pasqualino, R., Jones, A., Monasterolo, I., & Phillips, A. (2015). Understanding global systems today – a calibration of the world3–03 model between 1995 and 2012. *Sustainability, 7*(8), 9864–9889.

Pasqualino, R., Monasterolo, I., & Jones, A. (2019). An Integrated global food and energy security system dynamics model for addressing systemic risk. *Sustainability, 11*(14), 3995.

Rye, C. D., & Jackson, T. (2018). A review of EROEI-dynamics energy-transition models. *Energy Policy, 122,* 260–272.

Senge, P. M., & Forrester, J. W. (1980). Tests for building confidence in system dynamics models. *System Dynamics, TIMS Studies in Management Sciences, 14,* 209–228.

Steffen, W., Rockström, J., Richardson, K., Lenton, T. M., Folke, C., Liverman, D., . . . Crucifix, M. (2018). Trajectories of the earth system in the anthropocene. *Proceedings of the National Academy of Sciences, 115*(33), 8252–8259.

Sterman, J. (1981). *The energy transition and the economy: A system dynamics approach* (2 Vols.). MIT Alfred P. Sloan School of Management, Cambridge, MA.

Sterman, J. (2000). *Business dynamics: Systems thinking and modeling for a complex world.* Jeffrey J. Shelstad, Indianapolis.

World Bank Databank (WB). Available online: https://data.worldbank.org/ (accessed September 2019).

7 Conclusion

The purpose of this book

The purpose of this book is both to build clarity around the use system dynamics modelling, as well as address an important gap in the literature between the Limits to Growth study and today's decision making. In particular, a reassessment of global environmental limits, as well as the inclusion of financial and social variables such as prices and interest rates, and the representation of the economy based on a stock and flow consistent financial framework, have been developed. The analysis was presented both as a reassessment of the limits to growth in today's world based on the hot-house effect and an energy transition away from fossil fuels, as well as looking at the short-term consequences of shocks that could generate cascading impact across economic sectors and food security.

This book, and the online appendixes that accompany it, seek to bridge the gap between the real world and the world of models. Modelling is not a task performed by the few, but rather an activity we all do every time we face a problem in our life. The activity of global modelling is an extension of this.

Thus, Part I of this book provides a review of the Limits to Growth model and compares that with reality. Secondly, we provide a basic description of system dynamics to learn how the World3 model works. From a top-down perspective, the World3–03 model is presented, aiming to highlight the elements that impact the system behaviour, and showing how collapse and analysis are driven in the model. This is followed by a calibration of World3 with real-world data in Chapter 2, demonstrating how different the world evolved in comparison to the Limits to Growth scenarios. In Chapter 3, we provide a description of how the real world has evolved since Limits to Growth was first published, starting from the principles of capitalism, finance, and reasons why productivity and technology growth were considered the engine for prosperity.

The aim of Part I is to show how different models can be from the reality, and what the role of models are in society. The idea of a right or wrong model becomes secondary against the ability to use a model to understand large scale change over time. Building on this, Part II shows how the science of modelling and policy consultancy evolved. Chapter 4 shows the evolution of economic understanding of systems, including how different schools of thought defend their

DOI: 10.4324/9781315643182-9

own values. With the aim of comparing computer modelling schools, highlighting their strengths and complementarities, the system dynamics school is analysed in terms of its relationship with the economic profession since the time it was initially conceived (Forrester 1957). Thus both the Limits to Growth, and further work of the community, are analysed from the economic modelling perspective. Thus Chapter 4 provides further elucidation of those elements that, we believe, a system dynamics modeller should be aware of before engaging in economic modelling activities to influence system policy change. On the other hand, other economic communities should be aware of the potential of system dynamics as contributing to the behavioural, evolutionary, post-Keynesian, and institutional economic schools of thoughts while providing disciplined and rigorous formal modelling methods.

Chapters 5 and 6 provide a description of the ERRE model, starting from the framework emerging from the World3–03 model (Meadows et al. 2003), and the System Dynamics National Model as proposed in Sterman (1981) in the Energy Transition and the Economy model. We frame the resulting ERRE as a system dynamics model, which overlaps with neoclassical, evolutionary, behavioural, post-Keynesian, and ecological schools of economic thought. Tests and structures are highlighted to describe why the model fits in such a literature. Finally, statistical validation, analysis of resilience in the presence of short-term shocks, and long-term stress tests and scenarios are assessed to analyse the fat-tail extreme risks dependent on the interaction between economic growth, financial risk, and global resource limits.

The entire work was proposed to show how system dynamics modelling differs from, and provides value to, the standard general equilibrium and integrated assessment models, and how the use of non-linear relationships, behavioural economics, and bounded rationality of agents can be used as an extension to the former. The objective is to simplify the journey of both modellers and model users to extend this work and to perform their own based on the ERRE model framework. Simulation models are often seen as black box quantitative tools, often underestimated by potential users using the infamous sentence "all models are wrong." We argue here that models are the best approximation we have toward the solution of complex problems, and before being judged for their ability to solve problems they should be assessed with care. All models are questionable, however both the transparency of their assumptions, and the existing literature where they fit, should also be specified to allow criticism in an effective way. This is the objective of this book and the online appendixes alongside it.

How right was Limits to Growth?

Limits to Growth was the first report of the Club of Rome (Meadows et al. 1972). All models are wrong, however World3 has proven to be incredibly useful. In 1972, Limits to Growth caused controversy in the media of the time. Simplicity in the representation of knowledge linked to the difficulty of disentangling the world model to understand the dynamics of collapse, led to a huge impact of the Limits to Growth. Adding to the work of earlier scientists, and building further scientific consensus, alongside major persistent pollution events such as the Chernobyl nuclear accident, has led to significant policy change globally, shaping the world as it is today. Today, we are still in the midst of this debate with hundreds of models, all seeing the world from a different perspective, built for the purpose of policy influence and advice. Technology, institutions, and methods, have been widely tested, adopted and created, as well as institutionalised within governmental panels to support policy making in the most effective way.

The Limits to Growth advocated to stop exponential growth all over the world, at the time when its effects were less visible. Their prediction was to explain that there will always be limits to growth on a finite planet, and if we keep growing exponentially, overcoming any one of those limits will simply postpone the day of overshoot, since other limits will appear stopping growth, most likely forcing a global system decline. As this book has shown, modelling the future is very different from knowing about the future. Many trends that appeared in the real world in the last 50 years were not depicted by the Limits to Growth team. The impressive development of the service economy and finance are examples of those, as demonstrated in Chapter 2 of this book. Still exponential growth did not stop, and we now face the challenge of climate change, another problem to be tackled at the global system scale.

World3 did not capture elements on both the political and the ecological spheres. In particular, the functioning of the financial system, so key to today's economy, and its requirement to generate growth to maintain economic sustainability, is missing. The concepts of economic growth and labour productivity are shown as one of the main instruments, as advocated from the economic community, that can handle limits when they occur.

Among the limits in ecological systems, many have been generally predicted by the Limits to Growth. These include the issue of persistent pollution such as plastic in ecosystems, of organic pollutants in the air and in the soil. These are assessed to fundamentally cause serious damage to both people and ecosystems, despite being concentrated in some local areas of the world. However, while placing the Limits to Growth in the context of resource scarcity, food security, and climate change, we find that these are still the most challenging and extreme threats to the development of global society until the end of this century.

Thus some basic principles of the financial system, with their forward looking risk assessment activity, are depicted as driven by short-term gains, and are not suitable to support a sustainable transition alone. The concept of path dependency as highlighted with the lock-in effect of certain types of technologies is critical. The problem of the energy transition through a market driven solution, is shown as hopeless at best, with tackling climate change dependent on the complete electrification of a global renewable energy system within the next 20 to 30 years. This links with the systems of agriculture and food security, today highly dependent on the oil sector to keep feeding a growing population, highlighting possible solutions at the cost of developing new understandings of economic systems.

Given the complexity of this picture, and the level of interconnectedness among systems, a systems approach is needed. As the Sustainable Development Goals portray, the targeting of one single goal can easily decrease the system performance for other goals. It is only by addressing all (or at least the most) goals at the same time, that sustainability can be supported.

How useful are stock and flow consistent models of resources and environment?

Some of the greatest opponents to Limits to Growth were the other academic communities who used to engage in policy debate at the time it was published. Economists and econometricians above all attacked the conservative assumptions of the Limits to Growth in Scenarios 1 and 2 (scenarios with limited resources and scenarios with pollution collapse respectively), and rejected the approach of the system dynamics method and community.

The Limits to Growth can be considered as belonging to the family of ecological and evolutionary schools of thoughts, mostly focused on modelling the economy in a state of perpetual disequilibrium towards growth, while bounded by planetary limits. While neglecting financial variables, such as those used by policy makers to allocate budgets in an economy, the Limits to Growth model is limited in their usefulness for today's policy makers. On the other hand, by targeting financial variables (e.g. prices, debt, or interest rate) in a system model, as we do for the development of ERRE, requires a deeper analysis of the system.

The review of modelling methods revealed an interesting pattern to describe their evolution within modelling philosophies. Based on accounting principles, input-output analysis and econometrics are shown to provide the quantitative foundation for the many schools of thought today. Most important it appears that experienced modellers, aware of the limitations of their approach, often integrate more than one method at the same time to gain the advantages. General equilibrium models are described, alongside the integrated assessment models, representing the mainstream paradigm for policy analysis today. These two examples employ stocks and flows, and continuous time simulation for computing equilibria in the world economy, based on the Walras hypothesis. Differently from the system dynamics method, the assumption of linearity, rationality, and optimality in decision making opens these models to criticism. While the first often focuses on the dynamics of economic systems, the second enhances the spectrum to the economy-environment interaction. As a result they often model climate, energy, and agriculture to assess the impact of climate on human systems, and vice versa. Thus, the academic literature has partially moved in the direction of the Limits to Growth type of models. By relying on equilibrium, and optimal rationality, rather than disequilibrium, cognitive bias and bounded rationality they provide limitations in comparison to the method of the system dynamics.

Alongside these developments, the continuous work and advances of the system dynamics community allows the framing of the system dynamics school as fragmented from virtually all the various schools of thoughts present in economics.

System dynamics is founded on the use of stocks, flows, and feedback loops, and, while giving emphasis to disequilibrium and non-linear relationships as a means to quantify feedback forces, the school of evolutionary and behavioural economics takes a dominant role. In addition, by relying on the representation of organisations and on their rationally bounded capabilities, often targeted to improve some internal performance of an organisation, the mindset of the institutional and post-Keynesian economists is revealed to overlap greatly with the one of the system dynamicist.

In order to be able to provide effective policy advice, economic modelling approaches are necessarily stock and flow consistent. In order to transfer the complexity of their models into the language of policy makers, models are required to demonstrate a degree of realism by assuring that financial flows were consistent within every economy, and balance sheets are used to address the financial consistency of each sector in the economy.

All these considerations informed the Economic Risk, Resources and Environment (ERRE) model. The ERRE model finds agreement with, at least, five schools of economic thought. These are the neoclassical Solow school of thought (due to the characteristics of their production function, way of using technology and the overarching structure of investments), behavioural economic school (such that it employs non-linear feedback mechanisms describing cognitive capabilities and bounded rationality of decision makers), evolutionary school (such that it depicts path dependencies and allows the finding of equilibria if they exist rather than assuming them a priory), post-Keynesian (in relation to the behaviour of monetary policy in the model), and ecological (such that it captures environmental limits to address the interaction between growth and those limits).

Based on the analysis and differences between the World3 and the real world, we choose to focus the analysis on the interaction between financial risk, food security, global fossil fuel depletion, green energy transition, climate change, and governmental policies. The ERRE model can be considered as a stock and flow impact assessment model to address the financial risks emerging from the interaction between economic growth and environmental limits under the presence of shocks.

The added value in ERRE

The ERRE model is a means to bridge the gap between the recent past and the short- and long-term futures on our planet. The model uses the historical data from the year 2000 to provide a meaningful forecast for the future. However, negative feedback loops not present in historic data are captured endogenously in order to look at the bigger picture of the global system, and test possible solutions. This involves the impacts of depletion of fossil fuels and climate change, as well as green energy technology and carbon taxes.

Similarly to integrated assessment models that are built for this type of purpose, a question arises if these non-linear feedbacks from climate or energy depletion are too strong or not strong enough to be considered as a realistic assumption. On this we cannot provide a simple answer. The test provided in the ERRE model suggest the ability of the model to handle a large range of uncertainty, thus being suitable for comparative analysis with other system models of the same kind.

Often, integrated assessment models are used in conjunction with other general equilibrium economic models that focus on the modelling of the economy to be used as input-output. Thus for the perspective of the average modeller, the ERRE can be seen as the conjunction of different models each with a different name. For example, the financial structure can be given as the name FIN (1). The public policy structure as GOV (2). The energy resources as ENE (3), agriculture as AGRI (4), the household sector as HUMAN (5), the capital and goods sectors as ECON (6), and the climate module as CLIM (7). The careful integration of these models is, what in totality, we can call as the ERRE. Such a view, together with a suitable integration platform technology, can allow ERRE to be broken into smaller components, delegate the development of each component to internationally dispersed teams, and reintegrate the results together after improvements are made. Alternatively, in this way we can entirely substitute system structures with new models. For example, the climate module of ERRE is oversimplified in comparison to an average climate model. Those can be simply provided as objects, and plugged in the ERRE structure as additional elements.

A major difference between the ERRE economic sector and the standard used for computational general equilibrium models, is the set of assumptions that connect structures one to another. While both modelling approaches employ stocks, flows, and feedback loops as the building blocks of their structures, the ERRE adds the interpretation of decision making from the behavioural school of thought. That is non-linear feedback and limited cognitive capabilities of decision makers in the system. This is a very important addition due to the often irrational behaviour of people dealing with uncertainty on a daily basis. In addition, an understanding of the large uncertainty and interconnectedness of the complex interactions of heterogeneous agents is needed.

As a result, we argue the use of the ERRE, and the enhancement of existing system models with the ERRE structures, can provide a tool to generate deeper insights for policy recommendation.

What are the efforts involved in developing ERRE?

From the perspective of project management and execution, the development of the ERRE is a multidimensional experience. This is not just due to the number of variables that compose the model, which would make the ERRE a multi-loop 250th (and more) order system of differential equations. This is also due to the variety of views that have to be integrated in synergy to develop the system model. These include understanding systems, mathematical formulation and testing, engaging in the decision process from the user perspective, and providing a synthesis of the results obtained.

Due to this complexity, we believe that reflections on the modelling process to develop the ERRE are useful to those who are interested in engaging with similar questions using this model, and potentially to build their own. As a multidimensional experience, we mean the integration of a variety of skills and experiences that ultimately would require a multi-team effort. These have been divided in the three categories of (i) architectural and knowledge based experience, (ii) conceptual, mathematical and numerical formulation experience, and (iii) social impact driven experience. Table 7.1 shows these categories divided in ten skills, showing the particular tasks necessary to model the ERRE. We argue here that for each of

Table 7.1 Skill set to develop and update the ERRE model

Skill category	*Skill*	*Application of the skill for developing ERRE*
Architectural and knowledge based	1. Expert in human behaviour and decision making	o Ability to observe human behaviour and decision making as key component for modelling systems
	2. Subject experience in the systems to be modelled	o Financial – understanding of financial system and variables, and financial structures required to handle financial flows meaningfully o Industrial – understanding of industrial systems, decision processes and capacity constraints that intersect in the model o Geological – understanding of the resource limits problems and how to model that in realistic terms o Climatologist – understanding of climate processes and how they can feedback on the economy o Agricultural and biological – understanding of farming processes, and land management structures o Public system and policy – understanding of government financial structure and impact on the economy
	3. Expert in system science	o Boundaries and architectural perspective – ability to segment the reality in objects and think carefully about their input-output connections o Systemic – understanding of possible interconnections across systems and how these can emerge from the dynamic of the system o Synthesis – ability to develop simple theories out of the complexity of large scale models
	4. Expert in modelling theory and methods	o Economic theory – ability to frame the work in the existing economic literature o Modelling methods – general understanding of the methods to be put together for the development of the model

Skill category	Skill	Application of the skill for developing ERRE
Conceptual, mathematical, and numerical formulation	5. Expert in modelling (practice) and testing	o Mathematical formulation – strong emphasis of precision in structures of dynamic models o Manual sensing of mathematical and cognitive elements – use of non-linearity and feedback structures to model decision making o Simulation and behavioural structure – the ability to infer behaviour from system structure o Behavioural structure – understanding of simulation and how to use it to infer behaviour from the structure and causal tracing
	6. Expert in numerical analysis, databases and methods	o Econometric analysis – application of statistical analysis and econometric method wherever possible o Input-output structure – use of input-output to address the interconnection between systems o Understanding of metadata describing numerical value – correct interpretation of numerical values of the indicators that the model aim at representing o Output data analysis – ability to analyse numerical data output, both in terms of visualisation as well as in terms of statistical techniques (e.g. machine learning) to address model behaviour and implications
	7. Expert in enabling technology	o Good feeling for the computer instruments that allow the model, the data, and the analysis to be scalable
Social impact driven	8. Expert in history and politics	o Historical analysis – interest in the history of systems, as it is the major trigger to future expectations o Political – understanding of the structures necessary to influence policy
	9. Expert in strategy	o Strategic – understanding of the methods required to inform a strategy via scenario analysis o Futuristic – interpretation of futures based on the model inputs
	10. Expert in consulting and communication	o Empathic – ability to understand stakeholders needs, involved in the policy, financial, and industrial arena o Communication – ability to supply information in simple terms to non-experts

the sub-tasks, the three categories should be performed in parallel, constantly feeding back information one to another for the best success in the modelling process.

With architectural and knowledge based experience we mean the actual knowledge of the systems to study, how those systems can connect to each other, and the general understanding of the theory and methods necessary to structure the overarching architecture of the integrated system. In the case of the ERRE, we believe that the first of the skills in this category is dependent on the ability to observe and measure human behaviour and decision making, since this is a fundamental component of the system dynamics method and feedback modelling. This applies to the modelling of every firm, or any other elements that involves human decisions.

A second important requirement is the actual ability to understand a specific system. While most people develop that skill working within a particular sector of the economy over many years (e.g. a career in finance often requires very different thinking than a career in biology), a good system modeller should have both the ability to model the sector as well as a good feel on how each system does interconnect and impact on every other sector. The skill of modelling often requires an additional different mindset to the one necessary to understand the systems. Thus modelling the ERRE is a multidisciplinary project by construction. Ideally, one team of modellers should include someone capable of actually building the model (second category), and one person dedicated to provide the subject expertise in relation to each particular system. The model of every system might involve one subject expert, who can constantly evaluate if the model developed, and its behaviour, are consistent with their experience, and feedback to the those who do the practical work.

As each system might require a different mindset, different methods can be chosen to model some particular systems. At the level of project management, it is important to be sensitive to the various complex system methods, such that one can create synergies among those to answer every specific question. This understanding can provide the foundation for the system architecture, that can simplify the definition of modelling tasks and integration of those sub-models towards the purpose of the aggregated model. Finally, in the context of the ERRE it was important to review the economic theory and literature to capture what sort of thinking was required in each of the sections of the model. For example, it may be more useful to involve a climate scientist to model climate, whereas it might be more meaningful to involve a behavioural economist for investment decisions. Understanding the difference in mindset regarding methods and theories can support higher performance in the modelling process by delegating the right tasks to the right people.

With conceptual, mathematical, and numerical formulation we mean the actual modelling of ERRE in the computer, the process of human-model interaction, the data ingestion, and data analysis outcome of the model. This activity is heavily dependent on the other two, while adding precise understanding of data and computer rules to allow for the desired mathematical formulation of the system. The system dynamics method is generally based on the infographic representation of stocks and flows. This allows the development of system thinking while formulating systems, and it requires a manual sensitivity of model structures while simulating the relative behaviour. Testing is part of modelling and should not be distinguished from the activity of conceptualisation. The action of model formulation requires a careful interpretation of the system requirements, and the only way to address if the model formulation is meaningful is to simulate it. When dealing with large models (where large is a relative concept dependent on the ability of the modeller to formulate concepts), the addition, or amends to a previous structure, can change the behaviour of the entire system under study. Therefore testing that single structure would be an activity that requires the reinterpretation of all previously developed system structures.

Despite the comparison between model output and real world indicators being an important check to assess model meaningfulness, this activity takes lower relevance for the development of large models. First, a good model is one that is capable of capturing realistic behaviours for a wide range of model inputs. Secondly, the integration of various model structures in the same framework can lead to amendments to the ones that were previously developed, therefore fine tuning systems over time. For example, while attempting to generate a more meaningful price structure, amends to the production sector might be required. Forrester (2003, pp. 29–30), speaking about the System Dynamics National Model, argued:

> Some people have questioned the need for such a large and complex model. Indeed, many applications in education and in policy design might be better handled with a collection of far simpler models. But I have felt that it is important to have a model in which the major modes of economic behaviours exist simultaneously for examining how the different modes may interact. . . . After the larger system is understood, it will be desirable to revert to much simpler special purpose models.

In a similar way, the ERRE can be used both as a tool for addressing more complex and detailed issues, as well as a library of smaller models for the extraction of fine-tuned simple structures (e.g. price, capital, or labour) that can be used as the beginning for the development of new models.

The overarching system architecture is an important element for ingesting real data in the model, in particular around the initialisation of the model at the beginning of the simulation. For example, the six sectors' supply chain production structure is initialised as a small input-output table, whereas statistical techniques can be used to define the value of a parameter or a non-linear relationship. After data are ingested in the model, testing is the only activity necessary to reach a good meaningful system behaviour. The modeller should engage with the correct software that can capture all of these possibilities in the same platform. In the case of ERRE it would be important to employ software that support testing in the most efficient way before performing radical amends on the system. On the other hand, a good approach to testing could allow the scaling down of the modelling problem to simple rules that the computer can execute for the modeller any time that is requested. The larger the model the higher is the dependency of the model on efficient software and testing solutions. Given the variety of skills necessary to build a model in practice (in addition to the system skills presented in the previous category), more people should be involved at this level of modelling, often brainstorming solutions to technical problems, looking at issues from different perspectives. This should also be supported via feedback and interaction with the other categories to balance the final results towards the desired goal.

The third category, that we name as social impact driven, indicates all the soft and social skills that are required by the modeller to influence a decision, that ultimately is the purpose of the model. This includes the interaction with the user, empathy and communication skills, as well as the ability to provide a synthesis of the complex interactions in the model. At this level, political and historical perspectives are important to be considered, since the series of events that happened in the past force the team to act as detective to finds pattern that can explain the historical data. In fact, there exist a large difference between knowing how a system works in general (system understanding) and what actually happened in the real world that generates a specific behaviour (historical). For example, one can be an expert manager working in a firm, and have a good understanding of the processes involved in that firm. However, a fall in performance might indicate causes that would need to be further investigated. These events should be carefully modelled, thus improving the general system understanding. In addition, in order to influence strategic decisions, there exists various techniques to explore futures and show how the system under study might evolve at current knowledge. This might involve game theory, stress testing, scenario analysis, and batch simulations with probabilistic distributions.

Table 7.1 shows 27 tasks that, when integrated together, represent the complexity and effort required by individuals who are interested in developing models such as the ERRE. It is very important to recognise that having only the mathematical and technical ability cannot lead to successful models. On the other hand, improving on synthesis, communication, and empathy between the modeller and decision makers can often generate trade-offs between model complexity, and the ability of the modeller to explain behaviour from the structure. Each of these tasks can represent a career in modelling, thus suggesting that a multi-person effort, working in an integrated multidisciplinary environment, while focusing on the same issues one by one, is advised in comparison to single people projects. Every model, small or large, require the integration of most of these dimensions, each feeding back to the others. Political, strategic, communication, and historical understandings are necessary to engage in the policy making process, while mathematical, computing, and statistical understandings are required at the technical level. Ideally, one system expert (at least) should be engaged in every area the team is interested in modelling. These can be geological, environment, financial, or industrial, to provide model conceptualisation, and quality checks on the content of models. Most important, when interested in investigating a specific subject, idiosyncratic elements are necessary to be captured, based on the specific history of that system, requiring additional work for the entire team in order to catch that specific problem.

While the social impact category can be considered as soft skills, to be matured over years of disciplined application, the increasing size of the model implies harder technical problems arising from a more complex architecture of systems. This requires additional investments in developing platforms and algorithms that can analyse models efficiently, and allow dispersed teams in different subjects to work on the same platform.

What are the implications for short-term shocks?

One of the purposes of the ERRE is to provide insights regarding short-term shocks to support analysis of resilience in the context of extreme weather events and policy change. By short term we mean a shock that can be applied at the present time within a year time range, to show effects from one to five years and beyond (average policy agenda) with relative propagating effects across systems.

As our model employs decision making and perception delays at the core of its structure, it requires that a short enough time step within the model computation. In the case of the ERRE this results in a time step of approximately 11 days. The short-term time step supports the view of approaching a social response in the system, and opens the way to approach volatility that is difficult to capture in standard integrated assessment models, that are often run with a time step between one year and five years. Social responses to behaviour within the decision processes can open the way to a new line of research and support policy change today.

A second implication for short-term modelling in the ERRE, is the requirement to include additional structures, that were not available both in the World3–03 and Energy Transition and the Economy models, to capture that short-term shock. Due to our focus on financial risk and policy variables, structures such as inventories of food and fossil fuels, as well as the interaction between defaulted and operating capital assets, became fundamental. Ideally, a shorter term dynamic model could include many other structures, such as financing and short-term loans, hiring processes, and distribute the capital production pipelines among others. Depending on the focus more structures can be added, and other more long-term ones can be removed.

However, in the case of the ERRE model, the scale of the system provides an important constraint to the temporal analysis. Due to their inertia, a shock at the global (or national) scale can take months or years to register any significant change. Therefore, short-term shocks are applied to evaluate the response of the system to fossil fuels and agricultural land shocks in the one- to five-year time horizon, to demonstrate how this framework can be used to support analysis of resilience.

For the purpose of this model, the dynamic results in being sufficiently detailed. In particular, an agricultural asset loss shock shows increases to financial risk, and generates large increases in food price, with repercussion to the biofuels and energy market share. On the other hand, a production shock (or loss) in the fossil fuel industry demonstrates a good response of the model to the dynamics of the energy system and wider economy. In particular, a sudden lack in energy deliveries can generate recessions in the economy, inflation, and increases both energy and food prices. The model demonstrates that the impact of energy price on food price is larger than the other way around. Additional structures, such as the behaviour of investors as an alternative agent to firms and a better representation of the stock exchange sector can potentially add value to the behaviour generated by the model that is mostly driven by dynamics of capital production cycles coming from the supply chain and real economy.

Despite not being analysed in this book, additional sensitivities can be applied in order to search for mitigation policies to these shocks. For example, the hypothesis of storing additional food in inventories, or the option of including an energy utility sector that stores fossil fuels to mitigate shocks has the potential to reduce price instability and the impact of recessions.

Reaching ecological world limits in the 21st century

With ecological world limits we indicate some of those effects that can negatively impact the normal functioning of the economic system from 2030 to 2100. In the ERRE, these are represented by agricultural land limits, climate change and fossil fuel resources depletion. Stress testing in relation to technology development has been used to address which of these might be the most pressing, and which one has the less negative consequences when reaching those limits.

At the global scale, the study of agricultural land limits results in not being very meaningful. This is an issue that is mostly experienced at the local or national scale. Global historical data show that both agricultural land and forest land have been slightly decreasing in the last 20 years, while technology and fertilizer use is globally increasing productivity. In the real world, this increase in productivity is mostly concentrated in temperate zones and developed countries that can increase productivity with the same amount of agricultural land.

In the ERRE model, a steep land development cost curve starting the year 2000 allows a good fit of the model output to the data. This appears to show the limits are technically reached, while most increase is driven by productivity of each hectare of land. A national level analysis could reveal where that productivity is increasing, and where system pressures are worsening agriculture output. In ERRE, the exogenous productivity growth, supports increased productivity of both biofuels and food by reaching double the level of productivity in 2100 in comparison to the year 2000. This may hide the actual difficulties of the agricultural sector in responding to long-term shocks such as climate change or resource depletion in specific regions.

Scenarios 1 and 2 presented in Chapter 6 provide a simplistic sense of the effects of climate change on the food system. The climate crisis is a real anthropogenic phenomena with potential catastrophic consequences for every part of the economy. However, due to the difficulty in collecting historical data for comparison, we have to rely on uncertain sensitivity assumptions of the impact of future climate on the economy. Here we focused on the food system as an example to stress test the model. In the absence of significant mitigation efforts, the effects are negative. It could be possible to implement, for example, a dynamic carbon tax, increasing non-linearly, to mitigate the effect, or reduce the carbon emissions of agricultural capital through a shift of farming towards sustainable resources. This opens the way to model potential implications of a changing diet from households, as well as a technological shift in agriculture in the production of food.

Scenarios 3 and 4 provide a test of the hypothesis of an energy transition that can constrain an increasing temperature anomaly in the cases of (i) fossil fuel depletion and (ii) green technology growth. The general implications for economic growth are addressed. Fossil fuels is modelled without considering carbon storage capacity, whereas the energy transition is assumed to be led by renewable sources. These are assumed neither to generate carbon nor pollution, and no limit in terms of land availability or minerals for their construction are considered.

On the other hand, green energy is assumed to have a slow take up in the energy market due to technological and investment constraints.

Based on these assumptions slow growth in green energy, coupled with limited (conservative in comparison to current estimates) fossil fuels, can lead the world to collapse by the end of the century. On the other extreme, it appears that under the hypothesis of hot house, extremely positive green growth scenarios, would not find an easy way to keep temperature anomaly below +4 degrees by the end of the century in any case. This result is particularly negative given that a ×1000 increase in green labour productivity in one century is not sufficient to keep the world close to climate targets if the assumptions in the hot house scenario are correct. Uncertainty and risk analysis of those assumptions should be kept under consideration for future analysis.

Finally, Scenarios 5 and 6 seek the global limits of a green energy transition using a carbon tax applied to the fossil fuel industry. In particular, if the entire role of the carbon tax is to increase fossil energy prices to shift the burden of the transition to the market, then difficulties can arise. A carbon tax in Scenario 5 has to generate a +250% increase of the fossil fuel price beyond the market price in 2020 to be effective. The hypothesis of combining both a +250% carbon tax starting 2020, and a +9% exponential growth rate in green labour productivity over the entire century is the only option to reduce temperature anomaly to the +2 degrees climate target by the end of this century, using market forces alone. It is worth noting that this latter scenario of green technology corresponds to the assumption that EROEI from green energy can reach approximately 120 (i.e. 1 unit of energy can generate 120 units). This is highly unlikely, without considering the inclusion of currently non-existent technologies in the energy mix. Likewise, it is unlikely that there will be a +250% increase in fossil fuel price due to a carbon tax before this book has been published. Markets and technology, with only marginal contribution from government, cannot save the world.

Based on the long-term stress-testing and analysis of world limits, the ERRE partially confirms the results of the Limits to Growth study. Using a similar approach to the Limits to Growth, the ERRE provides a step forward for the world limits models based on resources, climate and agriculture interaction. The curves adopted to model limits and shocks are not as severe as in the Limits to Growth case, and the assumption of global resources depletion by mid-century is neglected. However, the analysis of social policy, and green growth, in the context of hot house effect does not look promising. The hypothesis of hot house effect represents one extreme scenario based on which all the ERRE analysis was built upon. In such an extreme but likely case, the options for green growth and carbon taxes remain insufficient in keeping the temperature increase within the climate target.

The ERRE model does not include societal responses to climate, technology growth in the overall economy is assumed to keep moving linearly with the time, and no energy efficiency has been considered for the most of productive sectors. As a result we are far from confirming this analysis as definitive in the case of the future that will be. All models are questionable, and require careful interpretation of their results before being used for policy advice. In the case of the ERRE, mathematical formulation of industries, fossil fuels, and green energy could improve the data fit to historical data. In addition, a deeper analysis of the climate system and its relationship with both agriculture and the rest of the economy could benefit the behaviour and precision of the model to inform policy. However, as it stands the ERRE represents a ground for model improvement both in terms of structure, mathematical formulation, and validation of its dynamics based on new data and events. Eventually it will support decision making towards a better future for all.

Can green growth save us?

The complexity of the climate crisis challenge is far beyond anything we have been accustomed to as humanity. It requires a system change, generating synergy at local, national, regional, and global levels. This requires citizens, governments, firms, and the scientific community to work closely together, each dealing with one part of the issue at stake.

The energy transition towards green technologies represents one of the major hopes for a solution of the climate change problem. However, the current state of technology means a massive electrification of the entire energy grid, and an exponential growth in renewable deployment. Thus green energy technology is far from being able to substitute fossil fuels quickly from its current base, without triggering profound consequences for the economy. On the other hand, without shutting down fossil fuels plants, climate change will simply worsen its effect on the society. There is a choice between economic uncertainty in the short term, against the worsening of human conditions on this planet for all future generations to come. The change is difficult but possible, and likely to require some sacrifice in terms of material belongings in the short term.

Concluding remarks

This book is a six-year effort of two scientists engaged in the understanding and modelling of systems, while finding collaboration with firms and scientists operating in the financial and energy sectors. The final objective is to influence the mental models of our readers, in relation to the topic of global sustainability, financial risk, and resilience. Starting from the Limits to Growth we aimed to build clarity around the major leverages and systems that interact with global society today, and for the next 80 years. We provide an analysis to highlight the challenges that we, citizens, governments, and the private sector will have to face to avoid catastrophic consequences by the end of the century.

Based on the analysis of historical data and future scenarios using the ERRE, it appears that, if the only metric to consider is market forces, green growth is unlikely to save us. Governments and regulators need to have strong engagement in the transition in every part of the world. They will need to cooperate amongst each other in the attempt to manage risks of transition. On the other hand, citizens should become more informed, engage with the sustainability problems, and most of all, be open to the change in demand that will support firms and governments in drastic changes towards a sustainable system.

Starting from a mental model of the entire world, and gradually explaining the structures of the World3–03 (Chapters 1 and 2), the comparison to the state of the world (Chapter 3), the explanation of methodologies and theories (Chapter 4), and the ERRE model structure and use (Chapter 5 and 6) we hope to have helped form a mental representation of the world that is a fair approximation of it. ERRE should help deal with the complex issue of a global sustainability transition, as a multidimensional, multidisciplinary problem that needs to involve everyone working in synergy in the both the short- and long-term futures.

The model is intended to support both a generic reader as well as educating a new generation of modellers who can engage in this modelling question, helping us shape a better future. In fact, when reading the book from the beginning to the end, we believe that an average analyst, could arrive here with a package of information that helps them to find a good framework to capture the evolution of today's global system, criticise the ERRE, help us improve it, and potentially build their own model.

In order to support clarity and criticism, the model has been made publicly available and we are happy to receive suggestions for further improvement from both academics and practitioners. We are interested in engaging in this dynamic debate until a system change which creates the dynamics for the better of both society and the environment. And we hope you can help us in making it happen.

References

Forrester J. (1957). *Dynamic models of economic systems and industrial organizations.* System Dynamics Group Memo D-0. Massachusetts Institute of Technology. Available online: http:// www.systemdynamics.org/

Forrester, J. W. (2003). Economic theory for the new millennium. *System Dynamics Review,* 29(1), 26–41.

Meadows, D. H., Meadows, D. L., & Randers, J. (2003). *The limits to growth: The 30-year update.* Routledge, Oxford, UK.

Meadows, D. H., Meadows, D. L., Randers, J., & Behrens, W. W. (1972). *The limits to growth.* Universe Books, New York, NY, USA.

Sterman, J. (1981). *The energy transition and the economy: A system dynamics approach* (2 Vols.). MIT Alfred P. Sloan School of Management, Cambridge, MA.

Index

21st Conference of Parties (COP21) 81,
   97, 118, 265, 266
3D farming 118
3D printing (Additive manufacturing)
   75, 76
80/20 rule 132, 230

ABM *see* agent-based; agent-based
   modelling
accelerated capital depreciation 210
accounting principle 179, 271
accumulation processes 9, 13, 14, 22, 23
adaptive behaviour 21, 155
adaptive technology 28, 33, 34, 35, 36, 37,
   39, 41, 43, 48, 55, 62
additive manufacturing *see* 3D printing
Advanced Research Projects Agency
   (ARPA, ARPAnet) 74
Africa 86, 96, 99, 116, 118, 120, 145
agent-based (ABM) 10, 132, 160, 161,
   162, 164, 200
agent-based modelling (ABM) 132, 160,
   161, 162, 164, 200
agricultural land 53, 92, 98, 109, 116, 184,
   189, 193, 203, 208, 209, 224, 226, 227,
   233, 234, 241, 242, 279, 280
agricultural policy 137
agricultural revolution 73
agriculture 8, 17, 19, 20, 23, 24, 27, 28,
   29, 30, 35, 36, 37, 38, 39, 41, 50, 55, 60,
   73, 81, 86, 89, 92, 94, 95, 96, 97, 98, 99,
   105, 108, 109, 112, 115, 116, 117, 120,
   138, 148, 178, 184, 193, 198, 202, 203,
   205, 208, 220, 224, 227, 231, 236, 237,
   240, 244, 249, 252, 253, 254, 263, 270,
   271, 273, 280, 281, 282
air pollution 32, 94, 103
aluminium 82, 85
Amazon 234

America 120
American Petroleum Institute (API) 87, 88
analysis of variance 139
Anthropocene 96, 118, 119
anthropogenic emissions (emissions) 8, 14,
   30, 80, 81, 85, 89, 95, 96, 97, 98, 101,
   115, 116, 117, 119, 136, 144, 145, 146,
   147, 148, 178, 184, 189, 220, 233, 234,
   244, 245, 249, 251, 252, 254, 257, 261,
   266, 280
API *see* American Petroleum Institute
aquaculture 116, 117
arable land 23, 24, 25, 28, 29, 35, 36, 39,
   52, 53, 55, 60, 61, 92, 94, 97, 116, 117,
   184, 233
archetypes 157, 158
ARPA *see* Advanced Research Projects
   Agency
ARPAnet *see* Advanced Research Projects
   Agency
Arrow 133, 141, 142, 143, 161, 178, 198, 199
Arthur, Bryan 160, 161
artificial intelligence 75
Asia 89, 99, 101, 104, 120
ASPO *see* Association for the Study of
   Peak Oil
assets 68, 69, 70, 71, 78, 81, 105, 106, 107,
   114, 145, 146, 163, 182, 184, 190, 191,
   193, 195, 208, 210, 213, 214, 240, 257,
   263, 279
Association for Evolutionary Economics 134
Association for the Study of Peak Oil
   (ASPO) 88, 89
atmosphere 14, 42, 80, 85, 95, 96, 97, 115,
   146, 147, 148, 244, 245
Australia 96
auxiliary variables 23, 182
aviation (avionic) 115
avionic *see* aviation

backlog 152, 153, 157
Baker criterion 155
balanced growth 79
balance sheet 71, 121, 179, 184, 189, 190, 193, 208, 224, 272
balance sheet matrix 189, 193, 208
balancing feedback 16, 23, 24, 25, 33, 34, 36, 151, 186, 189, 210, 212, 213, 214
bank 49, 51, 65, 69, 70, 71, 77, 78, 79, 80, 106, 121, 123, 153, 161, 163, 184, 185, 186, 189, 191, 192, 193, 195, 216, 217, 220, 223, 224, 225, 226, 227, 228, 240, 253, 254, 257
bank deposits 195
banking system 106, 153, 191, 212
Barabasi, A. L. 131, 162, 163
Bardi, U. 64, 81, 82, 83, 85, 87, 88, 101, 102, 104, 105
Barlas, Y. 17, 44, 155
Basel III 184
baseload 111, 112
base run (standard run) 6, 8, 27, 39, 40, 41, 42, 53, 144, 220, 227, 230, 234, 235, 236, 238, 241, 242, 243, 244, 266
battery storage 110, 112
Battiston, S. 107, 136, 163
Bayesian statistics 153
Behavioural economics 135, 269
behavioural prediction tests 234
behavioural testing 220
behavioural tests 177, 190, 216
behaviour anomaly tests 17
behaviour reproducibility 219
Beijing 103
Belgium 79
Berlin Wall 80
BGR *see* German Federal Institute of Geoscience and Natural Resources
BGS *see* British Geological Survey
bilateral matrix 137
bilateral trade flows 138, 144
Bio-energy 109, 112
biofuels 81, 94, 113, 114, 115, 116, 117, 118, 143, 184, 205, 224, 231, 232, 234, 240, 252, 254, 257, 279, 280
biomass 81, 94, 114, 116, 117
birth rate 48, 50, 55, 61
Black Monday 1987 75
Blind Men and the Matter of the Elephant 159
bonds (securities) 71, 72, 77, 78, 106, 192, 193, 195, 228
borrower 69, 70, 71, 106, 191

Boston 151
bottom-up 160, 211
boundaries 9, 11, 12, 15, 87, 98, 121, 140, 151, 155, 164, 177, 186, 200, 219
bounded rationality (rationally bounded) 16, 120, 135, 136, 143, 150, 157, 178, 182, 269, 271, 272
BP (British Petroleum) 86, 89
Brazil 86, 94
Brazil, Russia, India, China, South-Africa *see* BRICS
Bretton Woods 78, 79, 133
BRICS (Brazil, Russia, India, China, South-Africa) 138
British 67, 78, 85
British Geological Survey (BGS) 85
British Petroleum *see* BP
business as usual 35, 104, 191, 210, 212
business cycle 152, 180, 181, 232, 238

calcium 92
Caldarelli, G. 136, 162, 163
calibration 55, 58, 224
Cambridge Econometrics 141
capital charge rate 189, 208, 209, 210
capital discard 26, 27, 208, 210
capital investments 106, 153
capitalism 68, 72, 132, 133, 268
capital owners 210, 211
carbon 14, 81, 95, 96, 97, 98, 104, 111, 115, 120, 141, 146, 147, 148, 178, 215, 218, 233, 234, 236, 242, 243, 244, 245, 247, 249, 251, 252, 257, 258, 259, 260, 261, 262, 263, 266, 272, 280, 281
carbon capture storage (CCS) 266
carbon cycle 96, 147, 244
carbon dioxide 14, 95
carbon footprint 81, 266
Carbon from Deforestation 233
carbon tax (social cost of carbon) 120, 146, 148, 178, 215, 218, 236, 242, 243, 257, 258, 259, 260, 261, 262, 263, 272, 280, 281
Carnegie School 155
Carson, R. 103
cash flows 107, 193
casino finance 72
causal loop diagram 12, 16
CCS *see* carbon capture storage
Celsius 81, 97, 146, 245, 266
central bank 70
CERN 74
CES *see* Constant Elasticity of Substitution

CGE *see* Computable General Equilibrium
CGEM *see* Computable General
    Equilibrium
chaotic 157
Chatham House 138
Chernobyl 101, 270
Chicago School 133
China 85, 86, 89, 99, 104, 115, 116
Chinese 103
circular economy 105
classical economics 67
climate 8, 17, 18, 64, 73, 80, 81, 85, 89,
    92, 94, 95, 96, 97, 98, 99, 101, 106, 107,
    109, 113, 117, 118, 120, 121, 125, 136,
    141, 145, 146, 147, 148, 149, 159, 163,
    177, 178, 179, 184, 185, 186, 189, 209,
    215, 223, 225, 228, 234, 236, 240, 242,
    243, 244, 245, 247, 249, 253, 266, 270,
    271, 272, 273, 274, 276, 280, 281, 282
climate change 8, 18, 64, 80, 81, 85, 89,
    95, 96, 97, 98, 101, 107, 109, 113, 118,
    136, 145, 146, 147, 148, 149, 179, 209,
    225, 234, 236, 243, 249, 266, 270, 272,
    280, 282
climate crisis 280, 282
climate risk 89
climate stability 81
Climate Stress tests 163
closed loop economy 178, 193
closed loop supply chain (cradle to cradle)
    104, 189, 198, 204, 216
closed system economy 70, 224
Club of Rome (CoR) 3, 4, 5, 43, 61, 151, 269
coal 67, 68, 73, 81, 82, 85, 86, 87, 88, 89, 94,
    103, 108, 110, 111, 112, 114, 121, 144
Cobb, C. W. 143, 145, 147, 198, 199, 200,
    201, 203, 204, 207
coefficient of Pearson 230
cognitive decision rules 179
cognitive economists 135
co-integration 139, 145
Cold War 74, 80
collapse 4, 8, 15, 16, 24, 25, 26, 27, 28, 29,
    30, 33, 37, 38, 41, 42, 77, 79, 80, 101,
    134, 189, 215, 242, 252, 254, 257, 266,
    268, 269, 271, 281
commodity 9, 66, 67, 72, 85, 87, 137, 138,
    143, 189
commodity prices 142, 220
comparative advantage 67, 132
compensating feedback 15
complex networks 10, 132, 137, 160, 162,
    163, 164

complex systems 8, 10, 17, 108, 119, 120,
    131, 136, 160, 276
Computable General Equilibrium (CGE,
    CGEM) 136, 139, 141, 142, 143, 144,
    145, 146, 148, 150, 160, 162, 209, 218
computer modelling 8, 10, 269
Comtrade 138, 144
Conference of Parties (COP) 80, 103
conflicts 64, 78
Constant Elasticity of Substitution
    (CES) 143, 144, 178, 198, 199, 201,
    202, 203, 204
consumerism 64
consumers 27, 66, 69, 104, 137, 142, 143
consumption 20, 23, 27, 66, 68, 70, 74,
    82, 86, 99, 104, 105, 106, 109, 110, 113,
    114, 116, 117, 132, 137, 148, 178, 186,
    198, 205, 208, 228, 229, 242, 253, 257
consumption growth 182
continuous time 10, 11, 150, 151, 271
control engineering 151
conventional reserves 86, 87
COP *see* Conference of Parties
COP21 *see* 21st Conference of Parties
copper 82, 85, 92
CoR *see* Club of Rome
Costanza 9, 15, 107, 134, 157, 158
cost curve 233, 280
costs 23, 24, 25, 28, 33, 36, 39, 41, 66, 67,
    69, 70, 71, 73, 76, 77, 79, 82, 83, 85, 88,
    89, 94, 102, 109, 112, 113, 114, 115,
    116, 118, 137, 141, 142, 146, 147, 148,
    161, 186, 195, 200, 205, 207, 208, 210,
    212, 213, 214, 215, 223, 228, 229, 233,
    245, 258, 264, 265, 270, 280
counterintuitive 152
cradle to cradle *see* closed loop supply
    chain
credit 68, 69, 70, 71, 72, 209, 210, 225
credit market 72
C-Roads 18, 159
crops (maize, rice) 52, 53, 92, 94, 96, 99,
    101, 103, 116, 117, 123
crowding 31, 32, 50
crude oil 14, 68, 73, 82, 86, 121, 123
cryptocurrencies 75
cybernetics 131, 151
cycle 9, 77, 92, 96, 98, 110, 111, 141, 146,
    147, 148, 152, 184, 220, 230, 231, 236,
    239, 240, 242, 260, 279

Daly, H. 9, 134, 158
damage function 147, 149

DARPA *see* Defence Advanced Research
  Project Agency
DART *see* Dynamic Applied Regional
  Trade
Darwinian 134
data ingestion 219, 276
databases *see* dataset
dataset (databases) 9, 10, 49, 50, 51, 112,
  138, 140, 144, 177, 185, 218, 219, 220,
  223, 224, 225, 266, 275
DDT 101, 102, 103, 120
Debreu, G. 133, 141, 161
debt 64, 68, 69, 70, 71, 72, 77, 78, 79, 106,
  133, 153, 163, 177, 181, 182, 184, 186,
  190, 191, 192, 193, 195, 210, 211, 212,
  213, 214, 217, 220, 223, 224, 225, 226,
  227, 228, 230, 231, 236, 240, 253, 271
debt money 64, 68, 70, 71, 77, 106, 133,
  184
Debt Rank 163
decision making 14, 17, 135, 139, 143,
  144, 153, 155, 158, 162, 177, 179,
  189, 200, 219, 268, 271, 273, 275, 276,
  279, 282
decision making processes (decision
  processes) 10, 14, 16, 120, 219, 273, 274
decision processes *see* decision making
  processes
decision rules 150, 155, 156
decline 6, 24, 25, 41, 75, 83, 89, 225, 227,
  252, 270
decouple 58, 97, 109
decreasing marginal returns to productivity
  (marginally decreasing growth) 202, 227
deep uncertainty 18
default 69, 70, 78, 163, 211, 215, 228,
  229, 241
Defence Advanced Research Project
  Agency (DARPA) 74
deforestation 89, 92, 116, 231, 233, 234, 254
degrees 19, 51, 52, 81, 97, 146, 243, 244,
  245, 247, 248, 252, 257, 264, 265,
  266, 281
de-growth 109
delays 5, 15, 16, 21, 38, 41, 56, 59, 61, 96,
  150, 152, 158, 178, 179, 182, 198, 200,
  215, 225, 239, 241
delivery delays 152
demand 4, 27, 29, 33, 38, 63, 65, 66, 69,
  70, 75, 78, 83, 85, 86, 89, 92, 94, 98, 99,
  101, 109, 110, 112, 113, 114, 116, 117,
  118, 137, 138, 140, 141, 142, 143, 146,
  148, 151, 153, 178, 181, 182, 184, 186,

  189, 190, 191, 198, 199, 205, 208, 209,
  211, 213, 214, 215, 232, 238, 239, 240,
  242, 245, 249, 251, 257, 260, 265, 283
democracy 73
demographics 56, 59, 61, 180, 183
depletion 4, 21, 25, 40, 64, 80, 83, 85, 86,
  98, 113, 114, 117, 141, 157, 180, 182,
  186, 202, 215, 217, 225, 249, 250, 252,
  253, 257, 263, 281
depletion scenarios 242
depreciation 23, 209, 210
descriptive statistics 230
design 9, 62, 74, 78, 104, 154
development indicators 220
DICE *see* Dynamic Integrated Climate
  Economy
diet 101, 117, 266, 280
differential equations 17, 273
discard 20, 23, 24, 27, 28, 66, 143, 208
discount rate 107, 149, 210
discrete events 10, 150
disequilibrium 12, 64, 72, 77, 134, 137,
  141, 150, 157, 160, 179, 185, 186, 198,
  205, 209, 218, 220, 224, 225, 228, 229,
  249, 266, 271, 272
disequilibrium growth theory 134
disposable income 184
disruptive innovation 73
dividend pay-outs ratio 228, 229
dividends 190, 191, 195, 210, 225, 226,
  228, 229
Dosi, G. 161, 162
double-entry rule 193
Douglas, P. H. 143, 145, 147, 198, 199,
  200, 201, 203, 204, 207
Drake, Edwin 68
DSGE 143, 144
Dynamic Applied Regional Trade
  (DART) 148
dynamic change 14
dynamic hypothesis 219
Dynamic Integrated Climate Economy
  (DICE) 146, 147, 184
dynamics of growth 5, 6, 62, 64, 119, 146,
  177, 200, 214
Dynamic Stochastic General Equilibrium 143
Dynamo compiler 151

E3 *see* Economy, Energy, Environment
E3ME (E3MG) 140, 141
E3MG *see* E3ME
EAEC *see* European Atomic Energy
  Community

Earth 8, 14, 82, 88, 92, 95, 96, 98, 141, 185
ecological economics 134, 157
ecological school 179
econometric 16, 136, 139, 140, 141, 145, 151, 153, 154, 155, 160, 181, 219, 220, 275
econometrics 10, 139, 164, 271
economic growth (growth) 3, 4, 5, 8, 18, 20, 23, 24, 26, 29, 33, 39, 40, 41, 47, 60, 61, 62, 63, 64, 68, 70, 72, 76, 77, 78, 79, 81, 86, 87, 88, 89, 96, 97, 98, 102, 103, 106, 109, 116, 118, 120, 134, 141, 142, 146, 149, 159, 161, 177, 178, 179, 180, 184, 185, 186, 189, 190, 191, 195, 199, 214, 217, 225, 227, 228, 229, 234, 236, 237, 252, 253, 254, 257, 263, 264, 265, 266, 268, 269, 270, 271, 272, 280, 281, 282
Economic Risk, Resources and Environment (ERRE) 35, 44, 120, 121, 131, 136, 146, 159, 164, 177, 179, 180, 183, 184, 185, 186, 188, 189, 190, 192, 193, 195, 198, 200, 201, 202, 203, 204, 205, 208, 209, 210, 211, 212, 213, 214, 215, 216, 217, 218, 219, 220, 223, 224, 225, 227, 229, 231, 232, 233, 234, 236, 237, 238, 240, 242, 244, 247, 249, 253, 254, 257, 258, 265, 266, 267, 269, 271, 272, 273, 274, 275, 276, 277, 278, 279, 280, 281, 282, 283
economic theory 132, 133, 136, 137, 140, 155, 156, 159, 163, 177, 179, 181, 184, 198, 215, 276
economics 131, 132, 133, 136, 139, 145, 146, 152, 156, 157, 159, 163, 178, 179, 225, 271
economic transitions 180
Economy, Energy, Environment (E3) 140, 144, 177
economy in disequilibrium 220, 266
ecosystems 9, 11, 14, 19, 21, 24, 25, 30, 47, 63, 64, 65, 66, 81, 94, 97, 98, 99, 101, 104, 134, 148, 161, 234, 242, 266, 270
ECSC *see* Europena Coal and Steel Community
EEC *see* European Economic Community
EIA *see* Energy Information Administration
Eichner, A. S. 134
Einstein, Albert 74
electricity 37, 51, 74, 96, 102, 109, 110, 111, 112, 113, 114, 115, 254
electricity generation 110, 115, 254

electricity grid 74, 110
emergency *see* emergent property
emergent property (emergency) 65, 160
emissions *see* anthropogenic emissions
employment 67, 70, 73, 76, 78, 79, 133, 220, 231, 253, 256, 257
endogenous 150, 186, 218, 220
endogenous disequilibrium 218, 224, 228
endogenous disequilibrium tests 266
endogenous feedback 9
endogenous growth theory 135
endogenous money creation 143
endogenous stock variables 146
endogenous structure *see* feedback loop structure
endogenous variables 140
energy access 76
energy depletion *see* fossil fuel depletion
Energy Information Administration (EIA) 89, 220, 254
energy market 112, 184, 185, 186, 205, 257, 261, 279
energy requirements 207
energy retrofit 179, 185
Energy Returned on Energy Invested (EROEI) 87, 88, 190, 227, 252, 257, 263, 281
energy statistics 220
energy system 114, 115, 144, 148, 153, 252, 270, 279
energy transition 64, 68, 108, 109, 112, 114, 115, 116, 117, 120, 153, 157, 159, 181, 215, 228, 232, 250, 252, 254, 258, 262, 263, 268, 270, 272, 280, 281, 282
Energy Transition and the Economy (ETE) 180, 182, 184, 215, 279
Engels, Friedrich 68
England 68, 70, 143
Enigma 74
En-Roads 159
environment 8, 14, 21, 24, 30, 37, 74, 80, 102, 103, 104, 105, 117, 119, 140, 145, 149, 157, 159, 160, 271, 278, 283
environmental policy 80
environmental shocks 178, 186
equilibrium 12, 75, 132, 133, 136, 140, 141, 142, 143, 144, 145, 148, 152, 159, 161, 162, 164, 179, 186, 198, 208, 209, 218, 220, 224, 229, 237, 266, 269, 271, 273
equity 69, 72, 106, 193, 195, 228
eroding goals 158
EROEI *see* Energy Returned on Energy Invested

ERRE *see* Economic Risk, Resources and
Environment
error feedback and regulation 131
escalation 158
ESCIMO 184
ETE *see* Energy Transition and the
Economy
EU *see* European Union
Euler, L. 162
Eurace 161
Europe 70, 74, 80, 86, 96, 120, 143, 145, 253
European Atomic Energy Community
(EAEC) 79
European Commission 144
European Economic Community (EEC) 79
European Union (EU) 79, 80, 138, 144
European Coal and Steel Community
(ECSC) 79, 143
eutrophication 92, 99
evolutionary economics (Evolutionary school,
evolutionary modelling) 134, 157, 179
evolutionary hypothesis 186, 220
evolutionary modelling *see* evolutionary
economics
evolutionary school *see* evolutionary
economics
exogenous 11, 15, 18, 140, 144, 145, 147,
148, 149, 179, 180, 182, 186, 198, 201,
202, 203, 208, 210, 211, 212, 217, 218,
219, 220, 224, 225, 226, 234, 235, 238,
266, 280
exogenous shocks 201, 212, 219, 234, 238
exponential 21, 42, 96, 101, 152, 227, 263,
265, 270, 281, 282
exponential growth 21, 22, 23, 24, 25, 70,
73, 79, 98, 101, 186, 202, 228, 251, 252,
253, 254, 262, 263
exports 67, 78, 84, 89, 133, 182
extraction 3, 4, 19, 23, 28, 33, 39, 40, 41,
55, 66, 67, 81, 82, 83, 84, 85, 87, 88,
102, 113, 251, 252, 277
extreme behavioural scenario tests 236
extreme condition tests 17
extreme policy tests 236
extreme weather 85, 96, 177, 236, 237,
240, 278

FAO (FAOSTAT) 49, 52, 53, 77, 92, 94, 99,
101, 116, 117, 148, 220, 233, 234, 254
FAOSTAT *see* FAO
FAPRI-UK 143
farming 20, 73, 94, 109, 117, 118, 252,
274, 280

fat-tail 149, 218, 242, 269
Federal Reserve 70
feedback loop 8, 9, 10, 11, 12, 13, 14, 16,
19, 20, 21, 22, 23, 24, 25, 27, 29, 30, 33,
34, 35, 36, 43, 61, 72, 97, 98, 108, 134,
135, 145, 150, 151, 159, 177, 189, 191,
193, 210, 211, 212, 213, 214, 216, 218,
225, 272, 273
feedback loop dominance (loop
dominance) 9, 25, 151, 160
feedback loop structure (endogenous
structure) 11, 12, 13, 150, 214
feedback processes 140, 143, 148
feedback thinking 12
Fermi, Enrico 74
fertilizer *see* NPK fertilizers
Fiddaman, T. S. 9, 136, 184
FIMLOF *see* Full Information Maximum
Likelihood via Optimal Filtering
financial bubble *see* financial crisis
financial crisis (financial bubble) 78, 80,
136, 143, 145, 160, 163, 219, 225, 232
financial flows 75, 182, 189, 193, 195, 205,
272, 274
financial market 228, 229
financial networks 75, 76, 163
financial pressures 177
financial risk 105, 119, 184, 186, 189, 211,
214, 265, 269, 272, 279, 282
financial system 62, 64, 105, 106, 107,
119, 120, 134, 163, 178, 186, 195, 215,
270, 274
first industrial revolution 67, 73
Fish Banks 159
fisheries 99, 115, 116, 117
fixed point 179
fixes that fail 158
flight simulators 18, 159
floating goal 157
flow 10, 13, 14, 15, 16, 17, 25, 26, 36, 55,
66, 75, 78, 92, 98, 107, 111, 112, 121,
136, 137, 138, 143, 144, 146, 150, 151,
156, 159, 178, 179, 184, 186, 189, 193,
195, 200, 202, 208, 209, 210, 213, 216,
268, 271, 272, 273, 276
food poverty 89, 102, 103, 116, 118
food price 94, 184, 220, 229, 232, 236,
239, 249, 252, 257, 266, 279
Food Price Index 231, 253
food production loss 240, 245, 247, 267
food supply chain 53, 117
food system 116, 117, 184, 253, 280
food value added 230

food waste 53, 54, 99, 117
Ford, Henry 73
forecast 47, 89, 99, 140, 149, 154, 186,
  225, 247, 272
foreign exchange 72
foreign exchange market 72
forest 13, 20, 116, 148, 190, 231, 233, 234,
  254, 280
forest land 20, 116, 190, 231, 233, 234,
  254, 280
Forrester, J. 4, 5, 9, 10, 11, 15, 17, 18, 120,
  137, 151, 152, 153, 154, 155, 156, 157,
  180, 181, 219, 234, 236, 269, 277
fossil fuel depletion (energy depletion)
  148, 190, 236, 249, 263, 272, 280
fossil fuels 8, 65, 67, 68, 73, 81, 82, 85, 86,
  108, 109, 110, 112, 113, 114, 115, 119,
  120, 121, 146, 182, 184, 189, 217, 224,
  227, 228, 230, 231, 232, 234, 236, 237,
  238, 239, 240, 242, 249, 251, 252, 253,
  254, 257, 258, 260, 261, 262, 263, 264,
  265, 266, 268, 279, 280, 281, 282
fourth industrial revolution 75
France 79
free trade 64, 132
Friedman, M. 133
FTT *see* Future Technology
  Transformation
Fukushima 101
Full Information Maximum Likelihood via
  Optimal Filtering (FIMLOF) 154
Future Technology Transformation (FTT) 141

GAINS 144
Gallegati, M. 136, 162
game theory 146, 163, 278
gas turbines 111, 112, 113
GATT *see* General Agreement on Tariffs
  and Trade
GDP *see* Gross Domestic Product
GDP deflator 153
GDP growth 78, 227, 235
GEM-E3 144
General Agreement on Tariffs and Trade
  (GATT) 79, 80
general equilibrium 142, 145, 146, 162
Genetically Modified Organisms (GMO)
  103, 116
GENIE *see* Grid Enabled Integrated Earth
geological 83, 278
geo-politics 77
geothermal 110, 112, 113
German 74, 77, 78, 89

German Federal Institute of Geoscience
  and Natural Resources (BGR) 89
Germany 68, 77, 78, 86, 113
GISMO *see* Global Integrated
  Sustainability Model
Global Integrated Sustainability Model
  (GISMO) 148
Global Trade Analysis Project (GTAP) 144
GLOBIOM 149
GMO *see* Genetically Modified Organisms
goal-seeking 16
gold 70, 72, 77, 79, 82, 84, 133
gold standard 70, 72, 77, 79, 133
government 3, 14, 51, 71, 72, 77, 78, 118,
  119, 132, 142, 178, 182, 186, 189, 190,
  192, 193, 195, 216, 220, 223, 224, 225,
  226, 227, 230, 235, 253, 254, 258, 274,
  281
government debt 192, 193, 225, 236
government transfers 195
Granger, C. J. 139
great depression 133
green economy 64
green energy 108, 109, 113, 115, 120, 218,
  228, 242, 253, 254, 257, 263, 265, 272,
  281, 282
green growth 236, 243, 253, 257, 262, 263,
  264
greenhouse gas 80, 95, 97, 98
green revolution 73
green technology growth 255, 256
green transition 105, 107, 114, 115
Grid Enabled Integrated Earth (GENIE)
  141
Gross Domestic Product (GDP) 78, 133,
  147, 179, 186, 189, 220, 223, 225, 228,
  230, 231, 238, 253, 263
growth *see* economic growth
growth and underinvestment 158
growth paradigm 4, 79
growth theory 133, 135
GTAP *see* Global Trade Analysis Project

Haber-Bosch process 73
Hadley Centre 223
health services 21, 23, 29, 30, 52, 59
heating system 114, 115
heat pumps 114
heterogenous agents 273
Hiroshima 101
historical data 47, 48, 51, 57, 61, 144, 153,
  154, 182, 185, 219, 220, 224, 233, 282
Hitler 77, 78

holistic 150
Holocene 73, 96, 98, 146
hot house 98, 184, 185, 190, 218, 243,
    244, 245, 246, 262, 266, 281
household consumption 106
households 70, 71, 72, 104, 106, 110, 114,
    117, 153, 157, 161, 178, 182, 184, 185,
    186, 189, 190, 191, 192, 193, 195, 198,
    203, 204, 205, 208, 216, 217, 223, 224,
    226, 227, 228, 229, 231, 232, 236, 237,
    238, 242, 253, 257, 265, 266, 273, 280
HTML 74
HTTP 74
Hubbert, M. K. 83, 84, 86
Hubbert peak 83, 84, 86
human behaviour 179
human capital 65
human expectations 133
hurricane 96, 199
hydroelectricity 110, 111, 112
hyperinflation 77

IAM *see* integrated assessment model
IBRD *see* International Bank for
    Reconstruction and Development
IDA *see* International Development
    Association
IEA *see* International Energy Agency
IF *see* International Futures
IIASA *see* International Institute for
    Applied System Analysis
IIF *see* Institute of International Finance
IMAGE 147, 148
IMF *see* International Monetary Fund
impact assessment 144, 247, 272
Impact, Population, Affluence,
    Technology (IPAT) 148
imports 51, 77, 84, 133, 182
inclusive growth 118
income growth 238
India 86, 99, 116, 118
Indian 103, 159
Indian fable 159
indicator 23, 78, 80, 83, 118, 133, 162,
    180, 219, 220, 223, 230, 275, 277
industrial 3, 4, 5, 6, 8, 9, 20, 21, 23, 24, 25, 26,
    27, 28, 29, 30, 31, 32, 33, 34, 36, 38, 39, 40,
    41, 48, 50, 51, 52, 55, 60, 67, 68, 73, 75, 76,
    80, 81, 82, 85, 92, 94, 96, 97, 98, 102, 103,
    104, 107, 109, 110, 114, 116, 137, 141, 146,
    151, 153, 178, 180, 183, 190, 200, 205, 209,
    231, 234, 235, 243, 245, 248, 251, 254, 257,
    266, 267, 274, 275, 278

industrial capital 23, 27, 34, 39, 41, 49,
    56, 60
industrial dynamics 151
industrial growth 21, 26, 30, 31, 34, 58
Industrial output 23, 32
industrial revolution 75, 76, 96
industry 20, 23, 24, 27, 28, 30, 32, 39,
    51, 55, 74, 75, 82, 83, 85, 87, 96,
    101, 103, 109, 110, 114, 137, 138,
    142, 143, 189, 209, 257, 258, 260,
    261, 279, 281
inequality 64, 67, 71, 72, 76, 132, 134,
    163, 211
inflation 55, 70, 71, 145, 153, 157, 180,
    182, 195, 210, 211, 214, 225, 236, 237,
    238, 240, 252, 257, 260, 261, 263,
    265, 279
inflow 14, 193, 214
information 9, 11, 14, 15, 75, 137, 140, 143,
    150, 156, 163, 179, 182, 219, 275, 283
information base 153
information delays 148
information feedback 178
information processing 75, 76
information technology 60, 72
information theory 131, 155
initial condition 12, 232
innovation 66, 73, 75, 76, 80, 97, 135, 161
input-output analysis 137, 138, 164, 271
input-output tables 133, 137, 138, 139,
    141, 144, 145, 148, 277
instability 64, 77, 79, 134, 136, 214, 215,
    261, 263, 279
Institute of International Finance (IIF)
    195, 223
institutional economics 133, 134, 156
insurance 51, 77, 106, 153
integrated assessment 136, 141, 144, 145,
    149, 158, 159, 160, 162, 164, 271, 272,
    273, 279
integrated assessment model (IAM) 145,
    146, 148, 149, 150, 158
intended rationality (rational
    expectations) 135, 156
interest payments 195, 210
interest premium (risk premium) 106,
    211, 212
interest rate 69, 70, 71, 77, 106, 107, 145,
    153, 156, 178, 179, 181, 182, 184, 186,
    189, 190, 195, 210, 211, 212, 213, 215,
    229, 237, 240, 242, 257, 268, 271
Intergovernmental Panel on Climate
    Change (IPCC) 80, 85, 92, 95, 96, 97,

101, 109, 136, 145, 146, 147, 148, 149, 185, 223, 243, 245, 247, 248
International Bank for Reconstruction and Development (IBRD) 78, 79
International Development Association (IDA) 79
International Energy Agency (IEA) 85, 86, 89, 109, 114, 115, 120, 228
International Futures (IF) 148
International Institute for Applied System Analysis (IIASA) 5, 6, 152
International Monetary Fund (IMF) 78, 140
International Standard Industrial Classification (ISIC) 51
internet of things 75
inventory 14, 153, 157, 184, 213, 215, 238, 241, 242, 252
inventory-labour force *see* inventory-workforce
inventory-workforce (inventory-labour force) 152, 181, 184
investment function 26, 152, 153, 181, 199
invisible hand 151
IPAT *see* Impact, Population, Affluence, Technology
IPCC *see* Intergovernmental Panel on Climate Change
Iran 79, 86
Iraq 79, 86
IRENA 110, 112, 223, 224
iron 73, 82
ISIC *see* International Standard Industrial Classification
Israel 103
Italy 3, 70, 77, 79, 103

Jackson, T. 5, 18, 64, 65, 69, 71, 72, 76, 109, 136, 186, 191, 193, 227
Japan 86, 99, 101
Jevons, W. S. 114, 132, 137
Jevons Paradox 114

Kahneman, D. 135, 179
Kaldor, N. 134, 151, 160
Kalecki, M. 134, 151
Kalman filtering 154
Kaya Identity 148
Keynes, John Maynard 65, 74, 76, 78, 132, 133, 151
Keynesian 75, 133, 145, 159, 161
knowledge economy 75
Krugman, P. R. 134
Kuwait 79

Kuznets, S. 78, 133
Kuznet curve 133
Kyoto Protocol 80

labour 18, 33, 65, 66, 67, 70, 76, 77, 79, 89, 143, 153, 154, 178, 182, 186, 191, 198, 199, 200, 201, 202, 203, 204, 205, 207, 210, 211, 212, 213, 224, 227, 228, 231, 253, 257, 258, 261, 262, 263, 270, 277, 281
labour market 190
labour productivity 18, 67, 70, 76, 79, 182, 186, 201, 202, 227, 228, 253, 254, 257, 258, 261, 262, 263, 270, 281
land 8, 19, 20, 21, 23, 24, 25, 28, 29, 30, 31, 33, 35, 36, 37, 39, 40, 48, 49, 52, 53, 54, 55, 56, 57, 59, 60, 61, 64, 79, 81, 86, 88, 92, 95, 96, 97, 98, 101, 112, 114, 116, 117, 137, 146, 148, 152, 180, 184, 186, 202, 203, 205, 208, 215, 217, 224, 226, 227, 231, 233, 234, 240, 241, 254, 274, 280
land erosion 28, 36, 39, 53, 60, 96
land productivity 73, 94
land yield 28, 29, 30, 36, 37, 39, 40, 53, 60
Latin America 96, 145
Lavoie, M. 134, 136
League of Nations 78
LEAP 149
learning 11, 18, 113, 131, 135, 158, 159, 160, 162
lender *see* lending
lending (lender) 68, 69, 70, 190, 191, 195, 211, 240
Leontief, W. W. 133, 137, 198, 200, 201
leverage points 18, 151, 220
life expectancy 21, 23, 24, 26, 29, 30, 31, 32, 33, 36, 37, 38, 39, 48, 50, 55, 59, 61, 67
limits 4, 5, 8, 18, 25, 26, 33, 36, 39, 41, 42, 44, 47, 49, 55, 57, 58, 59, 60, 64, 77, 79, 102, 109, 119, 120, 121, 152, 177, 178, 180, 184, 185, 186, 189, 190, 200, 210, 211, 215, 218, 219, 236, 242, 243, 254, 262, 266, 268, 269, 270, 271, 272, 274, 280, 281
Limits to Growth 3, 4, 5, 19, 21, 24, 26, 29, 33, 35, 36, 37, 39, 41, 43, 44, 47, 48, 49, 53, 60, 61, 62, 79, 101, 102, 103, 104, 105, 119, 120, 152, 158, 162, 163, 164, 182, 186, 190, 215, 233, 254, 266, 268, 269, 270, 271, 281, 282
linear regression 139, 141, 145

liquefied natural gas (LNG) 88
liquidity 69, 70, 71, 77, 106, 179, 191,
    192, 193, 195, 211, 212, 213, 214, 215
lithium 82, 84, 113
LNG *see* liquefied natural gas
loan 69, 71, 106
long-term 21, 67, 70, 72, 76, 79, 99, 105,
    106, 107, 120, 133, 135, 140, 142, 143,
    145, 149, 150, 151, 153, 158, 177, 180,
    189, 210, 215, 218, 225, 236, 242, 243,
    266, 269, 272, 279, 280, 281, 283
long-term growth 106, 133, 136
lookup functions 15
loop dominance *see* feedback loop
    dominance
Lucas, P. 135
Lucas critique 135
Luxemburg 79

Maastrict Treaty 80
machine learning 75, 275
macroeconomic behaviour 178
macroeconomic theory 135
MAGICC 148
magnesium 82, 92
MAGNET 148
maize *see* crops
Malthus, T. R. 73, 151
Malthusian 73
MAPE *see* mean absolute percent error
marginally decreasing growth *see*
    decreasing marginal returns to
    productivity
marine 115
market 15, 52, 67, 69, 70, 72, 75, 77, 79,
    80, 82, 88, 94, 103, 105, 106, 107, 108,
    109, 110, 113, 114, 116, 119, 132, 134,
    135, 137, 141, 142, 143, 145, 154, 182,
    186, 189, 190, 200, 205, 217, 229, 240,
    251, 252, 256, 258, 260, 261, 263, 270,
    281, 282
mark-up 66
Marx, Karl 68
Mass, N. J. 120, 152, 180
Massachusetts Institute of Technology
    (MIT) 4, 9, 19, 46, 120, 151, 152,
    180, 217
material wealth 31
McKelvey, V. E. 82, 83
McKelvey diagram 83
Meadows, D. L. 3, 4, 5, 6, 8, 9, 11, 15, 18,
    19, 24, 30, 37, 41, 43, 47, 48, 50, 51, 52,
    54, 60, 62, 75, 77, 101, 102, 104, 105,

120, 137, 138, 140, 152, 154, 157, 159,
    179, 180, 181, 215, 254, 266, 269
mean absolute percent error (MAPE) 220,
    230, 231, 232, 234
mental data 9
mental model 283
mercury 101
Mesarovic, M. 5
MESSAGE 149, 168, 173
methane 88, 95
Met Office 223, 254
micro-economic foundations *see* micro-
    economic structure
micro-economic structure (micro-
    economic foundations) 143, 157, 178
Middle East 86, 89, 114
Millennium Development Goals 80, 81
Millennium Institute 158, 159
Miller, M. H. 133
mineral depletion 83
minerals 81, 82, 83, 84, 85, 87, 94, 102,
    113, 114, 115, 118, 119, 138, 280
Minsky, H. P. 134, 136
MIRAGE 149
MIT *see* Massachusetts Institute of
    Technology
model behaviour 43
model design 17
modelling process 146, 154, 155, 157, 273,
    275, 276
model simulation 17, 30, 39, 47, 154
model structure 15, 49, 50, 51, 185, 283
Modigliani, F. 133
Monash 144
monetary policy 120, 178, 182, 184, 215,
    225, 236
money 14, 65, 66, 69, 70, 71, 72, 75,
    77, 105, 106, 107, 120, 133, 138, 141,
    142, 143, 153, 170, 179, 181, 182,
    186, 189, 191, 195, 211, 217, 220,
    224, 225, 226, 227, 228, 231, 235,
    240, 253, 254
money creation 120, 141, 143, 179, 186,
    224, 225, 226, 235, 254
monoculture 92, 109
Monsanto 103
Montreal Protocol 80, 98
Muller, P. H. 102
multidimensional 273, 283
multidisciplinary 9, 276, 278, 283
multi-layer 195, 215
multiple equilibria 157
multiplier effect 31, 36

NAFTA *see* North American Free Trade
  Agreement
national accounting *see* national
  accounting systems
national accounting systems (national
  accounting) 137, 178, 209
national economy 154, 157
National Oceanic and Atmospheric
  Administration Earth Systems Research
  Laboratory 223
NATO *see* North Atlantic Treaty
  Organization
natural capital 65
natural gas liquids (NGL) 88
natural limits 25
natural process 14, 15, 23, 25, 146
negative effects of growth *see* negative
  impact of growth
negative feedback 20, 136
negative impact of growth (negative
  effects of growth) 25, 30, 39, 234
neoclassical economics (neoclassical
  school) 133, 134, 143, 178
neoclassical school *see* neoclassical
  economics
neoliberal 70
Netherlands 79
net present value (NPV) 107, 189, 210
network 66, 70, 74, 162, 163, 186, 188,
  208, 215, 218
Network theory 131
Newton, Isaac 134
NGL *see* natural gas liquids
Nigeria 99
nitrogen 73, 81, 92, 94, 98
nitrous oxides 95
Nixon, Richard 155
Nobel Prize 102, 135
noise 220, 230, 231, 232
non-conventional reserves 87
non-linear 9, 16, 26, 27, 37, 136, 141, 146,
  147, 148, 160, 180, 182, 189, 211, 218,
  219, 225, 247, 269, 272
non-linear adaptation *see* non-linear
  adaptive behaviour
non-linear adaptive behaviour (non-linear
  adaptation) 178, 198
non-linear behaviours 15
non-linear differential equations 151
non-linear feedback 9, 15, 157, 219, 272, 273
non-linearity 33, 34, 36, 38, 41, 275
non-linear relationship 15, 16, 25, 26, 27,
  29, 30, 33, 35, 36, 37, 39, 41, 43, 47, 48,

  52, 53, 150, 151, 180, 182, 189, 218,
  219, 269, 272, 277
non-persistent pollutant 21
non-renewable resources (non-renewables)
  8, 23, 37, 41, 49, 54, 70, 153, 193, 205,
  224, 237
non-renewables *see* non-renewable
  resources
Nordhaus, W. D. 136, 145, 146, 147,
  148, 152
North America 96
North American Free Trade Agreement
  (NAFTA) 80
North Atlantic Treaty Organization
  (NATO) 79, 80
NPK fertilizers (fertilizer) 81, 92,
  227, 280
NPV *see* net present value
nuclear *see* nuclear energy
nuclear energy (nuclear) 21, 74, 94,
  101, 102, 109, 110, 111, 182, 184,
  254, 270
nuclear waste 102

OECD *see* Organization for the Economic
  Co-operation and Development
Oil Producers Microworld 159
OLS *see* ordinary least square
OPEC *see* Organization of the Petroleum
  Exporting Countries
ordinary least square (OLS) 139
ores 81, 82, 83, 87
organic production 116
Organization for the Economic
  Co-operation and Development
  (OECD) 86, 94, 116, 145, 147
Organization of the Petroleum Exporting
  Countries (OPEC) 79, 86, 145, 153,
  182, 184
overshoot (overshooting) 4, 8, 25, 41, 48,
  64, 81, 153, 180, 182, 270
overshooting *see* overshoot
Oxford Economics 139, 140, 144, 145
ozone layer (stratospheric ozone) 80, 98

PAGE 149
paradigm 3, 4, 8, 24, 41, 62, 64, 67, 133,
  134, 139, 152, 160, 201, 271
parameter 15, 27, 39, 40, 51, 52, 53, 54,
  55, 57, 58, 60, 61, 143, 154, 199, 211,
  218, 224, 229, 238, 253, 263, 277
Pareto, V. 132, 142, 162, 230
Paris 44, 97

Partial Equilibrium (PE) 143
parts per million (ppm) 82, 97, 254
path dependency (path dependent) 108, 116, 160
path dependent *see* path dependency
PE *see* Partial Equilibrium
peak oil 79, 83, 88, 133, 153, 181
Peccei, Aurelio 3
pension funds 106
People Express 159
perception delay 178, 182, 279
perfect information *see* perfect rationality
perfect rationality (Perfect information) 14, 135, 155
Persian Gulf 85
persistent organic pollutants (POP, persistent pollution) 8, 19, 21, 25, 33, 37, 38, 39, 41, 50, 54, 55, 101, 102, 103, 120, 270
persistent pollution *see* Persistent organic pollutants
personal computers 74
Pestel, E. 5
pesticides 20, 23, 28, 98, 102, 103, 109, 116, 227
petroleum 68, 111, 115
phosphorus 81, 82, 92, 94, 98, 146
physical risk 105, 106
Piketty, T. 64, 71
PK *see* post-Keynesian
planetary boundaries 81, 89, 95, 98
platinum 82
POLES 149
policy agenda 136, 177, 279
policy analysis 144, 149, 179, 220, 225, 271
policy design 131, 156, 277
policy evaluation 139
policy levers 25, 119, 140, 178
policy makers 18, 97, 132, 141, 145, 152, 158, 159, 160, 193, 242, 271, 272
policy making 10, 14, 131, 132, 136, 145, 236, 270, 278
policy recommendation 8, 121, 149, 234, 273
policy testing 17
pollution 4, 6, 8, 21, 22, 27, 28, 37, 38, 39, 40, 41, 49, 50, 55, 57, 59, 60, 62, 64, 80, 81, 82, 89, 101, 103, 109, 114, 152, 180, 271, 280
POP *see* Persistent organic pollutants
population 4, 5, 6, 8, 18, 19, 20, 21, 22, 23, 24, 25, 27, 29, 32, 33, 36, 37, 41, 48, 50, 52, 54, 56, 59, 61, 62, 65, 71, 76, 89, 99, 103, 104, 116, 145, 147, 148, 162, 178, 184, 186, 208, 224, 225, 245, 253, 270
population dynamics 8, 24, 178
population growth 18, 21, 24, 26, 29, 30, 60, 73, 99, 116, 118, 145, 178, 182, 186, 189, 208, 209, 218, 235
positive feedback 12
post-growth 254
post-Keynesian (PK) 133, 140, 141, 143, 156, 157, 178, 179, 200, 269, 272
post-Keynesian economics (post-Keynesian school) 134, 143, 157, 179
post-Keynesian school *see* post-Keynesian economics
potassium 92, 94
poverty 4, 64, 67, 77, 80, 116
power generation (power plants) 110, 111
power plants *see* power generation
ppm *see* parts per million
Predicament of Mankind (problematique of mankind) 3, 4, 151
prices 19, 27, 66, 69, 70, 73, 77, 78, 79, 81, 82, 84, 85, 86, 89, 92, 94, 107, 108, 112, 114, 116, 121, 123, 142, 143, 145, 146, 153, 154, 163, 177, 178, 179, 180, 181, 182, 184, 186, 189, 195, 205, 207, 208, 210, 213, 214, 215, 220, 223, 224, 228, 229, 231, 232, 234, 236, 237, 238, 239, 240, 242, 245, 249, 251, 252, 253, 256, 257, 258, 260, 261, 262, 263, 264, 265, 266, 268, 271, 277, 279, 281
Primes model 144
Principles of Systems 151
printing money 195
private sector 66, 71, 182, 191, 192, 195, 211, 282
problematique of mankind *see* Predicament of Mankind
production function 137, 142, 143, 144, 178, 195, 198, 199, 200, 201, 202, 203, 204, 224, 272
productivity 23, 27, 28, 36, 37, 40, 53, 57, 59, 60, 66, 67, 75, 76, 83, 92, 94, 117, 120, 134, 186, 199, 200, 203, 205, 227, 253, 254, 257, 262, 263, 265, 268, 280
productivity growth 72, 74, 76, 77, 79, 94, 119, 135, 201, 202, 227, 253, 254, 258, 261
propensity for savings 228
prosperity 3, 78, 136, 268
protectionism 77
proven reserves 193, 252
public debt 71

purpose 8, 9, 11, 17, 18, 24, 43, 53, 55, 68, 73, 78, 79, 81, 105, 106, 120, 131, 144, 146, 148, 150, 153, 155, 156, 177, 180, 183, 184, 199, 200, 201, 209, 215, 219, 227, 233, 234, 262, 268, 270, 272, 276, 277, 279
putty-clay 181

quantitative easing 70, 71, 143
quantitative theory of monetary growth 133
Quesnay, F. (*Tableau of Economique*) 137

R3 *see* Resources, Risk and Resilience
Radiofrequency identification (RFID) 75
Radzicki, M. J. 134, 136, 156, 157, 158, 159, 178
rail 73, 115
RAINS 149
ramp growth 202, 227
Randers, J. 8, 43, 47, 60, 64, 66, 67, 71, 72, 78, 106, 108, 112, 184
rational expectations *see* intended rationality
rationally bounded *see* bounded rationality
raw materials 8, 66, 157
R coefficient of correlation (R square) 139, 220, 230, 232, 233, 234
real economy 72, 120, 143, 179, 180, 184, 186, 191, 205, 211, 279
recession 71, 136, 260
recycling 35, 81, 82, 83, 104
regression 139, 219
reinforcing feedback 23, 24, 97, 108, 212
REMIND 149
renewable energy growth 149
renewables 6, 8, 23, 33, 37, 41, 42, 43, 49, 54, 55, 70, 73, 81, 109, 110, 112, 113, 114, 115, 146, 153, 183, 184, 193, 202, 205, 217, 223, 224, 226, 227, 231, 232, 237, 251, 252, 253, 254, 257, 263, 270, 280, 282
renewables and nuclear 205
renewables productivity 228
research and development 21, 41, 74, 108, 113, 114, 135
reserves 79, 81, 82, 84, 85, 86, 87, 88, 89, 113, 195, 242, 251
reserves-to-production ratio (R/P) 83
resilience 98, 149, 177, 178, 236, 237, 265, 266, 282
resilience analysis 218, 269, 278, 279
resource depletion 33, 35, 41, 81, 84, 146, 153, 179, 189, 209, 215, 218, 242, 249, 250, 251, 266, 280

resources 3, 4, 6, 8, 18, 19, 21, 22, 23, 25, 33, 34, 35, 39, 40, 41, 55, 62, 64, 65, 66, 72, 78, 79, 81, 82, 83, 84, 85, 86, 88, 89, 113, 114, 117, 119, 121, 132, 134, 137, 141, 143, 144, 146, 153, 177, 178, 180, 181, 182, 183, 186, 189, 205, 213, 216, 237, 240, 242, 250, 251, 252, 253, 254, 257, 263, 265, 271, 273, 280, 281
Resources, Risk and Resilience (R3) 108, 177, 214
resource scarcity 8, 33, 64, 252, 270
Resource Trade database 138
retrofit 153
return on investment 190, 210
reusing 35
revenue 69, 70, 210, 211, 213, 214, 231, 253, 254, 258, 263
RFID *see* Radiofrequency identification
Ricardo, David (Ricardo) 67, 132
rice *see* crops
Richardson, J. 9, 10, 17, 131, 151, 174, 200
Rio Earth Summit 80
risk analysis (risk assessment) 70, 106, 121, 163, 180, 242, 243, 266, 270, 281
risk assessment *see* risk analysis
risk management 105
risk premium *see* interest premium
Rockström, J. 96, 97
Romer, P. M. 135
Roosevelt, Franklin D. 78
Roundup-Ready 103
R/P *see* reserves-to-production ratio
R square *see* R coefficient of correlation

Santa Fe Institute of Complexity 160
Saudi Arabia 79
savings 69, 71, 105, 106, 121, 184, 191, 192, 195, 225, 229, 231, 254
savings propensity 190
scenario 4, 6, 8, 18, 19, 24, 25, 26, 27, 28, 29, 30, 33, 35, 39, 41, 42, 43, 47, 48, 54, 55, 57, 58, 59, 60, 61, 62, 97, 104, 120, 131, 141, 144, 148, 149, 150, 151, 152, 153, 154, 159, 184, 185, 186, 215, 218, 220, 225, 234, 236, 237, 242, 243, 244, 245, 247, 248, 249, 252, 253, 254, 257, 258, 261, 265, 266, 268, 269, 271, 275, 281, 282
scenario analysis 8, 18, 26, 47, 234, 236, 275
Schumpeter, J. A. 132, 161, 167
SD *see* system dynamics

SDGs *see* Sustainable Development Goals
seams 82, 85
second industrial revolution 73
second principle of thermodynamics
134, 150
secular growth 133
secular stagnation 76, 80
securities *see* bonds
Senge, P. M. 11, 16, 17, 120, 152, 153,
154, 155, 158, 181, 219, 234, 236
sensitivities 236, 244, 279
sensitivity analysis 54, 154, 211, 236, 238,
242, 262
sensitivity test 16, 220, 252
sentiment 77, 118, 163
service capital 23, 51, 60
service output 23, 30, 50, 51, 52, 55, 56, 61
servo-mechanics 151
SFC *see* stock and flow consistency
shale *see* shale gas; shale oil
shale gas (shale) 88, 182
shale oil (shale) 88, 182
shift 15, 24, 25, 29, 60, 62, 76, 81, 89, 94,
103, 114, 116, 133, 134, 154, 240, 242,
257, 280, 281
shifting the burden 115, 158
shock 116, 163, 199, 218, 220, 236, 237,
238, 239, 240, 241, 242, 266, 278, 279
shocks analysis 266
short-term 96, 106, 138, 140, 145, 152,
153, 158, 177, 178, 180, 181, 184, 210,
214, 215, 218, 220, 223, 236, 237, 266,
268, 269, 270, 278, 279
silicon 82
Silicon Valley 160
Simon, H. A. 135, 155, 179
simulation 4, 5, 9, 10, 11, 15, 17, 18, 24,
25, 27, 30, 41, 48, 55, 57, 61, 120, 121,
141, 144, 148, 151, 153, 154, 161, 181,
182, 186, 199, 202, 203, 204, 205, 208,
209, 219, 224, 225, 227, 232, 234, 235,
238, 241, 242, 244, 247, 252, 253, 257,
271, 275, 277
slavery 67
Smith, Adam (Smith, *The Wealth of
Nations*) 67, 132, 151, 161
social capital 65
social cost of carbon *see* carbon tax
social response 119, 249, 279
society 4, 5, 8, 33, 36, 41, 42, 61, 62, 64,
65, 66, 67, 68, 71, 74, 76, 77, 89, 96, 97,
105, 118, 119, 120, 132, 134, 136, 145,
149, 152, 211, 268, 270, 282, 283

soil 21, 23, 30, 36, 73, 92, 96, 103, 117,
184, 270
soil erosion 23, 36
solar (solar photovoltaic) 107, 110, 112,
113, 182
solar photovoltaic *see* solar
Solow growth 178, 182, 186, 202
Soviet Union 74, 80
stagnation (steady state economy) 78, 134,
186, 202
standard run *see* base run
state variable 14, 17, 151
statistical *see* statistics
statistical analysis 219, 220
statistical test 139, 155
statistics (statistical) 139, 140, 153, 154,
155, 218, 219, 220, 232, 275, 277
steady state economy *see* stagnation
steam engine 67, 73
Steffen, W. 95, 97, 98, 104, 146, 149, 184,
185, 243, 262
Sterman, J. D. 5, 9, 11, 17, 18, 97, 108,
120, 152, 153, 154, 155, 156, 157,
159, 162, 179, 180, 181, 182, 184,
189, 193, 198, 201, 209, 215, 219,
224, 232, 258, 269
stock 13, 14, 15, 16, 17, 23, 25, 49, 51, 54,
56, 72, 75, 76, 77, 98, 106, 111, 121,
143, 146, 150, 151, 152, 159, 163, 178,
179, 180, 182, 184, 189, 191, 192, 193,
195, 203, 208, 209, 210, 216, 218, 219,
224, 228, 229, 234, 245, 268, 271, 272,
273, 276, 279
stock and flow consistency (SFC) 121,
178, 193, 195, 209
Stockholm 103, 120
Stockholm Convention 103, 120
stock market 77
stock price 229
strategy 11, 118, 154, 157, 236, 275
stratospheric ozone *see* ozone layer
stress test 163, 218, 236, 242, 269, 280
stress testing 220, 234, 236, 266, 278,
280, 281
structural causation 140
structure 9, 11, 12, 13, 14, 15, 16, 17, 26,
43, 48, 50, 61, 64, 78, 108, 118, 119,
120, 121, 137, 140, 141, 145, 152, 153,
154, 156, 157, 158, 160, 163, 177, 178,
181, 184, 185, 186, 189, 190, 193, 195,
205, 208, 209, 210, 211, 215, 216, 218,
228, 232, 233, 234, 249, 266, 272, 273,
274, 275, 276, 277, 278, 279, 282

subsistence food per capita 29
substitution 39, 68, 85, 198, 199, 202
success to the successful 158
supply 14, 15, 27, 53, 65, 66, 68, 70, 75, 76, 77, 78, 85, 86, 94, 101, 104, 110, 113, 116, 117, 121, 134, 138, 140, 142, 143, 145, 151, 178, 180, 181, 182, 184, 186, 198, 205, 208, 209, 211, 213, 217, 220, 225, 227, 229, 231, 238, 253, 275, 277, 279
supply and use tables 138
supply chains 15, 75, 104, 116, 178
sustainability 9, 64, 81, 89, 92, 105, 107, 112, 114, 116, 117, 118, 119, 120, 136, 147, 177, 180, 236, 242, 271, 282, 283
Sustainable Development Goals (SDGs) 81, 114, 118, 159
sustainable farming 117
Symphony model 161
synergy 26, 72, 75, 97, 108, 224, 273, 282, 283
systematic error 230, 232, 233, 234
system behaviour 9
system boundaries 150, 233
system dynamics (SD) 4, 5, 8, 9, 10, 11, 12, 13, 14, 15, 17, 18, 44, 61, 120, 121, 131, 132, 136, 137, 141, 145, 150, 151, 152, 154, 155, 156, 157, 158, 159, 160, 161, 162, 164, 181, 184, 185, 200, 209, 233, 269, 271, 272, 276, 277
System Dynamics National Model 120, 180, 269, 277
system improvement test 236
systemic risk 119, 163, 267
system policy science 105, 118, 119, 120, 121, 131
system pressures 186, 280
system theory 220
system thinking 8, 9, 61, 120, 131, 151, 160, 276

Tableau of Economique see Quesnay
table functions 15
tar sand 88
tax income 260
tax revenue 230, 231, 236, 253, 258
technology advancement 33
technology diffusion 84
technology growth 186, 198, 215, 225, 235, 242, 243
temperate 94, 96, 280
temperature *see* temperature anomaly
temperature anomaly (temperature) 92, 95, 96, 97, 110, 146, 147, 149, 190, 231,

234, 235, 236, 243, 244, 245, 247, 248, 249, 251, 252, 254, 257, 263, 264, 265, 266, 280, 281
test *see* testing
testing (test) 9, 10, 11, 15, 17, 18, 19, 25, 30, 47, 55, 103, 120, 121, 139, 140, 145, 147, 154, 178, 184, 185, 209, 211, 215, 218, 219, 224, 237, 243, 247, 253, 254, 261, 262, 266, 272, 273, 275, 276, 277, 280
Thaler, R. H. 131, 135, 179
Theil inequality statistics (Theil Statistics, unequal mean, unequal covariation) 155, 220, 230, 232
Theil Statistics *see* Theil inequality statistics
third industrial revolution 75
Threshold21 158
TIMER 148
tipping points 97, 247
titanium 82
top-down 11, 14, 43, 61, 131, 160, 268
topsoil 28, 92
total factor productivity 145, 147
trade 51, 64, 65, 67, 72, 73, 75, 77, 78, 79, 80, 84, 85, 118, 132, 133, 134, 138, 141, 144, 146, 160, 229, 278
trade networks 160
trade unions 77
tragedy of the commons 158
transistor 74
transition 23, 37, 70, 73, 80, 105, 108, 109, 114, 115, 118, 119, 120, 177, 180, 182, 236, 242, 250, 252, 254, 257, 260, 262, 263, 265, 270, 280, 281, 282
transition policy 243
transportation 67, 86, 88, 96, 110, 114, 115
Treaty of Paris 79
trickle-down effect 77
tsunami 101
Turing, Alan 74
Turner, G. M. 6, 8, 37, 47, 62
Tversky, A. 135, 179
typhoon 96
typology tests 162

uncertainty 4, 53, 84, 86, 98, 121, 149, 153, 219, 236, 242, 266, 267, 273, 281, 282
unemployment 64, 67, 77, 78, 79, 144
UNEP *see* United Nations Environmental Programme
unequal covariation *see* Theil inequality statistics

unequal mean *see* Theil inequality statistics
uneven growth rate 133
UNFCCC *see* United Nations Framework Convention on Climate Change
United Kingdom (UK) 44, 79, 86, 87, 143, 173
United Nations (UN) 3, 48, 49, 50, 76, 78, 79, 80, 81, 89, 94, 97, 99, 101, 114, 118, 138, 144, 185, 186, 225
United Nations Conference on Environment and Development 80
United Nations Environmental Programme (UNEP) 80, 147
United Nations Framework Convention on Climate Change (UNFCCC) 80, 97
United Nations Monetary and Financial Conference 78
United Nations Population Division (UNPD) 50, 185
United Nations Security Council 79
United States (US) 4, 44, 51, 55, 68, 70, 74, 75, 77, 78, 79, 80, 82, 83, 85, 88, 89, 92, 94, 103, 104, 120, 125, 126, 133, 138, 143, 152, 153, 155, 179, 181, 182, 209, 224, 253
United States Geological Survey (USGS) 82, 84, 85, 89, 104
University of Maryland 148
University of Missouri 143
UNPD *see* United Nations Population Division
uranium 82, 102
urban dynamics 151
urban stagnation 9
USGS *see* United States Geological Survey
utilitarianism 132
utility (utility function) 69, 104, 142, 149, 189, 190, 198, 201, 204, 216, 237, 279
utility function *see* utility

validation 121, 139, 155, 161, 218, 219, 224, 266, 269, 282
value added 51, 230
vector autoregression 140, 145
Venezuela 79, 87
Vensim 223
voluntarily unemployed 190
Von Neumann, John 74

wages 56, 66, 178, 181, 190, 195, 207, 217, 224, 226, 228
Walras, L. 132, 133, 134, 141, 142, 161, 271
waste 20, 21, 54, 70, 76, 81, 82, 101, 104, 117, 134, 150
water vapour 95
Watt, James 67
WB *see* World Bank
wealth 20, 25, 27, 59, 64, 71, 77, 89, 99, 212, 225, 228
Wealth of Nations *see* Adam Smith
WEC *see* World Energy Council
Weimar Republic 77
well-being 4, 21, 25, 36, 41, 64, 66, 67, 80, 132, 134, 149
wells 82, 85, 86
West Germany 79
wheat 72, 96, 123, 143
Wilson, Woodrow 68
wind 92, 107, 110, 112, 113
World Bank (WB) 51, 78, 106, 140, 227
World Bank Global Economic Monitoring 121, 123
World Dynamics 151, 152
World Energy Council (WEC) 86, 89, 128
world input-output table 138
World Trade Organization (WTO) 80, 85
World War I 77, 78
World War II 78
World Wide Web 74
World2 4, 151, 152
World3 4, 5, 6, 8, 18, 19, 20, 21, 23, 24, 25, 26, 27, 28, 29, 32, 33, 35, 36, 37, 39, 40, 41, 43, 47, 48, 49, 50, 51, 53, 54, 55, 57, 58, 60, 61, 62, 63, 101, 104, 119, 152, 154, 158, 180, 181, 183, 268, 269, 270, 272
World3–03 6, 19, 20, 22, 26, 41, 42, 43, 47, 49, 55, 62, 120, 131, 180, 182, 184, 215, 233, 268, 269, 279, 283
World3–03-Edited 49, 52, 53, 54, 56, 58, 225
World3–91 19, 47
World6 158
WTO *see* World Trade Organization
World3–91 19, 47
World6 158
WTO 80, 85

zinc 82, 92

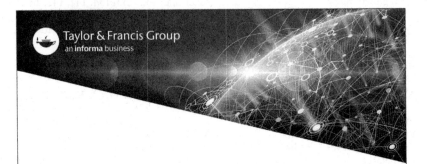

Printed in the United States
by Baker & Taylor Publisher Services

Printed in the United States
by Baker & Taylor Publisher Services